Mesopotamia, Syria and Transjordan in the Archibald Creswell Photograph Collection of the Biblioteca Berenson

Stefano Anastasio

with contributions by Spyros Koulouris and Francesco Saliola

ARCHAEOPRESS ARCHAEOLOGY

Archaeopress Publishing Ltd
Summertown Pavilion
18-24 Middle Way
Summertown
Oxford OX2 7LG

www.archaeopress.com

ISBN 978-1-80327-455-3 (print)
ISBN 978-1-80327-456-0 (ebook)

© Stefano Anastasio and Archaeopress 2023

All rights reserved. No part of this book may be reproduced, or transmitted, in any form or by any means, electronic, mechanical, photocopying or otherwise, without the prior written permission of the copyright owners.

This book is available direct from Archaeopress or from our website www.archaeopress.com

Contents

A martyr for Islamic architectural history, *by Spyros Koulouris* .... p. 1
   Processing the photo archive .... p. 2
   Archival descriptions .... p. 4
   Studying the past – working for the future .... p. 5
Introduction .... p. 7
Creswell and the Berenson Collection .... p. 11
   Biographical sketch .... p. 11
   Creswell photographer: the working method .... p. 12
   Creswell's legacy of photographs .... p. 15
   Creswell's collection at the Biblioteca Berenson .... p. 16
Mesopotamia, Syria and Transjordan in Creswell's photographs .... p. 19
   Mesopotamia, Syria and Transjordan at the end of World War I .... p. 19
   Photographers in Mesopotamia, Syria and Transjordan prior to Creswell's work .... p. 21
The sites and the monuments .... p. 27
   Mesopotamia .... p. 29
      Birecik .... p. 29
      Harran .... p. 41
      Samarra .... p. 55
      Qantarat Harba .... p. 73
      Baghdad .... p. 75
      Al-Madain – Taq Kisra .... p. 95
      Al-Ukhaidir .... p. 99
   Syria .... p. 113
      Ancient churches of Northern Syria: Qalat Siman, Qalb Lawzah and Ruweiha .... p. 113
      Aleppo .... p. 116
      Masyaf .... p. 180
      Hama .... p. 183
      Homs .... p. 191
      Damascus .... p. 199
   Transjordan .... p. 237
      Amman .... p. 237
      Iraq al-Amir .... p. 249
      Qusayr Amra .... p. 251
Conclusions .... p. 257
Appendixes .... p. 259
   1. Register of photographers in Mesopotamia, Syria and Transjordan between the 1840s and the 1930s .... p. 259
   2. Register of Creswell's photographs of the Biblioteca Berenson .... p. 275
   3. Synopsis of Creswell's photographs in the different archives .... p. 281
   4. Sites and monuments geolocation, *by Francesco Saliola* .... p. 299
Bibliographic references .... p. 305
Arabic Summary / موجز .... p. 317

List of Figures

Figure 1: Labels of one of the boxes where the Creswell photographs were put before the processing of the collection.

Figure 2: Platform that Creswell used to take photos of the mosaics at the Great Mosque of Damascus (photo by K.A.C. Creswell).

Figure 3: Mosaic at the Great Mosque of Damascus photographed by Creswell from the platform (photo by K.A.C. Creswell).

Figure 4: Ruins at Capernaum Synagogue (photo by K.A.C. Creswell).

Figure 5: Constantinople's city walls with letters indicating the towers (photo by K.A.C. Creswell).

Figure 6: Rhesion Gate (Mevlevihane Kapı), Istanbul (photo by K.A.C. Creswell).

Figure 7: Record in Harvard's Hollis Images catalog describing the Basilica of Hagia Sophia and related photographs.

Figure 8: Archibald Creswell, photographed by Jack Gordon.

Figure 9: Jerusalem, Dome of the Rock, published in Creswell 1932, fig. 491.

Figure 10: One of the earliest advertisements for a Chesterman tape, dated 1872.

Figure 11: Bernard and Mary Berenson at Villa I Tatti, March 1929.

Figure 12: Front (left) and back (right) of Berenson ID 133324.

Figure 13: The 'administrative areas' of Allenby's Administration of Occupied Enemy Territory, dated December 1918.

Figure 14: Joseph-Philibert Girault de Prangey. Aleppo, viewed from the Antioch Gate (1844).

Figure 15: Robert Byron. Damascus, Caravanserai. Date unknown (1930s).

Figure 16: Map of the photographed sites.

Figure 17: Birecik. The Citadel, looking north.

Figures 18-52: Birecik. Photos by K.A.C. Creswell in the Berenson Collection.

Figure 53: Harran. Drawing of the ruins, from Badger 1852.

Figure 54: Harran. The area of the Great Mosque at the time of Creswell and today.

Figure 55: Harran. The photographed monuments.

Figures 56-91. Harran. Photos by K.A.C. Creswell in the Berenson Collection.

Figure 92: Samarra. The site map and a sketch of the archaeological remains, published in Jones 1857.

Figure 93: Samarra. The Qubba al-Sulaibiya photographed in 1909 by H. Viollet, in 1930 by K.A.C. Creswell, and in 1983 by A. Northedge, after the restorations carried out in the 1970s.

Figure 94: Samarra. The al-Askari mosque and shrine in a photo taken in 1911 by G. Bell, and in 2006, after the bombing of the dome, but before the minarets were destroyed in 2007.

Figure 95: Samarra. Map of the phe photographed monuments.

Figures 96-135: Samarra. Photos by K.A.C. Creswell in the Berenson Collection.

Figure 136: The Qantarat Harba in a lithograph depicting the structure seen in 1847 by J.F. Jones and in a photograph of 1907 published by L. de Beylié.

Figures 137-139: Qantarat Harba. Photos by K.A.C. Creswell in the Berenson Collection.

Figure 140: Baghdad. The Zumurrud Khatun Mosque depicted by J.F. Jones (1857).

Figure 141: Baghdad at the beginning of the 19th century.

Figure 142: Baghdad. The Shaykh Maruf al-Kharkhi Mausoleum and the Zumurrud Khatun drawn by A. O'Callaghan (1899).

Figure 143: Baghdad. The 'Later East Baghdad', i.e., al-Rusafah, in the map drawn by Guy Le Strange.

Figures 144-197: Baghdad. Photos by K.A.C. Creswell in the Berenson Collection.

Figure 198: The Taq Kisra photographed by J. Dieulafoy (1885).

Figure: 199: The Taq Kisra. Map of Creswell's photographs.

Figures: 200-205: The Taq Kisra. Photos by K.A.C. Creswell in the Berenson Collection.

Figure 206: The Court of Honour of the al-Ukhaidir fortress, in a photo taken in 1907/1908 by L. Massignon and in a photo taken in 1930 by K.A.C. Creswell.

Figure 207: The al-Ukhaidir fortress. Map of the photographed monuments.

Figures 208-244: Al-Ukhaidir. Photos by K.A.C. Creswell in the Berenson Collection.

Figures 245-248: Qalat Siman. Photos by K.A.C. Creswell in the Berenson Collection.

Figure 249: Qalb Lawzah. Photo by K.A.C. Creswell in the Berenson Collection.

Figure 250: Ruweiha. Photo by K.A.C. Creswell in the Berenson Collection.

Figure 251: Aleppo. The map of the Citadel from Herzfeld 1954.

Figure 252: Aleppo. The area south of the Citadel, before and after the bombings of al-Khusrauriya Mosque and al-Sultaniya Madrasa.

Figure: 253: Aleppo. City map by Wagner & Debes, *c.* 1912.

Figures 254-473: Aleppo. Photos by K.A.C. Creswell in the Berenson Collection.

Figure: 474: Masyaf. The eastern front of the inner Castle in a Creswell's photo and today.

Figures 475-480: Masyaf. Photos by K.A.C. Creswell in the Berenson Collection.

Figure 481: Hama. View of the city, with a nouria on the left and the minaret of the al-Nuri Mosque on the right, in a watercolour of E. Fugmann (1930s).

Figure 482: Hama. Waterwheel on Orontes River (1898-1914).

Figures 483-502: Hama. Photos by K.A.C. Creswell in the Berenson Collection.

Figure 503: Homs. The Citadel.

Figure 504: Homs. Aerial view taken on May 1932 by the French Armée de l'Air.

Figures 505-522: Homs. Photos by K.A.C. Creswell in the Berenson Collection.

Figure 523: Damascus. Engraving of a late 19th century view of the city, taken from the Christian quarter.

Figure 524: Damascus. City map by Wagner & Debes, *c.* 1912.

Figures 525-661: Damascus. Photos by K.A.C. Creswell in the Berenson Collection.

Figure 662: Amman. The northern façade of the Umayyad Congregational Mosque.

Figure 663: Amman. Early photographs of the Roman Nimphaeum.

Figure 664: Amman. The restored right flank of north iwan of the Audience Hall.

Figure 665: Amman. Map of Creswell's photographs of the carved niches in the Audience Hall.

Figures 666-691: Amman. Photos by K.A.C. Creswell in the Berenson Collection.

Figure 692: Iraq al-Amir. Map of Creswell's photographs of the Qasr al-Abd.

Figures 693-695: Iraq al-Amir. Photos by K.A.C. Creswell in the Berenson Collection.

Figure 696: Qusayr Amra. Map of the photographed rooms.

Figure 697: Qusayr Amra. Details of the frescoes in Creswell's photos and today.

Figures 698-705: Qusayr Amra. Photos by K.A.C. Creswell in the Berenson Collection.

Image credits are included in the figures' captions.

A martyr for Islamic architectural history[1]
by Spyros Koulouris

Among architectural historians Archibald Creswell is seen as the doyen of Islamic architecture. His fame depends largely on his magnum opus *Early Muslim Architecture* and the great influence that this work had on future scholarship.[2] Creswell was a skilled photographer and the photographs he took during his expeditions between the 1910s and the 1930s have largely contributed to establishing his legacy and creating his myth. These cover a large geographical area from Baghdad to Kairouan and from Edirne to Cairo. It is not a coincidence that 3000 of the photographs are part of the Berenson photo archive, a collection that is considered to be the prototype of art historical photo archives.[3]

Based on the letters that Creswell sent to Berenson, it has long been deduced that the American art historian sponsored his friend's activity as a photographer. Now, an annotation on Mary Berenson's diary confirms BB's patronage, but most importantly it highlights that her husband's 'noble offer' was intended as a grant for Creswell's history of Arab architecture in Cairo and not only to support his photo campaign: 'We had a letter from Creswell in Cairo saying that the King has been told that he, Creswell, had spoken against him, so he refuses to continue the grant for work on his history of Arab architecture in Cairo. I wrote and said that we were willing to promise him £200 a year for 2 years to help him go on'.[4]

It is not an overstatement to say that Creswell's photo archive is an integral part of his publications and that his work as a scholar would not have been possible without measuring the monuments *in situ* and taking pictures of them.

For several decades, Creswell's photographs at I Tatti were housed in wooden boxes separate from the rest of the collection (Figure 1). It is one of the very few examples in the Berenson Library in which a group of

Figure 1: Labels of one of the boxes where the Creswell photographs were put before the processing of the collection.

photographs acquired before the 2000s has maintained its original location without getting mixed with other materials.[5] This is really surprising if we consider that a large number of other photographs coming from a variety of sources are filed in the Asian and Islamic collection. No less than 4000 images of art and architecture from various regions are arranged under this generic title. A large part of them concerns Chinese and Indian art, but there are also many images of Islamic art in private collections.[6] These photos arrived at I Tatti mainly through art dealers in France, and it is possible that they were proposals for new acquisitions, when Berenson was building up his art collection.[7] It is important to consider this documentation within the larger context of the Berenson Library. Indeed, along

---

[1] The title is an alteration of the way Mary Berenson described Creswell in her diary: a 'Sacred Victim' of Islamic architecture. *Berenson Library, Bernard and Mary Berenson papers, Mary Berenson Diary, 20 June 1922*, viewed 4 February 2022, https://nrs.harvard.edu/URN-3:VIT.BB:101410484?n=182.

[2] Creswell 1932, 1940.

[3] For the creation and development of the Berenson photo archive see: Gioffredi Superbi 2010; Pagliarulo 2011; Koulouris 2022. For a detailed file-level description of the collection see: *Berenson Library, Berenson Library photograph collection*, viewed 4 February 2022, https://id.lib.harvard.edu/ead/ber00047/catalog.

[4] *Berenson Library, Bernard and Mary Berenson papers, Mary Berenson Diary, 5 August 1922*, viewed 4 February 2022 (https://nrs.harvard.edu/URN-3:VIT.BB:101409302?n=241). As documented by the letters mentioned by Stefano Anastasio (see p. 12), Bernard Berenson supported Creswell's research for a long period, beyond the two years mentioned in the diary.

[5] The boxes also included photos sent to Berenson by Theron Damon after his trip in Istanbul in 1928, depicting monuments in Egypt, Constantinople, Adrianople, and Asia Minor. In addition to that, all Creswell articles were bound together by Berenson in two volumes under the title Creswelliana. This is the only case that this happens in the Berenson library. [Creswelliana], viewed 24 January 2023 (http://id.lib.harvard.edu/alma/990109421080203941/catalog).

[6] The images of India and south Asia include views of temples, caves and other religious buildings. They were obtained by the Johnston and Hoffmann studio based in Calcutta in 1914 approximately: *Berenson Library, Indian art and architecture photograph collection*, viewed 4 February 2022 (http://id.lib.harvard.edu/alma/990142118360203941/catalog). For the images of Japanese and Chinese art see: *Berenson Library, Bernard Berenson photograph collection of Chinese art*, viewed 4 February 2022 (http://id.lib.harvard.edu/alma/990147941220203941/catalog); *Berenson Library, Bernard Berenson photograph collection of Japanese art*, viewed 4 February 2022 (http://id.lib.harvard.edu/alma/990147919270203941/catalog). Of particular interest are eight panoramic photographs and rubbings of Han tombstones, as well as some beautiful photographs taken by the Japanese photographer Seiyō Ogawa.

[7] The provenance of the photographs is documented by the photographers' and art dealers' stamps or by annotations on their versos.

Figure 2: Platform that Creswell used to take photos of the mosaics at the Great Mosque of Damascus (photo by Archibald Creswell, Berenson ID 133577).

Figure 3: Mosaic at the Great Mosque of Damascus photographed by Creswell from the platform (photo by Archibald Creswell, Berenson ID 133604).

with the photographs, Berenson acquired books and photo albums about Islamic art and architecture, many of them quite rare.[8]

Processing the photo archive

In recent years there has been increasing interest among scholars for the Creswell photo archive. The destruction of cultural heritage sites in several parts of the Middle East has made people aware of the exceptional value of these photos. The photographs were already rehoused in acid-free containers to ensure long-term preservation when, in 2014, an attempt was made to describe the collection. The first solution that seemed to be appropriate was to create a collection-level bibliographic record. The materials could be searched in Hollis and generic information was provided about their provenance and content.[9] Considering the exceptional value of the photographs, in 2018 the library decided to process the entire collection and digitise it.[10] While the collection has maintained its original arrangement made by Berenson, there have been a few cases in which photographs not taken by Creswell were erroneously added to it. Thanks to I Tatti's internship programme we were able to figure out how many these photos were and remove them. At the same time interns transcribed Creswell's annotations from the versos of the prints and identified the monuments depicted.[11]

One of the great joys when working as an archivist is that you come across many hidden stories waiting to be discovered. Processing archives always brings surprises,

---

[8] The collection includes for example James Robertson's book with fine salt prints reproducing monuments in Istanbul (Roberts 1853) and the catalogue of the exhibition organised in Munich in 1910. Berenson was enthusiastic about this event (Sarre, Martin 1912; Sarre, Martin, Dreger 1912). All of these volumes have been digitised in high resolution and are accessible through Harvard's Hollis catalogue. For Berenson's interest on Islamic art see also: Rocke 2001; Casari 2014. Creswell himself acquired books for Berenson. In his letter dated 28 June 1923 (*Berenson Library, Bernard and Mary Berenson papers, Correspondence, Creswell-Berenson*, Box 37) he mentions two books about Islamic and Byzantine architecture that he found in the Librarie Paul Geuthner in Paris (13, Rue Jacob, VIe): one about Qusayr Amra and the other about the Church of St. Luke of Stiris, potentially at I Tatti now: Schultz, Barnsley 1901.

[9] *Berenson Library, Archibald Creswell photo archive*, viewed 4 February 2022 (http://id.lib.harvard.edu/alma/990142175150203941/catalog).

[10] The digitisation was supported by the Barakat Trust as part of the *Creswell Online Project*. At I Tatti a total of 2936 photographs were digitised using an Epson Expression 11000XL scanner and an IT8 calibration target. Both *.tiff and *.jpeg files were created at a 600 DPI resolution.

[11] My thanks go to the four interns that since 2014 have worked with enthusiasm on this project: Joan Chaker, Kathryn Kuhar, Gavin Moulton, and Serena Pellegrino.

while rediscovering what is supposed to be behind the camera is intriguing. In our case this is related to the technical difficulties that Creswell had to work out when taking photographs. The difficulties are highlighted by some photos that were found in the Byzantine art and architecture section of the Berenson photo archive. The series of images includes internal and external views of the Great Mosque of Damascus. The covering of the walls with coloured marbles and mosaics along with various architectural elements are documented in detail by numerous photographs. In one of them the British scholar decided to show the scaffolding he used to photograph the mosaics in the upper parts of the mosque's courtyard. It is impressive to see what it meant at the time to capture these artworks, when we compare this image with the one that depicts that specific detail taken from that point (Figures 2-3).[12]

When processing the collection, the photos were counted again. During this phase, it was possible also to check for unique images at the Berenson Library not owned by other institutions.[13] Although there is a lot of overlap, there are some important differences between the items held in various repositories. Creswell donated prints or negatives to different people and institutions. The prints should not be considered as copies of the same item. Each collection should be seen as an original archive in its own right living in a different context, as decided by Creswell. Collections in different locations tell different stories. For instance, the I Tatti collection can be seen as Berenson's intent to document the cultures around the Mediterranean and the connections between them, while Harvard's Fine Arts Library holdings are part of the bigger photograph collection of Arthur Kingsley Porter and the Victoria & Albert Museum's collection is part of the applied arts history proposed by the museum.[14]

Figure 4: Ruins at Capernaum Synagogue (photo by Archibald Creswell, Berenson ID 133971).

The study of the photographs at I Tatti revealed another interesting aspect of Creswell's work. The fact that he also photographed non-Islamic monuments on his trips. It is the case of numerous buildings in Palestine, Jordan, and Turkey that include Christian churches, Byzantine forts, Jewish synagogues, and various Roman monuments (Figure 4). A very interesting example is that of Constantinople's city walls. It seems that Creswell had a special interest in this structure as he took 31 photos of various parts of them. He captured the gates, houses, inscriptions, while he also numbered the defensive towers crowning the walls in an attempt to recreate their sequence (Figures 5-6). This fascinating series of photos does not only show the preservation condition of the walls at the time, but it also documents their surrounding areas, inside and outside the old city. The views of the Christian and Muslim cemeteries, the inhabited areas, and above all the landscape (now completely altered) offer a better understanding of what the city looked like before its expansion in the 20th century.

---

[12] The photographs taken by Creswell that in the past were erroneously filed with the Berenson photo archive were removed during the processing and put back with the rest of Creswell's photos. For an overview of the Byzantine collection of photographs see: *Berenson Library Byzantine art and architecture photograph collection*, viewed 4 February 2022 (https://id.lib.harvard.edu/ead/ber00023/catalog); see also Koulouris 2023.

[13] The largest part of the collections are at Harvard's Fine Arts Library, the Victoria & Albert Museum, and the Ashmolean Museum. These are available online and were checked in detail. This will soon be possible for the photos at the American University in Cairo. Recently, I came across 31 photos of Cairo owned by the Smithsonian's National Museum of Asian Art Archives: The Myron Bement Smith Collection. Freer Gallery of Art and Arthur M. Sackler Gallery Archives. Smithsonian Institution, Washington, D.C. Thanks to the archivist Ryan Murray, I was able to identify Creswell's handwriting on the versos. There seem to be further photographs taken by Creswell in existence in collections in Egypt and Germany, yet to be studied. Arthur Upham Pope also tried to acquire some photos for the Art Institute of Chicago, but this acquisition never took place: Kadoi 2016: 249.

[14] An additional element that makes I Tatti photographs

unique is that they have not been mounted, making it possible to read Creswell's annotations on the versos. Stefano Anastasio highlights how Creswell sometimes provided incorrect information about the names of the sites.

Figure 5: Constantinople's city walls with letters indicating the towers (photo by Archibald Creswell, Berenson ID 133412).

Figure 6: Rhesion Gate (Mevlevihane Kapı), Istanbul (photo by Archibald Creswell, Berenson ID 133419).

Archival description

With the digitised images being deposited at Harvard's digital repository system and plenty of time available at home during the first months of the COVID-19 pandemic in Italy, it seemed appropriate to catalogue the materials. As done with previous cataloguing projects at the Berenson Library, metadata included information about both the depicted monument (work record) and the photographic object (photograph record).[15] Harvard's Hollis Images catalogue allows browsing work records, in which related photograph records are attached (Figure 7).

It is not common practice to create finding aids for art historical photo archives. Institutions have opted traditionally to create item-level records for art related visual resources. Providing information for specific artworks or monuments depicted in a photograph is definitely something that most scholars need when making a search. However, it is often hard to understand in online catalogues the context to which the images belong. Although cataloguers dedicate a

---

[15] For the various terms describing built work types, subjects (general terms, decoration, or architectural elements), styles and periods, we used the *Getty's Art & Architecture Thesaurus (AAT)*, while for people's names we used the *Union List of Artist Names (ULAN)*. To geolocate the sites we opted for the *Thesaurus of Geographic Names (TGN)*.

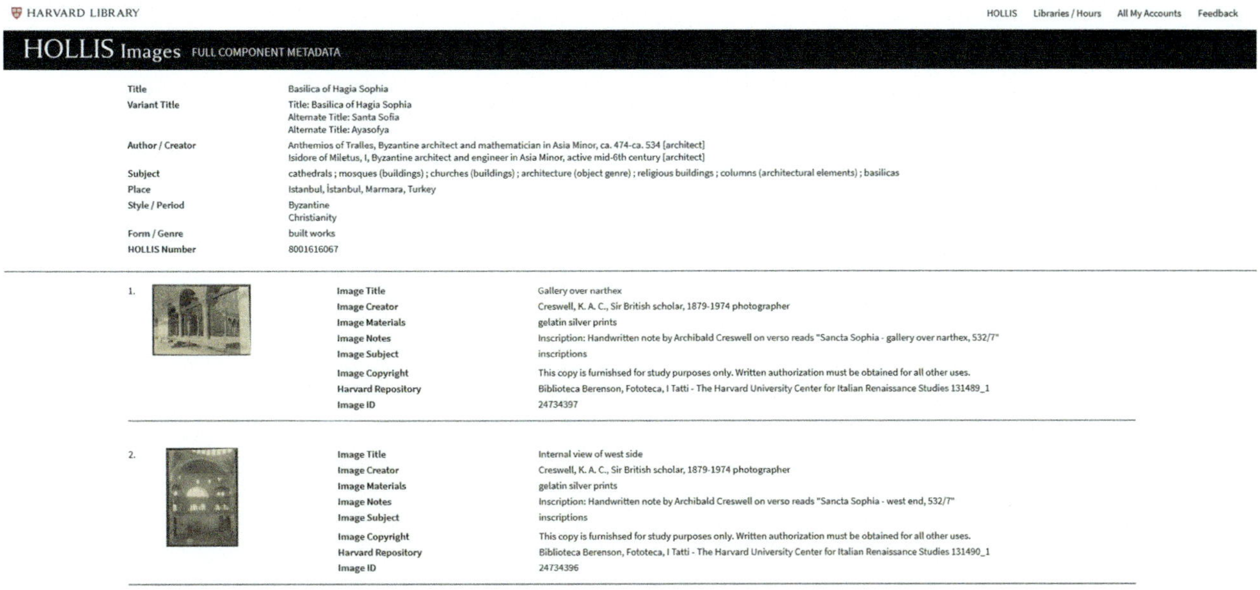

HARVARD LIBRARY — HOLLIS | Libraries / Hours | All My Accounts | Feedback

HOLLIS Images FULL COMPONENT METADATA

Title	Basilica of Hagia Sophia
Variant Title	Title: Basilica of Hagia Sophia Alternate Title: Santa Sofia Alternate Title: Ayasofya
Author / Creator	Anthemios of Tralles, Byzantine architect and mathematician in Asia Minor, ca. 474-ca. 534 [architect] Isidore of Miletus, I, Byzantine architect and engineer in Asia Minor, active mid-6th century [architect]
Subject	cathedrals ; mosques (buildings) ; churches (buildings) ; architecture (object genre) ; religious buildings ; columns (architectural elements) ; basilicas
Place	Istanbul, İstanbul, Marmara, Turkey
Style / Period	Byzantine Christianity
Form / Genre	built works
HOLLIS Number	8001616067

1.

Image Title	Gallery over narthex
Image Creator	Creswell, K. A. C., Sir British scholar, 1879-1974 photographer
Image Materials	gelatin silver prints
Image Notes	Inscription: Handwritten note by Archibald Creswell on verso reads "Sancta Sophia - gallery over narthex, 532/7"
Image Subject	inscriptions
Image Copyright	This copy is furnishsed for study purposes only. Written authorization must be obtained for all other uses.
Harvard Repository	Biblioteca Berenson, Fototeca, I Tatti - The Harvard University Center for Italian Renaissance Studies 131489_1
Image ID	24734397

2.

Image Title	Internal view of west side
Image Creator	Creswell, K. A. C., Sir British scholar, 1879-1974 photographer
Image Materials	gelatin silver prints
Image Notes	Inscription: Handwritten note by Archibald Creswell on verso reads "Sancta Sophia - west end, 532/7"
Image Subject	inscriptions
Image Copyright	This copy is furnishsed for study purposes only. Written authorization must be obtained for all other uses.
Harvard Repository	Biblioteca Berenson, Fototeca, I Tatti - The Harvard University Center for Italian Renaissance Studies 131490_1
Image ID	24734396

Figure 7: Record in Harvard's Hollis Images catalog describing the Basilica of Hagia Sophia and related photographs.

lot of effort in providing as detailed information as possible, sometimes they omit to link item records with the higher file, series, or collection level. That means losing information about the circumstances in which a photograph was taken and the relationship it has with other photographs or documents in the collection.

To avoid this happening, a finding aid was created for the Creswell photo archive. It provides some general information about the history of the collection and its creator, but it also allows us to describe the hierarchy of series, subseries, and files. At a later date, EAD digital objects were created which were linked to the item-level records of the single photographic prints. Both images, structural data, and descriptive metadata were combined into a IIIF Manifest and were delivered to users through a Mirador viewer. The information is now displayed in a structured way allowing easy access to the digitised objects and the description of the resources in a machine-readable way.[16]

Studying the past – working for the future

There are many future opportunities for the Creswell photographic archive. Although there is a lot of literature about the history and use of photo archives in Europe and the U.S. during the 19th and early 20th centuries, we still do not know a lot about how non-western art photographic reproductions were produced and circulated.[17]

Making these collections accessible to a larger audience will increase their visibility significantly. Stefano Anastasio highlights in this volume the exceptional value of these images to researchers, especially for the study and restoration of buildings in conflict areas like Syria.

The development of new technologies will revolutionise the way we study the past, and Digital Art History will have a central role in this transition.[18] In an attempt to disseminate as much information as possible and to make the best of these resources, the Berenson Library decided to include the Creswell photographs in the *Pharos* pilot project. Through this initiative, the images will be published in a linked open data environment together with millions of other photographs of artworks from different periods and cultures.[19] The new platform will allow the interconnection of data about sites, art, and architecture in the Middle East and North Africa with those originating from western art archives, thus creating a digital context in which new stories wait to be told.

Athens, January 24th, 2023

Spyros Koulouris

[16] *Berenson Library, Archibald Creswell photo archive*, viewed 4 February 2022 (https://id.lib.harvard.edu/ead/ber00045/catalog).

[17] Kadoi 2021.

[18] Resig 2014.

[19] Pharos 2016. For an overview of the innovative tools that this project will bring see Klic 2021.

Introduction

This volume presents the results of research that started in 2020 on the photographs of Mesopotamia, Syria and Transjordan in the Creswell collection, now at the Biblioteca Berenson of Villa I Tatti in Florence.

Keppel Archibald Cameron Creswell (1879-1974) was not only a pioneer in Islamic architecture studies, but also in the use of photography to document the architectural heritage of Egypt and the Near East.

As is well known, archaeology and photography flourished and developed together in the 19th century, in a relationship that has become increasingly close over time. The photographs covered in this volume date back to the 1920s-1930s — years which were particularly significant in the history of both disciplines. In those years the 'Middle East', as Alfred Thayer Mahan had first defined it a few years before,[20] assumed the role of strategic region for Western interests. As a result, it became a destination for travellers of all kinds and engaged in very different activities. From the point of view of archaeological research and study of antiquity in general, photographic documentation in those years increased considerably compared to the past. This happened because of the surge in archaeological research projects developed in a period that, after the fall of the Ottoman Empire, experienced the huge impact of European colonialism. Photographic techniques became accessible even to people who were not professional photographers, thus increasing the repertoires made directly by archaeologists, architects, engineers, geographers, and whoever else was directly involved in explorations and field work.

Creswell, therefore, was not the first person to photograph the monuments illustrated in his collection, but in many cases, he was the first true expert in architecture to do so.

Moreover, the fact that he photographed so many monuments in those years is of key significance for cultural heritage documentation: many of the monuments photographed, and especially many of their contexts, changed remarkably already in the immediately following years, due to the great urban changes initiated during the French and British Mandates and numerous archaeological excavations.

This would be more than sufficient to justify the attention paid to this collection.

However, there is also a further aspect of these photographs that is worth pointing out (and which, ultimately, is also the main reason that drove me into this research), which is the legacy of the Creswell collection: how it was formed, spread among different archives, and the fact that it is partly already known to the academic world but at the same time not yet catalogued or made accessible as a whole, with all the resulting methodological issues related to the work still to be done.

My personal interest in early photography for archaeology is quite recent and, I must admit, dictated by an almost random fact: in 2010 I started working at the Archaeological Museum of Florence where, 'thanks' to the perennial shortage of personnel, I found a place in the Photographic Archive, even if my skills could be generously defined as 'basic'. Since then, I began to study and deepen my understanding of this topic thanks to my work in the archive. For the most part, my job was to recover and enhance a large number of ancient photos, given that the Museum preserved (then and still now) many early documents, including photographs, yet to be inventoried.

Despite the experience gained in all these years, I still have the same feeling of initial 'discomfort' towards my work, driven by the awareness that I still lack the ability to balance an archaeological perspective with a photographic approach (it is always difficult for me to look at a photograph for the first time without being instinctively led to consider first of all its content rather than the photographic media used; this happens in most cases, and only sometimes the other way round). Obviously, this is a personal issue, but the general topic of the correct approach towards the use of early photographs for research deserves attention.

Today we are witnessing an increasing number of photographic repertoires of archaeological and historical-artistic interest which are accessible to the public, especially online. This is of course a good thing and we can only hope that this trend will continue. However, these collections of documents are often offered to the network without a critical study behind them, which takes into account both the history of the collection and an analysis of the subjects photographed. In these cases, the risk is that that repertoire, although theoretically accessible to all, in practice does not properly 'reach' the scholars of the disciplines for whom the information offered by the photographs could be important. But there is also an opposite problem in some ways. In the field of archaeological research — i.e., the one to which I belong and limit my remarks —, there has been a growing interest for some years now in the photographic archives of the 19th and early 20th century, with many projects focusing on the study, cataloguing and publication of documentation of photographic archives. Unfortunately, researchers with adequate archaeological expertise do not always have the same skills in archival research. In this case, the main risk is to use archival photography simply for gaining information on the represented subject, without considering all the details that can be obtained from studying the photographic *medium* as such: the photographer's *modus operandi*, the reason for

---
[20] Mahan 1902; Koppes 1976.

choosing that subject instead of another, or the reason for photographing it that way, the comparison with any similar photographs of the same period, etc., are all elements that cannot be overlooked if we wish to 'understand' what is represented in the photograph. Finally, shared standards and common practices on the criteria used for publishing data by the archaeological community would help compare information from different projects.[21]

Creswell's collection seemed to me, from the outset, an ideal subject to deal with these issues. Creswell's photographs, in fact, are already known: there are copies in various archives, some of which are accessible online. In addition, there are already some specific studies on the subjects of some of his photographs.[22] However, the data in the various archives are still catalogued and presented according to different systems and there is still no overall study of his work, especially with regard to the photographs of the geographic area in question.[23] This area was limited to Mesopotamia, Syria and Transjordan. The photographs dedicated to these regions can be considered similar and constitute a coherent group, compared to the groups of photographs of Turkey (mainly Istanbul) and North Africa. Palestine, also widely photographed by Creswell and which is certainly close to Syria and Transjordan, deserves a separate space of its own, in my opinion, especially when contextualising Creswell's work with that of scholars who had preceded him in photographing sites and monuments: from this viewpoint, there is such a huge amount of documentation on Palestine that needs to be processed, making its separate study quite justified. It seemed appropriate, therefore, to narrow down this work to the three regions mentioned above. Indeed, even with this limitation, the work proved to be extremely demanding and it soon became clear that a broader scope would have made the project more difficult to implement.

Many of the sites and monuments photographed by Creswell are known and still standing, but there are many others (especially in Aleppo and Damascus) that no longer exist, or have been significantly modified. Creswell's lack of knowledge of Arabic, and some uncertainties in the handwritten names of the places, did not help the research. Even the simple location of the monuments was, in some cases, a hard task and was possible only thanks to the help of colleagues and experts from the individual regions. For this reason, it was decided to offer the reader a map, created by Francesco Saliola, in order to geolocate the monuments photographed on Google My Maps. The possibility to use the same data on Google Earth, viewing them on satellite photos with different chronology, allows viewers to appreciate how the contexts in which the monuments are located have changed, at least in the last 30 years.

Technical notes — A few notes regard the criterion used for choosing the photos for publication and for dating the monuments. In parallel with the study for the publication, all the images, once digitised, were uploaded on Hollis Images, the Harvard University repository which the Biblioteca Berenson is a member of, and were then made available for consultation. For this reason, I thought it would be appropriate in the volume to publish the images by selecting them in some cases and reproducing just one shot if the same subject was photographed in a similar manner in other photographs. Where this occurs, the similar images are mentioned in the Appendix 2, so that the reader can easily find the images that complete the set of photographs of that monument online.

The photographs have been slightly resized in the catalogue; their external frame has been eliminated to make them of equal size and present them in a neat and orderly fashion. The full footprint of the photographs can still be appreciated in the digital versions uploaded on Hollis Images.

On the rear, most of the photographs have handwritten notes in pencil, detailing the pictured subjects. They are essential to recognise and interpret the subject, especially when portraying monuments that have disappeared. However, in a very few cases, the captions can be misleading: generally, they are written in Creswell's calligraphy, but in some cases, they have been clearly written by other unidentified people, probably at a later time. With regard to the notes in Creswell's calligraphy, it should be noted that he often writes Arabic names with obvious transliteration errors. The handwritten notes in the captions of the catalogue are always placed between quotation marks (e.g., 'Masyaf'.). They are followed by [Cres.] when they are written in Creswell's handwriting and by [Anon.] when the author is unknown (anonymous). A long dash — separates sentences/words that are visibly separated from each other (for example, the date of a monument is typically found in the upper right corner). Finally, many photographs have numbers on them, usually in the middle of the photographs. The numbers are written in pencil and are often not clearly legible. Most likely,

---

[21] Even during the academic publication of an archive catalogue, the same principle that governs the cataloguing of the archive must apply, according to which the user's interest and not that of the creator of the catalogue is essential Cf. *DACS 2019.0.3 - Describing Archives. A Content Standard*: xiv: 'Archivists make descriptive choices that impact how users find, identifiy, select and use archival records. To make wise choices about descriptive practices, archivists must develop and mantain an awareness of user needs and behaviours' (https://files.archivists.org/pubs/DACS_2019.0.3_Version.pdf).

[22] Northedge 1991; O'Kane 2009.

[23] An international project for reuniting all the archives in a single online platform has recently been launched: *The Creswell online network: documenting Islamic architecture through early photography* (Koulouris 2018).

they were added by one of Berenson's collaborators for a preliminary sorting of the photos in the collection in Florence. These numbers have not been included in the figure captions of this volume.

As for the dating of the monuments, this should always be understood as referring to the 'current era'; only in cases where this is earlier, the initials BCE (before current era) are indicated.

Finally, all URLs mentioned in the volume were last visited on December 20th, 2022.

Aknowledgments — This work could not have been possible without the great support of many colleagues and a number of institutions. My warmest thanks go to the staff of the Biblioteca Berenson, and especially to Spyros Koulouris, Giovanni Pagliarulo and Ilaria Della Monica, for allowing me to study and publish the photo collection.

Francesca Leoni, Alice Howard and Aimée Payton (Ashmolean Museum), Omniya Abdel Barr (Victoria & Albert Museum), Ola Seif (American University in Cairo), Joanne Bloom (Fine Arts Library, Harvard University) kindly provided information on the photos in the respective collections, allowing me to cross-check the data of the different archives.

Many colleagues provided valuable information on specific monuments and photos of their current state. In particular: Lidia Bettini, Laura Battini, Kathryn Brush, Janusz Byliński, Idris Bostan, Jennifer Celani, Giovanna De Palma, Gianluca Foschi, Piero Gilento, Haytham Hasan, Marc Lebeau, Balázs Major, Jean-Claude Margueron, Izabela Miszczak, Abdalrazzaq Moaz, Lobna Montasser, Giulia Annalinda Neglia, Alastair Northedge, Dick Osseman, Roberto Parenti, Pierre Sabatier, Eleanor Sheppard, Jehan Sherqo, Lasse Sommer Schütt, François Villeneuve, Daniel C. Waugh.

A special thanks goes to Ross Burns, who provided valuable assistance to locate several monuments in Syria.

Francesco Saliola developed the Google My Maps, Lisa Josephine Brucciani reviewed the English text of the volume, Chadi Hatoum translated the summary into Arabic, and Lucia Botarelli took care of resampling the images and of the volume's desktop layout.

Finally, my gratitude goes to David Davison, Ben Heaney, and Mike Schurer of the Archaeopress team for the highly professional assistance during the whole editorial process.

Firenze, January 24th, 2023
Stefano Anastasio

Creswell and the Berenson Collection

Biographical sketch

The figure of Archibald Creswell in the history of Islamic architectural studies is so well known that his biography has already been dealt with extensively in numerous articles and essays.[24] Here we will recall the key elements, underlining aspects related to his activity as a photographer and as the author of photographic collections that are currently spread across several institutions, including the Biblioteca Berenson.

Keppel Archibald Cameron Creswell was born in London on 13 September 1879, into a family originally from Nottingham (Figure 8). Keppel's father was a clergyman who later became a vicar, while his mother Margaret was the daughter of a solicitor in Rugby. He had a sister, Margaret. They lived at 12 Regent's Park Road.

He first attended Westminster School in London, between 1891 and 1896, where he excelled in his studies, especially in mathematics, and where he won awards for academic achievement. Tradition has it that the volume entitled *The seventh great oriental monarchy* (1876), i.e., the last volume of a series published by George Rawlison on the greatest periods of the ancient Near Eastern history, aroused Creswell's curiosity towards the East. In 1896, he moved to the City and Guilds Technical College in Finsbury, where he studied electrical engineering.

His first publication was in 1912, which curiously concerned occultism.[25] The following year, however, he published his first contribution to the subject of Islamic architecture, with an article entitled 'The origin of the Persian double dome' published in *The Burlington Magazine*.[26] The article, which was published in November 1913, was preceded in the August issue of the same magazine by a brief communication in the section 'Letters', regarding a Persian mihrab.[27]

In 1914, after brief work experiences at Siemens and then at Deutsche Bank, he submitted an application to join the Archaeological Survey of India, but the outbreak of World War I made him change his plans, preventing him from moving to India: 1916 was a year of major importance in Creswell's career, as he was appointed as Assistant Equipment Officer in the Royal Flying Corps and posted to Egypt which, from that moment onwards, became his adoptive homeland. In 1919, was promoted as Staff Captain of the Royal Air Force, and the following year, with the support of the keeper of the Ashmolean Museum, David George Hogarth, he was appointed Inspector under the British General Allenby's Military Administration of the Occupied Enemy Territory (see pp. 19-20).[28] This assignment allowed him to visit and catalogue a large number of monuments, for a survey that began in Aleppo and ended in Jerusalem, including Amman and Haifa as the other main stops.[29]

Figure 8: Archibald Creswell, photographed by Jack Gordon (courtesy American University in Cairo).

Under the patronage and with the financial support of King Fouad I of Egypt, he began working on the publication of the history of Islamic architecture, settling permanently in Cairo in 1920. The volumes of history of Islamic architecture that stemmed from this project are those that are most characteristic of his figure as a scholar: *Early Muslim architecture, Part 1* (1932) and *Part 2* (1940) and *Muslim architecture of Egypt, vol. I*, 1952, and *vol. II*, 1959. In 1958, *A Short account of early Muslim architecture* was also published, later revised by James Allan in 1989 and aimed at reaching a wider

---

[24] Combe 1965; Brisch 1974; Scanlon 1975; Hamilton 1991; AUC 2003; Anastasio 2020.
[25] Creswell 1912.
[26] Creswell 1913b.
[27] Creswell 1913a.
[28] Falls, Becke 1930: 608.
[29] A visit to Istanbul, that is widely represented in many of Creswell's photographs, which are not covered in this volume, also dates back to this period; Creswell mentions a trip 'in Constantinople in 1920' in a letter to Mary Whitall Smith, the wife of Bernard Berenson, dated 19 September 1928).

audience than just specialists.[30] It is probably in this early period of residence in Cairo that he first met Bernard Berenson, the art historian who, at least from 1922 was one of the patrons who supported Creswell's research, also financially (see p. 17).

In 1931 he became lecturer, and in 1934 tenured professor of Islamic Art and Archaeology at the Fouad University, a position he held until 1951, when he was forced to abandon the chair. In a letter kept at Villa I Tatti and dated 3 November 1952, Creswell informed Berenson that 'I was dismissed from the University last December, together with about 160 British officials still remaining in the Government service, as a reprisal for the events in the Canal Zone'. Nevertheless, his prestige was well known; among the various accolades and positions held, the following may be recalled: member of the Higher Council for the conservation of the Arab monuments (1939) and the trusteeship of the Palestine Archaeological Museum of Jerusalem (1949). The interruption of his teaching career at Fouad University and resulting loss in salary led to financial problems for Creswell, but he managed to find a solution thanks to fellowships from the Rockefeller Institute and, then, the Bollingen Foundation. In a letter dated 3 November 1952, Creswell informed Berenson that: 'Rockefeller Foundation decided that my work must continue (this without any action whatever on my part) and, after sending me a questionnaire, decided to pay me an annual sum exactly equal to my University salary for two years, as from June 1st 1952. So I am still floating'; in another letter, dated 11 September 1954, he wrote: 'Concerning myself, an application for a Bollingen Foundation Fellowship has been submitted with the support of (and on the suggestion on) Dr Badeau, late of the American University, Cairo. Prospects appear to be encouraging, but in any case it would not take effect until Jan 1st, 1955, whereas I have been living on my capital since June 1st – not a very pleasant sensation'.

The application was nevertheless fortunately successful, greatly easing Creswell's worries, as evidenced by a letter of 5 December 1954: 'As one of my staunchest allies I am sure you will be pleased to hear that I have just received official notification that the Bollingen Foundation has most generously granted me a fellowship for three years. You can imagine how relieved I am'. Bernard Berenson also supported Creswell financially, both earlier and in this period, as can be seen from other letters of thanks sent by Creswell.

1956 was another important year for Creswell, as the Suez crisis had a direct impact on his life. Fearing for the fate of his precious library, he decided to donate it to the American University of Cairo, while maintaining strict control over it and making it accessible only in a very limited way.[31] He was also appointed Distinguished Professor of Islamic Art and Architecture at the American University. In a letter to Berenson, dated 15 November 1957, Creswell summarises the situation: 'The American University here created a Chair of Muslim Architecture for me in April of last year, and that gave them a locus standi for intervening, through their Ambassador, on my behalf when I was told to leave the country within ten days on the 23rd of last November. I have been here all the time, except that I went home at the end of last June and returned at the beginning of October. I have two large rooms in the School of Oriental Studies, in which my library is installed. I have been able to continue my work, including planning mosques, etc., and have found everybody friendly, or at least indifferent'.

In 1973, a year after receiving Knighthood from the Queen, he was forced to leave Cairo: he had been a bachelor for his entire life and was no longer able to live alone self-sufficiently. Therefore, he returned to London, where he found refuge and care at the Congregation of the Alexian Brothers in Acton, where he died on 4 April 1974.

Creswell photographer: the working method

Many authors have focused on Creswell's method of carrying out his research and collecting documentation which, alongside serving as a basis for his publications, represents an extraordinary legacy of books, photographs, cards and notes. Here, I will particularly deal with Creswell's photographic documentation: what has reached us and how he produced it.[32]

With regard to Creswell's working method, it has been repeatedly emphasized that the guiding principle of all his work was the search for chronological order.[33] Creswell himself stated this in his writings, both directly and indirectly. For example, in the Introduction to the *Early Muslim architecture, Part 1*, the first sentence concerns the time span covered by the work, specifying that it went from 622 to 935 A.D. and that the final date had actually been changed compared to the original one. Creswell added 13 years so that the period taken into account could match one of the dates indicated by Leone Caetani in his *Islamic Chronographia*.[34] It is significant that Creswell decided to begin his first major work in this manner, as if emphasising the importance given to chronology, defined as 'the spinal column of history' in the same text. As further proof of this approach, it is worth recalling that his first two publications mentioned above, essentially deal with the chronology of the monuments examined.[35] All this

---

[30] Creswell 1932, 1940, 1952, 1958, 1959a. On Creswell's bibliography see Ettinghausen 1957; IAN 2004.
[31] Karnouk 1991; Tovell 1992, 1993.
[32] On Creswell's research method, and for a modern reinterpretation of his research, see Blair 1991; Grabar 1991; Raby 1991; Rogers 1991. On the activity of photographer: Fitzherbert 1991; Karnouk 1991; Warren N. 2009; Lederman 2015.
[33] On this subject, see Hamilton 1991: 130 especially.
[34] Creswell 1932: i.
[35] Creswell 1913a, 1913b.

is directly reflected in his working method: we know that during his trips he did his best to visit monuments in chronological order, so that his view of them was already arranged according to this principle.[36]

His notes, cards, drawings and photographs were ordered chronologically. This order was thus reflected in his finished work, where architectural development was explained through a sequence of monuments that followed one another in time: not by chance, it was said that Creswell's history of architecture is 'the biography of great buildings',[37] this being, for some scholars, a limitation of his work.[38]

Another aspect of key importance to understand Creswell's work as a photographer, is related to his great expertise in architectural graphic surveying. For Creswell, photographs were basically documentation illustrating what had been surveyed and filed: the method used for taking a photograph, therefore, had to be as consistent as possible with the method used for carrying out the surveys. He is well-known for his expertise in technical drawing, acquired since the years of the City and Guilds Technical College at Finsbury.[39] It cannot be too strongly emphasised that his ability not only led to exceptional accuracy and skill in the use of survey methods and tools, but to a real talent in solving practical problems, typical of architectural surveys, and in coming up at times with truly innovative solutions. This resulted in quite 'unique' surveys with an accuracy and thoroughness that are difficult to find in similar contemporary works.

An example may help to understand just how innovative this method was: in the first volume of *Early Muslim architecture*,[40] Creswell dedicates an appendix to illustrating the method followed to carry out an 'accurate plan' of the Dome of the Rock in Jerusalem. Given the complexity of the structure, 'owing to the piers, screens, etc', its accurate measurement 'from side to side' using traditional methods was prohibitive. Creswell, therefore, states that he used 'a 25-metre Chesterman tape', to determine a sequence of trilaterations, according to the scheme shown in Figure 9. The system is truly innovative and Creswell was well aware of this, to such an extent that he asked Mr F.S. Richards of the Survey of Egypt to carry out the data computation. Mr Richards '... was struck by the novelty of the problem, all the data obtained by me for the various triangles being sides, instead of angles as it is usually the case in a survey'. The margin of error, in the end, is indeed insignificant.

It may seem curious that, in illustrating his work, Creswell felt the need to point out that he used a '25-metre Chesterman tape'. However, we can compare

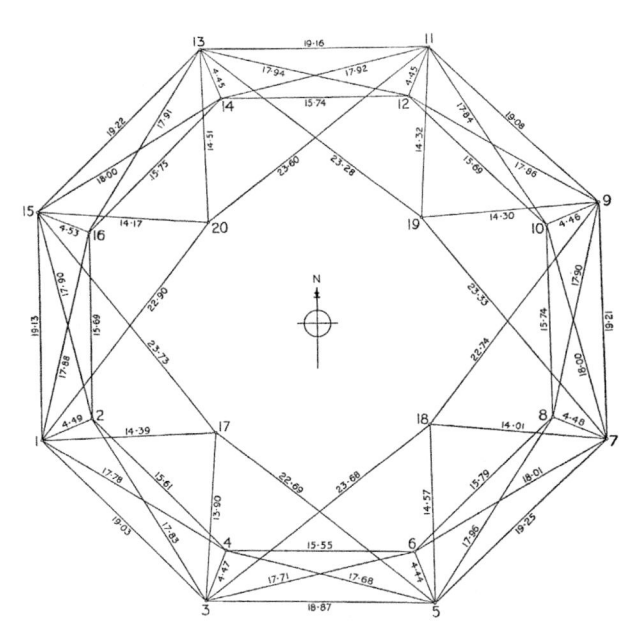

Figure 9: Jerusalem, Dome of the Rock, published in Creswell 1932, fig. 491 (original caption: 'diagram showing measurements taken to fix the true shape pf the two concentric octagons').

Figure 10: One of the earliest advertisements for a Chesterman tape, dated 1872 (https://www.gracesguide.co.uk/James_Chesterman_and_Co).

this statement to those made by contemporary scholars who mention the latest generation software or scanner they have used when describing their surveys. The new features, sophistication and level of detail of these tools are obviously of relevance for the data being illustrated. Actually, at the time of the Creswell's surveys, measuring tapes were already a century old: James Chesterman was granted with a patent for the steel tape in 1829.[41] However, at first the instrument was used almost exclusively for tailoring, and only occasionally in other fields.[42] A news item to publicise the tool, published in 1869 in the *Scientific American*, optimistically reports that the tool 'is extensively used by architects, surveyors, and contractors',[43] but

[36] Raby 1991: 7.
[37] Rogers 1991: 51.
[38] Raby 1991: 8; Draper 2005: 10.
[39] Hamilton 1991: 129.
[40] Creswell 1932: 412.

[41] Randy 2009.
[42] Eschner 2017.
[43] Anonymous 1869.

its diffusion was actually not so immediate and, above all, not consistent in all countries and in all fields and disciplines. This was because at the beginning it was not such a handy and effective tool as the modern version that we know today, and because it was also quite expensive. By scrolling through the various editions of the catalogue *A manual of the principal instruments used in American engineering and surveying*, published by W. and L.E. Gurley (Troy, N.Y.), we get a good idea of how the tool spread, at least in the United States. In the 1873 edition, exactly with regard to the Chesterman tape, it is stated that the tape was 'made of a ribbon of steel, which is joined at intervals, and wound up in a leather case, having a folding handle'. However, it is stressed that 'the great cost of the steel tape has always prevented its general use' (p. 129). Over time, the measuring tape began to be used more widely and different types were available, yet it continued to be a niche instrument. In the 1902 edition, for example, the entry 'tapes' is at the bottom of the catalogue's list of measuring instruments (p. 175), reporting that this tool is 'generally used in bridges, road and street works' (p. 237), as a complement to the rigid metre that continued to be the main instrument used. It was only in 1922, in the United States, that a new patent was granted to Hiram A. Farrand.[44] His instrument, compared to previous ones, was innovative because it was a 'measuring tape made of metallic ribbon curved to have a concavo-convex cross section and sufficiently flexible to permit of its being rolled or coiled [...] one object of the present invention is to provide a simple but inexpensive form of holder for the reception of a coil of tape of the type indicated'. It was the first metric tape, similar in every way to those still in use today, very practical and, therefore, widespread.

To sum up, we can say that the measuring tape, in Egypt and at the time of Creswell's surveys, was certainly an innovative and uncommon tool, especially if used in the field of architecture and art history. In my opinion, if Creswell felt the need to emphasise his use of the tape, it was because he did not simply use it to carry out traditional surveys, given that the flexible metric tape was much handier, but fully exploited its potential by making innovative surveys: indeed, while it would have been theoretically possible to take the measurements of the Dome of the Rock using a traditional rigid meter, it would have been very difficult in practical terms.[45] It is useful to consider this aspect when evaluating Creswell's work as a photographer, given that he saw photography as a tool for supporting monument surveys: when taking photographs, therefore, he on the one hand kept in mind a sort of chronological 'must'

and on the other tried to use the technical potential of his tools to the full. In this way, a photograph, if organised chronologically, 'spoke for itself'.[46]

The first impression we get when looking at Creswell's photographs but also when considering how they were collected, is of an activity that was carried out with meticulous care and attention to reach incredibly high levels of accuracy: Creswell personally devoted himself to all aspects of photography, without turning to other professional photographers, neither when taking the shots nor when developing and printing the photographs. He used different cameras and, above all, different lenses, privileging the telephotography wherever possible, to ensure the rendering of even the smallest details.[47] Unfortunately, I found no indication of the equipment used by Creswell in his early years as a photographer, including during his tenure as inspector under Allenby's administration.[48] Instead, there is more information about the following years, when his range of cameras and lenses became extremely rich and typical of a professional photographer. Creswell himself, in the Introduction to the first volume of his *Muslim architecture of Egypt*, provides information about his equipment: 'a Contessa Nettel (Stuttgart), 13×18cm, with a Zeiss double Protar, 18cm, and a supplement giving 15 and 13cm focus when required, and a wideangle Protar of 9cm; a Sinclair mahogany camera, 18×24cm, with a Zeiss Tessar, 24cm, a Goerz Dagor of 30cm, and two wide-angle Protars of 18 and 14cm'.[49] Several shots were often taken of the same subject, to capture any subtle light variations.

His meticulous attention and commitment, even physical, to always get the best shots is truly astonishing: see for example the photo of the scaffold used for the close-up shots of the mosaics of the Umayyad Mosque of Damascus (above, Figure 2). Photography, however, was used by Creswell not only to photograph monuments, but to exploit it to its maximum potential, especially if we keep in mind the years in which he worked: it is indeed noteworthy that Creswell was one of the first to use aerial photos for studying ancient architecture, for example, when he used the photographs taken by the French Aviation for studying the monuments of Raqqa.[50] Finally, he also took or acquired photographs to document written sources that could be of use

---

[44] See Patent US1402589A, available at https://patents.google.com/patent/US1402589A/en
[45] I would like to thank Roberto Parenti, who was the first to make me notice the quote of the measuring tape in Creswell's text.
[46] Karnouk 1991: 120. Karnouk also cites, at p. 117, an interview given by Creswell to the newspaper *al-Mussawar* in 1970, which unfortunately I have not been able to consult. According to Karnouk, in the interview, Creswell gave practical details about his fieldwork, which was divided into two main phases: first the reconstruction of the plan and then the study of the architecture, decorations and inscriptions.
[47] Karnouk 1991: 120.
[48] Fitzherbert 1991: 127.
[49] Creswell 1952: ix-x; a list of the cameras and lenses housed in Creswell's library in Cairo is given in Fitzherbert 1991: 127.
[50] Vernoit 1997: 6.

to his work. In a letter to Berenson dated 3 January 1958, he speaks of the Umayyad Mosque of Damascus and quotes the following: 'Ibn Shākir, c. 1360, wrote a History of Damascus, which he states is based on that of Ibn 'Asākir, c. 1180. Quatremère, when he translated Maqrīzī's Sulūk, under the title Histore des Sultans Mamlouks, in 1840, added as an Appendix a long translated extract from Ibn Shākir on the Great Mosque, so everybody interested in the mosque went straight to Quatremère and read the Appendix, and Ibn Shākir got a quite undeserved publicity! Following my principle — the only sound of — of always going back to the original sources, I had photographs made of about 14 pp. of the MS. of Ibn Asākin preserved at Damascus, which no Orientalist, even those living on the shot, had thought of doing, and the result was a pricked bubble'.
In the Introduction to the Early Muslim architecture mentioned above, there is an interesting observation by the author about the illustrations used for the book: Creswell emphasizes that he chose to publish the drawings 'to a simple scale, such as 1/50th, 1/100th, 1/200th, etc., so that dimensions can be taken off them with a centimetre scale, and the original size obtained immediately'.[51] This may seem a trivial matter, but in fact most contemporary publications reproduced scale drawings, but suited to the size of the print. Creswell's attention to this aspect means that he clearly knew what could be useful to readers who needed to check or further examine the data presented to them.
Consequently, his photographs were also published using accurate scales, as consistent as possible with those of the drawings. In the same text mentioned above he says: 'Whenever possible, that is to say, whenever flat, decorated surfaces are concerned, the photographs have been reproduced so as to represent the exact scale. [...] they are therefore tantamount to measured drawings, and dimensions can be obtained directly from them in the same way'.
We know that Creswell began taking photographs at a very early stage. Some photographs credited to Creswell were published in 1917 in a Cairo travel guide titled Rambles in Cairo.[52] As regards the photographs taken in Mesopotamia, Syria and Transjordan, it is not possible, to my knowledge, to precisely date them. Actually, the bulk of the collection consists in photos taken between July 1919 and May 1920, when Creswell served in the Allenby Administration. At that time, he was stationed in Aleppo and then in Amman, Haifa and Jerusalem.[53]

A proof of this is that almost all the photographs of Syrian and Jordanian sites, as well as those today in Turkey on the border with Syria (Harran, Birecik), belong to the batch of prints purchased by the Victoria & Albert Museum (V&A) in 1921. However, it cannot be excluded that some photos may date back to a different period. In two letters, dated 26 and 27 November 1923 and sent to Bernard Berenson and his wife, Mary Whitall Smith, respectively, he says that he had just made 'a trip of eighteen days archaeological research in Syria and Palestine with Sir John Marshall, Director General of Archaeology in India'. It is indeed possible that he took some photographs even on trips like this.[54] In several cases, the monuments photographed by Creswell were subject to excavations or photographed again at a later date and a comparison between the state of the monuments in the various photographs taken shows that Creswell's, overall, cannot be later than the 1920s. Only the photos of central Mesopotamia (Baghdad, Qantarat Harba, Samarra, Taq Kisra, Ukhaidir) are slightly later, since almost all correspond to the batch purchased by V&A in 1930. It is therefore most likely that they were taken on the occasion of a trip that Creswell made in the Spring of that year in Iraq.[55] The photographs of the Egyptian monuments is a different matter since they were obviously taken over a much longer period of time, until at least 1964.[56]

His work as photographer did not end on the site, but continued in his studio, i.e., the 'arsenal' according to Creswell's definition, where the photographs were mounted on Bristol-sheets and organised in books.[57] In addition to his own photographs, he bought and collected photographs of different authors, as well as adding several lantern slides to the negatives, which he used mainly for lectures.

Creswell's legacy of photographs

Creswell's legacy of photographs and slides is currently spread among different archives, as well as some minor private collections. Apart from the Biblioteca Berenson, discussed below, the main archives that hold Creswell's photographic legacy are the Ashmolean Museum in Oxford,[58] the American University in Cairo,[59] the

---

[51] Creswell 1932: xxiv.
[52] Devonshire 1917. On this subject, see also Lederman 2015.
[53] Hamilton 1991: 130: 'to compile an inventory, his first task, Creswell (now an Army Captain) was stationed initially at Aleppo, towards the extreme north of the area, then successively at Amman, Haifa, and Jerusalem. In this way, travelling by army transport, on horseback or by donkey, he was able to measure and photograph monuments from the Euphrates to the borders of Egypt'.

[54] It is worth remembering how Creswell, in the caption of the illustration of a mosaic of the Umayyad Mosque in Damascus published in Early Muslim Architecture, writes that it was photographed in 1925 (Creswell 1932, pl. 42.c; see below, Figure 564).
[55] Omniya Abdel Barr, pers. com.
[56] https://library.aucegypt.edu/libraries/rbscl/photographs/creswell-islamic-collection
[57] Karnouk 1991: 121 reports that Creswell had stated that the preparation of a sheet of paper required between 25 and 30 minutes, meaning that approximately 1067 hours, i.e., six hours a day for six months, was the time needed to produce the 2134 sheets of his collection.
[58] Fitzherbert 1991; Allan J. 2003.
[59] Burns K. 1991; O'Kane 2009.

Victoria & Albert Museum in London,[60] and the Fine Arts Library in Harvard.[61]

The Ashmolean Museum inherited Creswell's collection of negatives. The whole set consisted of about 2,400 unboxed negatives, 1,000 of which in glass. Furthermore, there were 55 cloth-bound books with half-plate negatives in numbered sleeves, meaning that the total amount could be close to 8,000.[62] In 1999, a good part of these images was digitised and published, at low resolution, on a CD-ROM. Currently, 5,659 photos are published online.[63]

The American University in Cairo (AUC) acquired its collection from Creswell in 1956, when he became professor of Islamic Art and Architecture at the same University. Creswell donated not only his photographic archive to AUC, but his personal library too. In 2004-2006 the collection was processed within a project sponsored by the Getty Foundation. The collection contains around 8,000 black and white printed photos, and around 1,000 glass slides, taken by Creswell between 1916 and 1964. The photo archive is organised according to Creswell's scheme, i.e., the photographs are sorted first by country, city, site and monument, and then in chronological order; for each subject, the photos are arranged in the following order: panoramic view, entrance, interior, particular features and decorative elements. A selection of photos of Egypt is currently available online.[64]

Another important batch of photographs is kept in London at the Victoria & Albert Museum (V&A). An initial purchase of about 2,600 printed photographs, in response to an offer by Creswell, was made by the Museum in September 1920. Further smaller batches of photographs were purchased in 1926, 1927, 1929, 1930 and 1939, bringing the total number of photographs in the collection to 3,341. In 1977, the collection was transferred from the National Art Library to the Department of Prints and Drawings and, thanks to a project for the cataloguing and digitalisation of the entire V&A collection, is now fully digitised and accessible online.[65]

Finally, the Fine Arts Library, at Harvard University, hosts a large batch of photographs. The collection comprises *c.* 2,800 photos, which are partly available online.[66] The photos were purchased at the end of 1923 or beginning 1924 by Arthur Kingsley Porter, a professor of Medieval Architecture at Harvard University between 1921 and 1933. His widow, Lucy Wallace, donated them in 1962, together with other photographs, to the Fine Arts Library. Porter was a friend of Berenson; therefore he was possibly the person who put Porter and Creswell into contact with each other.[67]

In most cases, the above-mentioned archives have replicas of the same images, although they are not exactly alike. In the Appendix 3 reference is made to any known replicas in other archives. Providing a complete synopsis of the archives is a quite difficult task (and the COVID-19 emergency made it even more challenging since it was not possible to visit the museums and examine the materials). However, thanks to the help and support of the archive keepers, these activities were at least partly carried out.[68] Hopefully, this work, which is certainly preliminary and yet to be completed, will be useful for the development of the international project currently in progress and designed to reunite all the archives in a single online accessible platform: *The Creswell online network: documenting Islamic architecture through early photography.*[69]

Creswell's collection at the Biblioteca Berenson

The photographs presented in this work are held in the archives of Villa I Tatti in Florence, where Bernard Berenson lived from 1900 until his death in 1959, and which currently houses The Harvard University Center for Italian Renaissance Studies.[70] Bernard Berenson, born Bernhard Valvrojenski in Butrimonys (Lithuania) on 26 June 1865, changed his name when his family, of Jewish origins, emigrated to the United States, settling in Boston in 1874. He showed a deep passion for art history from an early age, studying first at Boston University and then, from 1884, at Harvard. In 1887, he went on his first trip to Europe, where he furthered his knowledge of art history, especially Medieval and Renaissance, and soon matured a special interest in Italian painting. Over time, he became a well-known historian and critic of art, publishing several essays and acting as a consultant to collectors and museums, especially American ones. In 1900 he married Mary Whitall Smith and moved to Villa I Tatti with her,

---

[60] Lederman 2015; Owen 2017a-c.
[61] An introduction to the collection is available at https://library.harvard.edu/collections/middle-east-and-islamic-photographs
[62] Fitherbert 1991: 125; Allan 2003.
[63] https://collections.ashmolean.org/collection/search/new (search 'Creswell' under Person).
[64] http://digitalcollections.aucegypt.edu/digital/collection/p15795coll14 and https://dlmenetwork.org/library (search: 'Creswell').
[65] https://collections.vam.ac.uk/search/ (choose 'K.A.C. Creswell' under the suggested entries for 'Person').
[66] https://images.hollis.harvard.edu (search 'Creswell'

together with 'Fine Arts, Digital Images & Slides'. A large selection of images is also available at https://archnet.org/collections/12
[67] Joanne Bloom and Kathryn Brush, *pers. com.* Correspondence, notes, and biographical materials on A.K. Porter are included in the *Papers of Arthur Kingsley Porter, 1863-1957.* HUG 1706.102, Harvard University Archives.
[68] Francesca Leoni, Alice Howard and Aimée Payton (Ashmolean Museum), Ola Seif (American University in Cairo), Omniya Abdel Barr (Victoria & Albert Museum), Joanne Bloom (Fine Arts Library).
[69] Koulouris 2018.
[70] http://itatti.harvard.edu/about

on the hills of Settignano, near Florence (Figure 11). Thanks to his activity as a consultant, he acquired a remarkable fortune and managed to first purchase the property of I Tatti, which he had initially occupied as a tenant, and then expanded and embellished the estate. In short, I Tatti became a cultural cosmopolitan centre, equipped with a rich library of roughly 50,000 volumes, and an archive of photographs with particular focus on Italian Renaissance painting. Berenson bequeathed his estate and land, his works of art, and the archives to Harvard University, which now form the 'Villa I Tatti Research Center'.

Much has been written about Berenson and his method of study.[71] Here, it is interesting to note how he always emphasised the importance of photography as a tool for studying art history. Ever since his youth, he sought to purchase printed photos of art paintings, although his finances at the time were very low.[72] Over time, and having much more money available, he tried to build a photo library capable of containing as many photographs of art as possible, which would be of help to art history scholars. At present, the photographic collection has more than 300,000 items, the most part in black and white, and a small amount in colour. The collection and Berenson's research focused on Italian paintings and drawings from the fourteenth to the end of the sixteenth century, but Berenson also had a strong interest in the art of different civilizations, especially Byzantine, Oriental and Islamic art. To gain deeper knowledge of this sector he also went on several study trips in most of the countries on the shores of southern and eastern Mediterranean.[73] His relationship with Creswell is therefore linked to these areas of interest, and explains the presence of such a significant photo archive. Berenson's correspondence with various scholars and colleagues, including Creswell, is preserved in the archives of Villa I Tatti.[74] In all, there are 23 letters sent by Creswell to Berenson and his wife. In the earliest letter, dated 12 May 1922, Creswell speaks extensively of Mushatta, in Jordan, and writes of the forwarding to Berenson of 341 photographs (unfortunately without giving details about the subjects). In a slightly later letter, dated 17 August 1922, he thanks him 'for a long

Figure 11: Bernard and Mary Berenson at Villa I Tatti, March 1929 (Harvard University, Biblioteca Berenson, photo W629199_1).

series of kindnesses, culminating in your present generous offer'. In a letter to Mary, dated 28 June 1923, there is an interesting account of one of Creswell's trips to Italy during which, alongside meeting the Berensons, Creswell had the opportunity to visit other Italian places, and was particularly impressed by Pisa and its cathedral ('Dear Mrs. Berenson, I arrived at Pisa in good time and found the Cathedral enchanting. I think it is the most beautiful building of its kind in Italy. It satisfys all sorts of undefined architectural yearnings and canons of beauty, which I have always felt, but only half crystallized. The perfect repose of its smooth surfaces, the unusual presence of a triforium, and the beautiful way in which the latter is carried across the transepts, made me long to take off my hat to the tomb of the architect Busketus'). Berenson financed Creswell several times, especially in difficult times, for example, immediately after Creswell lost his professorship at Fouad University. In the correspondence preserved at I Tatti, Creswell thanks Berenson for different donations in letters dated 17 August 1922, 26 November 1923 and 4 October 1954. The photographs sent to Berenson therefore are not the result of actual sales, but are nevertheless related to Berenson's patronage activities. The Biblioteca Berenson preserves a total of 2930 gelatin silver prints, mainly 12×17cm or smaller. They

---

[71] Above all, see Pope-Hennessy 1988, with bibliography, and Gioffredi Superbi 2010, with a a focus on Berenson's relationship with photography.

[72] Gioffredi Superbi 2010: 290.

[73] On Berenson's interest in Islamic culture, see Casari 2014. In particular, a detailed list of the trips to study the Islamic world is given by Casari at footnote 34. One of these trips was dedicated to Syria and Palestine, in 1929.

[74] The letters are part of the collection *Bernard and Mary Berenson papers, Biblioteca Berenson, Tatti – The Harvard University Center for Italian Renaissance Studies,* https://hollisarchives.lib.harvard.edu/repositories/10/resources/6820. They were recently transcribed by Gavin Moulton (2018) and made available for this study through the assistance of Spyros Koulouris.

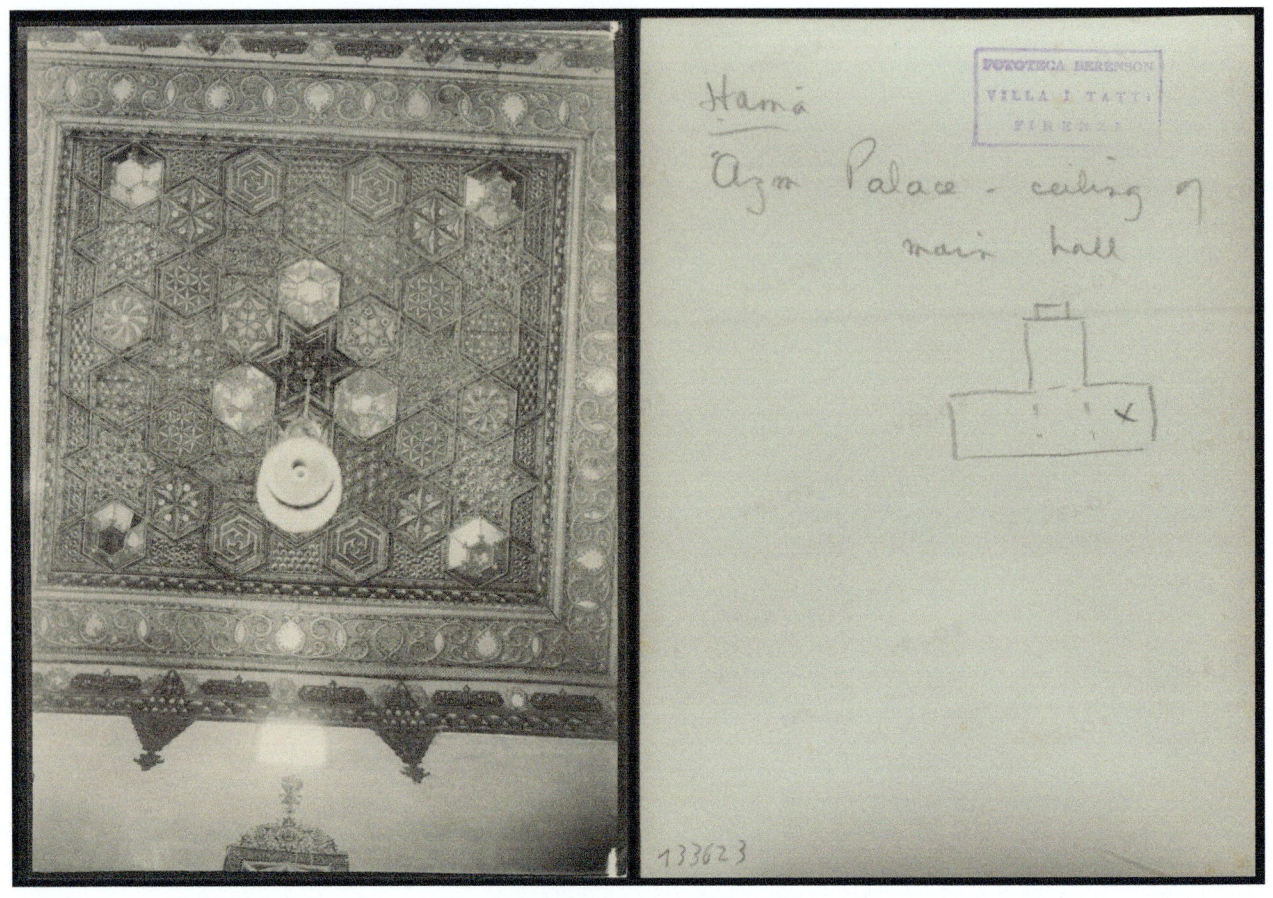

Figure 12: Front (left) and back (right) of Berenson ID 133324 (below, Figure 500).

are enclosed in transparent leaves in ring binders. The photos are sorted by country and then by city and/or specific site, and finally by monument. On the rear, many of them have handwritten notes, detailing the pictured subjects (Figure 12). The photographs concern sites and monuments in Egypt, Syria, Palestine, Iraq, Transjordan, Lebanon, Tunisia and Turkey. All the photos of the collection have been digitised and uploaded on Hollis Images.

Digitisation of the entire archive is still in progress and, as it continues, the images are gradually being uploaded (see p. 275).[75]

---

[75] https://images.hollis.harvard.edu/ (search 'Creswell' together with 'Berenson, Fototeca').

Mesopotamia, Syria and Transjordan in Creswell's photographs

Mesopotamia, Syria and Transjordan at the end of World War I

As said above (see p. 15), the bulk of the photos of Northern Mesopotamia, Syria and Transjordan, was taken between July 1919 and May 1920, while the photos of central Mesopotamia are perhaps slightly more recent (*c.* 1930).

As a photographer, Creswell paid attention exclusively to the architectural element. However, his photos are also of interest for what they tell us about the countryside and urban landscape where the monuments were located. They were indeed taken at a time of extraordinary change and transition from the end of the Ottoman rule to the beginning of the French and British mandates. The opportunity to visit the monuments during the inspection activities conducted in the territories of the Allenby Administration (Figure 13)[76] allowed Creswell to work in a privileged environment. He was able to photograph and document in a professional manner and, above all, quickly and consistently, the large number of monuments that we can admire today in his photo collection.

At the time of the Creswell's photographs, Mesopotamia, Syria and Transjordan were already well-known regions visited by Westerners, and by the British in particular. After a long period of 'abandonment', practically since the times of the Crusades, European interest for the Levant, intended mainly as a Syrian-Palestinian belt, resumed with the campaign of Egypt by Napoleon (1798-1801) and, from that moment onwards, did not stop. The Ottoman policy certainly contributed to this since it simply administered the regions, without fostering real integration with the local populations: if we exclude the religious domain, they felt the Turks were as distant as the Europeans. As regards also the study and protection of cultural heritage, it is no coincidence that the first initiatives were again European (for example, the constitution in 1881 in Egypt of the Committee for the Conservation of Monuments of Arab Art).[77]

Palestine and the neighbouring regions were, for Europeans, the scene of biblical events, and exercised a strong cultural appeal.[78]

Politically, it was from the beginning of the 20th century that awareness of the strategic importance of the region appeared, especially in Great Britain. The term 'Middle East' was coined to precisely indicate the area lying in the middle of India and Egypt and, for this reason, crucial to British interests.[79] This prolonged 'connection' between the West and the East and the expectations (especially of the Arab populations) towards France and Great Britain for the help that they could provide to local populations to achieve self-determination and independence, certainly favoured the development of a very close relationship and of a strong European presence that was fundamentally well accepted, until the end of the World War I. However, by the end of 1917, the 'Middle East affairs' became more complicated, especially following the revelation by the Russian government of the Sykes-Picot agreement, as well as the British promise to the Jews of a national home in Palestine enunciated in the so-called *Balfour Declaration.* However, this is not the place to define and discuss such a complex subject. What is necessary here is to briefly explain the historical context of Creswell's photographic activities.

After the Armistice of Moudros of 30 October 1918 and the Treaty of Sèvres of 10 August 1920, the Ottoman Sultanate renounced all its possessions outside Anatolia, which brought Mesopotamia, Syria and Transjordan (along with the rest of the Lebanese and Palestinian belt) to entering the orbit of the British and French, as established by the Sykes-Picot agreements signed on 16 May 1916.

In Mesopotamia, after the capture of Baghdad in 1917, the immediately strong presence of the British led to giving Britain the Mandate (received by the League of Nations in 1920) to administer Iraq in view of its future independence. The immediate anti-British uprisings convinced the British to abandon the direct mandate, favouring softer forms of control, with a kingdom entrusted to the Hashemite Faisal ben al-Hussayn, who had led the Arab Revolt in 1916, in August 1921. However, they retained military control and foreign policy, formally recognising the monarchy only in 1932. As said, we do not know exactly when Creswell took the photographs. It was certainly in this period of time, but no later than 1930.

---

[76] Cf. the description of the Allenby's 'administrative areas', as given in Falls-Becke 1930: 607: 'On the 23rd October (1918) Sir Edmund Allenby reported to the War office that he had issued fresh instructions for the military administration of enemy territory in Syria and Palestine already in his hands or likely to be occupied in the near future. There were to be three administrative areas, known as Occupied Enemy Territory South, Occupied Enemy Territory North, and Occupied Enemy Territory East. The first two comprised respectively the "Red" and "Blue" zones of the Sykes-Picot Agreement; the third such portions of Zones "A" and "B" of that agreement as came under the control of the Commander-in-Chef'.

[77] Diaz-Andreu 2007: 124.

[78] Diaz-Andreu 2007: 132-134.

[79] In 1902, Alfred Thayer Mahan, an American strategist, first used the term 'Middle East' in an essay entitled 'The Persian Gulf and international relations', published in the English journal *National Review* (Mahan 1902). He theorised that the British should extend its naval control over Persia and Mesopotamia, the middle lands between Egypt and India, already under British control.

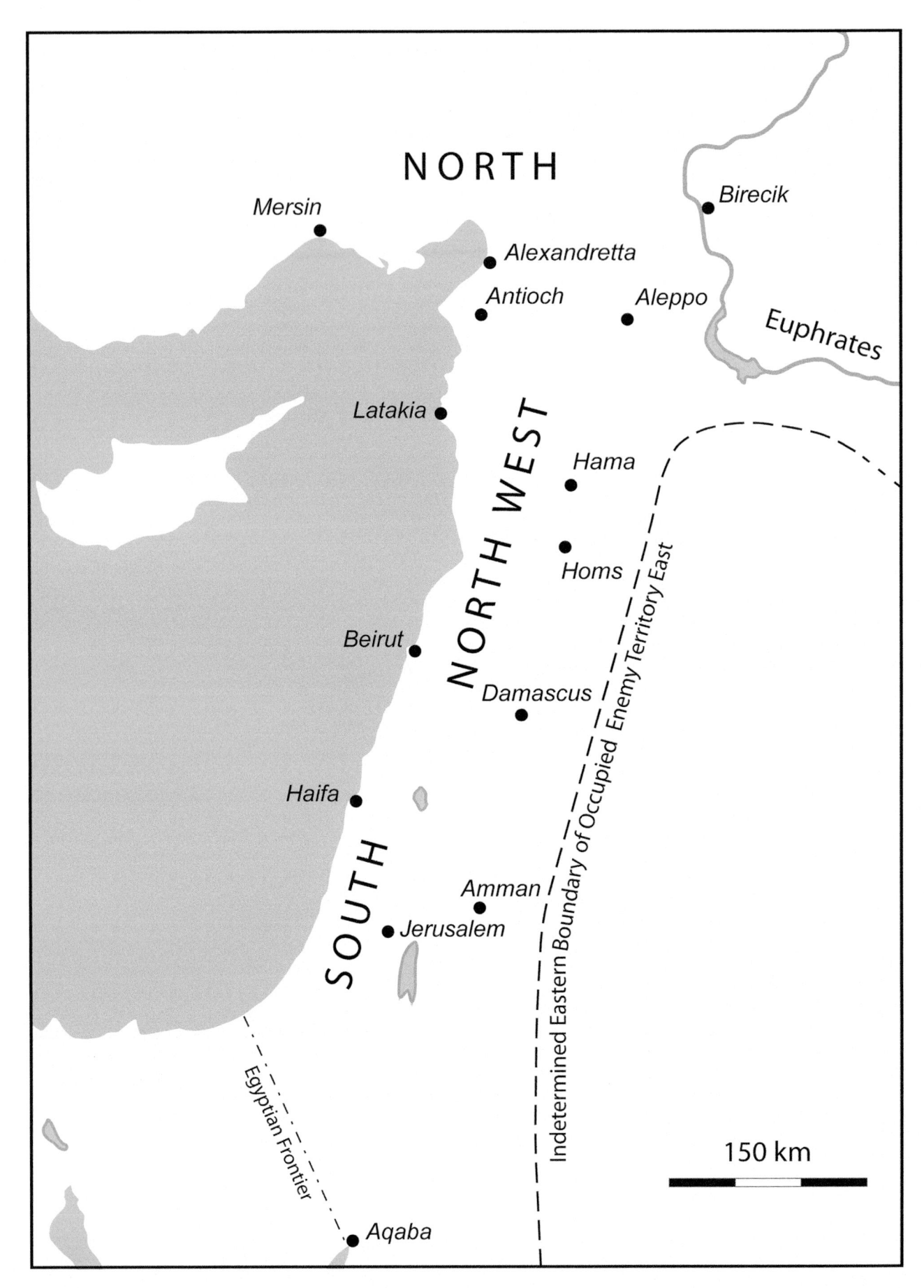

Figure 13: The 'administrative areas' of Allenby's Administration of Occupied Enemy Territory, dated December 1918 (map based on the sketch map n. 42 published in Falls, Becke 1930).

As for Syria, Creswell visited the country at a particularly delicate moment of political transition. It was exactly in 1919, during the brief existence of the so-called 'Kingdom of Syria', headed by the same Faisal ben al-Hussayn who, the following year, was removed by the French to shortly become the above mentioned King of Iraq. On 24 July 1920, the provisional Syrian government was dissolved and the French Mandate began, lasting until 1946.

In Transjordan the situation was different. In taking control of Syria, the French did not go south to Transjordan which consequently experienced a short period of 'power vacuum' immediately after the end of the war. This void was filled by the British, who in March 1921 included Transjordan in the Mandate for Palestine and placed the Emir Abdallah, the second son of Faisal ben al-Hussayn, on the throne of the new Emirate of Transjordan. Abdallah was proclaimed King by a plebiscite in 1921, but true independence was only achieved in 1932, with the official end of the British Mandate. Creswell's visit, therefore, took place immediately before the start of Abdallah's reign, in a period marked by the British negotiating and organising the constitution of the Emirate together with the Arabs of the region.

Photographers in Mesopotamia, Syria and Transjordan prior to Creswell's work

Besides these historical and political events, it is important to understand the context in which Creswell worked, with particular reference to photography. Much has been written about the history of photography in the Near East.[80] As might be expected, the first photographers and, later, the main development of photographic activity took place in the Syrian-Palestinian belt, where the European presence was most influential: the most important photographic studios were established in Beirut and Jerusalem.

Here, we will focus on the key aspects of the development of photography in the three regions examined — Mesopotamia, Syria and Transjordan — from the beginning of photographic practice to the period of Creswell's work. To support this general overview, Appendix 1 provides a review, which is certainly not exhaustive but representative, of the photographers known to have worked in these regions and throughout this time span.

Creswell photographed Mesopotamia, Syria and Transjordan, when the first successful photographic process had been developed nearly a century before, and had found immediate application in the East. The photographic method used, the daguerrotype, was presented in Paris on 7 January 1839: in November of the same year, the first daguerrotype was taken in Cairo (and was greeted by the Prefect of Cairo as the 'Devil's work'), and in December in Jerusalem.[81] We can say that about a decade passed between the first phase, featuring a real pioneering approach, and a more systematic and widespread production phase that strengthened and grew very quickly.

There are several reasons for this close relationship between photography and the Near East. First, technical factors played a key role. The landscapes and the light of Egypt and the Near East assured optimal conditions for early photographers: the early emulsions needed long exposure times, and the clear air and the strongly perpendicular light allowed posing times that were shorter than in most European countries.[82] In addition, advances in technology, as is known, were very rapid. The introduction of calotypes in the 1840s, which permitted the reproduction of multiple prints, allowed photographers to respond effectively to market demands and encouraged the circulation of their products. Furthermore, already in the 1850s the production of glass negative plates, first using wet collodion and then dry collodion increased the potential of photography, which was therefore gradually practiced and diffused.[83] Finally, it should be remembered that although the so-called half-tone process, which made it possible to reproduce photographs in book illustrations, dates back to the 1880s, even the photographs of previous years were an excellent basis for faithful engraving reproductions.[84] They guaranteed a true-to-life effect which was the first reason for the success of photography.

In addition, Europeans travelling to the Near East from the end of the 19th century were motivated by different reasons; yet, whatever these may have been, photography was always able to contribute to their purpose, ensuring they had adequate documentation and story-telling about their trips once back in Europe and America. The first to visit the Near East were missionaries and pilgrims, who wished to document their visits to Jerusalem and other biblical places,[85] yet there was already a significant increase in travellers and explorers as early as the 1840s. Often accompanied by painters and draftsmen, they visited the regions where biblical events had taken place and whose sites and monuments were becoming famous as a

---

[80] To mention just a few summary works: Onne 1980; Vaczek, Buckland 1981; Gavin 1982; O'Reilly 1983; Chevedden 1984; Nir 1985; Perez 1988; Howe 1997; Abujaber, Cobbing 2005; Bohrer 2011.

[81] Zevi 1984: 13; Howe 1997: 239.
[82] Zevi 1984: 14; Rosovsky 1997: 15.
[83] On these technical aspects, see in particular Zevi 1984: 12-13; Howe 1997: 24; Abujaber, Cobbing 2005: 225.
[84] Howe 1997: 45.
[85] Rosovsky 1997: 13; El-Hage 2000: 40-44; Diaz-Andreu 2007: 132; Bair 2011: 31. For a bibliography on ancient travellers in Syria, see also the *Bibliographie des récits de voyages* published on http://monummamluk-syrie.org

result of archaeological discoveries.[86] A separate issue regards the photography of scientific expeditions and research institutes, on which we will return later. Finally, some specific events gave new impetus to the development of photography: above all, the tour of the Levant made by the Prince of Wales in 1862, whose official photographer was Francis Bedford, and Kaiser Wilhelm II's 'oriental journey' in 1898, which was documented by numerous photographers who accompanied the court and used their photographs to record the journey (which also touched the regions considered in this study).[87]

Alongside the amateur photographer, the figure of the professional photographer soon developed in the Near East, both itinerant and operating in the photograph studios that were opened in the main cities.[88] Their production addressed a very wide market: views of sites and monuments intended directly for the European market, for the tourists who came to visit, as well as for scientific expeditions, publishing, portraits... The opportunity to have 'real' views of such far-away and evocative places provided an unstoppable impetus to the development of the photographic market in the region: a sentence by Félicien De Saulcy in his *Voyage en Terre Sainte* (1865), is best proof of this: 'D'ailleaurs, une bonne photographie vaut mieux que toutes les affirmations'.[89] It was to achieve these goals and meet these new demands that an ever-increasing number of photographers devoted themselves to field work, despite the enormous practical difficulties that this entailed, especially until the beginning of the 20th century. This aspect must always be kept in mind because it allows us to fully appreciate the photos that have been handed down to us from these early pioneers of photography, as well highlighted in a letter by Warren J. Moulton, who described the work of the photographer during an archaeological expedition led by Salah Merril in Transjordan in 1875: 'The work of the photographer was at all times exceedingly difficult and occasioned much delay. Wherever pictures were taken, it was necessary to set up a specially prepared tent for the development of the negatives, frequently water for this purpose had to be transported from great distances, even as far as sixteen miles. However, the excellent results of all this effort gave great satisfaction'.[90]

Another interesting aspect regards the nationality of the photographers, which to a certain extent went hand in hand with a different general approach to the art of photography.[91] At first, the photographers were almost exclusively European, with a prevalence of French and British,[92] but they were soon joined by local photographers, of whom we often know quite little (to my knowledge, the first professional Arab photographer in the region was probably George Sabunji, who opened a photography studio in Beirut in 1863).[93]

Besides nationality, it is above all the variety of interests and skills of the good number of photographers that led of course to different approaches and styles, since the early stages of photographic history.[94] We can imagine, therefore, that Creswell, like any other photographer of his time, both amateur and professional, was familiar with and had seen photographs of the countries where he worked; therefore, he must have been more or less knowingly influenced to a certain extent by the work of the photographers who had preceded him and those who worked on similar subjects during that period.

In this regard, it may be useful to say a few more words about a specific theme within the general topic of photography in the Near East, i.e., archaeological photography. This is an area to which Creswell's work is not entirely attributable, but it is certainly the most significant and similar for classifying and understanding his style and method.

It has often been emphasised how photography and Near Eastern archaeology grew and developed together from their very beginnings. In 1839, the photographic process was presented in Paris, and only three years later, in 1842, Richard Lepsius was the first to include a photo-camera in the equipment of his archaeological expedition to Egypt. Although Lepsius' approach was truly innovative, its results were not significant. The first successful use of a photo-camera in Near Eastern excavations was about ten years later, when Gabriel Tranchand took several photos during the 1852 excavations at Khorsabad, in Iraq.[95] Photography was

---

[86] Rosovsky 1997: 22.
[87] On the tour of Prince of Wales see Jacobson 2016: 67-68; Perez 1988: 134. On Kaiser Wilhelm II's journey see Scheffler 1998 and El-Hage 2000: 15-16.
[88] On itinerant photographers see in particular About 2015; on the photographers living here and working in photo studios, see directly the entries of Appendix 1.
[89] de Saulcy 1865: 105.
[90] Moulton J. 1926-1927: 64.
[91] On this point, which I believe may sometimes be overvalued, see in particular Chevedden 1984; Perez 1988: 84-85; Foliard 2016.
[92] Perez 1988: 74-76 offers an interesting distribution table which considers an overall period ranging from 1839 to 1885, to which period it refers exactly: the table shows that 40% of known photographers were French, followed by English (17.6%). On the contribution of Americans to the diffusion of photography, although focused on Palestine, see Hallote 2007.
[93] Sheehi *et al.* 2017. On the subject see also Apostolou 2013, and Hannoosh 2016. With regard to the diffusion of photography in the Ottoman Empire, the latter points out that 'The discovery of photography was reported in the official Ottoman state paper Takvim-i Vekayi ("Calendar of Events") on 28 October 1839, and the translation of Daguerre's manual on the daguerreotype was available in Istanbul before August 1841' (p. 4).
[94] On this specific aspect, which is also highlighted by various authors, reference should be made to Perez 1988: 93-95.
[95] See Bohrer 2011: 7-68 for a general summary on this subject.

used, increasingly but occasionally, in archaeological research for at least twenty years, while from the mid-1870s onwards, as a rule, photographers were included among the staff of the leading archaeological expeditions.

An aspect that favoured the development of this sector, was also the establishment of a number of research institutes dedicated to the exploration of Palestine, which in many cases gave life to real services or offices tasked with taking photographs of excavations and monuments.[96] The need to record the results of explorations and excavations with photographs soon became quite essential, not only for reasons of research, but also due to the increasing awareness of the need to document monuments often threatened by the risk of ruin and destruction. On this subject, worthy of note are the words of Basilius von Hitrowo who in 1896 wrote that due to the continuous changes and destruction of the archaeological heritage of Syria and Palestine 'in 10-20 years, there will probably be nothing else to search for, or to photograph'.[97] While undoubtedly overly apocalyptic, this prophecy shows a sensibility and awareness towards a problem that was already felt over a century ago and has become increasingly central today.

Despite this sort of 'primacy' held by Tranchand's calotypes, of the three regions considered here, Mesopotamia is certainly the one in which photography took longer to establish itself and spread. It must be said that, in some cases, it is simply the failure to preserve photographs that prevents us from evaluating the practice of photography. Indeed, we have news of travellers and researchers who took photographs, but we have no knowledge of their fate (see for example the names of Hormudz Rassam, Pierre Lottin, Major H. Ban, Léon Cahun, in the Appendix 1). Nevertheless, there continued to be a marked delay compared to western regions, including Syria and Transjordan, which is quite understandable given that the majority of photography studios were based in the largest cities closest to the Mediterranean, foremost Beirut and Jerusalem.[98]

In Syria, photography had been practiced since the 1840s, as confirmed by the work of photographers such as the Anglican Cleric Rev. George Wilson Bridges, or the better known Frédéric Auguste Antoine Goupil-Fesquet (also known for being the first to photograph Jerusalem, in December 1839) and Joseh-Philibert Girault de Prangey.[99] The first calotypes were taken in Damascus, probably as early as 1851, by Galen Claudius Wheelhouse (whose photographs were unfortunately destroyed), while Damascus is also documented in the photographs of one of the greatest photographers of the Near East who was active at the end of the 1850s: Francis Frith. The expedition of Emmanuel-Guillaume Rey documenting the crusader castles of Syria and Asia Minor also dates back to the late 1850s. The photographs of this expedition, which was dedicated to documenting architectural heritage, were taken by Louis-Constantin de Clerq and published in 1860. A peculiarity of early photography in Syria, is probably the fact that there were many photographers with extremely different styles: in addition to travellers, scientific explorers and photographers who took photographs for publishing and tourism, worthy of note are the works of photographers such as Ernst Benecke, whose photos taken in the 1850s captured the local people and their costumes, or Henry-Joseph Sauvaire, who documented the conflicts in Damascus in 1860, thus producing one of the first war photo reports. Another interesting feature is that female photographers had probably been operating in the country since the 1860s, most certainly Elizabeth Bowen Thompson, thus anticipating the works of the great female photographers of the 20th century (Gertrude Bell, Freya Stark, to quote the most famous names). Finally, the presence of local professional photographers is documented as early as the 1870s, such as Mahmoud al-Azm, who worked in Damascus. From a more strictly archaeological point of view, the presence of a good number of photographers throughout the country meant that many of them worked on commission, providing useful documentation for publications.[100] It was especially at the beginning of the 20th century that the production of specific photographic repertoires started, strictly related to the great archaeological expeditions.[101]

The photo-camera had already been introduced in Transjordan in 1844, when the Scottish physician George Skene Keith took some daguerrotypes of

---

[96] Just to mention a few of the main ones: the Palestine Exploration Fund (P.E.F.), which was established in 1865 and organised several archaeological surveys of the Holy Land, including Syria and Transjordan (Perez 1988: 77; Moscrop 1996; Abujaber, Cobbing 2005: 29; Jacobson 2016); the American Palestine Exploration Society (A.P.E.S.), established in 1870 (Perez 1988: 77; Howe 1997; Abujaber, Cobbing 2005: 33); the Deutscher Verein zur Erforsching Palastinas, established in 1877 (Perez 1988: 77); the American Colony Photo Department, established in 1898 (Bair 2011: 28).
[97] Hitrowo 1896: 137: 'In 10-20 Jahren wahrscheinlich nichts mehr zu untersuchen und zu photographiren übrig sein wird'.
[98] It is interesting to note that in the various editions of the *Baedeker Guide*, dedicated to the regions examined here, indications are given on where to find photographs and photographers for the large cities of Syria, such as Damascus and Aleppo, but not for Baghdad or other Iraqi cities.

---

[99] For information and bibliography on these and on the other photographers mentioned in this review, cf. the respective entries in Appendix 1.
[100] See, for instance, James Graham and Albert Poche in Appendix 1.
[101] See in particular, in Appendix 1, the entries on G. Cavalcanty, Max Fr. Von Oppenheiim, Th.E. Lawrence, R. Mouterde, A. Poidebard, L. Woolley.

Figure 14: Joseph-Philibert Girault de Prangey. Aleppo, viewed from the Antioch Gate. Date of creation: 1844. Daguerreotype, 18.9 × 24.1 cm. MET accession Nr: 2016.612 (https://www.metmuseum.org/art/collection/search/726483; image released under Open access license).

Jerash.[102] In 1851-1852 Leavitt Hunt and Nathan Felix Baker embarked on a *Grand Tour* of Greece, Egypt and the Levant, taking some photos in Petra.[103] However, it took about twenty years for archaeological photography to make a 'quantum leap' and become a regular practice of field work. The 1875 archaeological expedition by the American Palestine Exploration Society in the lands east of the Jordan river marked this change: photographic documentation was entrusted to Tancréde Dumas and was considered one of the expedition's main targets from the very beginning.[104] In 1876, part of the expedition's photos were published in an album that specifically addressed photographic documentation.[105] From this moment onwards, photography became a tool that was used systematically in field research and in the documentation of monuments.

Examining, albeit briefly, Creswell's predecessors and contemporaries makes it possible to better characterise his work and place him in the general context of the history of photography in the Near East: the result is the work of an amateur photographer, yet provided with professional skills and equipment, who used photography as a way to achieve a specific purpose, that is, documenting the architecture of what he was studying. For Creswell, therefore, photography was not so much a work of intrinsic value, but rather a tool that was successful if able to provide evidence of what had been documented through measurements, drawings and reliefs. The subject of the photo was always the focus of Creswell's attention, and photography had to achieve the versatility required to reproduce it as best as possible: for this reason, some subjects were photographed several times, from different shooting points or from the same one but with different lighting, and people, animals or other elements of the landscape never appear in his photographs,

---

[102] Mortensen 2018: 174.

[103] For a general sketch on the earliest photographs taken in Jordan, see Stapp 2008 and Anastasio 2022. See also Perez 1988; Abujaber, Cobbing 2005; Hannavy 2008, as well as table b. in Appendix 1, p. 273.

[104] Moulton J. 1926-1927: 64. On Tancréde Dumas see Appendix 1, p. 263

[105] ASOR 1876.

unless 'by mistake' or if strictly necessary. Given his attention to the architectural element, despite reservations owing to the varying consistency of the documentation available, there seems to be a strong reference to the work of Joseph-Philibert Girault de Prangey (Figure 14), especially for his particular interest in Islamic architecture, at a time when European attention was focused mainly on the pre-Islamic monuments. Another photographer who was more contemporary to Creswell and had, in my opinion, a similar technique was probably Robert Byron (Figure 15), the author of *The Road to Oxiana*,[106] not only for the almost exclusive attention to Islamic architecture, but also for the type of shots: especially the details of the interiors and the search for views from the outside, aimed at highlighting the monument that had to be devoid, as much as possible, of any external elements.

An aspect of Creswell's work that deserves special consideration, if we compare it to the work of photographers close to him, is undoubtedly the fact that he photographed a wide selection of monuments in a very short period of time, within a well-defined project and with consistent characteristics. Furthermore, he did so at a crucial time in the history of the monuments which, in many cases, would soon undergo radical and unfortunately often dramatic (especially following the events of recent history) changes.

Figure 15: Robert Byron. Damascus, Caravanserai. Date unknown (1930s). Negative B47/1778 (courtesy of the Conway Library, Courtauld Institute of Art. Released under CC BY-NC 4.0 licence).

---

[106] Byron's photos of the Near East date back to 1933-1934, therefore, they are later than those taken by Creswell and considered in this study. On Robert Byron see Appendix 1, pp. 261-262.

The sites and the monuments

Altogether, 18 sites photographed by Creswell in Mesopotamia, Syria and Transjordan are included in the Berenson Collection.

Most of the photographs in the collection (473) concern Syria, which is represented by 8 sites: among the large cities, Damascus and Aleppo are by far the most represented, while others such as Hama and Homs have a smaller number of photographs, probably a result of shorter inspections. Alongside the large cities, the collection also includes smaller sites, yet significant for their imposing monumental remains, well known at the time of Creswell's visit (Qalat Siman, Qalb Lawzah, Ruweiha, and Masyaf).

Mesopotamia is the second largest group, based on the number of photos preserved (232) and sites photographed (7). In fact, two distinct groups can be identified. The first is the largest group, corresponding to the sites of Babylonia, namely southern Mesopotamia (Bagdad, al Madain – Taq Kisra, Qantarat Harba, Samarra and, outside the Tigris valley, al-Ukhaidir), which were probably photographed in 1930. The second is represented by Birecik and Harran; although these sites should certainly be considered Mesopotamian, because situated inside the valley formed by the Tigris and Euphrates rivers, they are, however, much further north. They were indeed probably photographed at the same time as the Syrian sites, in 1919-1920.

Finally, Transjordan is by far the smallest group, in terms of number of photographs (38) and sites visited (3). While for two of these, Iraq al-Amir and Qusayr Amra, the number of photographs is limited, and most likely due to very short surveys, the repertoire regarding the citadel of Amman is considerable, with documentation particularly focused on the remains of a monument (the 'Audience Hall' of the Umayyad Palace) to which Creswell paid special attention.

The complete list of sites photographed is highlighted in the map of Figure 16, while a complete list of monuments organised by site can be found, in addition to the following paragraphs, in Appendix 2. See also Appendix 4 for a geolocation of sites and monuments on Google My Maps.

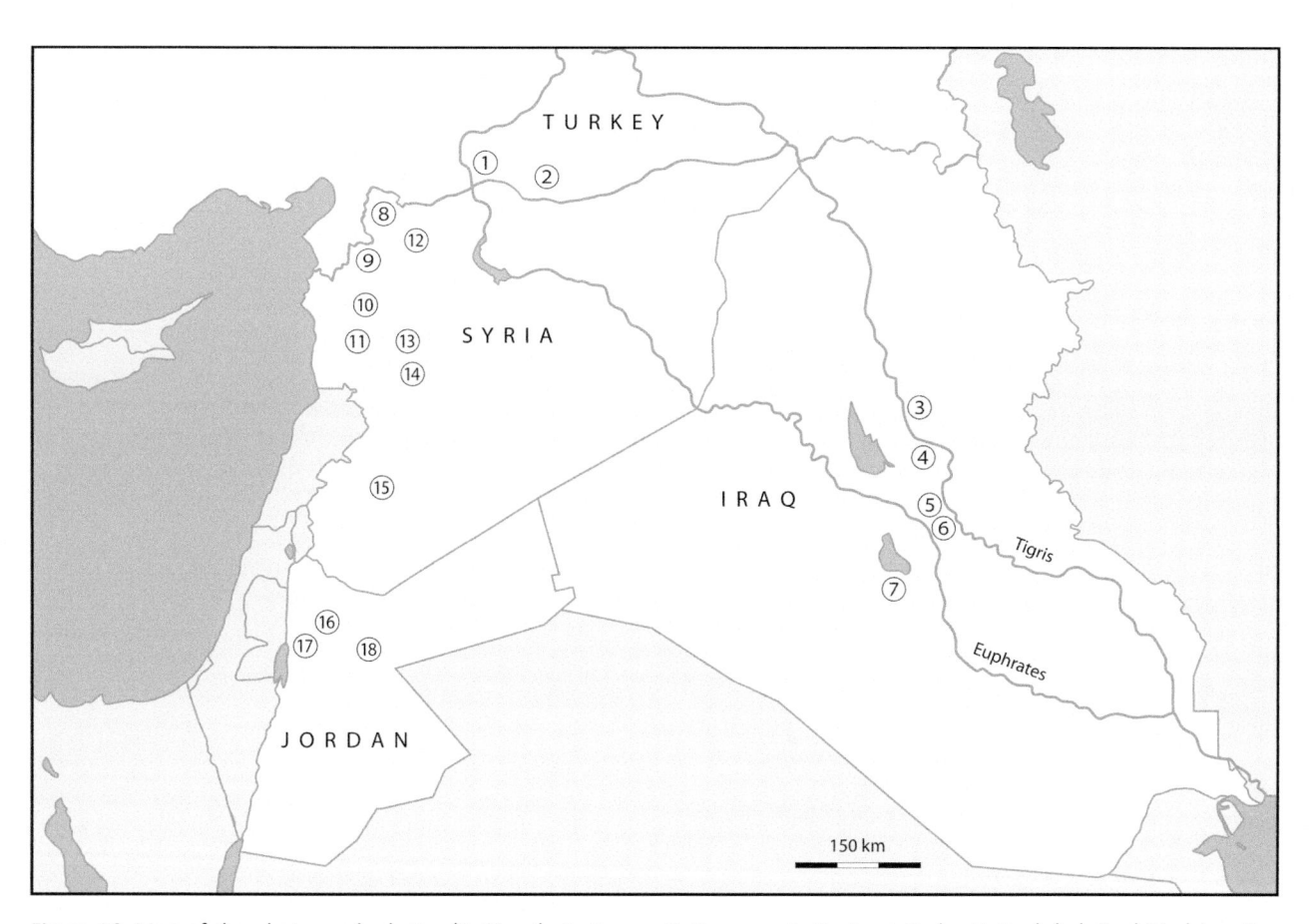

Figure 16: Map of the photographed sites (1: Birecik, 2: Harran, 3: Samarra, 4: Qantarat Harba, 5: Baghdad, 6: al-Madain – Taq Kisra, 7: al-Ukhaidir, 8: Qalat Siman, 9: Qalb Lawzah, 10: Ruweiha, 11: Masyaf, 12: Aleppo, 13: Hama, 14: Homs, 15: Damascus, 16: Amman, 17: Iraq al-Amir, 18: Qusayr Amra).

List of the photographed monuments for each site spotted in the map of fig. 16

1. *Birecik:* Castle (pp. 29-40).

2. *Harran:* Castle, City Walls, Great Mosque, Mazar of Shaikh Yahia (pp. 41-54).

3. *Samarra:* Abu Dulaf Mosque, al-Askari Shrine, Dar al-Khalifa, Great Mosque, Qasr al-Ashiq, Qubba al-Sulaibiya (pp. 55-72).

4. *Qantarat Harba:* Bridge (p. 73-74).

5. *Baghdad:* Suhrawardi Mosque and Mausoleum, al-Khulafa Minaret, al-Mirjaniya Madrasa, al-Mustansiriya Madrasa, Bab al-Wastani, Khan Mirjan, Mihrab of al-Khassaki Mosque, Qasr al-Abbasi, Shaykh Aquli Tomb, Shaykh Maruf al-Kharkhi Mausoleum, Zumurrud Khatun Mosque (pp. 75-94).

6. *Al-Madain:* Taq Kisra (pp. 95-98).

7. *Al-Ukhaidir:* Fortress (pp. 99-111).

8. *Qalat Siman:* Church of Saint Simeon Stylites (pp. 113-115).

9. *Qalb Lawzah:* Basilica (pp. 113-115).

10. *Ruweiha:* Bizzos Mausoleum (pp. 113-115).

11. *Aleppo:* al-Atrush Mosque, al-Bayada Mosque, al-Firdaws Madrasa, al-Halawiya Madrasa, al-Kamiliya Madrasa, al-Karimiya Mosque, al-Khusrauriya Mosque, al-Maqam Mosque, al-Muqaddamiya Madrasa, al-Qadi al-Mahmandar Mosque, al-Qiqan Mosque, al-Rumi Mosque, al-Safahiya Mosque, al-Sahibiya Madrasa, al-Shadhbakhtiya Madrasa, al-Sharafiya Madrasa, al-Shuaybiya Mosque, al-Sultaniya Madrasa, al-Tawashy Mosque, al-Zahiriya Madrasa, al-Zaki Mosque, Altunbugha Mosque, Arghun al-Kamili Bimaristan, Bab al-Hadid, Bab al-Jinan, Bab al-Maqam, Bab Antakya, Bab Qinnasrin, Bahramiya Mosque, Bahsita Mosque, Citadel, Citadel Mosque, City Walls, Great Mosque, Khan al-Jumruk, Khan al-Sabun, Khan al-Wazir, Khan al-Zait, Khan Qassabiya, Khan Utchan, Khanqah al-Farafra, Maqam Ibrahim al-Sulfi Mosque, Maqam Ibrahim fi al-Salihin, Maqam Ughulbak, Mashhad al-Husayn, Mashhad al-Muhassin, Masjid Yusuf, Musa Ibn Abdullah al-Nasiri Mausoleum, Nur al-Din Maristan, Qastal Bab al-Maqam, Qastal Sahat Bizza, Qastal Sakakini, Qastal Shabariq, Qubba Khayrbak, Shihab al-Din Ahmad al-Adrai Mausoleum, Takiya Shaykh Abu Bakr, Umm Malik al-Afdal Mausoleum, Zawiya al-Bazzaziya, Zawiya al-Haidary, Zawiya al-Junashiya (pp. 116-179).

12. *Masyaf:* Fortress (pp. 180-182).

13. *Hama:* al-Nuri Mosque, Azm Palace, Great Mosque (pp. 183-190).

14. *Homs:* Bab al-Masdud, Citadel, Great Mosque of al-Nuri (pp. 191-198).

15. *Damascus:* Abd al-Rahman ibn Abdallah al-Tashtadar Madrasa, Abu Abdallah Hasan ibn Salama Mausoleum, al-Adiliya Madrasa, al-Maridaniya Mosque, al-Nuriya al-Kubra Madrasa, al-Qaymari Maristan and Mausoleum, al-Rihaniya Madrasa, al-Sahiba Madrasa, al-Shamiya al-Kubra Madrasa, al-Sibaiya Madrasa, al-Zahiriya Madrasa, Ali al-Faranti Mausoleum, Amat al-Latif Mausoleum, Amir Kujkun al-Mansuri Mausoleum, Amir Tankiz Mosque and Mausoleum, Atabektya Mosque, Azm Palace, Bab al-Faraj, Bab al-Salam, Dar al-Hadith al-Ashrafiya al-Muqaddasiya, Hanabila Mosque, Izz al-Din Madrasa, Jaharkasiya Madrasa, Khan Asad Pasha, Khan Sulayman Pasha, Khatuniya Mausoleum, Nur al-Din Bimaristan, Raihan Mausoleum, Rukn al-Din Mausoleum, Saladin Mausoleum, Shaykh Muhammad ibn Ali ibn Nadif Mausoleum, Sinan Pasha Mosque, Takiya al-Sulaymaniya (pp. 199-236).

16. *Amman:* Umayyad Mosque, Nymphaeum, Qusayr al-Nuwaijis, Roman Theatre, Umayyad Palace (Audience Hall) (pp. 237-248).

17. *Iraq al-Amir:* Qasr al-Abd (pp. 249-250).

18. *Qusayr Amra* (pp. 251-255).

Mesopotamia

Birecik

Birecik is a small town in the province of Şanlıurfa in Turkey, on the bank of the River Euphrates. It corresponds to ancient Birtha, as found in classical sources, and to modern Biret al-Firat of the Ottoman Empire.[107]

The original core of the city probably rose on the left bank of the Euphrates, where a few remains of the fortress (the 'Castle'), representing the main monument of Birecik, can still be seen. The settlement, at least since the Middle Ages, developed first to the east, at the foot of the Castle, and later also on the other side.[108]

The first traces of occupation in the region date back to the Palaeolithic period, but the earliest finds that testify to a significant settlement belong to the Early Bronze age.[109] Since then, the history of the settlement was not broken by any interruptions, due to its strategic importance. Birecik is indeed located at the centre of a plain where the Euphrates, whose source lies almost 15km north, creates a navigable waterway towards the Mesopotamian plain.[110]

With specific reference to the Islamic period, the city was conquered by the Ayyubid armies in 1234 and, with its Castle, formed a solid bulwark against the Mongol invasion of 1259. The city was controlled by the Mamluks from 1262, before the final defeat of the Mongols in 1269, and came under Ottoman control only in 1516.[111] Birecik lost importance, at least partially, during the late Ottoman rule, especially following the construction of the Baghdad railway, which passed a little south of the city.[112]

Creswell visited Birecik during his service in the Allenby Administration (see p. 15), at a time of great change for the city and the region. Birecik was first occupied by the British and later by the French armies in 1919, until the occupation forces left the city in Summer 1920. The city continued to be quite important until the mid-1950s, when a bridge was built that is still one of Turkey's longest bridges over the Euphrates.[113]

Before Creswell, other European travellers had provided written descriptions of Birecik, starting back in the 17th century,[114] yet it must be said that there are few representations of the site in maps, drawings and,

Figure 17: Birecik. The Citadel, looking north (https://pbase.com/dosseman/beyazkale; courtesy of Dick Osseman, 2010).

above all, photographs. With regard to the latter, worth mentioning are a view of the city taken in 1881 by Maximillien-É.-É. Barry during the expedition of Ernest Chantre,[115] one taken in 1911 by Thomas E. Lawrence[116] and those, in the same year, by Gertrude Bell[117].

The standing architectural remains of Birecik date for the most part to the Mamluk and Ottoman periods, and consist mainly of the city walls, the Castle and a number of mosques in the city built around the Castle, two of which are of great architectural significance: the Great Mosque and the Çarsi Mosque.[118]

Creswell does not deal directly with Birecik in his *Early Muslim architecture*, nevertheless his photographic documentation is remarkable. The Berenson Collection contains 39 photographs of the city walls and the Castle. Very little of the city walls has survived today, especially to the north and south. Creswell's photographs are therefore particularly interesting, also because they portray three city gates (Figures 26-30).[119]

The Castle is a two-storey hexagonal building, with four corner towers facing each other, built on the cliff on the

---

[107] Durukan 2011: 37.
[108] Sinclair 1990: 157
[109] Engin 2003: 9, 13.
[110] Bostan 1992.
[111] About the history of the city from the Ayyubid conquest to the Ottoman period, see Bostan 1992: 187-188 and Durukan 2011: 37.
[112] The population of Birecik continued, nonetheless, to be notable, calculated as 8,600-10,000 people in the 1890s, with 450-500 shops in the city (Bostan 1992: 188).
[113] Bostan 1992: 188-189.
[114] Durukan 2011: 40-42.

[115] See the albumen print numbered as 103 in Barry 1881 (ID 2018.R.23 in the digitalised version).
[116] Lawrence 1939, pl. 13.
[117] A collection of 12 photos is published in the Gertrude Bell Archive, Album T 1911 and Album U 1911 (see p. 260). A further selection of photographs, including some by Max Fr. von Oppenheim is accessible in the Abdul Hamid II Collection of the Istanbul University, available at http://katalog.istanbul.edu.tr/client/en_US/defaulteng/ (search within 'II. Abdülhamid Han Fotoğraf Albümleri', subject: 'Birecik').
[118] On the latter, see Durkam 2011: 42, 45.
[119] On the present state of the walls and gates, see Sinclair 1990: 157 and Durukan 2011.

east bank of the Euphrates. It is built in clear limestone, hence the Arabic name Kal-i-Beuda, i.e., 'the white fortress', and housed several mosques, as described by various early travellers.[120] Six Arabic inscriptions are preserved in the Castle. They date back to the time of the Mamluk Sultan Berke Han (1277-1279) and of Sultan Kayitbay (1482-1483), to whom a major restoration of the building in 1482 is due.[121] Unfortunately, the Castle has not been the subject of archaeological investigations to date, although it has undergone restoration, even in recent years. A video with drone footage taken in 2019, available on the *T.C. Birecik Kaimakamlığı* official web channel allows viewers to appreciate the state of the monument.[122] In particular, the walls are the result of recent restorations and additions, especially on the south outer wall (Figure 17). Creswell's photographs allow us to grasp many details that are certainly fundamental in view of future restorations.

The set of photographs is completed by some shots taken inside the Castle. They document one of the mosques of the structure, located inside the south tower (Figures 50-52).

Figure 18: Birecik. The Citadel (signed and dated by K.A.C. Creswell, 1919). Berenson ID: 402895. Primary support 102x322mm; secondary support 20.8x48.2cm. Date of creation: 1919-1920.

---

[120] Durukan 2011: 40.
[121] Bostan 1992: 188; for a detailed description of the status of the Castle see Sinclair 1990: 157-159.
[122] http://www.birecik.gov.tr/birecik-kalesi2019

THE SITES AND THE MONUMENTS – MESOPOTAMIA

Figure: 19.
Subject: Birecik. The northern side of the walls.
Berenson ID: 133353.
Medium: gelatine silver print, 12×17cm.
Date of creation: 1919-1920.
Handwritten notes on the back: 'Birecik, The walls – N. side' [Cres.].
Ashmolean negative: EA.CA.6559.

Figure: 20.
Subject: Birecik. Ruined tower at the northeastern corner of the walls.
Berenson ID: 133352.
Medium: gelatine silver print, 12×17cm.
Date of creation: 1919-1920.
Handwritten notes on the back: 'Birecik, The walls – broken tower at N/E corner' [Cres.].
Ashmolean negative: EA.CA.6558.

Figure: 21.
Subject: Birecik. The eastern side of the walls.
Berenson ID: 133351.
Medium: gelatine silver print, 12×17cm.
Date of creation: 1919-1920.
Handwritten notes on the back: 'Birecik, The walls – E. side' [Cres.].
Ashmolean negative: EA.CA.6557.

Figure: 22.
Subject: Birecik. The southeastern corner of the walls.
Berenson ID: 133350.
Medium: gelatine silver print, 12×17cm.
Date of creation: 1919-1920.
Handwritten notes on the back: 'Birecik, The walls – S/E corner' [Cres.].
Ashmolean negative: EA.CA.6556.

Figure: 23.
Subject: Birecik. The southern side of the walls.
Berenson ID: 133347.
Medium: gelatine silver print, 12×17cm.
Date of creation: 1919-1920.
Handwritten notes on the back: 'Birecik, The walls – S. side' [Cres.].
Ashmolean negative: EA.CA.6553.

Figure: 24.
Subject: Birecik. The southern side of the walls.
Berenson ID: 133349.
Medium: gelatine silver print, 12×17cm.
Date of creation: 1919-1920.
Handwritten notes on the back: 'Birecik, The walls – S. side' [Cres.].
Ashmolean negative: EA.CA.6555.

THE SITES AND THE MONUMENTS – MESOPOTAMIA

Figure: 25.
Subject: Birecik. The southwestern corner of the walls.
Berenson ID: 133348.
Medium: gelatine silver print, 12×17cm.
Date of creation: 1919-1920.
Handwritten notes on the back: 'Birecik, The walls – S/W corner on Euphrates' [Cres.].
Ashmolean negative: EA.CA.6554.

Figure: 26.
Subject: Birecik. The northern gate.
Berenson ID: 133355.
Medium: gelatine silver print, 12×17cm.
Date of creation: 1919-1920.
Handwritten notes on the back: 'Birecik, N. Gate (of Qaytbay)' [Cres.].
Ashmolean negative: EA.CA.6561.

Figure: 27.
Subject: Birecik. The interior of the northern gate.
Berenson ID: 133356.
Medium: gelatine silver print, 12×17cm.
Date of creation: 1919-1920.
Handwritten notes on the back: 'Birecik, N. Gate – from within' [Cres.].
Ashmolean negative: EA.CA.6562.

Figure: 28.
Subject: Birecik. The eastern gate.
Berenson ID: 133357.
Medium: gelatine silver print, 12×17cm.
Date of creation: 1919-1920.
Handwritten notes on the back: 'Birecik, Remains of E. gate' [Cres.].
Ashmolean negative: EA.CA.6563.

Figure: 29 (left).
Subject: Birecik. The southeastern gate.
Berenson ID: 133365.
Medium: gelatine silver print, 12×17cm.
Date of creation: 1919-1920.
Handwritten notes on the back: 'Birecik, S/E gate' [Cres.].
Ashmolean negative: EA.CA.6565.

Figure: 30 (right).
Subject: Birecik. The interior of the southeastern gate.
Berenson ID: 133359.
Medium: gelatine silver print, 12×17cm.
Date of creation: 1919-1920.
Handwritten notes on the back: 'Birecik, S/E gate from within' [Cres.].
Ashmolean negative: EA.CA.6566.

Figure: 31.
Subject: Birecik. The northern end of the Citadel.
Berenson ID: 133373.
Medium: gelatine silver print, 12×17cm.
Date of creation: 1919-1920.
Handwritten notes on the back: 'Birecik, the Citadel – N. end' [Cres.].
Ashmolean negative: EA.CA.6580.

THE SITES AND THE MONUMENTS – MESOPOTAMIA

Figure: 32.
Subject: Birecik. The northern end of the Citadel.
Berenson ID: 133374.
Medium: gelatine silver print, 12×17cm.
Date of creation: 1919-1920.
Handwritten notes on the back: 'Birecik, the Citadel – N. end' [Cres.].
Ashmolean negative: EA.CA.6581.

Figure: 33.
Subject: Birecik. The eastern side of the Citadel.
Berenson ID: 133377.
Medium: gelatine silver print, 12×17cm.
Date of creation: 1919-1920.
Handwritten notes on the back: 'Birecik, the Citadel – E. side' [Cres.].
Ashmolean negative: EA.CA.6584.

Figure: 34 (left).
Subject: Birecik. The northern end of the Citadel.
Berenson ID: 133376.
Medium: gelatine silver print, 12×17cm.
Date of creation: 1919-1920.
Handwritten notes on the back: 'Birecik, the Citadel – N. end' [Cres.].
Ashmolean negative: EA.CA.6583.

Figure: 35 (right).
Subject: Birecik. The northern end of the Citadel.
Berenson ID: 133375.
Medium: gelatine silver print, 12×17cm.
Date of creation: 1919-1920.
Handwritten notes on the back: 'Birecik, the Citadel – N. end' [Cres.].
Ashmolean negative: EA.CA.6582.

Figure: 36.
Subject: Birecik. The minaret of the Great Mosque.
Berenson ID: 133384.
Medium: gelatine silver print, 12×17cm.
Date of creation: 1919-1920.
Handwritten notes on the back: 'Birecik, Minaret of Great Mosque' [Cres.].
Ashmolean negative: EA.CA.6592.

Figure: 37.
Subject: Birecik. The northern end of the Citadel.
Berenson ID: 133364.
Medium: gelatine silver print, 12×17cm.
Date of creation: 1919-1920.
Handwritten notes on the back: 'Birecik, the Citadel – N. end' [Cres.].
Ashmolean negative: EA.CA.6572.

Figure: 38.
Subject: Birecik. The southern end of the Citadel.
Berenson ID: 133369.
Medium: gelatine silver print, 12×17cm.
Date of creation: 1919-1920.
Handwritten notes on the back: 'Birecik, the Citadel – S. end' [Cres.].
Ashmolean negative: EA.CA.6576.

THE SITES AND THE MONUMENTS – MESOPOTAMIA

Figure: 39.
Subject: Birecik. The southern end of the Citadel.
Berenson ID: 133363.
Medium: gelatine silver print, 12×17cm.
Date of creation: 1919-1920.
Handwritten notes on the back: 'Birecik, the Citadel – S. end' [Cres.].
Ashmolean negative: EA.CA.6571.

Figure: 40 (left).
Subject: Birecik. Tower on the eastern side of the Citadel.
Berenson ID: 133371.
Medium: gelatine silver print, 12×17cm.
Date of creation: 1919-1920.
Handwritten notes on the back: 'Birecik, the Citadel – tower in center of east side' [Cres.].
Ashmolean negative: EA.CA.6578.

Figure: 41 (right).
Subject: Birecik. Inscription on a tower of the Citadel.
Berenson ID: 133372.
Medium: gelatine silver print, 12×17cm.
Date of creation: 1919-1920.
Handwritten notes on the back: 'Birecik, the Citadel – tower with inscription of Qayt Bay' [Cres.].
Ashmolean negative: EA.CA.6579.

Figure: 42.
Subject: Birecik. The southern side of the Citadel.
Berenson ID: 133370.
Medium: gelatine silver print, 12×17cm.
Date of creation: 1919-1920.
Handwritten notes on the back: 'Birecik, the Citadel – S. half' [Cres.].
Ashmolean negative: EA.CA.6577.

37

Figure: 43.
Subject: Birecik. The Citadel seen from the Euphrates.
Berenson ID: 133362.
Medium: gelatine silver print, 12×17cm.
Date of creation: 1919-1920.
Handwritten notes on the back: 'Birecik, the Citadel – from the river' [Cres.].
Ashmolean negative: EA.CA.6570.

Figure: 44.
Subject: Birecik. The Citadel seen from the Euphrates.
Berenson ID: 133361.
Medium: gelatine silver print, 12×17cm.
Date of creation: 1919-1920.
Handwritten notes on the back: 'Birecik, the Citadel – from the river' [Cres.].
Ashmolean negative: EA.CA.6569.

Figure: 45.
Subject: Birecik. The Citadel seen from the Euphrates.
Berenson ID: 133360.
Medium: gelatine silver print, 12×17cm.
Date of creation: 1919-1920.
Handwritten notes on the back: 'Birecik, from the river' [Cres.].
Ashmolean negative: EA.CA.6568.

THE SITES AND THE MONUMENTS – MESOPOTAMIA

Figure: 46.
Subject: Birecik. The Citadel, looking north.
Berenson ID: 133378.
Medium: gelatine silver print, 12×17cm.
Date of creation: 1919-1920.
Handwritten notes on the back: 'Birecik, the Citadel – interior, looking N' [Cres.].
Ashmolean negative: EA.CA.6586.

Figure: 47.
Subject: Birecik. The Citadel, looking south.
Berenson ID: 133379.
Medium: gelatine silver print, 12×17cm.
Date of creation: 1919-1920.
Handwritten notes on the back: 'Birecik, the Citadel – interior, looking S' [Cres.].
Ashmolean negative: EA.CA.6587.

Figure: 48.
Subject: Birecik, looking north.
Berenson ID: 133354.
Medium: gelatine silver print, 12×17cm.
Date of creation: 1919-1920.
Handwritten notes on the back: 'Birecik, looking N' [Cres.].
Ashmolean negative: EA.CA.6560.

Figure: 49.
Subject: Birecik. The southwestern corner of the Citadel.
Berenson ID: 133368.
Medium: gelatine silver print, 12×17cm.
Date of creation: 1919-1920.
Handwritten notes on the back: 'Birecik, the Citadel – S/w corner' [Cres.].
Ashmolean negative: EA.CA.6575.

Figure: 50 (left).
Subject: Birecik. Entrance to the mosque in the southern tower of the Citadel.
Berenson ID: 133381.
Medium: gelatine silver print, 12×17cm.
Date of creation: 1919-1920.
Handwritten notes on the back: 'Birecik, the Citadel – entrance to mosque in S. tower' [Cres.].
Ashmolean negative: EA.CA.6589.

Figure: 51 (right).
Subject: Birecik. Entrance to the mosque in the southern tower of the Citadel.
Berenson ID: 133380.
Medium: gelatine silver print, 12×17cm.
Date of creation: 1919-1920.
Handwritten notes on the back: 'Birecik, the Citadel – entrance to mosque in S. tower' [Cres.].
Ashmolean negative: EA.CA.6588.

Figure: 52.
Subject: Birecik. interior of the mosque in the southern tower of the Citadel.
Berenson ID: 133382.
Medium: gelatine silver print, 12×17cm.
Date of creation: 1919-1920.
Handwritten notes on the back: 'Birecik, Mosque in S. tower of Citadel – interior' [Cres.].
Ashmolean negative: EA.CA.6591.

Harran

Harran is located in the Turkish province of Şanlıurfa, around 16km from the Syrian border and within the Balih valley, a tributary of the Euphrates.

The settlement dates back at least to the Early Bronze Age (3rd millennium BCE).[123] This long history is testified not only by the findings of the excavations, but also by the characteristic shape of the main artificial mound, of about 130×100m, which corresponds to a typical 'tell' of the Mesopotamian landscape, formed as a result of the overlapping of archaeological levels over time. The whole standing architecture is Islamic and consists of the remains of the city walls, a mosque, a citadel and the so-called Mazar of Shaikh Yahia. The area of archaeological interest has been calculated as being around 78ht,[124] but most likely extends further, also considering that the archaeological investigation covered the area around the main mound summarily.

It is a site of great historical and religious importance for Jews, Christians and Muslims, since it was Abraham's dwelling before his journey to Palestine (*Genesis* 12: 4-5). Harran was also the Roman Charrae, where the Parthian army administered one of the most disastrous defeats to the Roman army, led by Marcus Licinius Crassus, in 53 BCE. Previously, since the site was an important crossroads for the caravan routes that connected Anatolia, Western Syria, Persia and central Mesopotamia, it had become particularly important under the Assyrian and Babylonian rules (8th-6th centuries BCE), when it was a place of worship of the Moon-god Sin. The strong presence of such a distinctive cult perhaps explains the reason why the city decided to maintain a well-defined religious identity, even after the Arab conquest. When Harran was conquered in 639 or 640, the population did not convert to Islam but declared to be Sabian, i.e., one of the religions tolerated by the early Umayyad caliphate.[125]

By a curious parallel, the site was home to the deposition of the last Assyrian ruler, Ashur-uballit II, following the conquest of the city (Assyrian Harranu) by the Medes and Babylonians in 610 BCE,[126] and also of the last Umayyad caliph, Marwan II, in 750, after the caliph moved the capital from Damascus to Harran.[127] Marwan II was responsible for the construction of a large mosque, which possibly stood right above the remains of the oldest temple of Sin. During the 11th century, it was the seat of the Numayrid dynasty (990-1081), which was in charge of the citadel's major renovations. The city maintained its prestige, due to its crucial position along the connecting roads, until the Ottoman period. Even the Mongol conquest, which caused the widespread destruction of buildings, did not

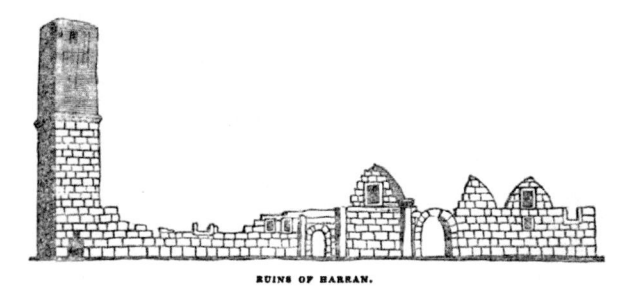

Figure 53: Harran. Drawing of the ruins, from Badger 1852: 432.

lead to a real control of the region, which, if anything, remained under Mamluk influence.

The city started to decline during the period of Ottoman rule. This is evidenced by the fact that Harran is described as a small village by the first European travellers in the early 19th century.[128] Among the visits made by the first Europeans, of interest is Francis R. Chesney's in 1835. In his travel report, Chesney reproduced the western gate and part of the walls, which appear well preserved.[129] Another drawing of the ruins was made about ten years later by George P. Badger,[130] an Anglican priest who visited the region in the early 1840s as a delegate to the Christians of the Church in Mesopotamia and Kurdistan: in the drawing, we can see a continuity between the walls of the mosque and the minaret (Figure 53). In 1879, the site was visited by Eduard Sachau, who among other things produced a first schematic map of the site.[131] With the beginning of the 20th century, news from travellers increased, including Conrad Preusser,[132] Gertrude Bell,[133] and Josef Strzygowski.[134] Lastly, worthy of note is a photographic survey of the site by Thomas E. Lawrence in 1911.[135]

The archaeological investigation began with a survey of the British Institute in Ankara by Seton Lloyd and William Brice in 1950,[136] which produced the first detailed map of the settlement. Later, excavations were carried out by David S. Rice between 1951 and 1956.[137]

---

[123] Çelik 2019.
[124] Yardımcı 2004a.
[125] Sinclair 1990: 29 for a summary on the history of the site.
[126] Boardmann 1991: 182.
[127] Bowsworth 2003.

[128] Sinclair 1990: 32.
[129] Chesney 1850: 115.
[130] Badger 1852: 341-342. He reported that 'traces of old foundations appears to have been encircled with a wall which joined on to the castle'.
[131] Sachau 1883: 217-226, with map at p. 223.
[132] Preusser 1911: 59-62.
[133] Bell, 1914: 152. A collection of 31 photos is published in the Getrude Bell Archive, Album T 1911 and Album U 1911 (see p. 260). A further selection of photographs, including some by Max Fr. von Oppenheim is accessible in the Abdul Hamid II Collection of the Istanbul University, available at http://katalog.istanbul.edu.tr/client/en_US/defaulteng/ (search within 'II.Abdülhamid Han Fotoğraf Albümleri', subject: 'Harran').
[134] van Berchem, Strzygowski 1910: 321-323.
[135] Lawrence 1939, pls 8-12.
[136] Lloyd, Brice 1951.
[137] Rice 1952, 1955. The Papers of Professor David Storm Rice relating to the Harran Excavation are available online, at

Figure 54: Harran. The area of the Great Mosque at the time of Creswell (left; below Figure 73) and today (right) (https://turkisharchaeonews.net/site/harran; courtesy of Izabela Miszczak, 2013).

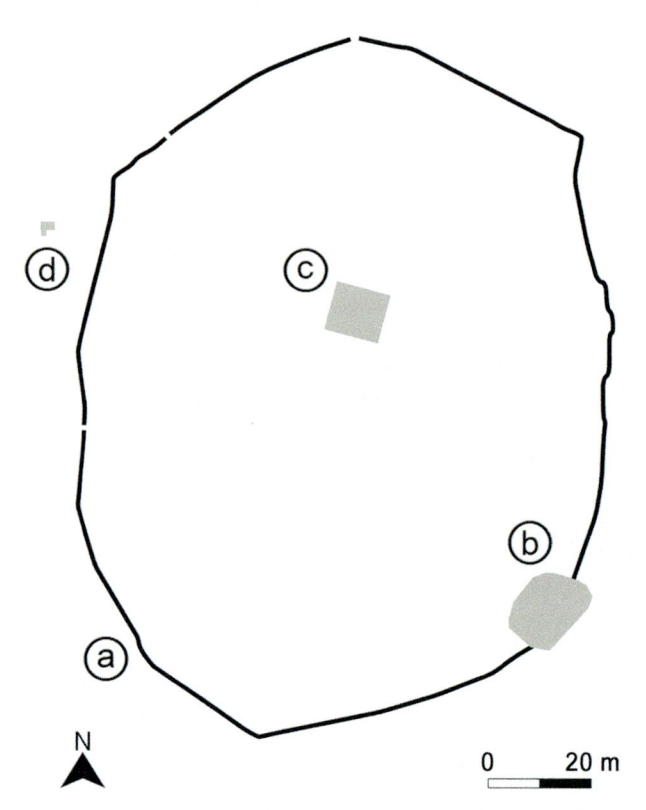

Figure 55: Harran. The photographed monuments; a: the city walls (Figures 56-59); b: the Castle (Figures 60-71); c: the Great Mosque (Figures 72-87); d: the Mazar of Shaikh Yahia (Figures 88-91).

A further important season of excavations took place in the early 1980s, when a Turkish expedition excavated the great mosque.[138] Since then, the investigation and restoration of the site has continued to this day, first under the direction of Nurettin Yardımcı (1983-2011)[139] and then of Mehmet Önal (from 2012 onwards).[140]

In his *Early Muslim architecture*, Creswell deals extensively with Harran, which he visited in 1919-1920, focusing mainly on the great mosque and the minaret.[141] From his description of the ruins, it is clear that they were insufficient to allow a sure reconstruction and interpretation of the original buildings, especially in the case of the mosque. For this reason, Creswell relied heavily on the descriptions of the archaeologists who had preceded him, Presseur in particular.[142] He also agreed with Ernst Herzfeld that the first installation of the mosque was Umayyad, later rebuilt in Saladin's time. However, he proposed a construction history featuring at least three distinct phases: the first dating back to the last Umayyad caliph (744-750), the second to Caliph al-Mamun (*c.* 830) and the third to the Saladin period, specifically to 1171-1184, based on the possible citation of the building in the account of the travels of the Arab traveller from Spain Ibn Jubayr.[143]

Creswell's general framework is still valid today. The Great Mosque is indeed notable, especially since it is one of the earliest examples of the Umayyad period, although the standing remains date back primarily to the Ayyubid period (Figures 72-87). A better understanding of the structure was, however, only gained in more recent years, compared to the earlier years of Creswell's visit, when the mosque was investigated by Rice.[144]

In addition to the mosque and the minaret, Creswell's photos portray all the remains that were then well visible: the city walls, dating back to the 12th century,[145] the 'Castle'[146] on the south-western border of the

---

https://archiveshub.jisc.ac.uk/search/archives/70088b89-2237-344e-a37c-e12dba671b96
[138] Nour 2017.
[139] Yardımcı 2004b.
[140] A summary of the state of research in Harran can be found in Önal, Mutlu S.I., Mutlu S. 2019.

[141] Creswell 1932: 406-409. See also Creswell 1958: 151-155.
[142] Creswell 1932: 406-407: 'I have attempted to plan the interior of the sanctuary, but it is impossible to suggest a reconstruction, for the irregularities are so curious and inexplicable'.
[143] Creswell 1932: 408-409. The text to which Creswell makes greatest reference is Herzfeld's text dated 1911.
[144] Sinclair 1990: 33-36.
[145] Sinclair 1990: 41.
[146] 'Castle/Qalat' is the name used by S. Lloyd and W. Brice (1991: 97), while Creswell wrote 'Citadel' in the captions of his photos. The visible remains of the Castle mainly belong to the

mound, and the Mazar of Shaikh Yahia, just outside the circuit of the walls, to the west.

The Castle was particularly well preserved at the time of Creswell, who took many photographs of it (Figures 60-71). It has a rectangular structure, with four angular circular towers, which partly protrude outside the walls.

A structure must have previously existed, based on the sources, but the visible remains are those of the Ayyubid construction, dating back to the 13th century.[147] The Mazar of Shaikh Yahia is dedicated to an ascetic of the 12th century, and the building was added to an already existing mosque probably built in the 10th/11th century (Figures 88-91).[148]

11th/12th centuries. Recently, two Greek inscriptions dating back to the 4th-6th centuries have been found in this building (Healey, Liddel, Önal 2020).

[147] Sinclair 1990: 36.
[148] Rice 1955; Sinclair 1990: 42. An early mention of this structure was already given by Badger (1852: 342), who reports the tradition according to which Christians identified the place of the sanctuary as the one where Terah, the father of Abraham, had been buried.

Figure: 56.
Subject: Harran. The northern side of the walls.
Berenson ID: 133633.
Medium: gelatine silver print, 12×17cm.
Date of creation: 1919-1920.
Handwritten notes on the back: 'Harran, walls – N side' [Cres.].
Ashmolean negative: EA.CA.6618.

Figure: 57.
Subject: Harran. The northern side of the walls.
Berenson ID: 133634.
Medium: gelatine silver print, 12×17cm.
Date of creation: 1919-1920.
Handwritten notes on the back: 'Harran, walls – N side' [Cres.].
Ashmolean negative: EA.CA.6619.

Figure: 58.
Subject: Harran. The western gateway.
Berenson ID: 133671.
Medium: gelatine silver print, 12×17cm.
Date of creation: 1919-1920.
Handwritten notes on the back: 'Harran, the W. gateway — 588 (1192)' [Cres.].
Ashmolean negative: EA.CA.6648.

Figure: 59.
Subject: Harran. Detail of the western gateway.
Berenson ID: 133672.
Medium: gelatine silver print, 12×17cm.
Date of creation: 1919-1920.
Handwritten notes on the back: 'Harran, The West gateway – detail — 588 (1192)' [Cres.].
Ashmolean negative: EA.CA.6650.

Figure: 60.
Subject: Harran. The southern side of the Castle.
Berenson ID: 133659.
Medium: gelatine silver print, 12×17cm.
Date of creation: 1919-1920.
Handwritten notes on the back: 'Harran. The Citadel – from the N' [Cres.].
Ashmolean negative: EA.CA.6637.

Figure: 61.
Subject: Harran. The northeastern side of the Castle.
Berenson ID: 133661.
Medium: gelatine silver print, 12×17cm.
Date of creation: 1919-1920.
Handwritten notes on the back: 'The Citadel from the S/W' [Cres.].
Ashmolean negative: EA.CA.6639.

Figure: 62.
Subject: Harran. The northern side of the Castle.
Berenson ID: 133662.
Medium: gelatine silver print, 12×17cm.
Date of creation: 1919-1920.
Handwritten notes on the back: 'Harran, The Citadel – from the S' [Cres.].
Ashmolean negative: EA.CA.6640.

Figure: 63.
Subject: Harran. The eastern side of the Castle.
Berenson ID: 133660.
Medium: gelatine silver print, 12×17cm.
Date of creation: 1919-1920.
Handwritten notes on the back: 'Harran – The Citadel – from the W' [Cres.].
Ashmolean negative: EA.CA.6638.

Figure: 64.
Subject: Harran. The eastern side of the Castle.
Berenson ID: 133664.
Medium: gelatine silver print, 12×17cm.
Date of creation: 1919-1920.
Handwritten notes on the back: 'Harran, The Citadel – from the W' [Cres.].
Ashmolean negative: EA.CA.6642.

THE SITES AND THE MONUMENTS – MESOPOTAMIA

Figure: 65.
Subject: Harran. The southwestern tower of the Castle.
Berenson ID: 133663.
Medium: gelatine silver print, 12×17cm.
Date of creation: 1919-1920.
Handwritten notes on the back: 'Harran, The Citadel – S/W. Tower' [Cres.].
Ashmolean negative: EA.CA.6641.

Figure: 66 (left).
Subject: Harran. Vaulted hall in the Castle.
Berenson ID: 133665.
Medium: gelatine silver print, 12×17cm.
Date of creation: 1919-1920.
Handwritten notes on the back: 'Harran, The Citadel, vaulted hall' [Cres.].
Ashmolean negative: EA.CA.6643.

Figure: 67 (right).
Subject: Harran. Vaulted hall in the Castle.
Berenson ID: 133666.
Medium: gelatine silver print, 12×17cm.
Date of creation: 1919-1920.
Handwritten notes on the back: 'Harran, The Citadel, Vaulted Hall' [Cres.].
Ashmolean negative: EA.CA.6644.

Figure: 68.
Subject: Harran. The upper level of the Castle.
Berenson ID: 133667.
Medium: gelatine silver print, 12×17cm.
Date of creation: 1919-1920.
Handwritten notes on the back: 'Harran, The Citadel – archway on the upper level' [Cres.].
Ashmolean negative: EA.CA.6645.

Figure: 69.
Subject: Harran. The upper level of the Castle.
Berenson ID: 133668.
Medium: gelatine silver print, 12×17cm.
Date of creation: 1919-1920.
Handwritten notes on the back: 'Harran, The Citadel – upper level' [Cres.].
Ashmolean negative: EA.CA.6646.

Figure: 70 (left).
Subject: Harran. The upper level of the Castle.
Berenson ID: 133669.
Medium: gelatine silver print, 12×17cm.
Date of creation: 1919-1920.
Handwritten notes on the back: 'Harran, The Citadel, vaulted hall on the N. side' [Cres.].
Ashmolean negative: EA.CA.6647.

Figure: 71 (centre).
Subject: Harran. The upper level of the Castle.
Berenson ID: 133670.
Medium: gelatine silver print, 12×17cm.
Date of creation: 1919-1920.
Handwritten notes on the back: 'Harran, The Citadel, doorway on the upper level' [Cres.].
Ashmolean negative: EA.CA.6649.

Figure: 72 (right).
Subject: Harran. The minaret of the Great Mosque.
Berenson ID: 133652.
Medium: gelatine silver print, 12×17cm.
Date of creation: 1919-1920.
Handwritten notes on the back: 'Harran, Great Mosque – minaret' [Cres.].
Ashmolean negative: EA.CA.678.

Figure: 73.
Subject: Harran. The area of the Great Mosque, looking northeast.
Berenson ID: 133641.
Medium: gelatine silver print, 12×17cm.
Date of creation: 1919-1920.
Handwritten notes on the back: 'Harran, Great Mosque – from S/W' [Cres.].
Ashmolean negative: EA.CA.6622.

Figure: 74.
Subject: Harran. The eastern inner side of the Great Mosque.
Berenson ID: 133640.
Medium: gelatine silver print, 12×17cm.
Date of creation: 1919-1920.
Handwritten notes on the back: 'Harran, Great Mosque – E side from within' [Cres.].
Ashmolean negative: EA.CA.673.
Published in Creswell 1932, pl. 81.c.

Figure: 75.
Subject: Harran. The eastern outer side of the Great Mosque.
Berenson ID: 133635.
Medium: gelatine silver print, 12×17cm.
Date of creation: 1919-1920.
Handwritten notes on the back: 'Harran, Great Mosque – E side' [Cres.].
Ashmolean negative: EA.CA.6621.

Figure: 76.
Subject: Harran. Detail of the eastern outer side of the Great Mosque.
Berenson ID: 133636.
Medium: gelatine silver print, 12×17cm.
Date of creation: 1919-1920.
Handwritten notes on the back: 'Harran, Great Mosque – E side' [Cres.].
Ashmolean negative: EA.CA.674.
Published in Creswell 1932, pl. 81.a.

Figure: 77.
Subject: Harran. Detail of the eastern outer side of the Great Mosque.
Berenson ID: 133639.
Medium: gelatine silver print, 12×17cm.
Date of creation: 1919-1920.
Handwritten notes on the back: 'Harran, Great Mosque – E side' [Cres.].
Ashmolean negative: EA.CA.676.
Published in Creswell 1932, pl. 81.b.

Figure: 78.
Subject: Harran. The central arch in the area of the Great Mosque.
Berenson ID: 133645.
Medium: gelatine silver print, 12×17cm.
Date of creation: 1919-1920.
Handwritten notes on the back: 'Harran – Great Mosque, central arch and sanctuary façade – outer face' [Cres.].
Ashmolean negative: EA.CA.6630.

THE SITES AND THE MONUMENTS – MESOPOTAMIA

Figure: 79.
Subject: Harran. The central arch in the area of the Great Mosque.
Berenson ID: 133647.
Medium: gelatine silver print, 12×17cm.
Date of creation: 1919-1920.
Handwritten notes on the back: 'Harran, Great Mosque, central arch of sanctuary from within' [Cres.].
Ashmolean negative: EA.CA.6625.

Figure: 80 (left).
Subject: Harran. Detail of the eastern side of the Great Mosque.
Berenson ID: 133638.
Medium: gelatine silver print, 12×17cm.
Date of creation: 1919-1920.
Handwritten notes on the back: 'Harran, Great Mosque – E side' [Cres.].

Figure: 81 (centre).
Subject: Harran. Detail of the eastern inner side of the Great Mosque.
Berenson ID: 133642.
Medium: gelatine silver print, 12×17cm.
Date of creation: 1919-1920.
Handwritten notes on the back: 'Harran, Great Mosque – inner side of E façade' [Cres.].
Ashmolean negative: EA.CA.6623.

Figure: 82 (right).
Subject: Harran. Detail of the eastern inner side of the Great Mosque.
Berenson ID: 133643.
Medium: gelatine silver print, 12×17cm.
Date of creation: 1919-1920.
Handwritten notes on the back: 'Harran, Great Mosque – inner side of E façade' [Cres.].
Ashmolean negative: EA.CA.6624.

Figure: 83 (left).
Subject: Harran. Pier of the Great Mosque.
Berenson ID: 133651.
Medium: gelatine silver print, 12×17cm.
Date of creation: 1919-1920.
Handwritten notes on the back: 'Harran, Great Mosque – back piers of sanctuary' [Cres.].
Ashmolean negative: EA.CA.675.
Published in Creswell 1932, pl. 81.e.

Figure: 84 (centre).
Subject: Harran. Pier of the Great Mosque.
Berenson ID: 133653.
Medium: gelatine silver print, 12×17cm.
Date of creation: 1919-1920.
Handwritten notes on the back: 'Harran, Great Mosque – back pier of sanctuary' [Cres.].
Ashmolean negative: EA.CA.6632.

Figure: 85 (right).
Subject: Harran. Detail of the masonry of the Great Mosque.
Berenson ID: 133649.
Medium: gelatine silver print, 12×17cm.
Date of creation: 1919-1920.
Handwritten notes on the back: 'Harran, Great Mosque – capital of engaged column of first pier' [Cres.].
Ashmolean negative: EA.CA.6628.

Figure: 86.
Subject: Harran. Remains of the mihrab of the Great Mosque.
Berenson ID: 133654.
Medium: gelatine silver print, 12×17cm.
Date of creation: 1919-1920.
Handwritten notes on the back: 'Harran, Great Mosque – base of mihrab' [Cres.].
Ashmolean negative: EA.CA.6633.

Figure: 87.
Subject: Harran.
Decorative element of the Great Mosque.
Berenson ID: 133655.
Medium: gelatine silver print, 12×17cm.
Date of creation: 1919-1920.
Handwritten notes on the back: 'Harran, Great Mosque ornament' [Cres.].
Ashmolean negative: EA.CA.6634.

Figure: 88.
Subject: Harran. The Mazar of Shaikh Yahia.
Berenson ID: 133673.
Medium: gelatine silver print, 12×17cm.
Date of creation: 1919-1920.
Handwritten notes on the back: 'Harran, Mazar of Shaikh Yahya — 592 (1196)' [Cres.].
Ashmolean negative: EA.CA.6651.

Figure: 89.
Subject: Harran. The Mazar of Shaikh Yahia.
Berenson ID: 133676.
Medium: gelatine silver print, 12×17cm.
Date of creation: 1919-1920.
Handwritten notes on the back: 'Harran, Mazar of Shaikh Yahya – W. Side' [Cres.].
Ashmolean negative: EA.CA.6654.

Figure: 90.
Subject: Harran. The Mazar of Shaikh Yahia.
Berenson ID: 133675.
Medium: gelatine silver print, 12×17cm.
Date of creation: 1919-1920.
Handwritten notes on the back: Harran, Mazar of Shaikh Yahya — 592 (1196)' [Cres.].
Ashmolean negative: EA.CA.6653.

Figure: 91.
Subject: Harran. The Mazar of Shaikh Yahia.
Berenson ID: 133674.
Medium: gelatine silver print, 12×17cm.
Date of creation: 1919-1920.
Handwritten notes on the back: 'Harran, Mazar of Shaikh Yahya — 592 (1196)' [Cres.].
Ashmolean negative: EA.CA.6652.

Samarra

Samarra is located on the eastern bank of the Tigris, about 100km north of Baghdad. It is one of the largest archaeological sites in the world, extending over 40km in length and with a maximum width of 8km. It covers more than 160km², with nearly 7,000 identified archaeological structures.[149]

Although traces of occupation date back to Protohistory (6th millennium BCE),[150] the site is mostly famous for having been the Abbasid capital for about half a century, between its founding by the Abbasid caliph al-Mutasim-Billah in 836, and 892.

It is not clear what spurred the caliph to create this new capital in an area of steppe that needed significant canalisation works for its irrigation. The historian al-Yaqubi describes the city in detail. He reports that it had become necessary to create a city separate from Baghdad, where non-Arab-speaking soldiers could resettle, and so reduce the friction with the local population.[151] The place chosen was probably the site of a settlement that already existed in the previous Sasanian period.[152] Al-Mutasim died in 842 and the city continued to be an imperial residence under his successor al-Wathiq (r. 842-847) who contributed to the city's growth, as did the subsequent caliph al-Mutawakil (r. 847-861). The works commissioned by al-Mutawakil were particularly valuable, with the construction of the Congregational Mosque and the spiral minaret which today is the most characteristic monument of Samarra. He expanded the city especially to the north of the previous boundaries, building what he called al-Mutawakliya. In the period of unrest that followed his death, Samarra began its decline. In 870, the situation returned to normal with the caliphate of al-Mutamid who continued to reside in Samarra, although effective power was held by his brother al-Muwaffaq, who returned to Baghdad. After the death of al-Mutamid in 892, the court officially returned to Baghdad, although Samarra was not entirely abandoned. One of the reasons that allowed Samarra not to disappear completely was the presence of the mausoleum of the Shiite imams Ali al-Hadi and Hasan al-Askari. We know that the city minted coins at least until 945, and that the Congregational Mosque of al-Mutawakil remained in use until at least the 11th century.[153]

Three main areas can be singled out in the Abbasid city: the earliest settlement of al-Mutasim, including the caliph's palace, the neighbourhoods of al-Qadisiya and Istabulat in the south, and the latest area of the city built by al-Mutawakil, in the north.[154]

The site was visited by European travellers in the 19th century.[155] The first meaningful visit was in 1847 by James F. Jones, to whom we owe a first map

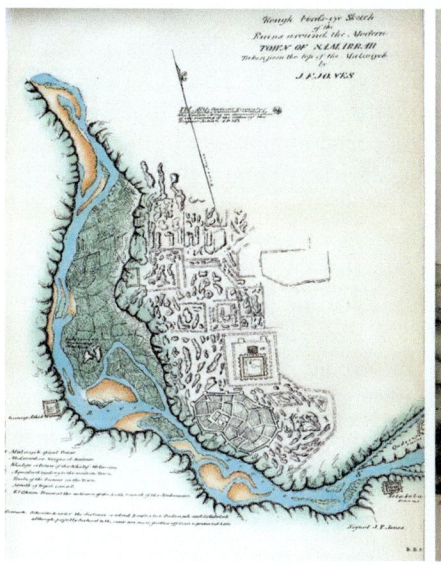

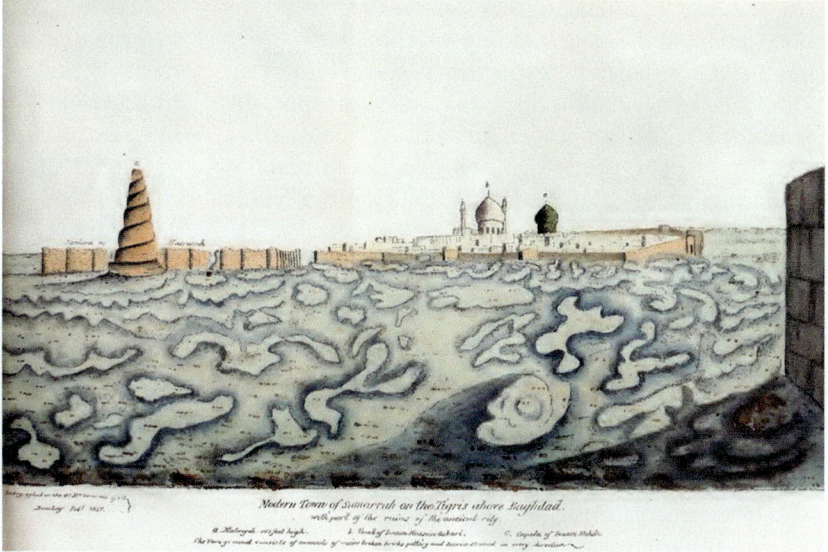

Figure 92: Samarra. The site map and a sketch of the archaeological remains, published in Jones 1857 (fig. not numbered).

and a sketch of the al-Askari shrine (Figure 92).[156] The first archaeological investigations were carried out in 1907 by Léon de Beylié, who photographically documented the site in a publication of the same

---

[149] Northedge, Kennet 2015/II.1. There is a wide literature available on the site. Fundamental for the historical-archaeological framework are the following titles: Jones 1857: 11-16; Viollet 1909, 1913; Sarre, Herzfeld 1911a; Herzfeld 1923, 1927, 1930, 1948b; Sarre 1925; Lamm 1928; al-Amid 1968; al-Janabi 1975, 1983; Northedge 1993, 2006, 2008, 2014; Robinson 2001; Leisten 2003; Northedge, Kennet 2015; Saba 2017.
[150] Breniquet 2008.
[151] Northedge 1995: 1039; On al-Yaqubi see Robinson 2003: 136, with bibliography, and Northedge 2008: 29-30.
[152] Northedge 2008: 49.

[153] On the late history see Northedge 2008: 239-246.
[154] Al-Janabi 1983: 306.
[155] For a summary on the topic see Northedge 1993: 144.
[156] Jones 1857: 11-17; the figures without map and sketch numbering are between pages 12 and 13.

Figure 93: Samarra. The Qubba al-Sulaibiya photographed a) in 1909 by H. Viollet (1909: fig. 6), b) in 1930 by K.A.C. Creswell (below, Figure 127), and c) in 1983 by a. Northedge, after the restorations carried out in the 1970s (courtesy by A. Northedge; published also in Northedge 2006, fig. 2).

year.[157] Immediately afterwards, between 1908 and 1910, Henry Viollet made some soundings in Dair al-Khalifa (see below).[158] Gertrude Bell visited the site between the two expeditions of de Beylié and Viollet, taking a rich batch of photographs.[159]

The history of the excavations of Samarra, however, is mainly linked to the research conducted between 1911 and 1913 by Ernst Herzfeld,[160] who excavated the main monuments and had direct contacts with Creswell. Herzfeld certainly deserves the credit of having investigated and laid the foundations for scientific research on the site, in spite of the difficulties encountered due to continually insufficient funds, considering the scale of the project and the evident logistical challenges. Nevertheless, the problem of the lack of adequate publication of Herzfeld's excavations still hinders full understanding of the site.[161] Since the 1930s, important excavation and restoration campaigns have been conducted on the site, especially by the Iraqi Department of Antiquities[162] and, since 1983, by Alastair Northedge, who currently handles an impressive work of publishing data on the whole excavations.[163]

The size of the settlement makes it particularly difficult to manage and survey the site,[164] which has been included in the *UNESCO World Heritage List* since 2007.[165]

Creswell focused much of his attention on Samarra, relying largely on the data made available by Herzfeld,[166] but also on personal observations collected during a short visit to the site, in Spring 1930. During his visit, he made reliefs of the Bab-al-Amma and, above all, of the Congregational Mosque (below). The plan he drew of the mosque is very accurate, especially if we consider the evidence visible at that time. Creswell wrote about Samarra in his *Early Muslim architecture* in distinct chapters,[167] following a chronological path: according to the order in his publication, the monuments photographed in the Berenson Collection are presented as follows (map in Figure 95).

Dar al-Khalifa.[168] This building, also referred to in the literature as Qasr al-Khalifa, was the residence of caliph al-Mutasim, who built it in 836. It is one of the most investigated buildings in Samarra, already inspected by de Beylié and Viollet, before being thoroughly excavated by Herzfeld.[169] In spite of this, only a small part has been excavated, compared to an overall estimated area of 176ht.[170] It is located in what was at the time the northern edge of the city, on a natural high ground. Today, there are three main elements: the main entrance with a triple iwan (i.e., the Bab al-Amma), in front of the Tigris, the audience or throne hall, originally decorated and surmounted by a dome, and a large swimming pool reserved for the caliph and his closest entourage. It is a structure that has undergone much looting, even after Herzfeld's excavations which reported of stucco decorations now lost (Figures 96-104).

---

[157] de Beylié 1907.
[158] Viollet 1909, 1913, with beautiful photos in pls 4-6. On this subject see also Rose 2017.
[159] A collection of 108 Bell's photos is published in the Getrude Bell Archive, Album L 1909 and Album V 1917-1918 (see p. 260).
[160] Herzfeld 1923, 1927, 1930, 1948; Sarre, Herzfeld 1911a, 1911b, 1920a, 1920b.
[161] On Herzfeld see Hauser 2003.
[162] For a summary see Northedge 2014: 78-82.
[163] Leisten 2003, Northedge 2014, Northedge, Kennet 2015.
[164] It is worth noting that, compared to over 6,300 buildings surveyed, only 9 of them retain significant standing remains (Northedge 1991: 74).
[165] In 2015 UNESCO signed an agreement for the *Conservation and Management of the World Heritage site of Samarra Archaeological City* (https://whc.unesco.org/pg_friendly_print.cfm?cid=82&id=1330&&). See also the report *State of conservation of the properties inscribed on the List of World Heritage in Danger* of the World Heritage Conmmitee (4 june 2021), at p. 25, https://

whc.unesco.org/archive/2021/whc21-44com-7B.Add-en.pdf. On the recent state of research in Samarra see also Northedge 2014.
[166] See Northedge 1991 for a detailed analysis of the relationship between Creswell and Herzfeld concerning the analysis of Samarra.
[167] See the references to the single monuments in the footnotes below.
[168] Creswell 1940: 233-237 and 1958: 260-266.
[169] See Northedge 2008: 133-150, with bibliography on the history of the research on this monument. Further bibliography, along with a description of the monument, can be found in the card of ARCHNET site 4205.
[170] Northedge 1993: 154.

Figure 94: Samarra. The al-Askari mosque and shrine in a) a photo taken in 1911 by G. Bell (courtesy of Gertrude Bell archive, NewCastle University, photo nr. V_034 from 'album 1917-1918, Iraq') and b) in 2006, after the bombing of the dome, but before the minarets were destroyed in 2007 (https://commons.wikimedia.org/wiki/File:Al-Askari_Mosque_2006.jpg; U.S. Federal Government image, released in Public domain).

Great Mosque.[171] It was built by the caliph al-Mutawakil (hence the alternative name of Jami al-Mutawakil) between 847 and 861 to replace the previous one, any remains of which have not yet been identified. Today, what remains above all is the large outer wall of the prayer hall (374×443m perimeter) and the famous minaret, also known as Malwiya. This is probably the most characteristic monument of Samarra on account of its counter-clockwise spiral shape with steps narrowing towards the cusp and its circular hall, with openings, on the top. The minaret is located on the north-eastern side of the complex and is built of brick and sandstone; it rests upon a square base of 32m per side and 52m in height. It was bombed in 2005, suffering extensive damage; in 2015, UNESCO drew up a plan for its restoration.[172] Already in 1968-1969 and then in the 1990s, the minaret had undergone significant restoration by the Iraqi Department of Antiquities, mainly consisting of partial reconstruction of the ramp. Therefore, today's structure differs significantly from the building photographed by Creswell (Figures 105-118).

Abu Dulaf Mosque.[173] The mosque was built between 859 and 861 by al-Mutawakil, when he expanded the city to the north. The mosque takes its name from a dignitary of the time, a famous patron.[174] Its shape recalls the Great Mosque: here, also, we find a large rectangular courtyard in bricks, with an outer perimeter of c. 360×350m, a central courtyard and a hypostyle prayer hall. It is well preserved especially on the north side, close to which stands the spiral minaret, 34m high (but originally it probably had one floor less). It was restored by the Department of Antiquities in the 1940s.[175] Creswell drew a plan, which however does not consider the later results following the Iraqi excavations (in particular, the remains of the resthouse for the caliph, behind the side of the mihrab) (Figures 119-126).

Qubba al-Sulaibiya.[176] This curious building rises on the right bank of the Tigris, in a once residential area with gardens. It has an octagonal plan, is surmounted by a dome and is built on a sort of wider platform, which raised the complex from the ground level by at least 2.5m.[177] The octagonal structure had eight openings leading to a corridor. In the centre, a square room of around 6m per side is surmounted by the dome. Its dating (875-900) is also linked to the material used and the construction technique, i.e., 'mud brick with a high gypsum content, interleaved with reed mats',[178] also used in Qasr al-Ashiq (below). Creswell agreed with Herzfeld's assumption that it was the mausoleum of al-Muntasir. However, it is still difficult today to interpret the building with certainty, even if from a certain point onwards it was definitely a sanctuary in memory of three individuals who were buried there but who have not been identified.[179] The building has been greatly

---

[171] Creswell 1940: 254-260 and 1958: 274-280.
[172] See Northedge 2008: 122-125 and the card of ARCHNET site 3828 for a bibliography on the researches on this monument.
[173] Creswell 1940: 278-282 and 1958: 280-285.
[174] See Northedge, Kennet 2015: I/155 and the card of ARCHNET site 3830 for a bibliography on the researches on this monument.

[175] The restoration can be clearly seen in the photo-repertoire published on ARCHNET.
[176] Creswell 1940: 283-286 and 1958: 287-289.
[177] See the card of ARCHNET site 3831, as well as Viollet 1909; Sarre, Herzfeld 1911a: 83-86; Abdu 1973; Leisten 2003: 72-78; Northedge 2006.
[178] Northedge 2006: 71.
[179] Herzfeld excavated the monument in just three days. He

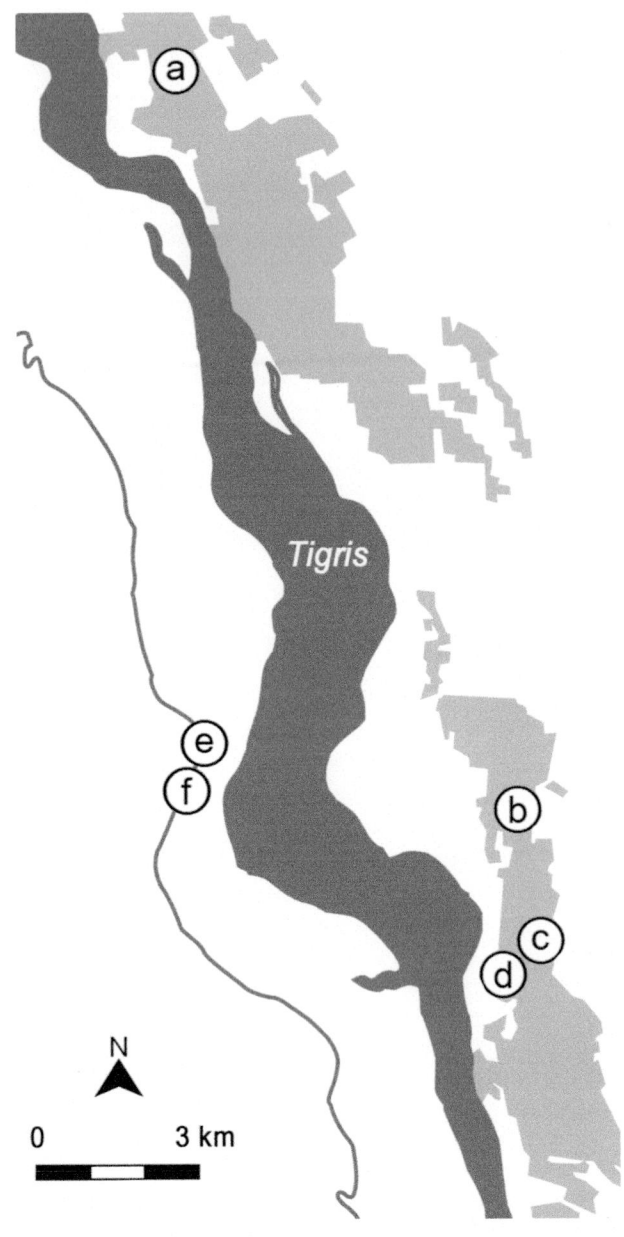

Figure 95: Samarra. Map of the phe photographed monuments; a: the Abu Dulaf Mosque (Figures 119-126); b: the Dar al-Khalifa (Figures 96-104); c: the Great Mosque (Figures 105-118); d: the al-Askari Shrine (Figures 134-135); e: the Qasr al-Ashiq (Figures 129-133); f: the Qubba al-Sulaibiya (Figures 127-128).

altered, compared to its original state of conservation, by Iraqi restoration carried out in the 1970s (Figure 93).[180] Creswell documented the monument when it was still without a dome,[181] and without the light reaching the base with the access ramps excavated during the Iraqi investigations (Figures 93, 127-128).

took only one photo (Northedge 1991: 81) and believed that the three burials were caliphs. Leisten (2003: 76-77) believed that it was originally a garden pavilion. Northedge suggested instead that it was a ka'aba model, described by al-Muqadasi in the 10th century (see Northedge 1991: 89 and 2003, with bibliography, for a detailed analysis of the different possible interpretations).
[180] Abdu 1973; Northedge 1991: 89.
[181] One of his photos is published in Viollet 1909, fig. 6.

Qasr al-Ashiq.[182] This building is located near the Qubba al-Sulaibiya. It is the last large palace built in Samarra by the caliph al-Mutamid, roughly dating back to between 877 and 882. After the death of the caliph, the palace continued to be inhabited and restored, until at least the 13th century.[183] It has a rectangular plan, with two walls, the outer one measuring 230×178m and the inner one 140×93m, separated by a moat. It is also one of the best preserved buildings in Samarra, although even in this case the current state is the result of restoration work carried out several times in the 1980s and 1990s.[184] It was a rather 'mysterious' building in Creswell's time, who nevertheless dated it correctly.[185] Herzfeld's excavations had been very few, and the situation became clearer only after the Iraqi excavations (Figures 129-133).

Al-Askari Shrine.[186] The so called al-Askari shrine, or Marqad al-Imamayn, is located near the mosque built by al-Mutasim. It was built by the Hamdanid Shiite Ruler Nasir al-Dawla (r. 929-967), and expanded significantly during the Buyid dynasty. The Buyids overthrew the Abbasids in 946, led by Muizz al-Dawla, who was also Shiite. He was responsible for the restoration of the mausoleum and the construction of the dome is probably due to him. The sanctuary contains the tombs of the two imams who were the tenth and eleventh successor of Ali, i.e., Hali al-Hadi and al-Hasan al-Askari. The latter was poisoned by caliph al-Mutamid in 874, who was jealous of the imams' prestige.[187] The general shape of the structure that we see today is the one defined during the Buyid phase: a central square burial chamber, about 15m per side, surmounted by a large dome. A hallway surrounds the burial chamber. The entrance is to the south, introduced by a large porch that is however more recent than the rest of the structure. The two minarets, 36m high, were originally decorated with a spiral motif that can be seen in the early photos. They were modified in 1905, when the golden dome was built, making the sanctuary renowned throughout the region,[188] although a similar cover had probably existed even before. In this regard, it is worth noting that after his visit in 1847,

[182] Creswell 1940: 361-364.
[183] See Northedge 2008: 233-236, with bibliography, and the card of ARCHNET site 4240 on the history of the research on this monument.
[184] Hamid 1974. In Northedge 2008, pls 86-89, some photographs clearly show the state of the building after restoration.
[185] Northedge 2008: 235.
[186] The monument was not considered in Creswell's *Early Muslim architecture*.
[187] On the building and in particular on the information handed down to us by Arab historians, see Northedge 2008: 246, and the card of ARCHNET site 5525.
[188] Even before Creswell's photo, the gold cover is particularly appreciated in some photographs taken in 1917, today in the Getrude Bell Archive, Album V 1917-1918, n. 34-36 (see p. 260).

Jones reported 'two handsome tombs, surmounted by cupolas; the larger being that erected over the remains of Imam Hussain Askari. It has recently been repaired, and, I believe, was formerly covered with gold similar to the cupolas of Kathemein, Kerbella, and Nejaf, but is now perfectly white, the present funds not being sufficient to give it its former splendour'.[189] In 2006 and 2007, the sanctuary was heavily damaged by two explosions, but its reconstruction began in 2009 (Figures 94, 134-135).[190]

---

[189] Jones 1857: 12. The second dome quoted by Jones refers to the dome of the neighbour shrine of the twelfth Imam, Muhammad al-Mahdi.
[190] Crowley 2014; Northedge 2014: 84-85. On the UNESCO website, a video-documentary on the destruction of the shrine is available at https://www.unesco.org/archives/multimedia/document-2801

Figure 96.
Subject: Samarra. The Dar al-Khalifa.
Berenson ID: 133229.
Medium: gelatine silver print, 12×17cm.
Date of creation: c. 1930.
Handwritten notes on the back: 'Samarra, Bab al-'Amma (remains of Khalif's palace)' [Cres.].
Ashmolean negative: EA.CA.6334.
Published in Creswell 1940, pl. 51.b; Creswell 1958, fig. 77.

Figure 97.
Subject: Samarra. The Dar al-Khalifa.
Berenson ID: 133217.
Medium: gelatine silver print, 12×17cm.
Date of creation: c. 1930.
Handwritten notes on the back: 'Samarra, Great Mosque' [sic] [Cres.].
Ashmolean negative: EA.CA.6333.
Published in Creswell 1940, pl. 51.a; Creswell 1958, fig. 76.

Figure 98.
Subject: Samarra. The Dar al-Khalifa.
Berenson ID: 133230.
Medium: gelatine silver print, 12×17cm.
Date of creation: c. 1930.
Handwritten notes on the back: 'Samarra, Bab al-'Amma (remains of Khalif's palace)' [Cres.].
Ashmolean negative: EA.CA.6335.

Figure 99.
Subject: Samarra. The Dar al-Khalifa.
Berenson ID: 133231.
Medium: gelatine silver print, 12×17cm.
Date of creation: c. 1930.
Handwritten notes on the back: 'Samarra, Bab al-'Amma – vault of side liwan' [Cres.].
Ashmolean negative: EA.CA.6339.
Published in Creswell 1940, pl. 51.c.

Figure 100 (left).
Subject: Samarra. The Dar al-Khalifa.
Berenson ID: 133232.
Medium: gelatine silver print, 12×17cm.
Date of creation: c. 1930.
Handwritten notes on the back: 'Samarra, Bab al-'Amma (remains of Khalif's palace)' [Cres.].
Ashmolean negative: EA.CA.6336.
Published in Creswell 1940, pl. 51.d.

Figure 101 (centre).
Subject: Samarra. The great iwan of the Dar al-Khalifa.
Berenson ID: 133233.
Medium: gelatine silver print, 12×17cm.
Date of creation: c. 1930.
Handwritten notes on the back: 'Samarra, Bab al-'Amma, showing trace of stucco ornament on arch of great iwan' [Cres.].
Ashmolean negative: EA.CA.6337.

Figure 102 (right).
Subject: Samarra. The great iwan of the Dar al-Khalifa.
Berenson ID: 133234.
Medium: gelatine silver print, 12×17cm.
Date of creation: c. 1930.
Handwritten notes on the back: 'Samarra, Bab al-'Amma – vault of great iwan' [Cres.].
Ashmolean negative: EA.CA.6338.

Figure 103.
Subject: Samarra. The Dar al-Khalifa.
Berenson ID: 133236.
Medium: gelatine silver print, 12×17cm.
Date of creation: c. 1930.
Handwritten notes on the back: 'Samarra, Bab al-'Amma (remains of Khalif's palace)' [Cres.].
Ashmolean negative: EA.CA.6342.

Figure 104.
Subject: Samarra. The Dar al-Khalifa.
Berenson ID: 133237.
Medium: gelatine silver print, 12×17cm.
Date of creation: c. 1930.
Handwritten notes on the back: 'Samarra, Bab al-'Amma (remains of Khalif's palace)' [Cres.].
Ashmolean negative: EA.CA.6343.

Figure 105.
Subject: Samarra. The Great Mosque, looking northwest.
Berenson ID: 133214.
Medium: gelatine silver print, 12×17cm.
Date of creation: c. 1930.
Handwritten notes on the back: 'Samarra, the Great Mosque, from the S.E' [Cres.].

THE SITES AND THE MONUMENTS – MESOPOTAMIA

Figure 106.
Subject: Samarra. The Great Mosque, looking northwest.
Berenson ID: 133223.
Medium: gelatine silver print, 12×17cm.
Date of creation: c. 1930.
Handwritten notes on the back: 'Samarra, the Great Mosque – S.W. side' [Cres.].
Ashmolean negative: EA.CA.6350.

Figure 107 (left).
Subject: Samarra. The minaret of the Great Mosque.
Berenson ID: 133225.
Medium: gelatine silver print, 12×17cm.
Date of creation: c. 1930.
Handwritten notes on the back: 'Samarra, the Great Mosque – minaret (Malwiya Tower)' [Cres.].
Ashmolean negative: EA.CA.6356.

Figure 108 (right).
Subject: Samarra. The minaret of the Great Mosque.
Berenson ID: 133226.
Medium: gelatine silver print, 12×17cm.
Date of creation: c. 1930.
Handwritten notes on the back: 'Samarra, the Great Mosque – minaret (Malwiya Tower)' [Cres.].
Ashmolean negative: EA.CA.6358.
Published in Creswell 1940, pl. 65.d.

Figure 109.
Subject: Samarra. The entrance façade and the minaret of the Great Mosque.
Berenson ID: 133224.
Medium: gelatine silver print, 12×17cm.
Date of creation: c. 1930.
Handwritten notes on the back: 'Samarra, the Great Mosque from the E' [Cres.].
Ashmolean negative: EA.CA.6355.
Published in Creswell 1940, pl. 64.c.

Figure 110.
Subject: Samarra. The base of the minaret of the Great Mosque.
Berenson ID: 133228.
Medium: gelatine silver print, 12×17cm.
Date of creation: c. 1930.
Handwritten notes on the back: 'Samarra, Great Mosque – base of minaret' [Cres.].
Ashmolean negative: EA.CA.6359.

Figure 111.
Subject: Samarra. Detail of the northwestern side of the Great Mosque.
Berenson ID: 133227.
Medium: gelatine silver print, 12×17cm.
Date of creation: c. 1930.
Handwritten notes on the back: 'Samarra, the Great Mosque – N.W side, showing take-off of wall of ziada' [Cres.].
Ashmolean negative: EA.CA.6354.
Published in Creswell 1940, pl. 65.c.

Figure 112.
Subject: Samarra. The southern corner of the Great Mosque.
Berenson ID: 133216.
Medium: gelatine silver print, 12×17cm.
Date of creation: c. 1930.
Handwritten notes on the back: 'Samarra, the Great Mosque, S. corner, showing take-off of wall of ziada' [Cres.].
Ashmolean negative: EA.CA.6347.
Published in Creswell 1940, pl. 65.b.

The Sites and the Monuments – Mesopotamia

Figure 113.
Subject: Samarra. The southeastern side of the Great Mosque.
Berenson ID: 133222.
Medium: gelatine silver print, 12×17cm.
Date of creation: c. 1930.
Handwritten notes on the back: 'Samarra, the Great Mosque – S.E. side' [Cres.].
Ashmolean negative: EA.CA.6345.

Figure 114.
Subject: Samarra. The southeastern side of the Great Mosque.
Berenson ID: 133220.
Medium: gelatine silver print, 12×17cm.
Date of creation: c. 1930.
Handwritten notes on the back: 'Samarra, the Great Mosque – southeast side' [Cres.].
Ashmolean negative: EA.CA.6346.
Published in Creswell 1940, pl. 65.a; Creswell 1958, fig. 83.

Figure 115.
Subject: Samarra. The southeastern side of the Great Mosque.
Berenson ID: 133221.
Medium: gelatine silver print, 12×17cm.
Date of creation: c. 1930.
Handwritten notes on the back: 'Samarra, the Great Mosque – S.E. side' [Cres.].
Ashmolean negative: EA.CA.6349.

Figure 116.
Subject: Samarra. The Great Mosque, with the minaret in the background.
Berenson ID: 133215.
Medium: gelatine silver print, 12×17cm.
Date of creation: c. 1930.
Handwritten notes on the back: 'Samarra, the Great Mosque, entrance in S.W. side' [Cres.].
Ashmolean negative: EA.CA.6353.

Figure 117 (left).
Subject: Samarra. Detail of a window of the Great Mosque.
Berenson ID: 133219.
Medium: gelatine silver print, 12×17cm.
Date of creation: c. 1930.
Handwritten notes on the back: 'Samarra, Great Mosque – windows in S wall' [Cres.].
Ashmolean negative: EA.CA.6363.
Published in Creswell 1940, pl. 66.b; Creswell 1958, fig. 84.

Figure 118 (right).
Subject: Samarra. Remains of the entrance to the Great Mosque.
Berenson ID: 133218.
Medium: gelatine silver print, 12×17cm.
Date of creation: c. 1930.
Handwritten notes on the back: 'Samarra, the Great Mosque, remains of entrance with opening above' [Cres.].
Ashmolean negative: EA.CA.6348.

Figure 119.
Subject: Samarra. The Abu Dulaf Mosque, looking north.
Berenson ID: 133238.
Medium: gelatine silver print, 12×17cm.
Date of creation: c. 1930.
Handwritten notes on the back: 'Samarra, Mosque of Abu Dulaf – from the S' [Cres.].
Ashmolean negative: EA.CA.6369.

Figure 120.
Subject: Samarra. The Abu Dulaf Mosque.
Berenson ID: 133239.
Medium: gelatine silver print, 12×17cm.
Date of creation: c. 1930.
Handwritten notes on the back: 'Samarra, Mosque of Abu Dulaf – from the W' [Cres.].
Ashmolean negative: EA.CA.6368.

Figure 121.
Subject: Samarra. The Abu Dulaf Mosque, looking east.
Berenson ID: 133243.
Medium: gelatine silver print, 12×17cm.
Date of creation: c. 1930.
Handwritten notes on the back: 'Samarra, Mosque of Abu Dulaf – looking E' [Cres.].
Ashmolean negative: EA.CA.6370.
Published in Creswell 1940, pl. 68.b.

Figure 122.
Subject: Samarra. The minaret of the Abu Dulaf Mosque.
Berenson ID: 133246.
Medium: gelatine silver print, 12×17cm.
Date of creation: c. 1930.
Handwritten notes on the back: 'Samarra, Mosque of Abu Dulaf – minaret, from the N' [Cres.].
Ashmolean negative: EA.CA.6378.
Published in Creswell 1940, pl. 71.e.

Figure 123.
Subject: Samarra. The Abu Dulaf Mosque, with the minaret in the background.
Berenson ID: 133241.
Medium: gelatine silver print, 12×17cm.
Date of creation: c. 1930.
Handwritten notes on the back: 'Samarra, Mosque of Abu Dulaf – central aisle of sanctuary' [Cres.].
Ashmolean negative: EA.CA.6380.

Figure 124.
Subject: Samarra. The Abu Dulaf Mosque: some piers and the minaret.
Berenson ID: 133245.
Medium: gelatine silver print, 12×17cm.
Date of creation: c. 1930.
Handwritten notes on the back: 'Samarra, Mosque of Abu Dulaf – northeast riwaq' [Cres.].
Ashmolean negative: EA.CA.6373.
Published in Creswell 1940, pl. 71.a.

Figure 125.
Subject: Samarra. The Abu Dulaf Mosque.
Berenson ID: 133247.
Medium: gelatine silver print, 12×17cm.
Date of creation: c. 1930.
Handwritten notes on the back: 'Samarra, Mosque of Abu Dulaf – from the W' [Cres.].
Ashmolean negative: EA.CA.6375.
Published in Creswell 1940, pl. 71.b.

THE SITES AND THE MONUMENTS – MESOPOTAMIA

Figure 126.
Subject: Samarra. The Abu Dulaf Mosque.
Berenson ID: 133242.
Medium: gelatine silver print, 12×17cm.
Date of creation: c. 1930.
Handwritten notes on the back: 'Samarra, Mosque of Abu Dulaf – sanctuary from the S.W' [Cres.].
Ashmolean negative: EA.CA.6381.
Published in Creswell 1940, pl. 71.d.

Figure 127.
Subject: Samarra. The Qubba al-Sulaibiya.
Berenson ID: 133254.
Medium: gelatine silver print, 12×17cm.
Date of creation: c. 1930.
Handwritten notes on the back: 'Samarra, Qubbat as-Slebiya' [Cres.].
Ashmolean negative: EA.CA.6383.

Figure 128.
Subject: Samarra. The Qubba al-Sulaibiya.
Berenson ID: 133253.
Medium: gelatine silver print, 12×17cm.
Date of creation: c. 1930.
Handwritten notes on the back: 'Samarra, Qubbat as-Slebiya' [Cres.].
Ashmolean negative: EA.CA.6384.
Published in Creswell 1940, pl. 79.a.

Figure 129.
Subject: Samarra. The southern side of the Qasr al-Ashiq.
Berenson ID: 133248.
Medium: gelatine silver print, 12×17cm.
Date of creation: c. 1930.
Handwritten notes on the back: 'Samarra, the Qasr al-'ashik – east side' [Cres.].
Ashmolean negative: EA.CA.6394.

Figure 130.
Subject: Samarra. The northern side of the Qasr al-Ashiq.
Berenson ID: 133249.
Medium: gelatine silver print, 12×17cm.
Date of creation: c. 1930.
Handwritten notes on the back: 'Samarra, the Qasr al-'ashik – north side' [Cres.].
Ashmolean negative: EA.CA.6395.
Published in Creswell 1940, pl. 115.b.

Figure 131.
Subject: Samarra. The northern side of the Qasr al-Ashiq.
Berenson ID: 133251.
Medium: gelatine silver print, 12×17cm.
Date of creation: c. 1930.
Handwritten notes on the back: 'Samarra, Qasr al-'ashik – north side' [Cres.].
Ashmolean negative: EA.CA.6391.
Published in Creswell 1940, pl. 116.c.

THE SITES AND THE MONUMENTS – MESOPOTAMIA

Figure 132.
Subject: Samarra. The northwestern corner of the Qasr al-Ashiq.
Berenson ID: 133252.
Medium: gelatine silver print, 12×17cm.
Date of creation: c. 1930.
Handwritten notes on the back: 'Samarra, Qasr al-'ashik – west side' [Cres.].
Ashmolean negative: EA.CA.6388.
Published in Creswell 1940, pl. 116.d.

Figure 133.
Subject: Samarra. The southern side of the Qasr al-Ashiq.
Berenson ID: 133250.
Medium: gelatine silver print, 12×17cm.
Date of creation: c. 1930.
Handwritten notes on the back: 'Samarra, Qasr al-'ashik – south side' [Cres.].
Ashmolean negative: EA.CA.6398.

Figure 134.
Subject: Samarra. The al-Askari Shrine.
Berenson ID: 133213.
Medium: gelatine silver print, 12×17cm.
Date of creation: c. 1930.
Handwritten notes on the back: 'Samarra' [Cres.]. 'Samarra was the second capital of the Abbasid caliphs, from 836-876' [Anon.].
Ashmolean negative: EA.CA.6331.

Figure 135.
Subject: Samarra. The al-Askari Shrine.
Berenson ID: 133255.
Medium: gelatine silver print, 12×17cm.
Date of creation: c. 1930.
Handwritten notes on the back: 'Samarra, Shrine of the 11th Īmam – Hasan al-'Askari dome covered with gilt tile' [Cres.].
Ashmolean negative: EA.CA.6332.

Qantarat Harba

Qantarat Harba, or rather the 'bridge of Harba', takes its name from the city of the same name which is located immediately to the south-east and on the route that joins Baghdad, Samarra and Tikrit.

The bridge was built in 1228 by the Abbasid caliph al-Mustansir (for this reason it is also known as al-Mustansir bridge) to connect the two banks of the old Dujail canal (Nahr Dujail) and was part of a larger project to implement an irrigation and water supply system in the region.[191]

It is an extremely important archaeological structure, as it is one of the very few examples of a well-preserved Abbasid bridge. It spans 54m in length and *c.* 12 in width and is supported on four pointed arches, spaced out with three niches. Today, the bridge is out of service and the arches mostly buried up in earth.[192]

Creswell's interest in this bridge, and his decision to visit and photograph it, most likely in 1930, is probably due to two very particular features: first, the bridge is built entirely of fired brick, without stone, and is the only one of its kind in Medieval Islamic architecture. Furthermore, the bridge has always been known and renowned for a long nashki inscription, which runs on both sides above the arches. As early as 1846, James F. Jones had made a detailed drawing of the bridge, depicting the parapet with the inscription as in excellent condition. A later photo of the bridge was taken by Léon de Beylié 1907 (Figure 136).[193] In both images, the channel already seems to be partially blocked.

Only three of Creswell's photographs have reached us, but they capture the bridge with good detail: an overview (Figure 137) shows that the arches were still largely blocked, as early as 1930. A second photograph (Figure 138) allows us to better evaluate the arches, at least the upper part where they are not obstructed by earth; a third photograph (Figure 139) illustrates a detail of the inscription, where the brick-laying technique around the inscription, with brick-edges projecting from the surface, can be appreciated.[194]

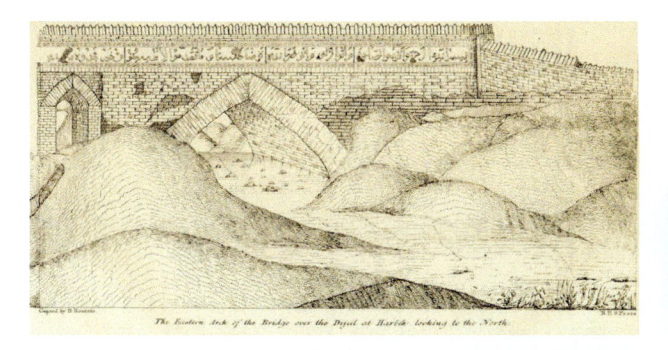

Figure 136: The Qantarat Harba in a lithograph depicting the structure seen in 1847 by J.F. Jones (1857: pl. after p. 252) and in a photograph of 1907 published by L. de Beylié (1907, fig. 26).

---

[191] Adamo 2020: 386-389.
[192] Michell 1978: 251. See also the card of ARCHNET site 3834.

[193] Jones 1857: 252-253.
[194] I would like to thank Jehan Sherqo for providing me with useful information and images of the current bridge, which allowed me to compare them with Creswell's photographs. The photos clearly show that the bridge is in rather good condition and that the arches have been at least partially restored in recent times.

Figure: 137.
Subject: The eastern side of the Qantarat Harba.
Berenson ID: 133256.
Medium: gelatine silver print, 12×17cm.
Date of creation: c. 1930.
Handwritten notes on the back: 'Harbi, Bridge of Mustansir – east side — 629 (1232)' [Cres.].
Ashmolean negative: EA.CA.6406.

Figure: 138.
Subject: The eastern side of the Qantarat Harba.
Berenson ID: 133257.
Medium: gelatine silver print, 12×17cm.
Date of creation: c. 1930.
Handwritten notes on the back: 'Harbi, Bridge of Mustansir – east side — 629 (1232)' [Cres.].
Ashmolean negative: EA.CA.6407.

Figure: 139.
Subject: Detail of the inscription on the eastern side of the Qantarat Harba.
Berenson ID: 133258.
Medium: gelatine silver print, 12×17cm.
Date of creation: c. 1930.
Handwritten notes on the back: 'Harbi, Bridge of Mustansir – east side — 629 (1232)' [Cres.].
Ashmolean negative: EA.CA.6408.

Baghdad

The capital of Iraq is located in the central region of the country, in a flood plain crossed by the river Tigris, which cuts the city in two. Here, the valley between the Tigris and the Euphrates widens in the direction of the Persian Gulf, having reached its narrower point in the region where the ancient capitals of Babylon, Seleucia, and Ctesiphon once rose.

Baghdad was the Abbasid capital between the mid-8th and 10th centuries, when it reached the peak of its splendour.[195] The city was originally built on the right bank of the Tigris, although today it is mostly on the left bank. It is likely that a settlement existed already in the pre-Islamic era, but the foundation of the city is traditionally dated 762, when the new capital was commissioned by the caliph al-Mansur, who moved the court here from Kufa. The new city was built as a circular city, bounded by a rampart and surrounded by a moat and city walls. Four gates looked towards Khorsan, Basra, Kufa and Syria. Its importance declined after 945, when power passed to the Buyid dinasty. It continued nevertheless to be highly influential until at least the mid-13th century, with a period of significant rebirth in the 11th century under the Seljuks, and after its recapture by the Abbasid caliph al-Nasr in 1186, when several construction projects were undertaken. It was sacked by the Mongols in 1258, but soon recovered, with the construction of new important buildings. After the Mongol period, the city also experienced new pillages and destruction of its architectural heritage, especially in 1401 with Timur and a century later, when it was the scene of a Sunni massacre at the hands of the Safavids. During the Ottoman occupation, although the city was less prominent, many ancient monuments were restored, and some new ones were built, especially during the governorship of Midhat Pasha, between 1869 and 1872.

On the eve of World War I, Baghdad was an important centre, with the largest population among other Iraqi cities and with the strongest concentration of diplomats and foreign residents. The *Baedeker Guide*, in its 1912 edition, reports a population of 200,000 inhabitants, 120,000 of which Muslims, 50,000 Jews, 15,000 Christians, with a hundred European residents, represented by the French, German, English, Austro-Hungarian, American and Russian consulates. It points out, however, that 'Il reste peu de chose des édifices de l'époque florissante de la ville'.[196]

Figure 140: Baghdad. The Zumurrud Khatun Mosque depicted by J.F. Jones (1857, plate after p. 311).

After the end of World War I, the British (who had invaded from the south and had quickly secured the strategic area of the Persian Gulf) set up in Baghdad the seat of the new king imposed, Faisal ben al-Hussayn, and in 1921 Baghdad became the capital of the new Iraqi state.

After World War II, the architecture of the city underwent profound changes. Between the 1950s and the 1980s, in particular, the possibility to assign contracts directly rather than through international competitions attracted the work of leading architects, including José Luis Sert, Alvar Aalto, Frank Lloyd Wright, le Corbusier, Gio Ponti, Walter Gropius.[197]

The most recent damage suffered took place in 1990 and 2003 with the Gulf Wars. During the Second Gulf War, Baghdad was bombed between April and March 2003 as part of the 'Iraq Freedom' operation. On that occasion, and in the period immediately after, many cultural monuments were damaged.

Although Baghdad is mentioned by several ancient Arab writers,[198] they describe a city that was completely different from the one that developed after the conquest by the Mongols, and whose monuments no longer existed when the first European travellers began to describe the city from the 18th century onwards (Figures 140-142).[199] It must be said that a detailed picture of the cultural heritage of the city is the result of recent works, since the first modern and systematic

---

[195] There is an extensive literature on Baghdad and its history: considering only some of the major works that focused on the historical development of the city, from which the information given in the summary proposed here is taken, we can mention: Lassner 1970; Wiet 1971; Kennedy 2005; al-Attar 2019. In addition, consider also the titles in the footnotes that follow, regarding the individual monuments.
[196] Baedeker 1912: 422-423.

[197] Janulardo 2015, with bibliography.
[198] Among these, worthy of mention are al-Khatib al-Baghdadi (11th century) and Ibn-Battuta (14th century). For a bibliography of the works of these and other medieval authors on the history of the city, see in particular Massignon 1912: 54-55; Khalil, Strika 1987: xiii-xiv.
[199] A useful list of the first European travellers describing Baghdad is given in Massignon 1912: 56. In particular, in addition to the works of Massignon (1910, 1912), information is also provided in Niehbur 1776-1780: II/239-270; Buckingham 1827: 371-380; Wellsted 1840: 254-279; Jones 1857: 303-402; Rousseau 1899: 1-14; Streck 1900; Le Strange 1901; Salmon 1904; Reuther 1910; Sarre, Herzfeld 1920a: 94-202; Coke 1927. After World War II, travel reports and studies quickly increased (a summary in Khalil, Strika 1987: xvi-xvii).

Figure 141: Baghdad the beginning of the 19th century (Parsons 1808, plate after p. 116).

survey of the monuments of the city was carried out by the Iraqi Department of Antiquities with the Italian Institute of Iraq between 1971 and 1976.[200]

Creswell photographed Baghdad in 1930, when it had been the Iraqi capital for less than ten years, and the general appearance of the city had not yet undergone radical changes compared to the period before World War I.[201] His photographs concern monuments located in different districts of the city, especially in al-Rusafa (Figure 143).

In a broad sense, the oldest monument to which Creswell paid attention was the al-Mansur Mosque, built as early as 762.[202] The mosque had been destroyed in antiquity, but Creswell photographed its famous marble mihrab, at that time located in the al-Khasiki mosque (built in 1069) and later moved first to the Museum of Qasr al-Abbasi and then to the Iraq Museum (Figures 144-148). It is a monument that had also received attention from other scholars.[203] Creswell dated it, as already Friedrich Sarre and Ernst Herzfeld, to the caliphate of al-Mansur, indicatively to 762.[204]

The architectural monuments photographed by Creswell, in chronological order according to the first date of construction, are the following.

Zumurrud Khatun.[205] This mausoleum was built by the Abbasid caliph al-Nasir li-Din Allah (r. 1180-1225) for his mother, Zumurrud Khatun, at the end of the 12th century. Its identification, often reported in the literature, as the mausoleum of Sitta Zubayda, wife of the Abbasid caliph Harun al-Rashid, is due to a misinterpretation of the first European travellers, which continues to be rooted in the tradition of studies.[206] The most striking architectural feature is the 9-layered tower, decorated with muqarnas and with a small dome on top, which covers the burial chamber: some openings in the muqarnas of the tower project a game of light inside the burial chamber. The monument has been extensively restored throughout its history but the main plan, with its octagonal base and stalactites covering system is a model that probably originated in Iraq (Figures 149-151).

Qasr al-Abbasi.[207] Located in the Maydan district, this rectangular two-storey brick building was probably built during the Abbasid caliphate of al-Mustansir (r. 1192-1242). The main entrance is on the west side, towards the Tigris. Its functional interpretation is still discussed, also due to the fact that only part of the original structure has been well preserved: traditionally, it is considered the building in which the caliph met dignitaries and visitors,[208] although it is possible that it could actually have been a madrasa (Figures 152-161).[209]

Suhrawardi Mosque and Mausoleum.[210] This complex includes a mosque and the shrine of Shaykh Umar Suhrawardi, within the famous cemetery of al-Wardiya. Shaykh Umar Suhrawardi was a legal scholar at Shafi School in the 13th century. The building was erected by the Abbasid caliph al-Nasir li Din Allah (r. 1180-1225) before the shaykh's death in the early 13th century. It was heavily restored many times, to such an extent that

---

[200] Khalil, Strika 1987.
[201] Creswell 1940: 1-38. A topographical map of the city, updated at the beginning of the 20th century, is published in Massignon 1912, pls 1-2.
[202] Creswell 1932, pl. 120:d.
[203] Buckingham 1827: 376-377; Sarre, Herzfeld 1911, pls 45-46 and 1920a: 139-144. It also appears in photos taken in 1907 by Henry Viollet (Viollet 1909, fig. 2), and in 1911 by Gertrude Bell (Getrude Bell Archive, Album Q 1911, n. 47-48, 53-55; see p. 260).
[204] Creswell 1932: 36, fig. 26. See also Creswell 1958: 179-182. The dating to the caliphate of al-Mansur had already been given in Sarre, Herzfeld 1920a: 142. See also Khoury 1998: 19 for a summary of the different dating proposals, and Khalil, Strika 1987: 49-50 for the general history of the monument and its movements in museums.

---

[205] Khalil, Strika 1987: 18-22. On this monument see also Wellsted 1840: 237-238; Rousseau 1899: 10; Le Strange 1901: 113-115; Massignon 1912: 108; Sarre, Herzfeld 1920a: 173-179; Michell 1978: 247. Early photos can be found in ARCHNET entry for site 1696, in the Gertrude Bell Archive, Album L 1909, n. 25, in the Matson Photo Collection, call nr. LC-USZ61-2006, LC-M33- 4589 [P&P], and LC-M33- 14493 [P&P]), and in the Lt. Roberts Middle Eastern Magic Lantern Slides Collection, image n 53 (see the entries 'Bell, Getrude', 'American Colony Photo Department' and 'Roberts, Lieutenant A.H.' in Appendix 1).
[206] See the caption 'Tomb of Lady Tobeideh' in the illustration in Jones 1857, reproduced here in Figure 140.
[207] Al-Janabi 1975: 61-71; Michell 1978: 247; Khalil, Strika 1987: 71-74. Early photos can be found in ARCHNET site 3835, and in the Gertrude Bell Archive, Album Q 1911, n. 47-48, 58-59 (see p. 260).
[208] Khalil, Strika 1987: 71-74.
[209] Michell 1978: 247.
[210] Khalil, Strika 1987: 51-53 and the ARCHNET site 4329. Early photos of this monument can be found in the Gertrude Bell Archive, Album L 1909 (see p. 260).

what we see today is essentially an Ottoman structure. Today, the complex has a rectangular courtyard adjoining a mosque and a tomb chamber, south of the mosque. The minaret has a polygonal base, cylindrical shaft with square Kufic decoration in glazed bricks and a frame of muqarnas, and a balcony. It was built in 1368 in the east of the courtyard, which is accessed by a large portal on the north-western side, with an iwan flanked by two niches (Figures 162-165).

Bab al-Wastani.[211] Built in 1221, it is one of the gates of the Abbasid city and is one of the best preserved (Figures 166-169).

Al-Mustansisriyya Madrasa.[212] This theological school was commissioned by the Abbasid caliph al-Mustansir Billah in 1227 and completed in 1234. It was the first example of 'universal' madrasa, because all orthodox rites were accepted. The construction was certainly different before the Mongol conquest and its destruction in 1258; nonetheless, it continued to be used and at least from the second half of the 18th century served as a caravanserai and a customs office.[213] After World War II, it underwent further changes and since 1960 has hosted the Museum of Islamic Art. Despite its long history, it is one of the few monuments of Baghdad to still retain its original features. Creswell's photos show the building nestled in a network of markets, in an environment, therefore, that has profoundly changed (Figures 170-177).[214]

Shaykh Maruf al Kharqi Mausoleum.[215] This mausoleum is located near the Zumurrud Khatun and is dedicated to the Sufi Maruf al-Kharqi, who died in 816. The mausoleum was destroyed by a fire in 1067, rebuilt and restored several times, also significantly altering the plan that was originally cross shaped and is difficult to date. An inscription dates the minaret to 1215, meaning that it is probably the earliest preserved part of the structure; the dome, on the contrary, is more recent, dating back to the Ottoman period (Figures 178-182).

Figure 142: Baghdad. The Shaykh Maruf al-Kharkhi Mausoleum and the Zumurrud Khatun drawn by A. O'Callaghan (Rousseau 1899: 10).

The al-Khulafa Minaret.[216] The minaret of the al-Khulafa mosque (otherwise known as al-Ghazi minaret, named after the nearby cotton suq) was the most characteristic of the city at the time of Creswell's visit. The mosque was probably built between 902 and 908 by the Abbasid caliph Muqtafi. It underwent significant restoration and reconstruction, especially in 1272, after it had been destroyed, or at least heavily damaged, by the Mongols in 1258. A madrasa was added in the 15th century, while more recently, in the 1960s, a new mosque connected to the minaret was built. The minaret was constructed in 1279, when the Ilkhanid dynasty took control of the city (1256-1353), but its style is most likely reminiscent of the style of the building that probably rose there before.[217] The minaret is made of bricks, on a 12-sided base, with a decoration consisting of a series of muqarnas that delimit a passageway, both at the base and just below the top. It is famous above all for the elaborate geometric decoration made of brick, on the outer surface. Part of the 13th-century structure, which unfortunately is now lost, can be reconstructed from Herzfeld's description (Figures 183-185).

Al-Mirjanya Madrasa.[218] Only a portion of this important madrasa, connected to a mosque and a mausoleum, remains today, specifically the entrance gate and the minaret. The building was largely destroyed after World War II to make way for the new Rashid Street. It was

---

[211] Jones 1857: 310; Le Strange 1901: 281; Sarre, Herzfeld 1920a: 151-156. Images of the gate are also published in Massignon 1912, pls 20-23, in a photo in the Gertrude Bell Archive, Album L 1909, n. L17 (see p. 260), and in the ARCHNET site 4326.

[212] Schmid, H. 1980. On the history of the monument see also Le Strange 1901: 266-267; Massignon 1912: 44-48; Sarre, Herzfeld 1920a: 161-170; al-Janabi 1975: 72-81; Mitchell 1978: 247-248; Khalil, Strika 1987: 65-70, as well as the ARCHNET site 3836.

[213] Niebuhr 1776-1780: II/241.

[214] On the general renovation of the neighbourhood in which the madrasa is located, see in particular al-Saffar 2018.

[215] On the life of the character and the history of the monument see Khalil, Strika 1987: 14-17. Among the descriptions of ancient travellers, noteworthy are those by Rousseau 1899, who portrays it in a drawing together with Zumurrud Khatun (Figure 142).

[216] Khalil, Strika 1987: 44. See also Le Strange 1901: 243; Massignon 1912: 41-44; Sarre, Herzfeld 1920a: 156-160; al-Janabi 1975: 113-125; Michell 1978: 248, besides the already mentioned Khalil, Strika 1987: 42-45. The minaret appears in several photos of ancient travellers: in particular one by Hermann Burchardt del 1894 (accessible on the database of the Ethnologisches Museum der Staatlichen Museen zu Berlin, Ident. Nr. 18/7), those published in Massignon 1912: 12-13, in the Gertrude Bell Archive, Album L 1909, n. 23 and Album Q 1911, n. 47-48 (see p. 260), and in the ARCHNET site 3842.

[217] Khalil, Strika 1987: 44.

[218] See Buckingham 1827: 375; Massignon 1912: 1-31; Al-Janabi 1975: 163-229; Michell 1978: 248; Khalil, Strika 1987: 46-50; Meinecke 1992: I/127; Parapetti 2017; see also the ARCHNET site 3844.

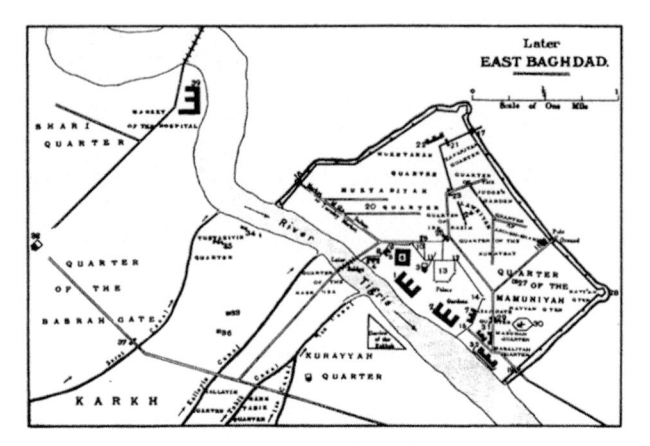

Figure 143: Baghdad. The 'Later East Baghdad', i.e., al-Rusafah, in the map drawn by Guy Le Strange (1901, map VIII).

built in 1357 in the period of the Jalayirid dynasty, and was a Sunna theological school. The name comes from Amin ad-Din Mirjan, Wali of Baghdad, who sponsored the construction. It was restored in 1785 at the time of Suleiman Pasha, and then in 1926, shortly before Creswell's visit. The access portal is quite remarkable with a pointed arch in a rectangular frame, of Seljuk inspiration, and is decorated with engraved stucco with terracotta inserts forming various decorative motifs. Recently, the prayer room was reconstructed inside the Iraq Museum (Figures 186-189).[219]

Khan Mirjan.[220] Built by Wali Amin al-Din Mirjan in 1358, as reported in the inscription at the entrance, it was originally made of bricks and wood. The building is rectangular, measuring 31.5×45m and arranged on two floors, with two entrances: one with a pointed arch from the adjacent Suq al-Thalutha and one from Dar al-Khilafa, now Samuel Street (Figures 190-195).

In addition to these buildings, Creswell photographed a wooden sarcophagus, known as one of the masterpieces of Islamic craftsmanship thanks to its refined floral decorations and nashki inscriptions, dating back to the 14th century. It was the sarcophagus of Imam Abdullah Ibn Mohammad Al-Aquli, who died in 1327, connected to the al-Aquliya mosque. Today the sarcophagus is located at the Iraq Museum (Figures 196-197).[221]

---

[219] Parapetti 2017. At p. 2 Parapetti reports that 'Too late, in September 1945, K.A.C. Creswell, one of the leading experts on Islamic architecture of the day, was invited by the government to visit the Mirjaniyah and express his opinion. Creswell reported: "The musalla of the Mirjaniya (...) is an outstanding monument of Muslim architecture, not only for its splendid ornaments (...) but also on account of the fact that it is the only example surviving in Iraq of this early type of triple-arched, laterally developed and domed, hall of prayer"'.

[220] See Michell 1978: 248; Khalil, Strika 1987: 75-77, and the ARCHNET site 15578.

[221] On the sarcophagus and on the inscription see in particular Massignon 1912: 31-40, with photos in pls 14-19; more recent information can be found in Khalil, Strika 1987: 57-58.

The Sites and the Monuments – Mesopotamia

Figure: 144.
Subject: Baghdad. The mihrab of the al-Khassaki Mosque.
Berenson ID: 133160.
Medium: gelatine silver print, 12×17cm.
Date of creation: c. 1930.
Handwritten notes on the back: 'Baghdad, mihrab from the Khasseki mosque' [Cres.].
Ashmolean negative: EA.CA.6264.
Published in Creswell 1940, pl. 120.d.

Figure: 145.
Subject: Baghdad. Detail of the mihrab of the al-Khassaki Mosque.
Berenson ID: 133162.
Medium: gelatine silver print, 12×17cm.
Date of creation: c. 1930.
Handwritten notes on the back: 'Baghdad, mihrab from the Khasseki mosque – detail' [Cres.].
Ashmolean negative: EA.CA.6265.

Figure: 146 (left).
Subject: Baghdad. Detail of the mihrab of the al-Khassaki Mosque.
Berenson ID: 133163.
Medium: gelatine silver print, 12×17cm.
Date of creation: c. 1930.
Handwritten notes on the back: 'Baghdad, mihrab from the Khasseki mosque – detail' [Cres.].
Ashmolean negative: EA.CA.6267.

Figure: 147 (right).
Subject: Baghdad. Detail of the mihrab of the al-Khassaki Mosque.
Berenson ID: 133164.
Medium: gelatine silver print, 12×17cm.
Date of creation: c. 1930.
Handwritten notes on the back: 'Baghdad, mihrab from the Khasseki mosque – detail' [Cres.].
Ashmolean negative: EA.CA.6266.

Figure: 148 (left).
Subject: Baghdad. Detail of the mihrab of the al-Khassaki Mosque.
Berenson ID: 133161.
Medium: gelatine silver print, 12×17cm.
Date of creation: c. 1930.
Handwritten notes on the back: 'Baghdad, mihrab from the Khasseki mosque – detail' [Cres.].
Ashmolean negative: EA.CA.6268.

Figure: 149 (centre).
Subject: Baghdad. The Zumurrud Khatun Mosque.
Berenson ID: 133189.
Medium: gelatine silver print, 12×17cm.
Date of creation: c. 1930.
Handwritten notes on the back: 'Baghdad, Mausoleum of Zubayda' [Cres.].
Ashmolean negative: EA.CA.6290.

Figure: 150. (right)
Subject: Baghdad. The Zumurrud Khatun Mosque.
Berenson ID: 133190.
Medium: gelatine silver print, 12×17cm.
Date of creation: c. 1930.
Handwritten notes on the back: 'Baghdad, Mausoleum of Zubayda' [Cres.].
Ashmolean negative: EA.CA.6291.

Figure: 151.
Subject: Baghdad. Inside the dome of the Zumurrud Khatun Mosque.
Berenson ID: 133191.
Medium: gelatine silver print, 12×17cm.
Date of creation: c. 1930.
Handwritten notes on the back: 'Baghdad, Mausoleum of Zubayda – vertical view of dome' [Cres.].
Ashmolean negative: EA.CA.6292.

THE SITES AND THE MONUMENTS – MESOPOTAMIA

Figure: 152.
Subject: Baghdad. a vaulted recess in the Qasr al-Abbasi.
Berenson ID: 133157.
Medium: gelatine silver print, 12×17cm.
Date of creation: c. 1930.
Handwritten notes on the back: 'Baghdad, Palace in the Citadel – vaulted recess' [Cres.].
Ashmolean negative: EA.CA.6285.

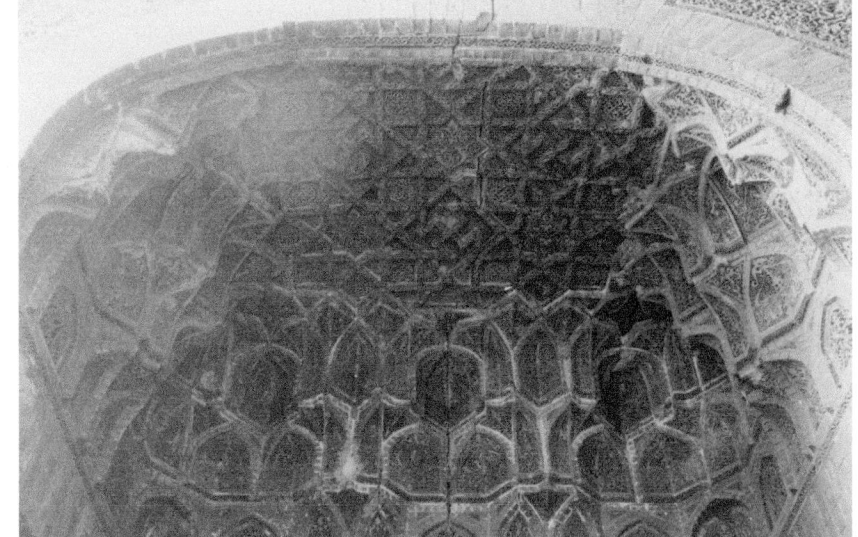

Figure: 153.
Subject: Baghdad. a vaulted recess in the Qasr al-Abbasi.
Berenson ID: 133158.
Medium: gelatine silver print, 12×17cm.
Date of creation: c. 1930.
Handwritten notes on the back: 'Baghdad, Palace in the Citadel – vaulted recess' [Cres.].
Ashmolean negative: EA.CA.6286.

Figure: 154.
Subject: Baghdad. a vaulted recess in the Qasr al-Abbasi.
Berenson ID: 133159.
Medium: gelatine silver print, 12×17cm.
Date of creation: c. 1930.
Handwritten notes on the back: 'Baghdad, Palace in the Citadel – vault of recess' [Cres.].
Ashmolean negative: EA.CA.6288.

Figure: 155.
Subject: Baghdad. Iwan in the Qasr al-Abbasi.
Berenson ID: 133146.
Medium: gelatine silver print, 12×17cm.
Date of creation: c. 1930.
Handwritten notes on the back: 'Baghdad, Palace in the Citadel – the iwan' [Cres.].
Ashmolean negative: EA.CA.6277.

Figure: 156.
Subject: Baghdad. Vault of iwan of the Qasr al-Abbasi.
Berenson ID: 133149.
Medium: gelatine silver print, 12×17cm.
Date of creation: c. 1930.
Handwritten notes on the back: 'Baghdad, Palace in the Citadel – decoration of vault of iwan' [Cres.].
Ashmolean negative: EA.CA.6275.

Figure: 157 (left).
Subject: Baghdad. Vault of iwan of Qasr al-Abbasi.
Berenson ID: 133151.
Medium: gelatine silver print, 12×17cm.
Date of creation: c. 1930.
Handwritten notes on the back: 'Baghdad, Palace in the Citadel – decoration of arch of iwan' [Cres.].
Ashmolean negative: EA.CA.6279.

Figure: 158 (right).
Subject: Baghdad. Detail of the decoration of an arch of the Qasr al-Abbasi.
Berenson ID: 133152.
Medium: gelatine silver print, 12×17cm.
Date of creation: c. 1930.
Handwritten notes on the back: 'Baghdad, Palace in the Citadel – decoration of arch of iwan' [Cres.].
Ashmolean negative: EA.CA.6280.

THE SITES AND THE MONUMENTS – MESOPOTAMIA

Figure: 159 (left).
Subject: Baghdad. Detail of a decoration in the Qasr al-Abbasi.
Berenson ID: 133154.
Medium: gelatine silver print, 12×17cm.
Date of creation: c. 1930.
Handwritten notes on the back: 'Baghdad, Palace in the Citadel – end of passage near iwan' [Cres.].
Ashmolean negative: EA.CA.6281.

Figure: 160 (centre).
Subject: Baghdad. a passage into the Qasr al-Abbasi.
Berenson ID: 133155.
Medium: gelatine silver print, 12×17cm.
Date of creation: c. 1930.
Handwritten notes on the back: 'Baghdad, Palace in the Citadel – entrance to a room' [Cres.].
Ashmolean negative: EA.CA.6283.

Figure: 161 (right).
Subject: Baghdad. Detail of a decoration in the Qasr al-Abbasi.
Berenson ID: 133156.
Medium: gelatine silver print, 12×17cm.
Date of creation: c. 1930.
Handwritten notes on the back: 'Baghdad, Palace in the Citadel – vault of passage' [Cres.].
Ashmolean negative: EA.CA.6282.

Figure: 162.
Subject: Baghdad. The Suhrawardi Mosque and Mausoleum.
Berenson ID: 133192.
Medium: gelatine silver print, 12×17cm.
Date of creation: c. 1930.
Handwritten notes on the back: 'Baghdad, Mausoleum of Shaykh Omar' [Cres.].
Ashmolean negative: EA.CA.6306.

83

Figure: 163.
Subject: Baghdad. The Suhrawardi Mosque and Mausoleum.
Berenson ID: 133194.
Medium: gelatine silver print, 12×17cm.
Date of creation: c. 1930.
Handwritten notes on the back: 'Baghdad, Mausoleum of Shaykh Omar' [Cres.].
Ashmolean negative: EA.CA.6307.

Figure: 164.
Subject: Baghdad. The Suhrawardi Mosque and Mausoleum.
Berenson ID: 133193.
Medium: gelatine silver print, 12×17cm.
Date of creation: c. 1930.
Handwritten notes on the back: 'Baghdad, Mausoleum of Shaykh Omar' [Cres.].
Ashmolean negative: EA.CA.6308.

Figure: 165.
Subject: Baghdad. Entrance to the Suhrawardi Mosque and Mausoleum.
Berenson ID: 133195.
Medium: gelatine silver print, 12×17cm.
Date of creation: c. 1930.
Handwritten notes on the back: 'Baghdad, Mausoleum of Shaykh Omar – entrance to mausoleum' [Cres.].
Ashmolean negative: EA.CA.6309.

THE SITES AND THE MONUMENTS – MESOPOTAMIA

Figure: 166.
Subject: Baghdad. The Bab al-Wastani.
Berenson ID: 133171.
Medium: gelatine silver print, 12×17cm.
Date of creation: c. 1930.
Handwritten notes on the back: 'Baghdad, the Bab al-Wustani' [Cres.].
Ashmolean negative: EA.CA.6328.

Figure: 167.
Subject: Baghdad. The Bab al-Wastani.
Berenson ID: 133172.
Medium: gelatine silver print, 12×17cm.
Date of creation: c. 1930.
Handwritten notes on the back: 'Baghdad, the Bab al-Wustani' [Cres.].
Ashmolean negative: EA.CA.6327.

Figure: 168.
Subject: Baghdad. Inside the Bab al-Wastani.
Berenson ID: 133174.
Medium: gelatine silver print, 12×17cm.
Date of creation: c. 1930.
Handwritten notes on the back: 'Baghdad, the Bab al-Wustani – inner exit' [Cres.].
Ashmolean negative: EA.CA.6325.

Figure: 169.
Subject: Baghdad. Inside the Bab al-Wastani.
Berenson ID: 133173.
Medium: gelatine silver print, 12×17cm.
Date of creation: c. 1930.
Handwritten notes on the back: 'Baghdad, the Bab al-Wustani – interior' [Cres.].
Ashmolean negative: EA.CA.6326.

Figure: 170.
Subject: Baghdad. The al-Mustansiriya Madrasa, looking north.
Berenson ID: 133175.
Medium: gelatine silver print, 12×17cm.
Date of creation: c. 1930.
Handwritten notes on the back: 'Baghdad, the Mustansiriya Madrasa – looking N' [Cres.].
Ashmolean negative: EA.CA.6294.

Figure: 171.
Subject: Baghdad. The al-Mustansiriya Madrasa, looking southeast.
Berenson ID: 133178.
Medium: gelatine silver print, 12×17cm.
Date of creation: c. 1930.
Handwritten notes on the back: 'Baghdad, the Mustansiriya Madrasa – looking S.E' [Cres.].
Ashmolean negative: EA.CA.6295.

THE SITES AND THE MONUMENTS – MESOPOTAMIA

Figure: 172.
Subject: Baghdad. The upper part of the southeastern façade of the al-Mustansiriya Madrasa.
Berenson ID: 133177.
Medium: gelatine silver print, 12×17cm.
Date of creation: c. 1930.
Handwritten notes on the back: 'Baghdad, the Mustansiriya Madrasa – detail of S.E. facade' [Cres.].
Ashmolean negative: EA.CA.6296.

Figure: 173.
Subject: Baghdad. The court of the al-Mustansiriya Madrasa.
Berenson ID: 133180.
Medium: gelatine silver print, 12×17cm.
Date of creation: c. 1930.
Handwritten notes on the back: 'Baghdad, the Mustansiriya Madrasa – centre of S.W side of court' [Cres.].
Ashmolean negative: EA.CA.6298.

Figure: 174.
Subject: Baghdad. Entrance to the southwestern side of the court of the al-Mustansiriya Madrasa.
Berenson ID: 133181.
Medium: gelatine silver print, 12×17cm.
Date of creation: c. 1930.
Handwritten notes on the back: 'Baghdad, the Mustansiriya Madrasa – entrance in S.W. side of court' [Cres.].
Ashmolean negative: EA.CA.6299.

Figure: 175.
Subject: Baghdad. Inscription on the northeastern façade of the al-Mustansiriya Madrasa.
Berenson ID: 133182.
Medium: gelatine silver print, 12×17cm.
Date of creation: c. 1930.
Handwritten notes on the back: 'Baghdad, the Mustansiriya Madrasa – inscription on N.E facade' [Cres.].
Ashmolean negative: EA.CA.6300.

Figure: 176.
Subject: Baghdad. Detail of the inscription on the northeastern façade of the al-Mustansiriya Madrasa.
Berenson ID: 133184.
Medium: gelatine silver print, 12×17cm.
Date of creation: c. 1930.
Handwritten notes on the back: 'Baghdad, the Mustansiriya Madrasa – detail of inscription on N.E facade' [Cres.].
Ashmolean negative: EA.CA.6302.

Figure: 177.
Subject: Baghdad. Inscription on the northeastern façade of the al-Mustansiriya Madrasa.
Berenson ID: 133183.
Medium: gelatine silver print, 12×17cm.
Date of creation: c. 1930.
Handwritten notes on the back: 'Baghdad, the Mustansiriya Madrasa – inscription on N.E facade' [Cres.].
Ashmolean negative: EA.CA.6301.

THE SITES AND THE MONUMENTS – MESOPOTAMIA

Figure: 178.
Subject: Baghdad. The Shaykh Maruf al-Kharkhi Mausoleum.
Berenson ID: 133165.
Medium: gelatine silver print, 12×17cm.
Date of creation: c. 1930.
Handwritten notes on the back: 'Baghdad. Mausoleum of Shaykh Maruf al-Kharki' [Cres.].
Ashmolean negative: EA.CA.6269.

Figure: 179 (left).
Subject: Baghdad. The Shaykh Maruf al-Kharkhi Mausoleum.
Berenson ID: 133166.
Medium: gelatine silver print, 12×17cm.
Date of creation: c. 1930.
Handwritten notes on the back: 'Baghdad. Mausoleum of Shaykh Maruf al-Kharki' [Cres.].
Ashmolean negative: EA.CA.6270.

Figure: 180 (centre).
Subject: Baghdad. The Shaykh Maruf al-Kharkhi Mausoleum.
Berenson ID: 133167.
Medium: gelatine silver print, 12×17cm.
Date of creation: c. 1930.
Handwritten notes on the back: 'Baghdad. Mausoleum of Shaykh Maruf al-Kharki' [Cres.].
Ashmolean negative: EA.CA.6272.

Figure: 181 (right).
Subject: Baghdad. The Shaykh Maruf al-Kharkhi Mausoleum.
Berenson ID: 133169.
Medium: gelatine silver print, 12×17cm.
Date of creation: c. 1930.
Handwritten notes on the back: 'Baghdad. Mausoleum of Shaykh Maruf al-Kharki – minaret' [Cres.].
Ashmolean negative: EA.CA.6273.

Figure: 182 (left).
Subject: Baghdad. The Shaykh Maruf al-Kharkhi Mausoleum.
Berenson ID: 133170.
Medium: gelatine silver print, 12×17cm.
Date of creation: c. 1930.
Handwritten notes on the back: 'Baghdad. Mausoleum of Shaykh Maruf al-Kharki – minaret' [Cres.].
Ashmolean negative: EA.CA.6274.

Figure: 183 (centre).
Subject: Baghdad. The minaret of the al-Khulafa Mosque.
Berenson ID: 133203.
Medium: gelatine silver print, 12×17cm.
Date of creation: c. 1930.
Handwritten notes on the back: 'Baghdad, minaret in the Suq al-Ghazl' [Cres.].
Ashmolean negative: EA.CA.6303.

Figure: 184 (right).
Subject: Baghdad. The minaret of the al-Khulafa Mosque.
Berenson ID: 133202.
Medium: gelatine silver print, 12×17cm.
Date of creation: c. 1930.
Handwritten notes on the back: 'Baghdad, minaret in the Suq al-Ghazl' [Cres.].
Ashmolean negative: EA.CA.6304.

Figure: 185 (left).
Subject: Baghdad. The minaret of the al-Khulafa Mosque.
Berenson ID: 133204.
Medium: gelatine silver print, 12×17cm.
Date of creation: c. 1930.
Handwritten notes on the back: 'Baghdad, minaret in the Suq al-Ghazl' [Cres.].
Ashmolean negative: EA.CA.6305.

Figure: 186 (right).
Subject: Baghdad. Entrance to the al-Mirjaniya Madrasa.
Berenson ID: 133187.
Medium: gelatine silver print, 12×17cm.
Date of creation: c. 1930.
Handwritten notes on the back: 'Baghdad, Mirianiya Madrasa – entrance' [Cres.].
Ashmolean negative: EA.CA.6318.

THE SITES AND THE MONUMENTS – MESOPOTAMIA

Figure: 187.
Subject: Baghdad. The upper part of the al-Mirjaniya Madrasa.
Berenson ID: 133185.
Medium: gelatine silver print, 12×17cm.
Date of creation: c. 1930.
Handwritten notes on the back: 'Baghdad, Mirianiya Madrasa – upper part of facade of sanctuary' [Cres.].
Ashmolean negative: EA.CA.6320.

Figure: 188.
Subject: Baghdad. The dome of the al-Mirjaniya Madrasa.
Berenson ID: 133186.
Medium: gelatine silver print, 12×17cm.
Date of creation: c. 1930.
Handwritten notes on the back: 'Baghdad, Mirianiya Madrasa – dome of mausoleum' [Cres.].
Ashmolean negative: EA.CA.6321.

Figure: 189.
Subject: Baghdad. The courtyard of the al-Mirjaniya Madrasa, looking north.
Berenson ID: 133188.
Medium: gelatine silver print, 12×17cm.
Date of creation: c. 1930.
Handwritten notes on the back: 'Baghdad, Mirianiya Madrasa – sahn looking N' [Cres.].
Ashmolean negative: EA.CA.6319.

Figure: 190.
Subject: Baghdad. The Khan Mirjan.
Berenson ID: 133196.
Medium: gelatine silver print, 12×17cm.
Date of creation: c. 1930.
Handwritten notes on the back: 'Baghdad, Khan Orthma' [Cres.].
Ashmolean negative: EA.CA.6310.

Figure: 191.
Subject: Baghdad. Inside the Khan Mirjan.
Berenson ID: 133199.
Medium: gelatine silver print, 12×17cm.
Date of creation: c. 1930.
Handwritten notes on the back: 'Baghdad, Khan Orthma – interior' [Cres.].
Ashmolean negative: EA.CA.6313.

Figure: 192 (left).
Subject: Baghdad. Inside the Khan Mirjan.
Berenson ID: 133197.
Medium: gelatine silver print, 12×17cm.
Date of creation: c. 1930.
Handwritten notes on the back: 'Baghdad, Khan Orthma, vaulting system' [Cres.].
Ashmolean negative: EA.CA.6314.

Figure: 193 (right).
Subject: Baghdad. Inside the Khan Mirjan.
Berenson ID: 133198.
Medium: gelatine silver print, 12×17cm.
Date of creation: c. 1930.
Handwritten notes on the back: 'Baghdad, Khan Orthma, vaulting system' [Cres.].
Ashmolean negative: EA.CA.6315.

THE SITES AND THE MONUMENTS – MESOPOTAMIA

Figure: 194.
Subject: Baghdad. Inside the Khan Mirjan.
Berenson ID: 133200.
Medium: gelatine silver print, 12×17cm.
Date of creation: c. 1930.
Handwritten notes on the back: 'Baghdad, Khan Orthma – vaulting system' [Cres.].
Ashmolean negative: EA.CA.6316.

Figure: 195.
Subject: Baghdad. inside the Khan Mirjan.
Berenson ID: 133201.
Medium: gelatine silver print, 12×17cm.
Date of creation: c. 1930.
Handwritten notes on the back: 'Baghdad, Khan Orthma – brackets of gallery' [Cres.].
Ashmolean negative: EA.CA.6317.

Figure: 196.
Subject: Baghdad. The wooden sarcophagus of Shaykh al-Aquli.
Berenson ID: 133205.
Medium: gelatine silver print, 12×17cm.
Date of creation: c. 1930.
Handwritten notes on the back: 'Baghdad, Tarbut of Shaykh aquili' [Cres.].
Ashmolean negative: EA.CA.6322.

Figure: 197.
Subject: Baghdad. The wooden sarcophagus of Shaykh al-Aquli.
Berenson ID: 133206.
Medium: gelatine silver print, 12×17cm.
Date of creation: c. 1930.
Handwritten notes on the back: 'Baghdad, Tarbut of Shaykh aquili' [Cres.].
Ashmolean negative: EA.CA.6324.

Al-Madain – Taq Kisra

The name Taq Kisra (alternatively, Ayvan Kisra) refers to the remains of a large Sasanian palace. Its construction began at the time of Khosrau I in the mid-6th century in the area of the two nearby cities of Seleucia and Ctesiphon, which the Arabs called al-Madain after the fall of the Sasanian empire.

Although Taq Kisra is a pre-Islamic monument, it is easy to understand why it was included in the catalogue of sites photographed by Creswell. It is indeed one of the most famous and impressive monuments in Mesopotamia, thanks to the large brick-vault, 25.5m high, with bricks held together by plaster mortar. The vault cuts the facade that unfortunately is partly collapsed, yet still visible in some photographs of the 1880s.[222]

Taq Kisra was investigated by Ernst Herzfeld between 1907 and 1908[223] and then excavated by a German expedition. A first campaign was directed in 1927-1928 by Oscar Reuther[224] and a second, together with the Metropolitan Museum of New York, by Ernst Kühnel in 1931-1932.[225]

Much work was subsequently carried out on the site, mainly aimed at ensuring the best conservation of the monument; the stability of the building is clearly threatened due to water infiltration. In particular, an Italian mission in the mid-1960s laid the foundations for a first survey and the exact understanding of the structure.[226] Subsequently, the Directorate General for Iraqi Antiquities conducted significant restoration work, which continued in the 1970s and 1980s, even during the period of the war with Iran.

Figure 198: The Taq Kisra photographed by J. Dieulafoy 1885 (Dieulafoy 1885, pls. 3-6).

---

[222] Creswell discusses this monument in his chapter on al-Ukhaidir (Creswell 1940: 87, fig. 72). On the history of the research at Taq Kisra see Keall 2011, with bibliography.

[223] Sarre, Herzfeld 1920a: 60-89.
[224] Reuther 1930.
[225] Upton 1932. The photographer of the expedition was Oswin H.-W. Puttrich-Reignard (see in Appendix 1).
[226] Bruno 1966.

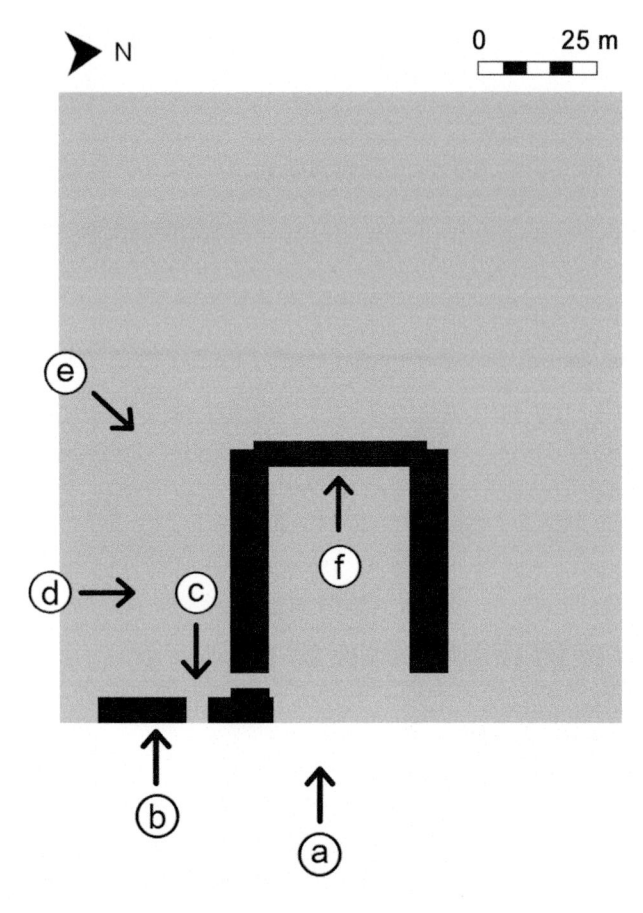

Figure: 199: The Taq Kisra. Map of Creswell's photographs (the arrow indicates the direction of the shots); a: Figure 200; b: Figure 203; c: Figure 204; d: Figure 201; e: Figure 202; f: Figure 205.

More recently, in 2015, a Czech mission carried out a new digital survey, with simulations to investigate the effects of self-weight and of environmental factors on the structure.[227]

The site's monumentality and proximity to Baghdad are the reasons why Taq Kisra is probably the most photographed pre-Islamic monument in Mesopotamia. Particularly noteworthy are the photos, taken as early as 1885, by Jean Dieulafoy and published in *L'art antique de la Perse* (authored by her husband, Marcel Dieulafoy).[228] The photos allow us to appreciate the state of the monument before an important collapse following a flood in 1888 (Figure 198).

The peculiarity of the monument, located in a flat area, with no other structures nearby, has always made the Taq Kisra an ideal monument for photography. In early photographs, we notice the repetition of a rather frequent pattern when shooting monuments like this one: that is, first wide panoramas, from all sides, and then a series of more detailed photographs.[229] Creswell followed this pattern and indeed, in his collection, we see general views, taken from different angles, and detailed photos that, curiously, do not so much concern the vault, but the standing blind façade and the opening on the back of the iwan (Figure 199). These subjects are not among the most commonly taken by photographers prior to and contemporary with Creswell, and this makes Creswell's photos particularly interesting.

---

[227] Chandra Makoond 2015.
[228] Dieulafoy 1885. On Jean Dieulafoy, see the entry dedicated to her in Appendix 1 (p. 263).
[229] On this methodological aspect, see in particular Bohrer 2011: 17-18. In the rich collection of photographs of the monument before Creswell's visit, those taken in 1909 by Gertrude Bell (altogether 17 photos published in the Gertrude Bell Archive, Album K 1909 and Album L 1909, see p. 260) and those taken in 1932 for the American Colony Photo Department (Library of Congress, Washington D.C: call numbers: LC-M33 4660-4661, 14470-14471, 14379-14387) are noteworthy.

THE SITES AND THE MONUMENTS – MESOPOTAMIA

Figure: 200.
Subject: The Taq Kisra, looking west.
Berenson ID: 133207.
Medium: gelatine silver print, 12×17cm.
Date of creation: c. 1930.
Handwritten notes on the back: 'Ctesiphon, Taq-i-Kisra' [Cres.].
Ashmolean negative: EA.CA.6262.

Figure: 201.
Subject: The Taq Kisra, looking north.
Berenson ID: 133211.
Medium: gelatine silver print, 12×17cm.
Date of creation: c. 1930.
Handwritten notes on the back: 'Ctesiphon, Taq-i-Kisra – from the S' [Cres.].
Ashmolean negative: EA.CA.6330.

Figure: 202.
Subject: The Taq Kisra, looking northeast.
Berenson ID: 133210.
Medium: gelatine silver print, 12×17cm.
Date of creation: c. 1930.
Handwritten notes on the back: 'Ctesiphon, Taq-i-Kisra – from the S.W.' [Cres.].
Ashmolean negative: EA.CA.6257.

Figure: 203 (left).
Subject: Detail of the façade of the Taq Kisra.
Berenson ID: 133208.
Medium: gelatine silver print, 12×17cm.
Date of creation: c. 1930.
Handwritten notes on the back: 'Ctesiphon, Taq-i-Kibra – detail of façade' [Cres.].
Ashmolean negative: EA.CA.6261.

Figure: 204 (centre).
Subject: Back of the façade of the Taq Kisra.
Berenson ID: 133212.
Medium: gelatine silver print, 12×17cm.
Date of creation: c. 1930.
Handwritten notes on the back: 'Ctesiphon, Taq-i-Kisra – back of façade' [Cres.].
Ashmolean negative: EA.CA.6329.

Figure: 205 (right).
Subject: Detail of a doorway of the Taq Kisra.
Berenson ID: 133209.
Medium: gelatine silver print, 12×17cm.
Date of creation: c. 1930.
Handwritten notes on the back: 'Ctesiphon, Taq-i-Kisra – doorway at back of great iwan' [Cres.].
Ashmolean negative: EA.CA.6258.

Al-Ukhaidir

The remains of al-Uhkaidir lie *c.* 120km south-west of Baghdad. It is positioned therefore outside the valley of the Tigris, in a region that today is of steppe but that, at the time the architectural complex was built, was certainly greener since cultivated using irrigation systems with water drawn from the Tigris.

To the contemporary visitor, al-Ukhaidir nowadays appears as an imposing building that stands alone in the desert: large rectangular city walls in mud-bricks, with circular corner towers and semi-circular towers along the outer perimeter, of *c.* 630×530m. The walls contain a rectangular building, i.e., a fortified palace, of 175×169m, built mainly in gravel mixed with mortar, with little use of mud-bricks. A smaller building is attached on the eastern side, always within the main wall, while a larger one rises outside the main wall, immediately to the south-east, which was probably a caravanserai.

The architectural complex is interpreted as being an Abbasid fortified residence, built in the second half of the 8th century. Creswell assumed that it was built by Isa Ibn Moussa (721-783/4), the nephew of the Caliph al-Masur. This is still the most likely hypothesis.[230]

The site was known since ancient times, and is mentioned by Pietro della Valle, who visited it in 1625.[231] Although there are other mentions of visits to the monument between the 17th and 18th century (unfortunately not always faithful), it was only at the beginning of the 19th century that it was actually rediscovered and investigated. In particular, Louis Massignon was the first to carry out on-field research between 1907 and 1908, publishing scientific reports of his studies,[232] while Gertrude Bell visited al-Ukhaidir in 1909, dedicating an important monograph to the site.[233] Between 1909 and 1910, the site was excavated by Oscar Reuther,[234] while in more recent years, systematic excavations and restoration have been carried out several times, especially between the mid-1960s and mid-1980s.[235]

Creswell visited the site in 1930 at an ideal moment: the site had been partially investigated and was therefore accessible compared to its initial ruinous state, thanks to the works conducted by Massignon and Reuther. However, it had not yet been modified by the most

Figure 206: The Court of Honour of the al-Ukhaidir fortress, a) in a photo taken in 1907/1908 by L. Massignon (1910: pl. 15) and b) in a photo taken in 1930 by K.A.C. Creswell (below, fig. 221). The condition of the structure is basically the same.

invasive and restorative interventions of the following years. If we compare Creswell's photographs with the pictures published in the works of Massignon and Reuther,[236] we see that the state of conservation of the standing structures had not changed significantly, while there is a considerable difference with the building's current state, in which a large amount of masonry has been restored and integrated (Figure 206).

As is well known, Creswell devoted much attention to the site of al-Ukhaidir in the first volume of his *Early Muslim architecture*.[237] Although the very wide selection of photographs was used for publication, it is interesting to note that the legacy preserved in the archives contains many photographs not published by Creswell, which therefore greatly expands the photographic repertoire that can be used to assess the state of conservation of the monument, before recent restorations.

In the specific case of the Berenson Collection, out of the 37 preserved photographs, as many as 17 are not used in publications, and are included in the following figures.

---

[230] Creswell 1940: 20-100.
[231] Della Valle 1843: 847 (*lettera XI, Aleppo, 5 agosto 1625*. The site is quoted as 'Casr Chaider').
[232] Massignon 1909, 1910.
[233] Bell 1914; see pp. ix-xi for a summary of previous research. A collection 167 Bell's photos is published in the Getrude Bell Archive, Album K 1909 and Album P 1911 (see p. 260), while other images are published in Bell 1911, figg. 73-111. Also noteworthy is a series of photographs taken in the 1920s by Arthur L.F. Smith, published in Album Nr. 6 of his collection, within the ID series 46-61 (see p. 270), although recorded without captions.
[234] Reuther 1912.
[235] Al-Husayni 1966; Hasan K.I. 1977; Killick, Roaf 1983.

[236] Massignon 1909, figs I, III-IV, and 1910: pls 1-23; Reuther 1912.
[237] Creswell 1932: 1-50; see also later in Creswell 1958: 192-203.

In addition to some general views, ample space is given to the details of the gateways and the outer wall, moved by semi-circular towers and blind arches; inside, the photographic sequence reveals a path that runs from the main gateway on the north side, through a vaulted covered vestibule, to the main central court of the palace, i.e., the so-called 'Court of Honour', and the iwan which is located immediately to the south. Creswell showed particular interest in this element (now reconstructed) because, in the arch that introduces the iwan, higher than the adjacent structures, he recognised an example of pishtaq, i.e., the rectangular frame built around the arched openings, typical of Iranian architecture.

The collection is completed by some photos dedicated to the rooms on the east and west sides ('bayts' in Creswell's description), to the mosque on the northern side, immediately to the side of the vestibule at the entrance, and to the two 'Annexes' (according to a terminology introduced by Massignon): a T-shaped complex placed within the circle of the walls and on the east side of the palace (the 'Inner Annexe'), and a building outside the outer wall, immediately to the north (the 'Outer' or 'Northern Annexe'), probably to be interpreted as a sort of caravanserai. The latter was largely excavated only from the mid-1970s, and at the time of Creswell's visit only the remains of the part close to the outer wall were visible.

Despite the importance of the monument was also recognised by its inclusion in the 2007 *UNESCO Tentative List*,[238] recent reports show that it is in poor condition, due to substantial abandonment and absence of adequate maintenance.[239]

Thanks to the large number of shots taken on the site, Creswell's photographic repertoire is probably the leading iconographic source, after Bell's,[240] that allows the original state of the ruins to be assessed. It offers valuable information for restoration work, critical to the preservation of this imposing yet fragile monument.

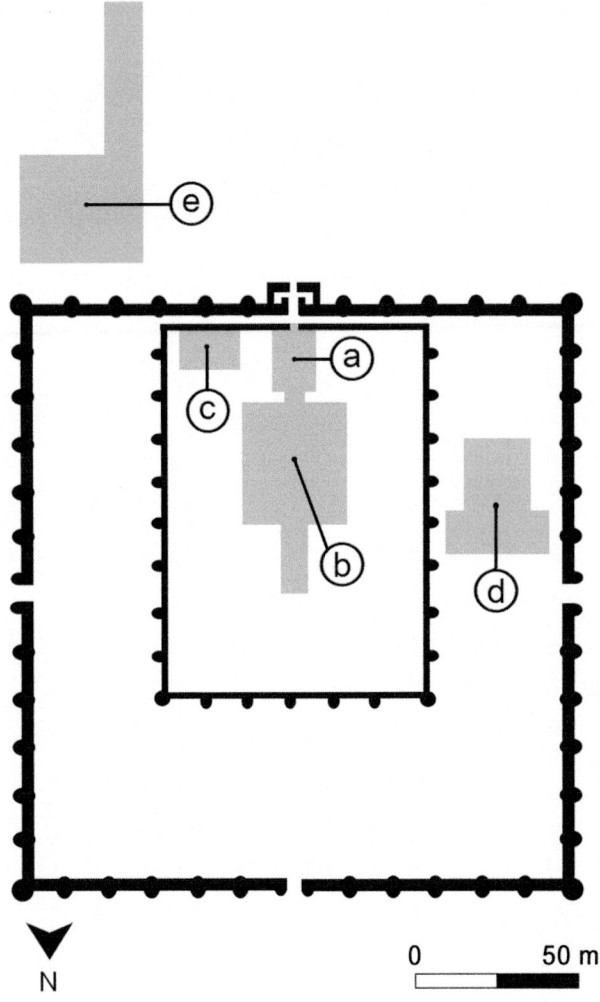

Figure 207: The al-Ukhaidir fortress. Map of the photographed monuments; a: the Vestibule (Figure 210); b: the Great Hall (Figures 221-228); c: the Mosque (Figures 233-239); d: the Inner Annexe (Figure 241); e: the Outer Annexe (Figure 242-244).

Creswell's photographs in Florence portray almost all the architectural elements considered in the analysis of the complex (Figures 208-244).

---

[238] *UNESCO Tentative List 07/07/2000* (https://whc.unesco.org/en/tentativelists/1467).

[239] Bassem 2015. It should be noted that recent remote sensing analyses have made it possible to assess the state of the site as a whole, identifying a significant number of areas of archaeological interest, the excavation of which would certainly allow a better understanding of the monument (Abdulrazzaq 2020).

[240] See in the Getrude Bell Archive, Album K 1909, n. K081-K179 and Album P 1911, n. P140-P203 (see p. 260).

Figure: 208.
Subject: The eastern façade of the al-Ukhaidir fortress.
Berenson ID: 133264.
Medium: gelatine silver print, 12×17cm.
Date of creation: c. 1930.
Handwritten notes on the back: 'S. Mesopotamia, Ukhaidir – east façade' [Cres.].
Ashmolean negative: EA.CA.6414.
Published in Creswell 1940, pl. 6.a.

Figure: 209.
Subject: The al-Ukhaidir fortress, looking southeast.
Berenson ID: 133259.
Medium: gelatine silver print, 12×17cm.
Date of creation: c. 1930.
Handwritten notes on the back: 'S. Mesopotamia, Ukhaidir – from the N.W' [Cres.].
Ashmolean negative: EA.CA.6438.

Figure: 210.
Subject: The northern vestibule of the al-Ukhaidir fortress.
Berenson ID: 133276.
Medium: gelatine silver print, 12×17cm.
Date of creation: c. 1930.
Handwritten notes on the back: 'S. Mesopotamia, Ukhaidir – north vestibule' [Cres.].
Ashmolean negative: EA.CA.6443.
Published in Creswell 1940, pl. 10.a; Creswell 1958, fig. 49.

Figure: 211 (left).
Subject: Hallway inside the al-Ukhaidir fortress.
Berenson ID: 133275.
Medium: gelatine silver print, 12×17cm.
Date of creation: c. 1930.
Handwritten notes on the back: 'S. Mesopotamia, Ukhaidir – tranverse passage leading out of vestibule' [Cres.].
Ashmolean negative: EA.CA.6445.
Published in Creswell 1940, pl. 10.b.

Figure: 212 (right).
Subject: The great hall of the al-Ukhaidir fortress.
Berenson ID: 133277.
Medium: gelatine silver print, 12×17cm.
Date of creation: c. 1930.
Handwritten notes on the back: 'S. Mesopotamia, Ukhaidir – the great hall' [Cres.].
Ashmolean negative: EA.CA.6456.
Published in Creswell 1940, pl. 10.d.

Figure: 213 (left).
Subject: The great hall of the al-Ukhaidir fortress.
Berenson ID: 133274.
Medium: gelatine silver print, 12×17cm.
Date of creation: c. 1930.
Handwritten notes on the back: 'S. Mesopotamia, Ukhaidir – the great hall' [Cres.].

Figure: 214 (right).
Subject: The western gate of the al-Ukhaidir fortress.
Berenson ID: 133265.
Medium: gelatine silver print, 12×17cm.
Date of creation: c. 1930.
Handwritten notes on the back: 'S. Mesopotamia, Ukhaidir – west entrance' [Cres.].
Ashmolean negative: EA.CA.6431.
Published in Creswell 1940, pl. 8.a.

Figure: 215.
Subject: The inner side of the western gate of the al-Ukhaidir fortress.
Berenson ID: 133268.
Medium: gelatine silver print, 12×17cm.
Date of creation: c. 1930.
Handwritten notes on the back: 'S. Mesopotamia, Ukhaidir – west entrance from within' [Cres.].
Ashmolean negative: EA.CA.6433.
Published in Creswell 1940, pl. 8.c.

THE SITES AND THE MONUMENTS – MESOPOTAMIA

Figure: 216.
Subject: Detail of the northern side of the al-Ukhaidir fortress.
Berenson ID: 133263.
Medium: gelatine silver print, 12×17cm.
Date of creation: c. 1930.
Handwritten notes on the back: 'S. Mesopotamia, Ukhaidir – detail of north façade' [Cres.].
Ashmolean negative: EA.CA.6439.
Published in Creswell 1940, pl. 9.c.

Figure: 217.
Subject: a staircase inside the al-Ukhaidir fortress.
Berenson ID: 133270.
Medium: gelatine silver print, 12×17cm.
Date of creation: c. 1930.
Handwritten notes on the back: 'S. Mesopotamia, Ukhaidir – northwest corner of enclosure' [Cres.].
Ashmolean negative: EA.CA.6436.

Figure: 218 (left).
Subject: Detail of the eastern façade of the al-Ukhaidir fortress.
Berenson ID: 133266.
Medium: gelatine silver print, 12×17cm.
Date of creation: c. 1930.
Handwritten notes on the back: 'S. Mesopotamia, Ukhaidir – detail of E. façade' [Cres.].
Ashmolean negative: EA.CA.6420.
Published in Creswell 1940, pl. 6.c.

Figure: 219 (right).
Subject: Detail of the eastern façade of the al-Ukhaidir fortress.
Berenson ID: 133267.
Medium: gelatine silver print, 12×17cm.
Date of creation: c. 1930.
Handwritten notes on the back: 'S. Mesopotamia, Ukhaidir – detail of E. façade' [Cres.].
Ashmolean negative: EA.CA.6421.
Published in Creswell 1940, pl. 6.b.

Figure: 220.
Subject: Detail of the southern façade of the al-Ukhaidir fortress.
Berenson ID: 133269.
Medium: gelatine silver print, 12×17cm.
Date of creation: c. 1930.
Handwritten notes on the back: 'S. Mesopotamia, Ukhaidir – detail of S. façade' [Cres.].
Ashmolean negative: EA.CA.6419.

Figure: 221.
Subject: The northern side of the Court of Honour of the al-Ukhaidir fortress.
Berenson ID: 133290.
Medium: gelatine silver print, 12×17cm.
Date of creation: c. 1930.
Handwritten notes on the back: 'S. Mesopotamia, Ukhaidir – north façade of main court' [Cres.].
Ashmolean negative: EA.CA.293.
Published in Creswell 1958, fig. 52.

Figure: 222.
Subject: The northern side of the Court of Honour of the al-Ukhaidir fortress.
Berenson ID: 133278.
Medium: gelatine silver print, 12×17cm.
Date of creation: c. 1930.
Handwritten notes on the back: 'S. Mesopotamia, Ukhaidir – N. façade of main court' [Cres.].
Ashmolean negative: EA.CA.296.

Figure: 223.
Subject: The western side of the Court of Honour of the al-Ukhaidir fortress.
Berenson ID: 133279.
Medium: gelatine silver print, 12×17cm.
Date of creation: c. 1930.
Handwritten notes on the back: 'S. Mesopotamia, Ukhaidir – main court, west side' [Cres.].
Ashmolean negative: EA.CA.6470.
Published in Creswell 1940, pl. 14.b.

Figure: 224.
Subject: The eastern side of the Court of Honour of the al-Ukhaidir fortress.
Berenson ID: 133284.
Medium: gelatine silver print, 12×17cm.
Date of creation: c. 1930.
Handwritten notes on the back: 'S. Mesopotamia, Ukhaidir – east façade of main court' [Cres.].
Ashmolean negative: EA.CA.6468.
Published in Creswell 1940, pl. 13.a.

Figure: 225.
Subject: Niche in the western side of the Court of Honour of the al-Ukhaidir fortress.
Berenson ID: 133283.
Medium: gelatine silver print, 12×17cm.
Date of creation: c. 1930.
Handwritten notes on the back: 'S. Mesopotamia, Ukhaidir – E. façade of main court, detail' [Cres.].
Ashmolean negative: EA.CA.6472.
Published in Creswell 1940, pl. 13.c.

Figure: 226.
Subject: The southern side of the Court of Honour of the al-Ukhaidir fortress.
Berenson ID: 133280.
Medium: gelatine silver print, 12×17cm.
Date of creation: c. 1930.
Handwritten notes on the back: 'S. Mesopotamia, Ukhaidir – main court, south side' [Cres.].
Ashmolean negative: EA.CA.6480.

Figure: 227.
Subject: The southern side of the Court of Honour of the al-Ukhaidir fortress.
Berenson ID: 133281.
Medium: gelatine silver print, 12×17cm.
Date of creation: c. 1930.
Handwritten notes on the back: 'S. Mesopotamia, Ukhaidir – main court, south side' [Cres.].
Ashmolean negative: EA.CA.6479.
Published in Creswell 1958, fig. 53.

Figure: 228.
Subject: Two people into the Court of Honour of the al-Ukhaidir fortress.
Berenson ID: 133282.
Medium: gelatine silver print, 12×17cm.
Date of creation: c. 1930.
Handwritten notes on the back: 'S. Mesopotamia, Ukhaidir – exit in S.E. corner of main court' [Cres.].
Ashmolean negative: EA.CA.6478.

THE SITES AND THE MONUMENTS – MESOPOTAMIA

Figure: 229.
Subject: The southern side of the minor court of the al-Ukhaidir fortress.
Berenson ID: 133272.
Medium: gelatine silver print, 12×17cm.
Date of creation: c. 1930.
Handwritten notes on the back: 'S. Mesopotamia, Ukhaidir – second court looking N' [Cres.].
Ashmolean negative: EA.CA.6496.
Published in Creswell 1940, pl. 16.b

Figure: 230.
Subject: Creswell's Room 32 of the al-Ukhaidir fortress.
Berenson ID: 133289.
Medium: gelatine silver print, 12×17cm.
Date of creation: c. 1930.
Handwritten notes on the back: 'S. Mesopotamia, Ukhaidir – Room N°32' [Cres.].
Ashmolean negative: EA.CA.6484.
Published in Creswell 1940, pl. 15.d.

Figure: 231.
Subject: Creswell's Room 32 of the al-Ukhaidir fortress.
Berenson ID: 133288.
Medium: gelatine silver print, 12×17cm.
Date of creation: c. 1930.
Handwritten notes on the back: 'S. Mesopotamia, Ukhaidir – vaulting of Room N°32' [Cres.].
Ashmolean negative: EA.CA.6488.

Figure: 232.
Subject: Creswell's Room 33 of the al-Ukhaidir fortress.
Berenson ID: 133286.
Medium: gelatine silver print, 12×17cm.
Date of creation: c. 1930.
Handwritten notes on the back: 'S. Mesopotamia, Ukhaidir – Room N°33' [Cres.].
Ashmolean negative: EA.CA.6495.

Figure: 233.
Subject: Remains of a vault in the mosque of the al-Ukhaidir fortress.
Berenson ID: 133294.
Medium: gelatine silver print, 12×17cm.
Date of creation: c. 1930.
Handwritten notes on the back: 'S. Mesopotamia, Ukhaidir – court of ruined mosque – showing remains of vaulting' [Cres.].
Ashmolean negative: EA.CA.6503.
Published in Creswell 1940, pl. 18.e.

Figure: 234.
Subject: Remains of a vault in the mosque of the al-Ukhaidir fortress.
Berenson ID: 133295.
Medium: gelatine silver print, 12×17cm.
Date of creation: c. 1930.
Handwritten notes on the back: 'S. Mesopotamia, Ukhaidir – ruined mosque – E. end of vault' [Cres.].
Ashmolean negative: EA.CA.6511.
Published in Creswell 1940, pl. 19.a.

THE SITES AND THE MONUMENTS – MESOPOTAMIA

Figure: 235.
Subject: Remains of a vault in the mosque of the al-Ukhaidir fortress.
Berenson ID: 133293.
Medium: gelatine silver print, 12×17cm.
Date of creation: c. 1930.
Handwritten notes on the back: 'S. Mesopotamia, Ukhaidir – ruined mosque – E. end of vault' [Cres.].
Ashmolean negative: EA.CA.6513.
Published in Creswell 1940, pl. 19.c.

Figure: 236.
Subject: Remains of a vault in the mosque of the al-Ukhaidir fortress.
Berenson ID: 133292.
Medium: gelatine silver print, 12×17cm.
Date of creation: c. 1930.
Handwritten notes on the back: 'S. Mesopotamia, Ukhaidir – ruined mosque – W. end of vault' [Cres.].

Figure: 237.
Subject: The mihrab of the mosque of the al-Ukhaidir fortress.
Berenson ID: 133291.
Medium: gelatine silver print, 12×17cm.
Date of creation: c. 1930.
Handwritten notes on the back: 'S. Mesopotamia, Ukhaidir – mosque, mihrab of [sic]' [Cres.].
Ashmolean negative: EA.CA.6512.

Figure: 238 (left).
Subject: a doorway of the mosque of the al-Ukhaidir fortress.
Berenson ID: 133287.
Medium: gelatine silver print, 12×17cm.
Date of creation: c. 1930.
Handwritten notes on the back: 'S. Mesopotamia, Ukhaidir – mosque, entrance from within' [Cres.].
Ashmolean negative: EA.CA.6507.

Figure: 239 (right).
Subject: The entrance of the mosque of the al-Ukhaidir fortress.
Berenson ID: 133285.
Medium: gelatine silver print, 12×17cm.
Date of creation: c. 1930.
Handwritten notes on the back: 'S. Mesopotamia, Ukhaidir – mosque, entrance from interior' [Cres.].
Ashmolean negative: EA.CA.6504.

Figure: 240.
Subject: The main bulding inside the al-Ukhaidir fortress.
Berenson ID: 133271.
Medium: gelatine silver print, 12×17cm.
Date of creation: c. 1930.
Handwritten notes on the back: 'S. Mesopotamia, Ukhaidir – main building and enclosure walls' [Cres.].

Figure: 241.
Subject: The Inner annex of the al-Ukhaidir fortress.
Berenson ID: 133273.
Medium: gelatine silver print, 12×17cm.
Date of creation: c. 1930.
Handwritten notes on the back: 'S. Mesopotamia, Ukhaidir – annexe on east side of palace' [Cres.].
Ashmolean negative: EA.CA.6526.

THE SITES AND THE MONUMENTS – MESOPOTAMIA

Figure: 242.
Subject: The Outer annex of the al-Ukhaidir fortress.
Berenson ID: 133261.
Medium: gelatine silver print, 12×17cm.
Date of creation: c. 1930.
Handwritten notes on the back: 'S. Mesopotamia, Ukhaidir – outbuildings on north side' [Cres.].
Ashmolean negative: EA.CA.6529.

Figure: 243.
Subject: The Outer annex of the al-Ukhaidir fortress.
Berenson ID: 133260.
Medium: gelatine silver print, 12×17cm.
Date of creation: c. 1930.
Handwritten notes on the back: 'S. Mesopotamia, Ukhaidir – outbuildings on north side' [Cres.].
Ashmolean negative: EA.CA.6530.
Published in Creswell 1940, pl. 21.c.

Figure: 244.
Subject: The Outer annex of the al-Ukhaidir fortress.
Berenson ID: 133262.
Medium: gelatine silver print, 12×17cm.
Date of creation: c. 1930.
Handwritten notes on the back: 'S. Mesopotamia, Ukhaidir – outbuildings on north side from the E' [Cres.].
Ashmolean negative: EA.CA.6533.

Syria

Ancient churches of Northern Syria: Qalat Siman, Qalb Lawzah and Ruweiha

During his travels as an inspector for the Allenby Administration, Creswell visited the limestone massif region in upper central Syria. Archaeologically speaking, this is a very interesting region because, between the Late Roman period and the Islamic conquest, hundreds of villages were founded in the vast plateau that extends roughly between the cities of Aleppo, Antioch and, to the south, Apamea. Annual rainfall was sufficient to sustain agriculture, especially the cultivation of the olive tree, and allowed sheep and goat herding. Between the end of the 5th and the beginning of the 7th century, the region was the destination of many pilgrims who visited Qalat Siman, i.e., the place where, according to tradition, St. Symeon Stylites lived on the top of a pillar for about 40 years. Therefore, these were important villages for Late Antiquity Christianity. A large number of churches were built here, many of which have been preserved until modern times in exceptionally good condition, due to the good quality of the local limestone and the long phase of partial abandonment of the region after the 8th century. Thanks to all this, in 2011, some 40 villages of this area became part of the *UNESCO World Heritage List*, and were subsequently listed on the *World Heritage in Danger List* in 2013.[241]

The region was first subject to archaeological investigation by Melchior de Vogüé, between 1861 and 1863.[242] Howard C. Butler provided a new survey between 1899 and 1909, producing documentation consisting of maps, architectural drawings and photographs that were the basis for all subsequent studies.[243] The region was little known, partly because of its extremely low population in the modern era. In 1933, a new survey was carried out by Georges Tchalenko, giving rise to a new interest in this important evidence of Syrian Late Antiquity.[244] Since the 1970s, the region has been systematically investigated, mainly by the Institut français du Proche-Orient, which added excavations to the surface surveys.[245]

Although the architectural interest of these sites concerns monuments prior to the Islamic period, Creswell took a limited number of photographs of some of the most significant monuments. They were well known at the time of his visit, since the standing remains were well-preserved although not yet excavated by archaeologists: the three sites documented by Creswell's photographs in the Biblioteca Berenson, are Qalat Siman, Qalb Lawzah and Ruweiha.

Qalat Siman is undoubtedly the most important and well-known site in the region.[246] At the end of the 5th century, a martyrium was built there, around the column that according to tradition had hosted the first Stylite, St Symeon, for 40 years. Between the 6th and 10th century, other buildings were added to the martyrium, creating a large architectural complex: it was equipped with a baptistery, houses for pilgrims, a cemetery, fortifications, and was able to respond to the needs of what had become one of the most important destinations of Christian East pilgrims. Between 2007 and 2010, the site was excavated by French archaeologists, but the excavations were interrupted by the Civil War,[247] which caused considerable damage to the complex, mainly due to a Russian air strike in 2016.[248]

Creswell took at least four photographs (Figures 245-248) at this site, all capturing architectural details and none with panoramic or overall views. The same set of photos of the site may also be found in the archives of the Ashmolean Museum and the Victoria & Albert Museum, suggesting that Creswell did actually take only these shots.

Only one photograph is dedicated to the basilica of *Qalb Lawza*. Built in the 5th century,[249] it is a noteworthy monument since it features two twin square towers that line the arched entrance and can be considered a forerunner of the European Romanesque. Creswell's

---

[241] See the UNESCO report *Ancient Villages of Northern Syria* at https://whc.unesco.org/en/list/1348/. For a general picture, see Tchalencko G. 1953; Tate 1992; Foss 1996; Burns R. 1992: 141-143.

[242] de Vogüé 1865.

[243] Butler *et al.* 1907-1930, especially vol. 2B/6.

[244] Tchalenko G. 1953.

[245] Tate 1992. See also Foss 1996 for a summary of research in the region.

[246] de Vogüé 1865: 141-154; Butler *et al.* 1907-1930 (2/B:6): 281-284; van Berchem, Fatio 1914: 222-225; Butler 1929: 97-105; Tchalenko, Loosley, Leeming 2019. G. Bell took an interesting set of photos (Bell 1919: 274-281). See also ARCHNET, site 4325 and Burns R. 1992: 272-275.

[247] Biscop, Sodini 1989 and Pieri 2015, with bibliography.

[248] http://whc.unesco.org/en/news/1499. UNESCO 2016: p. 25 reports that, in addition to damage reported since 2013, 'stones from the archaeological sites are being used as building material': moreover: 'Illegal constructions are reported in the sites of Saint Simeon (inside the citadel, outside towards the south, main gate, near the south-western church, close to the Triumphal Arch)': also 'illegal quarries', 'illicit excavations' and 'collapse of stones' are reported. See further information in the *SOC Report by the State Party 2017* (p. 34), downloadable at https://whc.unesco.org/en/soc/3542. See also Alyehia, al-Issa 2016.

[249] de Vogüé 1865: 135-138; Butler 1929: 71-73; Tchalenko G. 1974; Loosley 2012: 227. See also ARCHNET, site 4314 and Burns R. 1992: 244-246. The site does not appear to have suffered much damage following the Syrian Civil War (cf. the *SOC Report by the State Party 2014*, downloadable at https://whc.unesco.org/en/soc/2914. At p. 17 it is reported that 'Qalb Luzeh of the church is completely intact apart from breaking four stones of the apse').

photograph shows an architectural detail of a pier of the structure (Figure 249).

Equally, only one photograph depicts the *Mausoleum of Bizzos in Ruweiha*.[250] The site is significant because it hosts one of the largest churches in the region, erected in the 6th century, next to the limestone tomb built for its patron, Bizzos. Creswell's photograph (Figure 250) portrays the inner base of the dome. Creswell dedicated a large paragraph in his *Early Muslim architecture* to the dome, accompanied by the hand drawn plan of the mausoleum, and pointed out 'the particular importance of this building for students of Muhammadan architecture, on account of the fact that it is the only ancient structure in Northern Syria that preserves a full example of a cubical building with a doomed roof (...) a prototype of the weli, such a characteristic building of the Muhammadan period in Syria, and of the domed mausoleums of the Muslim period of Egypt'.[251]

---

[250] de Vogüé: 1865: 102; Sachau 1883: pls 17-18; Butler *et al.* 1907-1930 (2/B:3): 142-148; Bell 1919: 253; Butler 1929: 205; Tchalenko 1953; Burns R. 1992: 268-269; Loosley 2012: 237.

[251] Creswell 1932: 310, with the plan of the mausoleum reproduced in the same page, at fig. 371.

Figure: 245 (left).
Subject: Qalat Siman. The Church of Saint Simeon Stylites.
Berenson ID: 133908.
Medium: gelatine silver print, 12×17cm.
Date of creation: 1919-1920.
Handwritten notes on the back: 'Qal'at Siman, doorway into east arm of church' [Cres.].
Ashmolean negative: EA.CA.6010.

Figure: 246 (right).
Subject: Qalat Siman. The Church of Saint Simeon Stylites.
Berenson ID: 133909.
Medium: gelatine silver print, 12×17cm.
Date of creation: 1919-1920.
Handwritten notes on the back: 'Qal'at Siman, angle pier of the s. near octagon' [Cres.].
Ashmolean negative: EA.CA.6011.

Figure: 247 (left).
Subject: Qalat Siman. The Church of Saint Simeon Stylites.
Berenson ID: 133920.
Medium: gelatine silver print, 12×17cm.
Date of creation: 1919-1920.
Handwritten notes on the back: ' Qal'at Siman' [Cres.].
Ashmolean negative: EA.CA.6012.

Figure: 248 (right).
Subject: Qalat Siman. The Church of Saint Simeon Stylites.
Berenson ID: 133907.
Medium: gelatine silver print, 12×17cm.
Date of creation: 1919-1920.
Handwritten notes on the back: 'Qal'at Siman, pier of arch' [Cres.].
Ashmolean negative: EA.CA.6009.

Figure: 249 (left).
Subject: Qalb Lawzah. A pier in the Basilica.
Berenson ID: 133916.
Medium: gelatine silver print, 12×17cm.
Date of creation: 1919-1920.
Handwritten notes on the back: 'Qalb Luzeh, double windows with curious pier' [Cres.].
Ashmolean negative: EA.CA.6023.

Figure: 250 (right).
Subject: Ruweiha. The setting of the dome of the Bizzos Mausoleum.
Berenson ID: 133948.
Medium: gelatine silver print, 12×17cm.
Date of creation: 1919-1920.
Handwritten notes on the back: 'Ruweiha, Mausoleum of Bizzos setting of dome' [Cres.].
Ashmolean negative: EA.CA.6030.
Published in Creswell 1932, fig. 371.

Aleppo

Aleppo is located in north-western Syria, about 40km from the Turkish border, at an altitude of *c.* 300m asl in a valley crossed by the river Qwayq, which flows close to the city. It is a very favourable location, owing to the availability of water from the river, and the presence of a well-defensible rocky outcrop.[252] At least since the 3rd millennium BCE, it became an important crossroads of the routes that connected Anatolia to Palestine and Mesopotamia, and the latter to the regions on the Mediterranean coast.

Little is known of the city's early history, which is mentioned in the Ebla archives in the second half of the 3rd millennium BCE. The city was quite important in the 2nd millennium BCE, especially between the 18th and 17th centuries, when it was the capital of one of the most influential kingdoms of the region, called Yamhad, before being destroyed by the Hittites around 1600 BCE.[253] The city grew over time, especially from the Hellenistic period and then in Roman times, when Aleppo was the second largest city in the region, preceded only by Antioch. Despite the information from written sources, however, we know very little about the architectural history of the city throughout the period preceding the Muslim conquest in 637, after a period of Byzantine domination which started in 395. Remains of the 1st millennium BCE have been found mainly from excavations in the Citadel,[254] while traces of the Hellenistic period can chiefly be recognised in the orthogonal street grid of the current Old city.[255] Actually, not much has reached us about the city's architecture during the whole first part of the Islamic period, until around the 10th century, apart from the descriptions of ancient and modern travellers.[256] During the Umayyad and Abbasid periods, the city was only of provincial importance. It began to assume a more significant role from the Hamdanid period, when in the middle of the 10th century Sayf al-Dawla, made it his capital, embellishing Aleppo with new buildings. The whole period that followed, until 13th century, was marked by political instability, due first to the continuous contrasts with the Byzantines[257] and then with events related to the Crusades. Nonetheless, Aleppo managed to enjoy relatively stable and prosperous phases, especially in the 12th century, under the Zanjid dynasty, which contributed largely to the architectural development of the city, with important new buildings. In particular, the reign of Nur-al-Din (1146-1173) led to the first unification of Aleppo and Damascus under a single ruling and to significant changes in the urban layout of the city, notably through the construction of fortifications on the Citadel and new city walls.[258]

Despite the destruction caused by the Mongols in the mid-13th century (which, almost completely destroyed the circuit of city walls), a number of previous buildings of the Ayyubid period (1176-1260) were still standing at the time of Creswell's visit and were the subject of several photographs.[259] These mostly concern monuments of the Mamluk period (1260-1516), during which the city's appearance underwent various changes: it was in this specific period that the definitive route of the city walls was defined, the Citadel was restored and enlarged, and the first khans were built in the city centre (previously, they were located only in several suburban neighbourhoods).[260] The history of the Mamluk period was also marked by the need to cope with phases of partial economic and social decline, which also had an impact on the state of its architecture with several buildings being destroyed. The crisis following the plague of 1348 is worth recalling as well as the conquest by Timur's army in 1400, when the city was sacked, before being soon recovered by the Mamluks.[261] During the Ottoman period, which began in 1516, the urban layout did not change a great deal initially, but the defensive structures of the walls and Citadel certainly lost their function, because the city was within the empire and no longer needed to respond to threats.[262] The main consequence of this was a growth that no longer took into account the division of the *intra* and *extra muros* zones, and an increase in market areas, also due to the economic growth of the city.[263] Even during the Ottoman period, the architectural history of the city had to cope with destructive events, such as a strong earthquake in 1822[264] which led to many building

---

[252] According to tradition, the settlement arose on the Citadel, where Abraham stopped to milk his sheep, during his journey from Canaan to Jerusalem (Gaube 2007: 73).
[253] For mention of the city of the 3rd millennium BCE in the archives of Ebla and on Yamhad see Liverani 1988: 209-210 and 391-395 respectively.
[254] van Berchem, Fatio 1914: 210-218; Anonymous 1931; Michell 1978: 231; Meinecke 1992: I/181-184; Allen 1999: chapter 5; Gonnella, Khayyata, Kohlmeyer 2005; ARCHNET site 2812.
[255] Gaube 2007: 75.
[256] On the sources of early Islamic geographers and early European travellers see Herzfeld 1955: 1-6; Kafescioğlu 1999: 79-82; Gaube 2007: 85-89; Gonnella 2007: 109.
[257] The temporary Byzantine conquest of the city in 962 led to significant destruction of the city's buildings (Gaube 2007: 85).

---

[258] Gonnella 2007: 106. It is worth remembering that, just before the beginning of the Zanjid period, the city suffered numerous damages following an earthquake in 1138 (Lafi 2017, footnote 12).
[259] An interesting recent photographic review on the Ayyubid architectural heritage can be found in Hammad 2004.
[260] Gaube 2007: 91-92.
[261] On the architecture of the Mamluk period, primary reference should be made to the fundamental work by Meinecke 1992, especially I/112-115, 132-135, 180-188, 208-211.
[262] On the architecture of the Ottoman period, see Moaz 1998; Raymond 1998; Kafescioğlu 1999.
[263] Gaube 2007: 92 and 101.
[264] UNESCO/UNITAR 2018: 14. The impact of the earthquake was significant, with damage particularly to the Citadel, which was subsequently abandoned, and a large part of the

reconstruction and restoration plans. Regardless of these destructive episodes, the 19th century brought major changes to the urban layout, especially following the Tanzimat reforms of 1839,[265] which shaped the future economic, social, and architectural changes of the city. More specifically, in the second half of the century, new neighbourhoods were built in the west and from 1882 the city also developed beyond the north-western corner of the city walls, beyond Bab al-Faraj. From this moment onwards, we can speak of a 'Modern city', distinct from the pre-19th century 'Old city'. Beginning in the late 1850s, regulations were enacted for the protection and management of cultural heritage, which were further regulated later, under the French Mandate. During this period, the Institut français d'études arabes de Damas, which was founded in 1922, began a detailed cataloguing and study of the city's monuments.

A comparison with the photos kept at the Victoria & Albert Museum clearly indicates that all the photos of Aleppo from the Berenson Collection can be dated to the period of the 1919-1920 trip. Creswell visited Aleppo at a crucial moment of its history, since prior to the publication of the researches carried out by the first scholars who devoted themselves to cataloguing and systematically describing the monuments, foremost Jean Sauvaget[266] and Ernst Herzfeld.[267] Creswell, therefore, photographed a city that was still little known in terms of its architectural history, except for the descriptions of ancient and modern travellers.[268] In addition to his poor knowledge of the Arabic language, this is certainly also the reason why it is sometimes difficult to identify the monuments from his captions, because he misspelled their names. Probably, many of the monuments photographed were completely unknown to Creswell, who recorded their name simply based on what he heard when talking to the local people.

Regardless of these details, the photographs taken by Creswell in Aleppo are of great value, first of all because they portray a truly large number of monuments (as many as 60 in the Berenson Collection). His photographic legacy is indeed one of the richest and most detailed among those handed down to us from the various early photographers who worked in the city.[269]

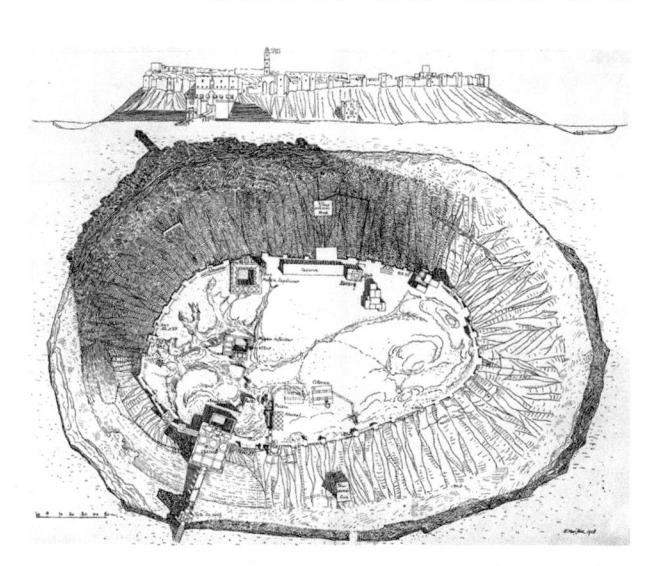

Figure: 251. Aleppo. The map of the Citadel from Herzfeld 1954, pl. 25.

It should also be recalled that the photos are probably dated prior to a great fire that destroyed part of the city in 1920.[270] More generally, they portray Aleppo before the urban transformations of the 20th century[271] and, especially in this first part of the century, due to the Syrian Civil War: the result of the bombardments, shelling, fires and street combats, mainly between 2012 and late 2016, had devastating effects on the city's cultural heritage. The comparison between Creswell's photos and the current panorama is merciless: the mosque of Khusrauriya, in the area immediately south of the Citadel, is unfortunately only one of many examples of the intense devastation suffered by many monuments (Figure 252).[272]

---

urban fabric was completely destroyed.
[265] Kawtharani 2013.
[266] Sauvaget 1931.
[267] Herzfeld 1954, 1955, 1956.
[268] Among the publications preceding Creswell's visit, those of Sachau 1883: 105-108 (figs at p. 458-459) and van Berchem, Fatio 1914: 207-221 deserve special mention.
[269] Given the importance of Aleppo, it was obviously portrayed by most of the first photographers who reached Syria. It is worth noting that the 1912 edition of the *Baedeker Guide*, quotes at least two stable photographic studios in Aleppo: those of Missirliyan and Cloris Thévenet (Baedeker 1912: 370).

[270] Gaube 2007: 78.
[271] Particularly in the mid-1950s, a general urban renewal project led to a large number of expropriations and demolitions in historic neighbourhoods, such as Bab al-Faraj, al-Judayda and the west areas of Bab al-Jinan, and strongly reshaped the urban fabric. See especially UNESCO/UNITAR 2018: 14-16 for a summary of the history of the protection of monuments in Syria in the second half of the 20th century, which led in 1986 to the declaration of the Old City as 'UNESCO World Heritage property' (https://whc.unesco.org/en/list/21/9).
[272] There are now many documents and reports that allow us to assess the damage suffered by the architectural heritage of Aleppo. Among these, the *40th Session of the World Heritage Committee* (Istanbul, 2016) available at https://whc.unesco.org/archive/2016/whc16-40com-7AAdd-en.pdf, that reports damages 'to the Great Umayyad Mosque, Mosque al-Utrush, Madrasa al-Adiliyya, Madrasa al-Sultania, the Citadel, the New Serail (Grand Serail), the Hotel Carlton, Matbakh al-Ajami, Khan al-Shouna, Khan al-Saboun and Khan al-Wazeer as well as additional severe damages to the Maronite Church. In addition, severe damage has been reported at Khan Slaimanyeh (Haj Musa), Suq al-Haddadin, Suq al-Zarb, Suq al-Sagha, part of Suq al-Suweiqa and at Madrasa al-Shathbakhtiyya (al-Shaikh Maarouf Mosque) destroyed by underground explosions. Minor damage is reported at Aslan Dede Mosque, al-Hayaat Mosque, al-Dabagah Mosque, and

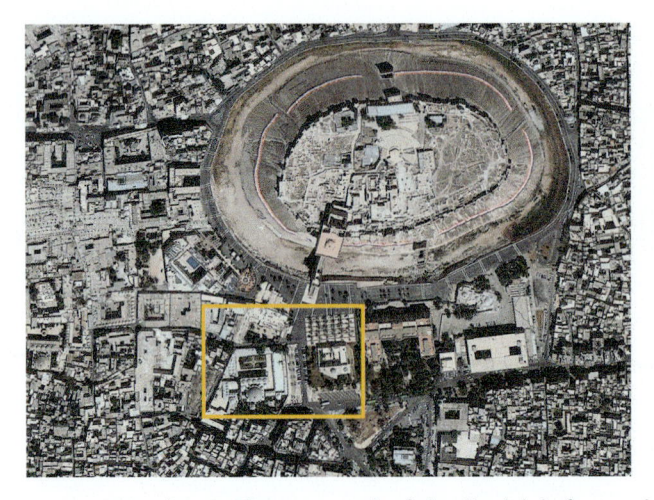

Mesopotamia, Syria and Transjordan in the Creswell Collection

Figure: 252. Aleppo. The area south of the Citadel, before and after the bombings of al-Khusrauriya Mosque and al-Sultaniya Madrasa (in the yellow box in the photo on the left; below, Figures 357-362 and 459-461). Google Earth, Image © 2022 MaxarTechnologies; date of photo on the left: 9 august 2011, date of photo on the right: 29 September 2017.

Although Aleppo is not one of the places most considered by Creswell in his publications, he took countless photos there (this is actually the largest group of the entire collection analysed in this study, counting 257 photographs). Most of them focus on three subjects: the Citadel, the City walls with their gates and the Great Mosque. The rest of the photos portray various types of monuments (mosques, madrasas,[273] hospitals, mausoleums, fountains...), in a time span between the Abbasid and Ottoman periods. Below is a review of the monuments represented and illustrated in the catalogue, organised considering first the three main subjects listed above and then all the others, grouped chronologically. For details on building chronology and location of individual monuments, see Appendix 4 directly.

The Citadel (Figures 254-273) has a very ancient history as witnessed by deep soundings that have brought to light structures of the 1st millennium BCE.[274] However, the structure we see today dates back mainly to the Zanjid and Ayyubid periods (12th century). The construction underwent restoration and modifications in later periods. Under the Ottomans, after losing its defensive function, it became home to barracks and was partially dismantled after the earthquake of 1822, since many of the fortification's stones were used to build new buildings in the lower town; at the same time, restoration was carried out on some buildings inside the Citadel.[275] Creswell's photographs depict the Citadel when the main Ottoman building works had already been completed but prior to the commencement of the restoration and excavations by the French in the 1930s.[276] Creswell's photographs portray the Citadel as a whole, with various panoramic shots from different sides, the Citadel (or Upper) Mosque, constructed in 1213/1214 under the patronage of Ayyubid Sultan al-Malik al-Zahir Ghazi (Figure 274), and the Maqam Ibrahim al-Sulfi Mosque, dedicated to the prophet Abraham (Figures 275-277). This latter monument was built in the Zanjid period (12th century) and restored, probably after the Mongol conquest of the city in 1260; for this reason, its current appearance mainly reflects the Mamluk building phase. Some photographs of inside the Citadel are quite noteworthy because they portray structures that today have significantly changed from the past, following important restorations: this is particularly the case of the so-called Throne Hall (Figures 268-270).[277]

Creswell also paid great attention to the city walls, mainly dating back to the Ayyubid and Mamluk periods between the 13th and 16th centuries (Figures 278-286), with shots that mostly portray structures that have now disappeared or deeply changed. Many photographs capture some of the city gates: Bab al-Jinan, built in the Hamdanid period (10th century) and then remodelled in the Mamluk period (early 16th century), but demolished in the early 20th century to broaden a street (Figure 287);[278] Bab Antakya, probably the oldest, built in the

---

Suq Qara Qumash'. A map with air photos and details of the damaged structures can be found in the document *SOC Report by the State Party 2015* (p. 27), at https://whc.unesco.org/en/soc/3183 and in *SOC Report by the State Party 2014* (p. 10), at https://whc.unesco.org/en/soc/2914. See also the UNESCO annual reports at http://whc.unesco.org/en/soc/3345

[273] The photographs and reliefs dedicated to the madrasas were later used by Creswell in a publication in which he objected to the prevailing opinion that the cruciform plant of the madrasas was Syrian (or even more oriental), proposing instead an Egyptian origin (Creswell 1922: 43).

[274] Gonnella, Khayata, Kholmeyer 2005; see above, footnote 254.

[275] Gonnella 2007: 109-110.

[276] See van Berchem, Fatio 1914: 213-218 for a description just before Creswell's visit, and the view in Figure 251 (from Herzfeld 1954, pl. 25) for an overview prior to the French excavations.

[277] Gonnella 2012.

[278] Herzfeld 1955: 43-44; Gaube, Wirth 1984: 370.

THE SITES AND THE MONUMENTS – SYRIA

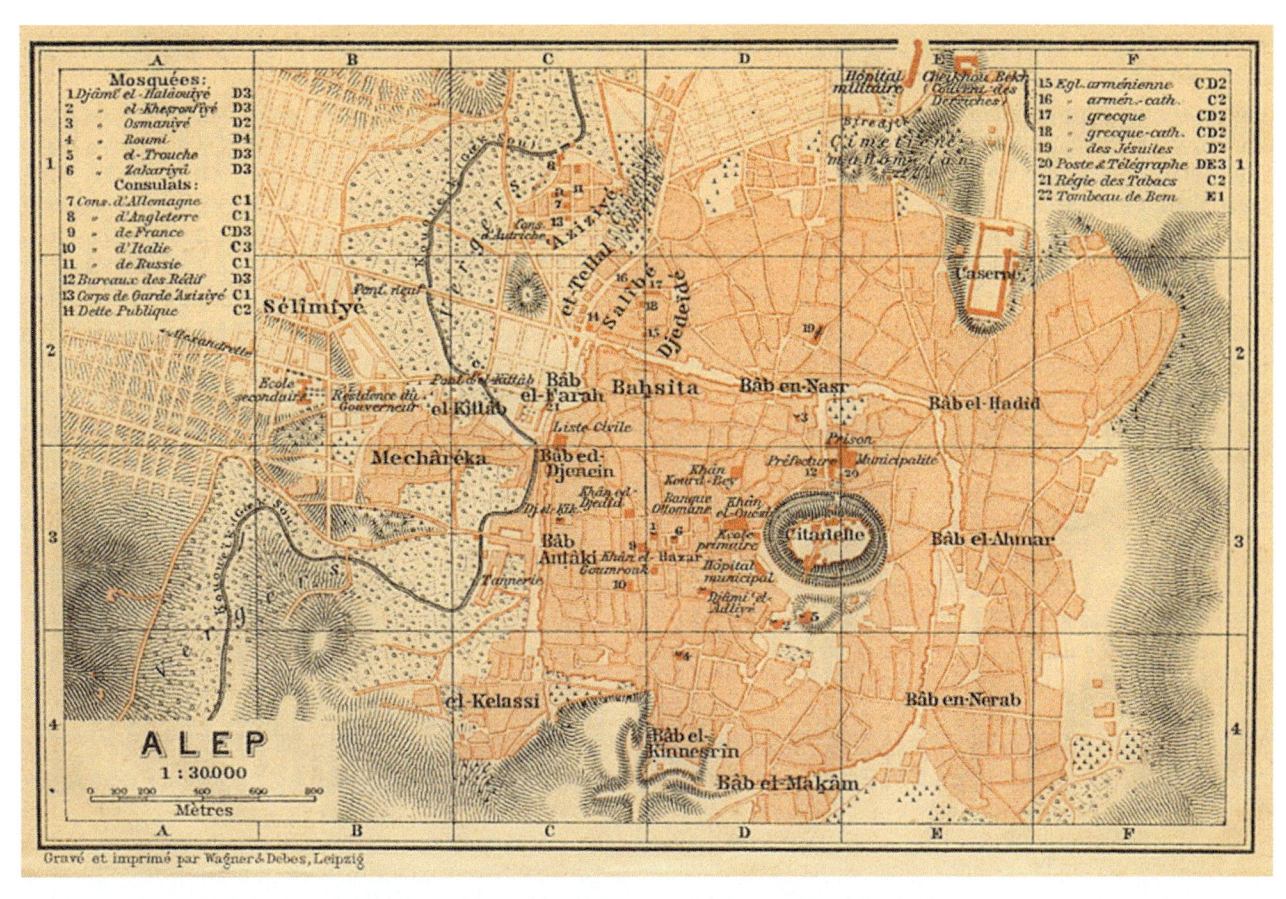

Figure: 253. Aleppo. City map by Wagner & Debes, c. 1912 (folding map in Baedeker 1912).

Hamdanid period but later radically remodelled in the Ayyubid period (13th century), with further later repairs and restoration in the 14th-15th centuries (Figures 288-290);[279] Bab Qinnasrin, also erected in the Hamdanid period (10th century) but completely rebuilt in the Mamluk period and heavily damaged during the recent Syrian Civil War (Figures 291-295);[280] Bab al-Maqam, built in the Ayyubid period (13th century), which is worthy of note for its original construction with three openings and no towers (Figure 296);[281] Bab al-Hadid, also known as the Iron Gate, which was first built in the Ayyubid period (13th century), but later remodelled during the Mamluk period (16th century). This last gate was also severely damaged during the Syrian Civil War and has recently been restored (Figure 297).[282]

The third subject of the main group of photos is the Great Mosque,[283] i.e., the largest mosque in Aleppo, mainly built in the Umayyad, Zangid, Seljuk, and Mamluk (8th-13th century) periods. In this case, Creswell's photographs (Figures 298-307) are an extremely valuable source of documentation, given that this mosque is one of the monuments most severely damaged by the recent Syrian Civil War. The conflict caused the collapse of its famous minaret in 2013, after restoration of both the minaret and the courtyard in 2003.[284]

Outside these three main groups, many other monuments are represented in Creswell's photographs: most are located in the area immediately behind the Citadel and in the whole area to the west, up to the circuit of the ancient walls, while some also outside the circuit wall, to the north and south. The following list is sorted by chronological periods, each of which ordered alphabetically.

Evidence of the Abbasid period (8th-9th century) has almost completely disappeared in modern Aleppo. Indeed, only one monument photographed dates back (at least as regards its foundation) to this period. This

---

[279] Herzfeld 1955: 47-56; Burns R. 1992: 43; Meinecke 1992: I/181, II/278; ARCHNET site 2870.

[280] Herzfeld 1955: 59-65; Gaube, Wirth 1984: 388; Meinecke 1992: I/181, II/322; ARCHNET site 2871.

[281] Gaube, Wirth 1984: 385. It has been suggested that the gate had ceremonial purposes (Tabbaa 1997: 67-69).

[282] Gaube, Wirth 1984: 379; Burns R. 1992: 55; Meinecke 1992: I/184, II/458; ARCHNET site 2873.

[283] Creswell 1932: 325; 1940: 377. Further bibliography: Herzfeld 1943: 34-35, 1948a: 118-120; Michell 1978: 231; Gaube, Wirth 1984: 357; Burns R. 1992: 40-41; Meinecke 1992: I/52-55; Allen 1999: chapter 4; Takieddine, Abd al-Ghafour 2022c;

ARCHNET site 1804.

[284] A project for the restoration of the structure began in 2020, in an attempt to save what remained still standing: see UNESCO 2016: 17 and UNESCO 2019: 63. Photographic documentation of the work in progress can be found in the *SOC Report by the State Party 2019* (pp. 7-17), at https://whc.unesco.org/en/soc/3866

monument is the Mashhad al-Muhassin,[285] the oldest Shiite shrine, built in 962 (Figures 308-310). However, once again the standing remains belong predominantly to the Zanjid and Ayyubid periods (12th century).

The Maqam Ibrahim fi al-Salihin is the third mosque dedicated to Abraham, after the two on the Citadel, and was founded by the Seljuk sultan Malikshah at the end of the 11th century (Figure 311).[286]

The following monuments belong to the Zanjid Period (12th century): al-Shuaybiya Mosque, built on the site of an earlier Umayyad mosque. It was remodelled several times and has recently been restored (Figures 312-315);[287] Nur al-Din Maristan, with the entrance and the door frame being the only original remaining structure (Figures 316-319);[288] al-Halawiya Madrasa (Figures 320-323)[289] and al-Muqaddamiya Madrasa (Figures 324-327),[290] both built on the remains of Byzantine churches. A large part of the monuments photographed by Creswell dates back to the Ayyubid period (1175-1260): the Mashhad al-Husayn, a Shiite sanctuary and mosque, built in the 13th century, is worthy of mention.[291] The monument was destroyed in 1919 or 1920, so shortly after Cresswell's visit, when it was used as a powder keg, and was rebuilt after World War II. Creswell portrays it in many photographs showing both the outside and inside of the building (Figures 328-338). An additional, large group of photographs portrays the al-Firdaws Madrasa, built in the 13th century, outside the Medieval city walls;[292] in this case also, Creswell photographed both the exterior and the interior, with great attention to the building details (Figures 339-350). The rest of the monuments are instead portrayed by Creswell with a fewer but nonetheless significant number of photographs for each monument, often focused not so much on overall views but individual architectural elements that were considered particularly distinctive and interesting. In some cases, Creswell's photographic documentation is noteworthy because it represents monuments that were damaged during the recent Syrian Civil War: for example, the al-Shadhbakhtiya Madrasa, which had already been partially destroyed in the 19th century to make room for the adjacent market (Figures 351-356)[293] and the al-Sultaniya Madrasa (Figures 357-362).[294] The Ayyubid group is completed by the following monuments: al-Kamiliya Madrasa (Figures 363-368),[295] al-Karimiya Mosque (Figure 369),[296] al-Sharafiya Madrasa (Figures 370-377),[297] al-Zahiriya Madrasa (Figures 378-385),[298] Khanqah al-Farafra (Figures 386-388),[299] and the Umm Malik al-Afdal Mausoleum, named Darwishiya Mausoleum by Creswell (Figures 389-390).[300] The last monument mentioned here is Masjid Yusuf: it is described in detail by Creswell as the 'Mazjid of Jusuf bin Muhammmad ibn al-Malik az-Zahin' and dated to 1260, that is, the passage between the Ayyubid and Mamluk periods. In this case, the structure was already largely in ruins at the time of Creswell's visit, as can be clearly seen from the photographs: to my knowledge, neither the location nor the exact historical context is clear (Figures 391-392).

The period most represented in Creswell's photographs is certainly the Mamluk period, spanning between the 14th and 15th centuries. This is certainly also due to the large number of standing architectural remains that could be photographed. Again, these are monuments that are only in some cases portrayed in their entirety; more often, they are represented by individual architectural elements and decorative details, both outside and inside the buildings. The list includes the following monuments: al-Atrush Mosque, damaged during the recent Syrian Civil War (Figures 393-397);[301] al-Bayada Mosque, built during the 14th century, but largely modified by later additions (Figures 398-399);[302]

---

[285] Creswell discusses this monument in his chapter on the development of the squinch (Creswell 1940: 109, fig. 100). Further bibliography: Herzfeld 1955: 193-201, 236-248; Gaube, Wirth 1984: 410; Burns R. 1992: 56; Meinecke 1992: I/16, 20, 52/II: 12; Allen 1999: chapter 4; ARCHNET site 1810.

[286] Herzfeld 1955: 175-182; Gaube, Wirth 1984: 411; Burns R. 1992: 50; ARCHNET site 4244.

[287] Herzfeld 1955: 222-227; Burns R. 1992: 43; Allen 1999: chapter 2; Raby 2004; ARCHNET site 3718.

[288] Allen 1999: chapter 2; ARCHNET site 4229.

[289] Herzfeld 1955: 205-222; Gaube, Wirth 1984: 353; Burns R. 1992: 41; Takieddine, Ad al-Ghafour 2022b; ARCHNET site 1805.

[290] Herzfeld 1955: 233-236; Burns R. 1992: 43; Allen 1999: chapter 2; ARCHNET site 1813. It is mentioned as 'Madrasa Khan al-Tutun' in Creswell's captions on the photographs.

[291] Gaube, Wirth 1984: 410; Burns R. 1992: 56; Meinecke 1992: I/16, 20, 52, 93, II/12; Allen 1999: chapter 5; Hammad 2004: 7; ARCHNET site 1811.

[292] van Berchem, Fatio 1914: 218-221; Herzfeld 1956: 297-302; Michell 1978: 231; Gaube, Wirth 1984: 411; Burns R. 1992: 48-49; Meinecke 1992: I/73, 89; Allen 1999: chapter 8; Hammad 2004: 4-5; Takieddine, Abd al-Ghafour 2022a; ARCHNET site 1803.

[293] Herzfeld 1956: 255-260; Burns R. 1992: 42; ARCHNET site 1819.

[294] UNESCO 2016: 17. Further bibliography: Herzfeld 1955: 276; Gaube, Wirth 1984: 382; Burns R. 1992: 47; Meinecke 1992: I/34, 54; ARCHNET site 1821.

[295] Herzfeld 1956: 305-306; Gaube, Wirth 1984: 346; Meinecke 1992: I/54; Allen 1999, chapter 8; Hammad 2004: 12-16; ARCHNET site 1808.

[296] Herzfeld 1956: 315-319; Gaube, Wirth 1984: 388; ARCHNET site 4332.

[297] Herzfeld 1956: 312-315; Gaube, Wirth 1984: 361; Meinecke 1992: I/94, 114; Allen 1999, chapter 8; ARCHNET site 1820.

[298] Herzfeld 1956: 273-276; Gaube, Wirth 1984: 411; Burns R. 1992: 112; Meinecke 1992: I/55; Allen 1999, chapter 8; ARCHNET site 1826.

[299] Herzfeld 1956: 302-305; Gaube, Wirth 1984: 377; Burns R. 1992: 55; Hammad 2004: 17-20; ARCHNET site 4247.

[300] Kafescioğlu 1999: 74; ARCHNET site 4337.

[301] UNESCO 2016: 17. Further bibliography: Gaube, Wirth 1984: 381; Herzfeld 1956: 362-366; Meinecke 1992: I/184-186, II/294-297; Daiber 2022e; ARCHNET site 1825.

[302] Herzfeld 1956: 349-350; ARCHNET site 4331.

al-Maqam Mosque (Figures 400-401);[303] al-Qadi al-Mahmandar Mosque, built in the 14th century but with a minaret reconstructed in 1946; this monument also suffered damages during the Civil Syrian War (Figure 402);[304] al-Qiqan Mosque, probably built in the late Mamluk period and worthy of note because, among the building stones, one contains a Hittite relief dating back to the late 2nd millennium BCE (Figures 403-404);[305] al-Rumi Mosque (Figures 405-408),[306] al-Safahiya Mosque (Figures 409-411),[307] al-Sahibiya Madrasa (Figures 412-416),[308] al-Tawashy Mosque, built in the 14th century, and restored in the Ottoman period (Figures 417-418);[309] al-Zaki Mosque (Figure 419);[310] Altunbugha Mosque (Figures 420-426),[311] Arghun al-Kamili Bimaristan (Figures 427-434),[312] Bahsita Mosque, where Creswell photographs the curious mihrab (Figure 435),[313] Maqam Ughlulbak (Figure 436),[314] Musa Ibn Abdullah al-Nasiri Mausoleum (Figures 437-439),[315] Qubba Khayrbak (Figure 440-443),[316] Shihab al-Din Ahmad al-Adrai Mausoleum (Figures 444-445),[317] Zawiya al-Bazzaziya (Figure 446),[318] Zawiya al-Haidary, no longer existing to my knowledge, whose original location was possibly in the Bab Nairab al-Qasilah area (Figures 447-448);[319] Zawiya al-Junashiya, also no longer existing to my knowledge, and originally located in the Bab al-Nasr area (Figures 449-450).[320]

In addition to these religious monuments, Creswell also photographed some khans, now partly demolished, such as Khan al-Sabun (Figures 451-452),[321] Khan Qassabiya (Figure 453)[322] and Khan Utchan (Figure 454),[323] as well as some fountains: Qastal Bab al-Maqam, on the east side of Bab al-Maqam (Figure 455);[324] Qastal Sahat Bizza (Figure 456),[325] Qastal Sakakini (Figure 457)[326] and Qastal Shabariq, the latter no longer existing to my knowledge and possibly located in the Bab Nairab al-Qasilah area (Figure 458).[327]

A smaller number of photographs concern the monuments of the Ottoman period, with documentation that is very interesting because the photographs often portray structures that have been completely destroyed: this is especially the case, mentioned above, of the complex of the al-Khusrauriya Mosque, i.e., the first Ottoman monument of the city, built in the 16th century by architect Mimar Sinan.[328] It was almost completely destroyed in 2014-2015, during the Syrian Civil War (Figures 459-461; see Figure 252 above for a shocking comparison between the state of the monument at Creswell's time and today).

The other monuments photographed are the Bahramiya Mosque (Figures 462-463),[329] the Takiya Shaykh Abu Bakr (Figures 464-467),[330] and some khans: Khan al-Zait, now demolished, originally located south of the Great Mosque (Figure 468),[331] Khan al-Jumruk (Figure 469),[332] Khan al-Wazir, partly demolished during the French Mandate to make way for new roads (Figures 470-471).[333]

---

[303] Herzfeld 1956: 321-322; ARCHNET site 4334.
[304] Herzfeld 1956: 361-362; ARCHNET site 1812.
[305] Herzfeld 1956: 407-408; ARCHNET site 4249.
[306] Herzfeld 1956: 344-345; Gaube, Wirth 1984: 388; ARCHNET site 1815.
[307] Herzfeld 1956: 368; Meinecke 1992: I/181, II/352; ARCHNET site 1816.
[308] Herzfeld 1956: 340-342; Burns R. 1992: 42; Meinecke 1992: I/181-352; ARCHNET site 4341.
[309] Herzfeld 1956: 349; Gaube, Wirth 1984: 384; ARCHNET site 1822.
[310] Meinecke 1992: I/181, II/298; ARCHNET site 4246.
[311] Herzfeld 1956: 324-326; Gaube, Wirth 1984: 381; Burns R. 1992: 48; Meinecke 1992: I/70, II/175; ARCHNET site 1823.
[312] Herzfeld 1956: 332-338; Gaube, Wirth 1984: 387; ARCHNET site 1801.
[313] Herzfeld 1956: 330-331; Meinecke 1992: I/113-115, II/216; ARCHNET site 4330.
[314] Meinecke 1992: I/183, II/409; Abd al-Razik 2019; ARCHNET site 4339.
[315] Meinecke 1992: I/53, II/115; ARCHNET site 4338.
[316] Gaube, Wirth 1984: 410; ARCHNET site 5343.
[317] ARCHNET site 4251.
[318] Meinecke 1992: II/273; ARCHNET site 4340.
[319] ARCHNET site 4335.
[320] Herzfeld 1956: 359-361; ARCHNET site 4335.
[321] Gaube, Wirth 1984: 360; Burns R. 1992: 42; Meinecke 1992: I/185, 199, II/435; ARCHNET site 2153.
[322] Gaube, Wirth 1984: 351; Herzfeld 1956: 403-404; Meinecke 1992: I/182; ARCHNET site 4243.
[323] Herzfeld 1956: 406.
[324] Herzfeld 1956: 368-369.
[325] Meinecke 1992: I/184, II/276.
[326] ARCHNET site 4203.
[327] Herzfeld 1956: 327-329; Meinecke 1992: I/112, II/203; ARCHNET site 4199.
[328] Burns R. 1992: 47; Kafescioğlu 1999: 71-72; ARCHNET site 1809.
[329] Gaube, Wirth 1984: 349; ARCHNET site 1802.
[330] Gaube, Wirth 1984: 408; Watenpaugh 2005; ARCHNET site 4250.
[331] Kafescioğlu 1999: 75.
[332] Gaube, Wirth 1984: 355; Burns R. 1992: 43; ARCHNET site 2154.
[333] Michell 1978: 231; Gaube, Wirth 1984: 366; Burns R. 1992: 42; Meinecke 1992: I/210; ARCHNET site 2865.

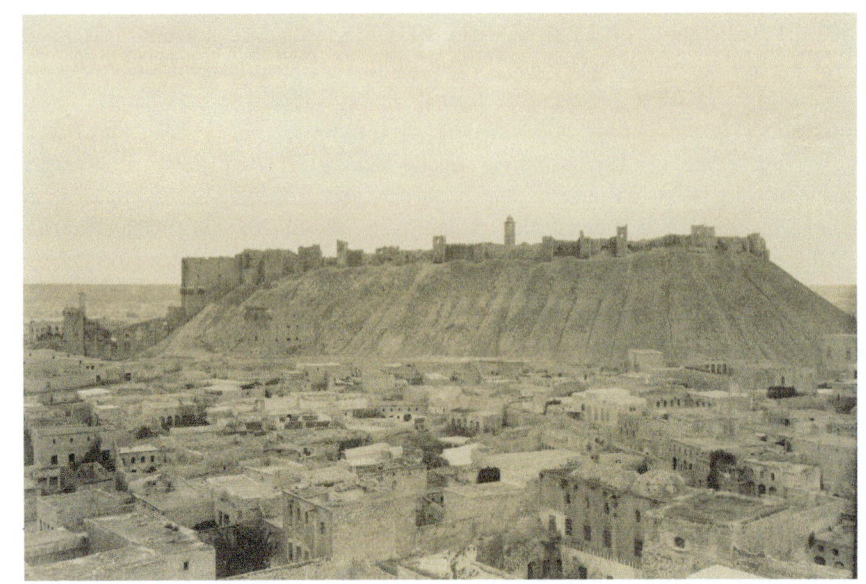

Figure: 254.
Subject: Aleppo. The Citadel, looking west.
Berenson ID: 133980.
Medium: gelatine silver print, 12×17cm.
Date of creation: 1919-1920.
Handwritten notes on the back: 'Aleppo, The Citadel from the S/E — chiefly 600/11 (1203/15)' [Cres.].
Ashmolean negative: EA.CA.5683.

Figure: 255.
Subject: Aleppo. The Citadel, looking southeast.
Berenson ID: 133981.
Medium: gelatine silver print, 12×17cm.
Date of creation: 1919-1920.
Handwritten notes on the back: 'Aleppo, The Citadel, from the N/W — chiefly 600/11 (1203/15)' [Cres.].
Ashmolean negative: EA.CA.5681.

Figure: 256.
Subject: Aleppo. The Citadel, looking southwest.
Berenson ID: 133982.
Medium: gelatine silver print, 12×17cm.
Date of creation: 1919-1920.
Handwritten notes on the back: 'Aleppo, The Citadel, from the N/E — chiefly 600/11 (1203/15)' [Cres.].
Ashmolean negative: EA.CA.5682.

THE SITES AND THE MONUMENTS – SYRIA

Figure: 257.
Subject: Aleppo. The Citadel, looking east.
Berenson ID: 133983.
Medium: gelatine silver print, 12×17cm.
Date of creation: 1919-1920.
Handwritten notes on the back: 'Aleppo, The Citadel – from the W — chiefly 600/11 (1203/15)' [Cres.].
Ashmolean negative: EA.CA.5680.

Figure: 258.
Subject: Aleppo. The Citadel, looking north.
Berenson ID: 133984.
Medium: gelatine silver print, 12×17cm.
Date of creation: 1919-1920.
Handwritten notes on the back: 'Aleppo, The Citadel from the S — chiefly 600/11 (1203/15)' [Cres.].
Ashmolean negative: EA.CA.5696.

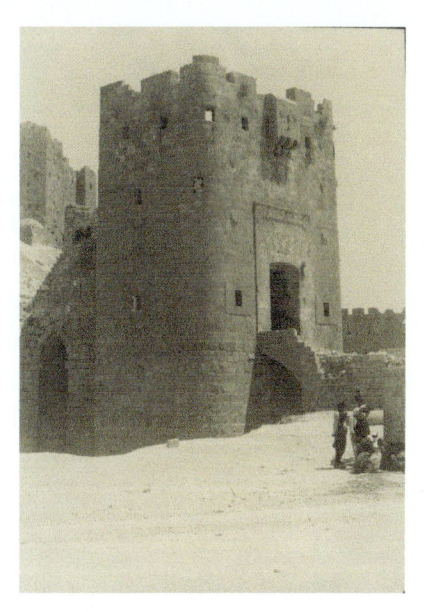

Figure: 259.
Subject: Aleppo. The entrance to the Citadel.
Berenson ID: 133985.
Medium: gelatine silver print, 12×17cm.
Date of creation: 1919-1920.
Handwritten notes on the back: 'Aleppo, The Citadel – entrance — chiefly 600/11 (1203/15)' [Cres.].
Ashmolean negative: EA.CA.5688.

Figure: 260.
Subject: Aleppo. The bridge at the entrance of the Citadel.
Berenson ID: 133991.
Medium: gelatine silver print, 12×17cm.
Date of creation: 1919-1920.
Handwritten notes on the back: 'Aleppo, The Citadel – bridge from the ante entrance to inner — 600/11 (1203/15)' [Cres.].
Ashmolean negative: EA.CA.5692.

Figure: 261 (left).
Subject: Aleppo. Tower on the southern side of the Citadel.
Berenson ID: 134012.
Medium: gelatine silver print, 12×17cm.
Date of creation: 1919-1920.
Handwritten notes on the back: 'Aleppo, The Citadel – Tower of al-Phury — chiefly 600/11 (1203/15)' [Cres.].
Ashmolean negative: EA.CA.5687.

Figure: 262 (right).
Subject: Aleppo. Tower on the northern side of the Citadel.
Berenson ID: 134016.
Medium: gelatine silver print, 12×17cm.
Date of creation: 1919-1920.
Handwritten notes on the back: 'Aleppo, The Citadel – N. side — chiefly 600/11 (1203/15)' [Cres.].
Ashmolean negative: EA.CA.5685.

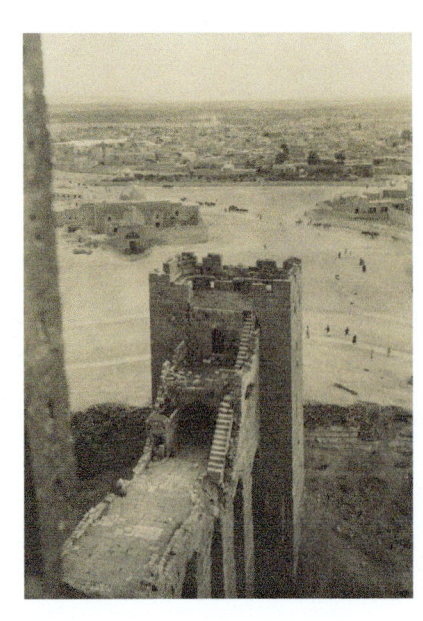

Figure: 263 (left).
Subject: Aleppo. The glacis of the Citadel.
Berenson ID: 134017.
Medium: gelatine silver print, 12×17cm.
Date of creation: 1919-1920.
Handwritten notes on the back: 'Aleppo, The Citadel – glacis — chiefly 600/11 (1203/15)' [Cres.].
Ashmolean negative: EA.CA.5686.

Figure: 264 (right).
Subject: Aleppo. The entrance to the Citadel, seen from the inside.
Berenson ID: 134018.
Medium: gelatine silver print, 12×17cm.
Date of creation: 1919-1920.
Handwritten notes on the back: 'Aleppo, The Citadel – reverse of entrance — chiefly 600/11 (1203/15)' [Cres.].
Ashmolean negative: EA.CA.5691.

Figure: 265 (left).
Subject: Aleppo. The glacis on the northern side of the Citadel.
Berenson ID: 133986.
Medium: gelatine silver print, 12×17cm.
Date of creation: 1919-1920.
Handwritten notes on the back: 'Aleppo, The Citadel – glacis on N. side — chiefly 600/11 (1203/15)' [Cres.].
Ashmolean negative: EA.CA.5684.

Figure: 266 (centre).
Subject: Aleppo. The inner entrance of the Citadel.
Berenson ID: 133987.
Medium: gelatine silver print, 12×17cm.
Date of creation: 1919-1920.
Handwritten notes on the back: 'Aleppo, The Citadel – inner entrance from top of ante — chiefly 600/11 (1203/15)' [Cres.].
Ashmolean negative: EA.CA.5693.

Figure: 267 (right).
Subject: Aleppo. The entrance to the Citadel.
Berenson ID: 133988.
Medium: gelatine silver print, 12×17cm.
Date of creation: 1919-1920.
Handwritten notes on the back: 'Aleppo, The Citadel – from the W — chiefly 600/11 (1203/15)' [Cres.].
Ashmolean negative: EA.CA.5690.

Figure: 268.
Subject: Aleppo. The Throne Hall of the Citadel.
Berenson ID: 134009.
Medium: gelatine silver print, 12×17cm.
Date of creation: 1919-1920.
Handwritten notes on the back: 'Aleppo, The Citadel – great hall over entrance — chiefly 600/11 (1203/15)' [Cres.].
Ashmolean negative: EA.CA.5699.

Figure: 278.
Subject: Aleppo. The western side of the City Walls.
Berenson ID: 134251.
Medium: gelatine silver print, 12×17cm.
Date of creation: 1919-1920.
Handwritten notes on the back: 'Aleppo, The Walls – W. side' [Cres.].
Ashmolean negative: EA.CA.5626.

Figure: 279.
Subject: Aleppo. The western side of the City Walls.
Berenson ID: 134252.
Medium: gelatine silver print, 12×17cm.
Date of creation: 1919-1920.
Handwritten notes on the back: 'Aleppo, The Walls – W. side' [Cres.].
Ashmolean negative: EA.CA.5627.

Figure: 280.
Subject: Aleppo. a tower with carved lions on the western side of the City Walls.
Berenson ID: 134253.
Medium: gelatine silver print, 12×17cm.
Date of creation: 1919-1920.
Handwritten notes on the back: 'Aleppo, The Walls – W. Side – tower with lions' [Cres.].
Ashmolean negative: EA.CA.5628.

THE SITES AND THE MONUMENTS – SYRIA

Figure: 281.
Subject: Aleppo. a lion carved on a tower on the western side of the City Walls.
Berenson ID: 133990.
Medium: gelatine silver print, 12×17cm.
Date of creation: 1919-1920.
Handwritten notes on the back: 'Aleppo, The walls – W. Side – lion on tower' [Cres.].
Ashmolean negative: EA.CA.5629.

Figure: 282.
Subject: Aleppo. another tower with carved lions on the western side of the City Walls.
Berenson ID: 134254.
Medium: gelatine silver print, 12×17cm.
Date of creation: 1919-1920.
Handwritten notes on the back: 'Aleppo, The Walls – W. Side – another tower with lions' [Cres.].
Ashmolean negative: EA.CA.5630.

Figure: 283.
Subject: Aleppo. The southern side of the City Walls.
Berenson ID: 134255.
Medium: gelatine silver print, 12×17cm.
Date of creation: 1919-1920.
Handwritten notes on the back: 'Aleppo, The Walls – S. side' [Cres.].
Ashmolean negative: EA.CA.5631.

Mesopotamia, Syria and Transjordan in the Creswell Collection

Figure: 284.
Subject: Aleppo. a tower on the southern side of the City Walls.
Berenson ID: 134256.
Medium: gelatine silver print, 12×17cm.
Date of creation: 1919-1920.
Handwritten notes on the back: 'Aleppo, The Walls – S. side' [Cres.].
Ashmolean negative: EA.CA.5632.

Figure: 285.
Subject: Aleppo. a tower on the northern side of the City Walls.
Berenson ID: 134257.
Medium: gelatine silver print, 12×17cm.
Date of creation: 1919-1920.
Handwritten notes on the back: 'Aleppo, The Walls – S. side' [Cres.].
Ashmolean negative: EA.CA.5634.

Figure: 286.
Subject: Aleppo. a tower on the City Walls.
Berenson ID: 134258.
Medium: gelatine silver print, 12×17cm.
Date of creation: 1919-1920.
Handwritten notes on the back: 'Aleppo, The Walls – N. side. Tower with lions' [Cres.].
Ashmolean negative: EA.CA.5635.

Figure: 287.
Subject: Aleppo. The Bab al-Jinan.
Berenson ID: 134268.
Medium: gelatine silver print, 12×17cm.
Date of creation: 1919-1920.
Handwritten notes on the back: 'Aleppo. Tower next Bab Geneina' [Cres.].
Ashmolean negative: EA.CA.5625.

Figure: 288.
Subject: Aleppo. The Bab Antakya.
Berenson ID: 134259.
Medium: gelatine silver print, 12×17cm.
Date of creation: 1919-1920.
Handwritten notes on the back: 'Aleppo, Antioch Gate' [Cres.].
Ashmolean negative: EA.CA.5636.

Figure: 289.
Subject: Aleppo. The Bab Antakya.
Berenson ID: 134260.
Medium: gelatine silver print, 12×17cm.
Date of creation: 1919-1920.
Handwritten notes on the back: 'Aleppo, Antioch Gate' [Cres.].
Ashmolean negative: EA.CA.5637.

Figure: 290.
Subject: Aleppo. Passage way inside the Bab Antakya.
Berenson ID: 134261.
Medium: gelatine silver print, 12×17cm.
Date of creation: 1919-1920.
Handwritten notes on the back: 'Aleppo, Antioch Gate – vault of passage way' [Cres.].
Ashmolean negative: EA.CA.5638.

Figure: 291.
Subject: Aleppo. The Bab Qinnasrin.
Berenson ID: 134262.
Medium: gelatine silver print, 12×17cm.
Date of creation: 1919-1920.
Handwritten notes on the back: 'Aleppo, Qinnasirn Gate' [Cres.].
Ashmolean negative: EA.CA.5639.

Figure: 292.
Subject: Aleppo. The Bab Qinnasrin.
Berenson ID: 134263.
Medium: gelatine silver print, 12×17cm.
Date of creation: 1919-1920.
Handwritten notes on the back: 'Aleppo, Qinnasirn Gate' [Cres.].
Ashmolean negative: EA.CA.5640.

THE SITES AND THE MONUMENTS – SYRIA

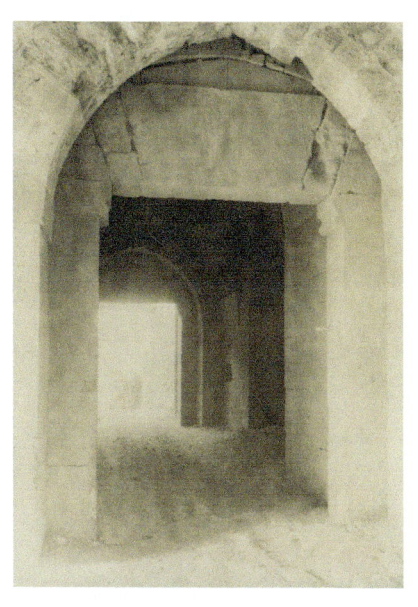

Figure: 293 (left).
Subject: Aleppo. The interior of the Bab Qinnasrin.
Berenson ID: 134264.
Medium: gelatine silver print, 12×17cm.
Date of creation: 1919-1920.
Handwritten notes on the back: 'Aleppo, Qinnasirn Gate – interior' [Cres.].

Figure: 294 (centre).
Subject: Aleppo. The interior of the Bab Qinnasrin.
Berenson ID: 134265.
Medium: gelatine silver print, 12×17cm.
Date of creation: 1919-1920.
Handwritten notes on the back: 'Aleppo, Qinnasirn Gate – interior' [Cres.].
Ashmolean negative: EA.CA.5641.

Figure: 295 (right).
Subject: Aleppo. The interior of the Bab Qinnasrin.
Berenson ID: 134266.
Medium: gelatine silver print, 12×17cm.
Date of creation: 1919-1920.
Handwritten notes on the back: 'Aleppo, Qinnasirn Gate – exit of interior' [Cres.].
Ashmolean negative: EA.CA.5642.

Figure: 296.
Subject: Aleppo. The Bab al-Maqam.
Berenson ID: 134267.
Medium: gelatine silver print, 12×17cm.
Date of creation: 1919-1920.
Handwritten notes on the back: 'Aleppo, Bab al-Maq'am' [Cres.].
Ashmolean negative: EA.CA.5644.

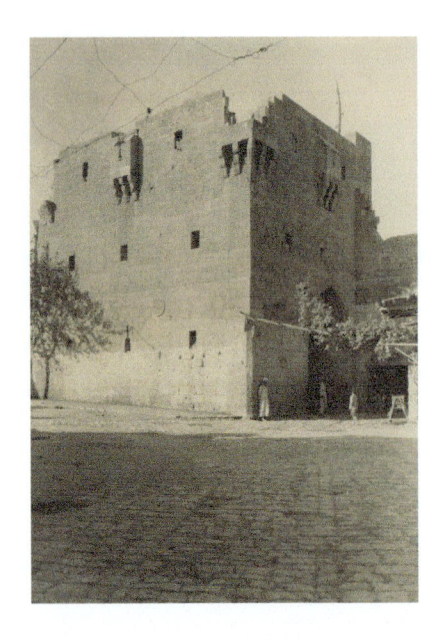

Figure: 297 (left).
Subject: Aleppo. The Bab al-Hadid.
Berenson ID: 134269.
Medium: gelatine silver print, 12×17cm.
Date of creation: 1919-1920.
Handwritten notes on the back: 'Aleppo, Bab al-Hadid' [Cres.].
Ashmolean negative: EA.CA.5643.

Figure: 298 (right).
Subject: Aleppo. The Great Mosque, seen from the minaret.
Berenson ID: 134242.
Medium: gelatine silver print, 12×17cm.
Date of creation: 1919-1920.
Handwritten notes on the back: 'Aleppo, The Great Mosque sahn from the minaret' [Cres.].
Ashmolean negative: EA.CA.5646.

Figure: 299.
Subject: Aleppo. The Great Mosque, looking north.
Berenson ID: 134241.
Medium: gelatine silver print, 12×17cm.
Date of creation: 1919-1920.
Handwritten notes on the back: 'Aleppo, The Great Mosque sahn looking N' [Cres.].
Ashmolean negative: EA.CA.5645.

Figure: 300 (left).
Subject: Aleppo. The minaret of the Great Mosque.
Berenson ID: 134243.
Medium: gelatine silver print, 12×17cm.
Date of creation: 1919-1920.
Handwritten notes on the back: 'Aleppo, The Great Mosque – minaret' [Cres.].
Ashmolean negative: EA.CA.5653.

Figure: 301 (right).
Subject: Aleppo. The minaret of the Great Mosque.
Berenson ID: 134244.
Medium: gelatine silver print, 12×17cm.
Date of creation: 1919-1920.
Handwritten notes on the back: 'Aleppo, The Great Mosque – minaret' [Cres.].
Ashmolean negative: EA.CA.5654.

THE SITES AND THE MONUMENTS – SYRIA

Figure: 302 (left).
Subject: Aleppo. The entrance to the sanctuary of the Great Mosque.
Berenson ID: 134245.
Medium: gelatine silver print, 12×17cm.
Date of creation: 1919-1920.
Handwritten notes on the back: 'Aleppo, The Great Mosque – entrance to sanctuary' [Cres.].
Ashmolean negative: EA.CA.5647.

Figure: 303 (centre).
Subject: Aleppo. Interior of the Great Mosque.
Berenson ID: 134246.
Medium: gelatine silver print, 12×17cm.
Date of creation: 1919-1920.
Handwritten notes on the back: 'Aleppo, The Great Mosque – interior' [Cres.].
Ashmolean negative: EA.CA.5648.

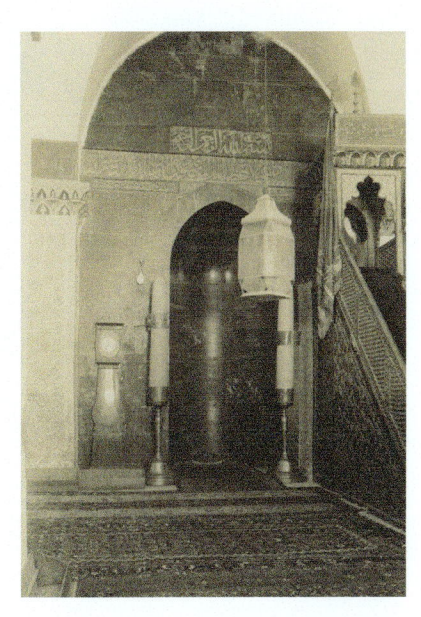

Figure: 304 (right).
Subject: Aleppo. Interior of the Great Mosque.
Berenson ID: 134247.
Medium: gelatine silver print, 12×17cm.
Date of creation: 1919-1920.
Handwritten notes on the back: 'Aleppo, The Great Mosque – interior' [Cres.].
Ashmolean negative: EA.CA.5649.

Figure: 305 (left).
Subject: Aleppo. The shrine of the Prophet Zakariya in the Great Mosque.
Berenson ID: 134248.
Medium: gelatine silver print, 12×17cm.
Date of creation: 1919-1920.
Handwritten notes on the back: 'Aleppo, The Great Mosque – shrine of Zakariyya' [Cres.].
Ashmolean negative: EA.CA.5650.

Figure: 306 (right).
Subject: Aleppo. Mihrab of the Great Mosque.
Berenson ID: 134249.
Medium: gelatine silver print, 12×17cm.
Date of creation: 1919-1920.
Handwritten notes on the back: 'Aleppo, The Great Mosque – mihrab' [Cres.].
Ashmolean negative: EA.CA.5651.

Figure: 307.
Subject: Aleppo. Tile panels of the Great Mosque.
Berenson ID: 134250.
Medium: gelatine silver print, 12×17cm.
Date of creation: 1919-1920.
Handwritten notes on the back: 'Aleppo, The Great Mosque – tile panels' [Cres.].
Ashmolean negative: EA.CA.5652.

Figure: 308.
Berenson ID: 134034.
Subject: Aleppo. The Mashhad al-Muhassin.
Medium: gelatine silver print, 12×17 cm.
Date of creation: 1919-1920.
Handwritten notes on the back: 'Aleppo, Mashhad of Sheykh Mohsin — 609 (1211/13)' [Cres.].
Ashmolean negative: EA.CA.5714.

Figure: 309 (left).
Berenson ID: 134037.
Subject: Aleppo. The entrance to the Mashhad al-Muhassin.
Medium: gelatine silver print, 12×17 cm.
Date of creation: 1919-1920.
Handwritten notes on the back: 'Aleppo, Mashhad of Sheyk Mohsin entrance — 609 (1211/3)' [Cres.].
Ashmolean negative: EA.CA.5715.

Figure: 310 (right).
Berenson ID: 134038.
Subject: Aleppo. Interior of the Mashhad al-Muhassin.
Medium: gelatine silver print, 12×17 cm.
Date of creation: 1919-1920.
Handwritten notes on the back: 'Aleppo, Mashhad of Sheykh Moshin – dome & pendentives — 609 (1211/13)' [Cres.].
Ashmolean negative: EA.CA.5718.

Figure: 311.
Berenson ID: 134302.
Subject: Aleppo. Interior of the Maqam Ibrahim fi al-Salihin.
Medium: gelatine silver print, 12×17 cm.
Date of creation: 1919-1920.
Handwritten notes on the back: 'Aleppo, as-Salihin – room behind mihrab' [Cres.].
Ashmolean negative: EA.CA.5823.

Figure: 312.
Berenson ID: 133992.
Subject: Aleppo. The al-Shuaybiya Mosque.
Medium: gelatine silver print, 12×17 cm.
Date of creation: 1919-1920.
Handwritten notes on the back: 'Aleppo, Jami ash-Shaibiyeh — 545 (1150)' [Cres.].
Ashmolean negative: EA.CA.5662.

Figure: 313.
Berenson ID: 133993.
Subject: Aleppo. The al-Shuaybiya Mosque.
Medium: gelatine silver print, 12×17 cm.
Date of creation: 1919-1920.
Handwritten notes on the back: 'Aleppo, Jami ash-Shaibiyeh — 545 (1150)' [Cres.].
Ashmolean negative: EA.CA.5663.

Figure: 314 (left).
Berenson ID: 133995.
Subject: Aleppo. The al-Shuaybiya Mosque.
Medium: gelatine silver print, 12×17 cm.
Date of creation: 1919-1920.
Handwritten notes on the back: 'Aleppo, Jami ash-Shaibiyeh — 545 (1150)' [Cres.].
Ashmolean negative: EA.CA.5664.

Figure: 315 (centre).
Berenson ID: 133994.
Subject: Aleppo. Detail of the masonry of the al-Shuaybiya Mosque.
Medium: gelatine silver print, 12×17 cm.
Date of creation: 1919-1920.
Handwritten notes on the back: Aleppo, 'Jami ash-Shaibiyeh — 545 (1150)' [Cres.].
Ashmolean negative: EA.CA.5666.

Figure: 316 (right).
Berenson ID: 134286.
Subject: Aleppo. The Nur al-Din Maristan.
Medium: gelatine silver print, 12×17 cm.
Date of creation: 1919-1920.
Handwritten notes on the back: 'Aleppo, Muristan of Nur ad-Din – interior looking N.' [Cres.].
Ashmolean negative: EA.CA.5675.

Figure: 317 (left).
Berenson ID: 134287.
Subject: Aleppo. The entrance to the Nur al-Din Maristan.
Medium: gelatine silver print, 12×17 cm.
Date of creation: 1919-1920.
Handwritten notes on the back: 'Aleppo, Muristan of Nur ad-Din – entrance' [Cres.].
Ashmolean negative: EA.CA.5672.

Figure: 318 (right).
Berenson ID: 134288.
Subject: Aleppo. Interior of the Nur al-Din Maristan.
Medium: gelatine silver print, 12×17 cm.
Date of creation: 1919-1920.
Handwritten notes on the back: 'Aleppo, Muristan of Nur ad-Din – entrance' [Cres.].
Ashmolean negative: EA.CA.5673.

The Sites and the Monuments – Syria

Figure: 319.
Subject: Aleppo. interior of the Nur al-Din Maristan.
Berenson ID: 134285.
Medium: gelatine silver print, 12×17cm.
Date of creation: 1919-1920.
Handwritten notes on the back: 'Aleppo, Muristan of Nur ad-Din – interior looking W' [Cres.].
Ashmolean negative: EA.CA.5674.

Figure: 320.
Subject: Aleppo. The al-Halawiya Madrasa.
Berenson ID: 134272.
Medium: gelatine silver print, 12×17cm.
Date of creation: 1919-1920.
Handwritten notes on the back: 'Aleppo, The Madrasa Halawiya' [Cres.].
Ashmolean negative: EA.CA.5658.

Figure: 321.
Subject: Aleppo. Interior of the al-Halawiya Madrasa.
Berenson ID: 134273.
Medium: gelatine silver print, 12×17cm.
Date of creation: 1919-1920.
Handwritten notes on the back: 'Aleppo, The Madrasa Halawiya –interior' [Cres.].
Ashmolean negative: EA.CA.5657.

Figure: 322.
Subject: Aleppo. Detail of the interior of the al-Halawiya Madrasa.
Berenson ID: 134270.
Medium: gelatine silver print, 12×17cm.
Date of creation: 1919-1920.
Handwritten notes on the back: 'Aleppo, The Madrasa Halawiya' [Cres.]. 'Jami el-Halawiyeh. Kindness Capt. Creswell. p. 232 photo 49' [Anon.].
Ashmolean negative: EA.CA.5655.

Figure: 323.
Subject: Aleppo. Mihrab of the al-Halawiya Madrasa.
Berenson ID: 134274.
Medium: gelatine silver print, 12×17cm.
Date of creation: 1919-1920.
Handwritten notes on the back: 'Aleppo, The Madrasa Halawiya – under mihrab in liwan' [Cres.].
Ashmolean negative: EA.CA.5659.

Figure: 324.
Subject: Aleppo. The al-Muqaddamiya Madrasa.
Berenson ID: 133999.
Medium: gelatine silver print, 12×17cm.
Date of creation: 1919-1920.
Handwritten notes on the back: 'Aleppo, Madrasa Khan at-Tulun – façade of sanctuary — 564 (1168/9)' [Cres.].

Figure: 325 (left).
Subject: Aleppo. Interior of the al-Muqaddamiya Madrasa.
Berenson ID: 134003.
Medium: gelatine silver print, 12×17cm.
Date of creation: 1919-1920.
Handwritten notes on the back: 'Aleppo, Madrasa Khan at-Tutun sanctuary — 564 (1168/9)' [Cres.].
Ashmolean negative: EA.CA.5670.

Figure: 326 (centre).
Subject: Aleppo. Entrance to the al-Muqaddamiya Madrasa.
Berenson ID: 134001.
Medium: gelatine silver print, 12×17cm.
Date of creation: 1919-1920.
Handwritten notes on the back: 'Aleppo, Madrasa Khan at-Tutun – entrance — 564 (1168/9)' [Cres.].
Ashmolean negative: EA.CA.5669.

Figure: 327 (right).
Subject: Aleppo. Mihrab of the al-Muqaddamiya Madrasa.
Berenson ID: 134000.
Medium: gelatine silver print, 12×17cm.
Date of creation: 1919-1920.
Handwritten notes on the back: 'Aleppo, Madrasa Khan at-Tutun – mihrab — 564 (1168/9)' [Cres.].
Ashmolean negative: EA.CA.5671.

Figure: 328.
Subject: Aleppo. The inner eastern side of the Mashhad al-Husayn.
Berenson ID: 134028.
Medium: gelatine silver print, 12×17cm.
Date of creation: 1919-1920.
Handwritten notes on the back: 'Aleppo, Mashhad of Huseyn – sahn – east side — 608 (1211/2)' [Cres.].
Ashmolean negative: EA.CA.5704.

Figure: 329.
Subject: Aleppo. The inner southern side of the Mashhad al-Husayn.
Berenson ID: 134029.
Medium: gelatine silver print, 12×17cm.
Date of creation: 1919-1920.
Handwritten notes on the back: 'Aleppo, Mashhad of Huseyn – sahn – south side — 608 (1211/2)' [Cres.].
Ashmolean negative: EA.CA.5705.

Figure: 330.
Subject: Aleppo. The sanctuary of the Mashhad al-Husayn.
Berenson ID: 134030.
Medium: gelatine silver print, 12×17cm.
Date of creation: 1919-1920.
Handwritten notes on the back: 'Aleppo, Mashhad of Huseyn – iwan on W side of sahn — 608 (1211/2)' [Cres.].

Figure: 331 (left).
Subject: Aleppo. The entrance to the Mashhad al-Husayn.
Berenson ID: 134025.
Medium: gelatine silver print, 12×17cm.
Date of creation: 1919-1920.
Handwritten notes on the back: 'Aleppo, Mashhad of Huseyn – entrance — 608 (1211/2)' [Cres.].
Ashmolean negative: EA.CA.5700.

Figure: 332 (right).
Berenson ID: 134027.
Subject: Aleppo. Detail of the entrance to the Mashhad al-Husayn.
Medium: gelatine silver print, 12×17 cm.
Date of creation: 1919-1920.
Handwritten notes on the back: 'Aleppo, Mashhad of Huseyn – vault of entrance bay — 608 (1211/2)' [Cres.].
Ashmolean negative: EA.CA.5703.

Figure: 333 (left).
Subject: Aleppo. Detail of the entrance to the Mashhad al-Husayn.
Berenson ID: 134026.
Medium: gelatine silver print, 12×17cm.
Date of creation: 1919-1920.
Handwritten notes on the back: 'Aleppo, Mashhad of Huseyn – entrance — 608 (1211/2)' [Cres.].

Figure: 334 (centre).
Subject: Aleppo. Detail of the entrance to the Mashhad al-Husayn.
Berenson ID: 134024.
Medium: gelatine silver print, 12×17cm.
Date of creation: 1919-1920.
Handwritten notes on the back: 'Aleppo, Mashhad of Huseyn – entrance — 608 (1211/2)' [Cres.].
Ashmolean negative: EA.CA.5701.

Figure: 335 (right).
Subject: Aleppo. Interior of the Mashhad al-Husayn.
Berenson ID: 134031.
Medium: gelatine silver print, 12×17cm.
Date of creation: 1919-1920.
Handwritten notes on the back: 'Aleppo, Mashhad of Huseyn – sanctuary — 608 (1211/2)' [Cres.].
Ashmolean negative: EA.CA.5706.

Figure: 336 (left).
Subject: Aleppo. Mihrab of the Mashhad al-Husayn.
Berenson ID: 134032.
Medium: gelatine silver print, 12×17cm.
Date of creation: 1919-1920.
Handwritten notes on the back: 'Aleppo, Mashhad of Huseyn – mihrab — 608 (1211/2)' [Cres.].
Ashmolean negative: EA.CA.5707.

Figure: 337 (right).
Subject: Aleppo. Dome of the Mashhad al-Husayn.
Berenson ID: 134035.
Medium: gelatine silver print, 12×17cm.
Date of creation: 1919-1920.
Handwritten notes on the back: 'Aleppo, Mashhad of Huseyn – dome to left of entrance — 608 (1211/2)' [Cres.].
Ashmolean negative: EA.CA.5708.

Figure: 338.
Subject: Aleppo. Interior of the Mashhad al-Husayn.
Berenson ID: 134033.
Medium: gelatine silver print, 12×17cm.
Date of creation: 1919-1920.
Handwritten notes on the back: 'Aleppo, Mashhad of Huseyn – pendentives of dome over mihrab — 608 (1211/2)' [Cres.].

Figure: 339.
Subject: The al-Firdaws Madrasa, looking southwest.
Berenson ID: 134063.
Medium: gelatine silver print, 12×17cm.
Date of creation: 1919-1920.
Handwritten notes on the back: 'Aleppo (Firdaus), Jami and Madrasa Firdaus – from the N/E — 633 (1235/6)' [Cres.]. 'Aleppo. Firusi Cemetery – p. 229 photo 46' [Anon.].
Ashmolean negative: EA.CA.5837.

Figure: 340.
Subject: The al-Firdaws Madrasa, looking northeast.
Berenson ID: 134064.
Medium: gelatine silver print, 12×17cm.
Date of creation: 1919-1920.
Handwritten notes on the back: 'Aleppo (Firdaus), Jami and Madrasa Firdaus – from the S/W — 633 (1235/6)' [Cres.].
Ashmolean negative: EA.CA.5844.

THE SITES AND THE MONUMENTS – SYRIA

Figure: 341.
Subject: The southern side of the al-Firdaws Madrasa.
Berenson ID: 134065.
Medium: gelatine silver print, 12×17cm.
Date of creation: 1919-1920.
Handwritten notes on the back: 'Aleppo (Firdaus), Jami and Madrasa Firdaus – S. side — 633 (1235/6)' [Cres.].
Ashmolean negative: EA.CA.5843.

Figure: 342.
Subject: The eastern side of the al-Firdaws Madrasa.
Berenson ID: 134066.
Medium: gelatine silver print, 12×17cm.
Date of creation: 1919-1920.
Handwritten notes on the back: 'Aleppo (Firdaus), Jami and Madrasa Firdaus – E side — 633 (1235/6)' [Cres.].
Ashmolean negative: EA.CA.5839.

Figure: 343.
Subject: The eastern side of the al-Firdaws Madrasa.
Berenson ID: 134070.
Medium: gelatine silver print, 12×17cm.
Date of creation: 1919-1920.
Handwritten notes on the back: 'Aleppo (Firdaus), Jami and Madrasa Firdaus – E. side — 633 (1235/6)' [Cres.].
Ashmolean negative: EA.CA.5840.

Figure: 344.
Subject: The courtyard of the al-Firdaws Madrasa.
Berenson ID: 134071.
Medium: gelatine silver print, 12×17cm.
Date of creation: 1919-1920.
Handwritten notes on the back: 'Aleppo (Firdaus), Jami and Madrasa Firdaus – sahn looking N/W — 633 (1235/6)' [Cres.].
Ashmolean negative: EA.CA.5850.

Figure: 345 (left).
Subject: The courtyard of the al-Firdaws Madrasa.
Berenson ID: 134139.
Medium: gelatine silver print, 12×17cm.
Date of creation: 1919-1920.
Handwritten notes on the back: 'Aleppo (Firdaus), Jami & Madrasa Firdaus – sahn – N. liwan — 633 (1235/6)' [Cres.].
Ashmolean negative: EA.CA.5851.

Figure: 346 (centre).
Subject: The courtyard of the al-Firdaws Madrasa.
Berenson ID: 134140.
Medium: gelatine silver print, 12×17cm.
Date of creation: 1919-1920.
Handwritten notes on the back: 'Aleppo (Firdaus), Jami & Madrasa Firdaus – sahn, S. side — 633 (1235/6)' [Cres.].
Ashmolean negative: EA.CA.5849.

Figure: 347 (right).
Subject: The courtyard of the al-Firdaws Madrasa.
Berenson ID: 134143.
Medium: gelatine silver print, 12×17cm.
Date of creation: 1919-1920.
Handwritten notes on the back: 'Aleppo (Firdaus), Jami & Madrasa Firdaus – sahn – E side — 633 (1235/6)' [Cres.].
Ashmolean negative: EA.CA.5847.

Figure: 348 (left).
Subject: Interior of the al-Firdaws Madrasa.
Berenson ID: 134146.
Medium: gelatine silver print, 12×17cm.
Date of creation: 1919-1920.
Handwritten notes on the back: 'Aleppo (Firdaus), Jami & Madrasa Firdaus – sanctuary — 633 (1235/6)' [Cres.].
Ashmolean negative: EA.CA.5846.

Figure: 349 (centre).
Subject: Interior of the al-Firdaws Madrasa.
Berenson ID: 134147.
Medium: gelatine silver print, 12×17cm.
Date of creation: 1919-1920.
Handwritten notes on the back: 'Aleppo (Firdaus), Jami & Madrasa Firdaus – hall on W. side of sahn — 633 (1235/6)' [Cres.].
Ashmolean negative: EA.CA.5857.

Figure: 350 (right).
Subject: mihrab of the al-Firdaws Madrasa.
Berenson ID: 134148.
Medium: gelatine silver print, 12×17cm.
Date of creation: 1919-1920.
Handwritten notes on the back: 'Aleppo (Firdaus), Jami & Madrasa Firdaus – mihrab — 633 (1235/6)' [Cres.].
Ashmolean negative: EA.CA.5856.

Figure: 351.
Subject: Aleppo. The façade of the al-Shadhbakhtiya Madrasa.
Berenson ID: 134002.
Medium: gelatine silver print, 12×17cm.
Date of creation: 1919-1920.
Handwritten notes on the back: 'Aleppo, Madrasa of Shad Bakhr – façade of sanctuary — 589 (1193)' [Cres.].
Ashmolean negative: EA.CA.5679.

Figure: 352.
Subject: Aleppo. The northern iwan of the al-Shadhbakhtiya Madrasa.
Berenson ID: 134008.
Medium: gelatine silver print, 12×17cm.
Date of creation: 1919-1920.
Handwritten notes on the back: 'Aleppo, Madrasa of Shad Bakhr – N. liwan — 589 (1193)' [Cres.].
Ashmolean negative: EA.CA.5678.

Figure: 353 (left).
Subject: Aleppo. The al-Shadhbakhtiya Madrasa.
Berenson ID: 134004.
Medium: gelatine silver print, 12×17cm.
Date of creation: 1919-1920.
Handwritten notes on the back: 'Madrasa of Shad Bakhr – entrance — 589 (1193)' [Cres.].

Figure: 354 (centre).
Subject: Aleppo. The inner side of the entrance to the al-Shadhbakhtiya Madrasa.
Berenson ID: 134005.
Medium: gelatine silver print, 12×17cm.
Date of creation: 1919-1920.
Handwritten notes on the back: 'Aleppo, Madrasa of Shad Bakhr – inner side of entrance — 589 (1193)' [Cres.].
Ashmolean negative: EA.CA.5677.

Figure: 355 (right).
Subject: Aleppo. Dome of the al-Shadhbakhtiya Madrasa.
Berenson ID: 134007.
Medium: gelatine silver print, 12×17cm.
Date of creation: 1919-1920.
Handwritten notes on the back: 'Aleppo, Madrasa of Shad Bakhr – dome and pendentives — 589 (1193)' [Cres.].
Ashmolean negative: EA.CA.7984.

Figure: 356.
Subject: Aleppo. Mihrab of the a-Shadhbakhtiya Madrasa.
Berenson ID: 134006.
Medium: gelatine silver print, 12×17cm.
Date of creation: 1919-1920.
Handwritten notes on the back: 'Aleppo, Madrasa of Shad Bakhr – mihrab — 589 (1193)' [Cres.].
Ashmolean negative: EA.CA.5676.

Figure: 357.
Subject: Aleppo. The al-Sultaniya Madrasa.
Berenson ID: 134054.
Medium: gelatine silver print, 12×17cm.
Date of creation: 1919-1920.
Handwritten notes on the back: 'Aleppo, Madrasa as-Sultaniya — 620 (1223)' [Cres.].
Ashmolean negative: EA.CA.5721.

Figure: 358.
Subject: Aleppo. The al-Sultaniya Madrasa.
Berenson ID: 134055.
Medium: gelatine silver print, 12×17cm.
Date of creation: 1919-1920.
Handwritten notes on the back: 'Aleppo, Madrasat as-Sultaniya – N. side — 620 (1223)' [Cres.].
Ashmolean negative: EA.CA.5722.

Mesopotamia, Syria and Transjordan in the Creswell Collection

Figure: 359.
Subject: Aleppo. The entrance to the al-Sultaniya Madrasa.
Berenson ID: 134056.
Medium: gelatine silver print, 12×17cm.
Date of creation: 1919-1920.
Handwritten notes on the back: 'Aleppo, Madrasa as-Sultaniya – inner side of entrance — 620 (1223)' [Cres.].
Ashmolean negative: EA.CA.5723.

Figure: 360.
Subject: Aleppo. The entrance to the al-Sultaniya Madrasa.
Berenson ID: 134057.
Medium: gelatine silver print, 12×17cm.
Date of creation: 1919-1920.
Handwritten notes on the back: 'Aleppo, Madrasa as-Sultaniya – entrance — 620 (1223)' [Cres.].
Ashmolean negative: EA.CA.5724.

Figure: 361.
Subject: Aleppo. The façade of the sanctuary of the al-Sultaniya Madrasa.
Berenson ID: 134058.
Medium: gelatine silver print, 12×17cm.
Date of creation: 1919-1920.
Handwritten notes on the back: 'Aleppo, Madrasa as-Sultaniya – façade of sanctuary — 620 (1223)' [Cres.].

THE SITES AND THE MONUMENTS – SYRIA

Figure: 362.
Subject: Aleppo. The mihrab of the al-Sultaniya Madrasa.
Berenson ID: 134060.
Medium: gelatine silver print, 12×17cm.
Date of creation: 1919-1920.
Handwritten notes on the back: 'Aleppo, Madrasa as-Sultaniya – mihrab — 620 (1223)' [Cres.].

Figure: 363.
Subject: Aleppo. The al-Kamiliya Madrasa.
Berenson ID: 134275.
Medium: gelatine silver print, 12×17cm.
Date of creation: 1919-1920.
Handwritten notes on the back: 'Aleppo (Firdaus) – Madrasa Kamiliya – from the N/W' [Cres.].
Ashmolean negative: EA.CA.5865.

Figure: 364.
Subject: Aleppo. The al-Kamiliya Madrasa.
Berenson ID: 134278.
Medium: gelatine silver print, 12×17cm.
Date of creation: 1919-1920.
Handwritten notes on the back: 'Aleppo (Firdaus)– Madrasa Kamiliya – façade of sanctuary' [Cres.].
Ashmolean negative: EA.CA.5868.

Figure: 365.
Subject: Aleppo. The entrance to the al-Kamiliya Madrasa.
Berenson ID: 134276.
Medium: gelatine silver print, 12×17cm.
Date of creation: 1919-1920.
Handwritten notes on the back: 'Aleppo (Firdaus) – Madrasa Kamiliya – entrance' [Cres.].
Ashmolean negative: EA.CA.5866.

Figure: 366.
Subject: Aleppo. The courtyard of the al-Kamiliya Madrasa.
Berenson ID: 134280.
Medium: gelatine silver print, 12×17cm.
Date of creation: 1919-1920.
Handwritten notes on the back: 'Aleppo (Firdaus) – Madrasa Kamiliya – sahn looking W' [Cres.]
Ashmolean negative: EA.CA.5870.

Figure: 367 (left).
Subject: Aleppo. The interior of the al-Kamiliya Madrasa.
Berenson ID: 134282.
Medium: gelatine silver print, 12×17cm.
Date of creation: 1919-1920.
Handwritten notes on the back: 'Aleppo (Firdaus)– Madrasa Kamiliya – sanctuary looking E' [Cres.]
Ashmolean negative: EA.CA.5872.

Figure: 368 (right).
Subject: Aleppo. Mihrab of the al-Kamiliya Madrasa.
Berenson ID: 134283.
Medium: gelatine silver print, 12×17cm.
Date of creation: 1919-1920.
Handwritten notes on the back: 'Aleppo (Firdaus)– Madrasa Kamiliya – mihrab' [Cres.].
Ashmolean negative: EA.CA.5873.

THE SITES AND THE MONUMENTS – SYRIA

Figure: 369 (left).
Subject: Aleppo. The entrance to the al-Karimiya Mosque.
Berenson ID: 134168.
Medium: gelatine silver print, 12×17cm.
Date of creation: 1919-1920. Handwritten notes on the back: 'Aleppo, Jami al-Karimiya — 654 (1256).
Ashmolean negative: EA.CA.5745.

Figure: 370 (centre).
Subject: Aleppo. The courtyard of the al-Sharafiya Madrasa.
Berenson ID: 134158.
Medium: gelatine silver print, 12×17cm.
Date of creation: 1919-1920.
Handwritten notes on the back: 'Aleppo, Madrasa Sharafiya – sahn S. side — c. 640 (1242/3)' [Cres.].
Ashmolean negative: EA.CA.5741.

Figure: 371 (right).
Subject: Aleppo. The entrance to the al-Sharafiya Madrasa.
Berenson ID: 134157.
Medium: gelatine silver print, 12×17cm.
Date of creation: 1919-1920.
Handwritten notes on the back: 'Aleppo, Madrasa Sharafiya – entrance — c. 640 (1242/3)' [Cres.].
Ashmolean negative: EA.CA.5735.

Figure: 372.
Subject: Aleppo. The nortwestern corner of the courtyard of the al-Sharafiya Madrasa.
Berenson ID: 134159.
Medium: gelatine silver print, 12×17cm.
Date of creation: 1919-1920.
Handwritten notes on the back: 'Aleppo, Madrasa Sharafiya – sahn – N/W corner — c. 640 (1242/3)' [Cres.].
Ashmolean negative: EA.CA.5738.

Figure: 373.
Subject: Aleppo. The nortwestern corner of the courtyard of the al-Sharafiya Madrasa.
Berenson ID: 134160.
Medium: gelatine silver print, 12×17cm.
Date of creation: 1919-1920.
Handwritten notes on the back: 'Aleppo, Madrasa Sharafiya – sahn – N/E corner — c. 640 (1242/3)' [Cres.].
Ashmolean negative: EA.CA.5740.

Figure: 374.
Subject: Aleppo. The eastern side of the courtyard of the al-Sharafiya Madrasa.
Berenson ID: 134162.
Medium: gelatine silver print, 12×17cm.
Date of creation: 1919-1920.
Handwritten notes on the back: 'Aleppo, Madrasa Sharafiya – sahn east side — c. 640 (1242/3)' [Cres.].
Ashmolean negative: EA.CA.5739.

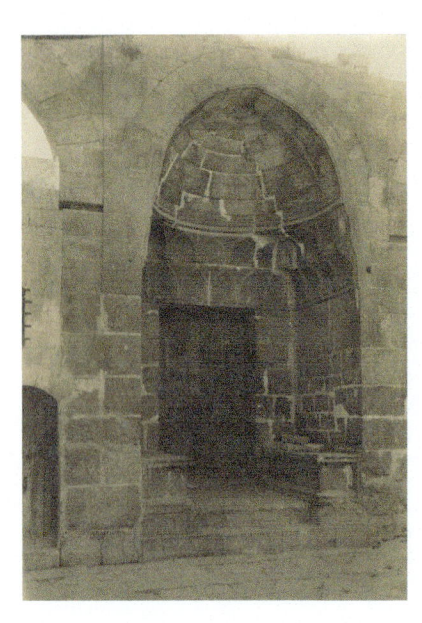

Figure: 375.
Subject: Aleppo. The inner side of the entrance to the al-Sharafiya Madrasa.
Berenson ID: 134163.
Medium: gelatine silver print, 12×17cm.
Date of creation: 1919-1920.
Handwritten notes on the back: 'Aleppo, Madrasa Sharafiya – inner side of entrance — c. 640 (1242/3)' [Cres.].
Ashmolean negative: EA.CA.5736.

The Sites and the Monuments – Syria

Figure: 376 (left).
Subject: Aleppo. Muqarnas in the al-Sharafiya Madrasa.
Berenson ID: 134165.
Medium: gelatine silver print, 12×17cm.
Date of creation: 1919-1920.
Handwritten notes on the back: 'Aleppo, Madrasa Sharafiya – dome over mihrab — c. 640 (1242/3)' [Cres.].
Ashmolean negative: EA.CA.5737.

Figure: 377 (right).
Subject: Aleppo. Mihrab of the al-Sharafiya Madrasa.
Berenson ID: 134166.
Medium: gelatine silver print, 12×17cm.
Date of creation: 1919-1920.
Handwritten notes on the back: 'Aleppo, Madrasa Sharafiya – mihrab — c. 640 (1242/3)' [Cres.].
Ashmolean negative: EA.CA.5743.

Figure: 378.
Subject: Aleppo. The courtyard of the al-Zahiriya Madrasa.
Berenson ID: 134040.
Medium: gelatine silver print, 12×17cm.
Date of creation: 1919-1920.
Handwritten notes on the back: 'Aleppo (Firdaus), Madrasa of Malik az-Zahir – façade of sanctuary — 613 (1216/7)' [Cres.].

Figure: 379.
Subject: Aleppo. The courtyard of the al-Zahiriya Madrasa.
Berenson ID: 134043.
Medium: gelatine silver print, 12×17cm.
Date of creation: 1919-1920.
Handwritten notes on the back: 'Aleppo (Firdaus) Madrasa of Malik az-Zahir – façade of sanctuary — 613 (1216/7)' [Cres.].
Ashmolean negative: EA.CA.5834.

Figure: 380.
Subject: Aleppo. The courtyard of the al-Zahiriya Madrasa.
Berenson ID: 134044.
Medium: gelatine silver print, 12×17cm.
Date of creation: 1919-1920.
Handwritten notes on the back: 'Aleppo (Firdaus) Madrasa of Malik az-Zahir capital of column — 613 (1216/7)' [Cres.].
Ashmolean negative: EA.CA.5830.

Figure: 381.
Subject: Aleppo. The courtyard of the al-Zahiriya Madrasa.
Berenson ID: 134042.
Medium: gelatine silver print, 12×17cm.
Date of creation: 1919-1920.
Handwritten notes on the back: 'Aleppo (Firdaus) Madrasa of Malik az-Zahir – S/E corner — 613 (1216/7)' [Cres.].
Ashmolean negative: EA.CA.5829.

Figure: 382.
Subject: Aleppo. The entrance to the al-Zahiriya Madrasa.
Berenson ID: 134049.
Medium: gelatine silver print, 12×17cm.
Date of creation: 1919-1920.
Handwritten notes on the back: 'Aleppo (Firdaus) Madrasa of Malik az-Zahir entrance — 613 (1216/7)' [Cres.].

The Sites and the Monuments – Syria

Figure: 383.
Subject: Aleppo. Detail of the entrance to the al-Zahiriya Madrasa.
Berenson ID: 134046.
Medium: gelatine silver print, 12×17cm.
Date of creation: 1919-1920.
Handwritten notes on the back: 'Aleppo (Firdaus) Madrasa of Malik az-Zahir – vault of entrance bay — 613 (1216/7)' [Cres.].
Ashmolean negative: EA.CA.5824.

Figure: 384.
Subject: Aleppo. The courtyard of the al-Zahiriya Madrasa.
Berenson ID: 134048.
Medium: gelatine silver print, 12×17cm.
Date of creation: 1919-1920.
Handwritten notes on the back: 'Aleppo (Firdaus) Madrasa of Malik az-Zahir – E liwan — 613 (1216/7)' [Cres.].
Ashmolean negative: EA.CA.5825.

Figure: 385.
Subject: Aleppo. The courtyard of the al-Zahiriya Madrasa.
Berenson ID: 134050.
Medium: gelatine silver print, 12×17cm.
Date of creation: 1919-1920.
Handwritten notes on the back: 'Aleppo (Firdaus) Madrasa of Malik az-Zahir – N/W corner — 613 (1216/7)' [Cres.].
Ashmolean negative: EA.CA.5833.

Figure: 386.
Berenson ID: 134151.
Subject: Aleppo. The façade of the sanctuary of the Khanqah al-Farafra.
Medium: gelatine silver print, 12×17 cm.
Date of creation: 1919-1920.
Handwritten notes on the back: 'Aleppo, Ribat Khanqan – façade of sanctuary — 635 (1237/8)' [Cres.].
Ashmolean negative: EA.CA.5730.

Figure: 387 (left).
Berenson ID: 134155.
Subject: Aleppo. Mihrab of the Khanqah al-Farafra.
Medium: gelatine silver print, 12×17 cm.
Date of creation: 1919-1920.
Handwritten notes on the back: 'Aleppo, Ribat Khanqan – mihrab — 635 (1237/8)' [Cres.].
Ashmolean negative: EA.CA.5732.

Figure: 388 (right).
Berenson ID: 134156.
Subject: Aleppo. Interior of the Khanqah al-Farafra.
Medium: gelatine silver print, 12×17 cm.
Date of creation: 1919-1920.
Handwritten notes on the back: 'Aleppo, Ribat Khanqan – pendentives — 635 (1237/8)' [Cres.].
Ashmolean negative: EA.CA.5731.

Figure: 389.
Berenson ID: 134061.
Subject: Aleppo. The Umm Malik al-Afdal Mausoleum.
Medium: gelatine silver print, 12×17 cm.
Date of creation: 1919-1920.
Handwritten notes on the back: 'Aleppo (Firdaus) Darwishiya Mausoleum — 621 (1220)' [Cres.].
Ashmolean negative: EA.CA.5835.

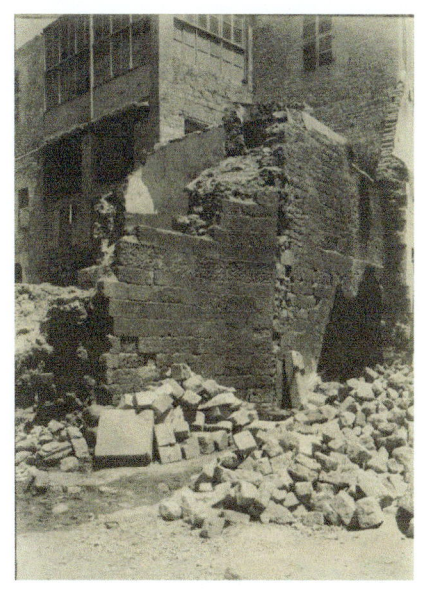

Figure: 390 (left).
Berenson ID: 134062.
Subject: Aleppo. Interior of the Umm Malik al-Afdal Mausoleum.
Medium: gelatine silver print, 12×17 cm.
Date of creation: 1919-1920.
Handwritten notes on the back: 'Aleppo (Firdaus) Darwishiya Mausoleum – interior — 621 (1220)' [Cres.].

Figure: 391 (centre).
Berenson ID: 134167.
Subject: Aleppo. The ruins of the Masjid Yusuf.
Medium: gelatine silver print, 12×17 cm.
Date of creation: 1919-1920.
Handwritten notes on the back: 'Masjid of Jusuf bin Muhammmad ibn al-Malik az-Zahr — 658 (1260)' [Cres.].
Ashmolean negative: EA.CA.5733.

Figure: 392 (right).
Berenson ID: 134303.
Subject: Aleppo. The ruins of the Masjid Yusuf.
Medium: gelatine silver print, 12×17 cm.
Date of creation: 1919-1920.
Handwritten notes on the back: 'Aleppo, Masjid of Yusuf ibn Muhammad ibn Malik az-Zahn – fragment' [Cres.].
Ashmolean negative: EA.CA.5734.

Figure: 393.
Berenson ID: 134208.
Subject: Aleppo. The al-Atrush Mosque.
Medium: gelatine silver print, 12×17 cm.
Date of creation: 1919-1920 .
Handwritten notes on the back: 'Aleppo, Jami al-Atrush — 801/12 (1398/1409)' [Cres.].
Ashmolean negative: EA.CA.5780.

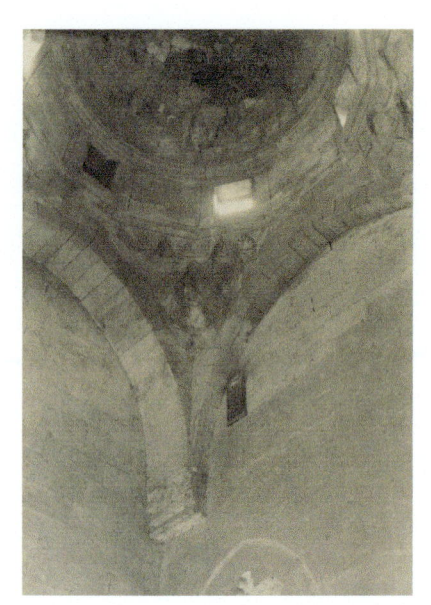

Figure: 394 (left).
Berenson ID: 134209.
Subject: Aleppo. The northern entrance to the al-Atrush Mosque.
Medium: gelatine silver print, 12×17 cm.
Date of creation: 1919-1920.
Handwritten notes on the back: 'Aleppo, Jami al-Atrush – N. entrance — 801/12 (1398/1409)' [Cres.].
Ashmolean negative: EA.CA.5781.

Figure: 395 (centre).
Berenson ID: 134210.
Subject: Aleppo. The courtyard of the al-Atrush Mosque.
Medium: gelatine silver print, 12×17 cm.
Date of creation: 1919-1920.
Handwritten notes on the back: 'Aleppo, Jami al-Atrush – sahn west side — 801/12 (1398/1409)' [Cres.].
Ashmolean negative: EA.CA.5783.

Figure: 396 (right).
Berenson ID: 134212.
Subject: Aleppo. Interior of the al-Atrush Mosque.
Medium: gelatine silver print, 12×17 cm.
Date of creation: 1919-1920.
Handwritten notes on the back: 'Aleppo, Jami al-Atrush – pendentives of mausoleum — 801/12 (1398/1409)' [Cres.].
Ashmolean negative: EA.CA.5785.

Figure: 397.
Berenson ID: 134213.
Subject: Aleppo. A fallen capital of the al-Atrush Mosque.
Medium: gelatine silver print, 12×17 cm.
Date of creation: 1919-1920.
Handwritten notes on the back: 'Aleppo, Jami al-Atrush – fallen capital — 801/12 (1398/1409)' [Cres.].
Ashmolean negative: EA.CA.5784.

THE SITES AND THE MONUMENTS – SYRIA

Figure: 398.
Berenson ID: 134171.
Subject: Aleppo. The façade of the al-Bayada Mosque.
Medium: gelatine silver print, 12×17 cm.
Date of creation: 1919-1920.
Handwritten notes on the back: 'Aleppo, Jami al-Bayada – façade — 710 (1310)' [Cres.].
Ashmolean negative: EA.CA.5747.

Figure: 399.
Berenson ID: 134172.
Subject: Aleppo. The entrance to the al-Bayada Mosque.
Medium: gelatine silver print, 12×17 cm.
Date of creation: 1919-1920.
Handwritten notes on the back: 'Aleppo, Jami al-Bayada – entrance — 710 (1310)' [Cres.].
Ashmolean negative: EA.CA.5748.

Figure: 400.
Berenson ID: 134169.
Subject: Aleppo. The al-Maqam Mosque.
Medium: gelatine silver print, 12×17 cm.
Date of creation: 1919-1920.
Handwritten notes on the back: 'Aleppo (Firdaus) Jami al-Maqamat — 703 (1303)' [Cres.].
Ashmolean negative: EA.CA.5860.

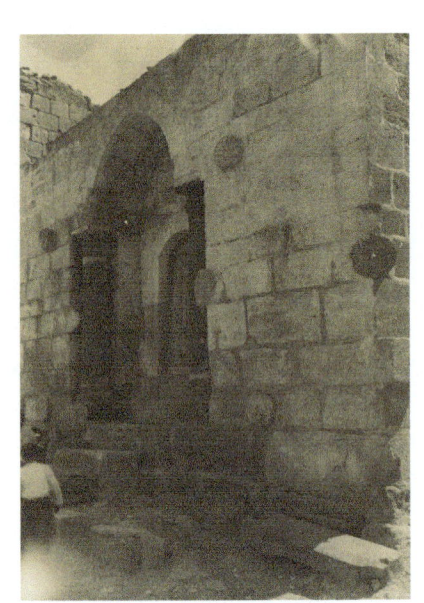

Figure: 401 (left).
Berenson ID: 134170.
Subject: Aleppo. A blazon on a a wall of the al-Maqam Mosque.
Medium: gelatine silver print, 12×17 cm.
Date of creation: 1919-1920.
Handwritten notes on the back: Aleppo (Firdaus) Qatal Maqamat blazon of polo master — 703 (1303)' [Cres.].
Ashmolean negative: EA.CA.5861.

Figure: 402 (centre).
Berenson ID: 134301.
Subject: Aleppo. The façade of the al-Qadi al-Mahmandar Mosque.
Medium: gelatine silver print, 12×17 cm.
Date of creation: 1919-1920.
Handwritten notes on the back: 'Aleppo, Jami al-Qady – façade of sanctuary' [Cres.].
Ashmolean negative: EA.CA.5746.

Figure: 403 (right).
Berenson ID: 134293.
Subject: Aleppo. The entrance to the al-Qiqan Mosque.
Medium: gelatine silver print, 12×17 cm.
Date of creation: 1919-1920.
Handwritten notes on the back: 'Aleppo, Mosque of Qiqan' [Cres.].
Ashmolean negative: EA.CA.5660.

Figure: 404 (left).
Berenson ID: 134294.
Subject: Aleppo. Interior of the al-Qiqan Mosque.
Medium: gelatine silver print, 12×17 cm.
Date of creation: 1919-1920.
Handwritten notes on the back: 'Aleppo, Mosque of Qiqan – interior' [Cres.].
Ashmolean negative: EA.CA.5661.

Figure: 405 (right).
Berenson ID: 134202.
Subject: Aleppo. The entrance to the al-Rumi Mosque.
Medium: gelatine silver print, 12×17 cm.
Date of creation: 1919-1920.
Handwritten notes on the back: 'Aleppo, Jami Manglybugha – entrance — 767 (1365/6)' [Cres.].
Ashmolean negative: EA.CA.5775.

Figure: 406.
Berenson ID: 134203.
Subject: Aleppo. The minaret of the al-Rumi Mosque.
Medium: gelatine silver print, 12×17 cm.
Date of creation: 1919-1920.
Handwritten notes on the back: 'Aleppo, Jami Manglybugha – minaret — 767 (1365/6)' [Cres.].
Ashmolean negative: EA.CA.5774.

Figure: 407.
Berenson ID: 134204.
Subject: Aleppo. The courtyard of the al-Rumi Mosque.
Medium: gelatine silver print, 12×17 cm.
Date of creation: 1919-1920.
Handwritten notes on the back: 'Aleppo, Jami Manglybugha – sahn – east side — 767 (1365/6)' [Cres.].
Ashmolean negative: EA.CA.5777.

Figure: 408 (left).
Berenson ID: 134205.
Subject: Aleppo. Muqarnas in the al-Rumi Mosque.
Medium: gelatine silver print, 12×17 cm.
Date of creation: 1919-1920.
Handwritten notes on the back: 'Aleppo, Jami Manglybagha – top of L side entrance — 767 (1365/6)' [Cres.].
Date of creation: 1919-1920.
Ashmolean negative: EA.CA.5776.

Figure: 409 (right).
Berenson ID: 134216.
Subject: Aleppo. The entrance to the al-Safahiya Mosque.
Medium: gelatine silver print, 12×17 cm.
Date of creation: 1919-1920.
Handwritten notes on the back: 'Aleppo, Jami as-Safahiya – entrance — 828 (1424/5)' [Cres.].
Ashmolean negative: EA.CA.5787.

Figure: 410.
Berenson ID: 134217.
Subject: Aleppo. The al-Safahiya Mosque.
Medium: gelatine silver print, 12×17 cm.
Date of creation: 1919-1920.
Handwritten notes on the back: 'Aleppo, Jami as-Safahiya — 828 (1424/5)' [Cres.].
Ashmolean negative: EA.CA.5786.

Figure: 411.
Berenson ID: 134218.
Subject: Aleppo. The mihrab of the al-Safahiya Mosque.
Medium: gelatine silver print, 12×17 cm.
Date of creation: 1919-1920.
Handwritten notes on the back: 'Aleppo, Jami as-Safahiya – interior — 828 (1424/5)' [Cres.].
Ashmolean negative: EA.CA.5788.

Figure: 412.
Berenson ID: 134184.
Subject: Aleppo. The al-Sahibiya Madrasa.
Medium: gelatine silver print, 12×17 cm.
Date of creation: 1919-1920.
Handwritten notes on the back: 'Aleppo – Zawriyat as-Sahibiya — 750 (1349)' [Cres.].
Ashmolean negative: EA.CA.5764.

THE SITES AND THE MONUMENTS – SYRIA

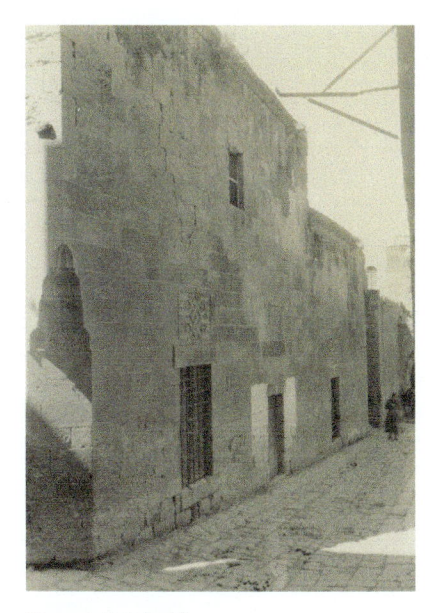

Figure: 413 (left).
Berenson ID: 134185.
Subject: Aleppo. The al-Sahibiya Madrasa.
Medium: gelatine silver print, 12×17 cm.
Date of creation: 1919-1920.
Handwritten notes on the back: 'Aleppo – Zawriyat as-Sahibiya – facade — 750 (1349)' [Cres.].
Ashmolean negative: EA.CA.5760.

Figure: 414 (centre).
Berenson ID: 134186.
Subject: Aleppo. Mihrab of the al-Sahibiya Madrasa.
Medium: gelatine silver print, 12×17 cm.
Date of creation: 1919-1920.
Handwritten notes on the back: 'Aleppo – Zawriyat as-Sahibiya – mihrab under small dome — 750 (1349)' [Cres.].
Ashmolean negative: EA.CA.5762.

Figure: 415 (right).
Berenson ID: 134187.
Subject: Aleppo. Mihrab of the al-Sahibiya Madrasa.
Medium: gelatine silver print, 12×17 cm.
Date of creation: 1919-1920.
Handwritten notes on the back: 'Aleppo – Zawriyat as-Sahibiya – mihrab under large dome — 750 (1349)' [Cres.].
Ashmolean negative: EA.CA.5763.

Figure: 416.
Berenson ID: 134188.
Subject: Aleppo. The entrance to the al-Sahibiya Madrasa.
Medium: gelatine silver print, 12×17 cm.
Date of creation: 1919-1920.
Handwritten notes on the back: 'Aleppo – Zawriyat as-Sahibiya – entrance bay — 750 (1349)' [Cres.].
Ashmolean negative: EA.CA.5761.

Figure: 417.
Berenson ID: 134230.
Subject: Aleppo. The al-Tawashy Mosque.
Medium: gelatine silver print, 12×17 cm.
Date of creation: 1919-1920.
Handwritten notes on the back: 'Aleppo, Jami al-Jawashy — 944 (1537/8)' [Cres.].
Ashmolean negative: EA.CA.5801.

Figure: 418 (left).
Berenson ID: 134231.
Subject: Aleppo. The antrance to the al-Tawashy Mosque.
Medium: gelatine silver print, 12×17 cm.
Date of creation: 1919-1920.
Handwritten notes on the back: 'Aleppo, Jami al-Jawashy – entrance — 944 (1537/8)' [Cres.].
Ashmolean negative: EA.CA.5802.

Figure: 419 (right).
Berenson ID: 134219.
Subject: Aleppo. The northern entrance to the al-Zaki Mosque.
Medium: gelatine silver print, 12×17 cm.
Date of creation: 1919-1920.
Handwritten notes on the back: 'Aleppo, Jami az-Zaky – Northern entrance — 893 (1487/8)' [Cres.].
Ashmolean negative: EA.CA.5790.

Figure: 420.
Berenson ID: 134173.
Subject: Aleppo. The Altunbugha Mosque.
Medium: gelatine silver print, 12×17 cm.
Date of creation: 1919-1920.
Handwritten notes on the back: 'Aleppo, Jami Altunbugha — 718 (1318)' [Cres.].
Ashmolean negative: EA.CA.5749.

THE SITES AND THE MONUMENTS – SYRIA

Figure: 421 (left).
Berenson ID: 134176.
Subject: Aleppo. The courtyard of the Altunbugha Mosque.
Medium: gelatine silver print, 12×17 cm.
Date of creation: 1919-1920.
Handwritten notes on the back: 'Aleppo, Jami Altunbugha – entrance — 718 (1318)' [Cres.].
Ashmolean negative: EA.CA.5750.

Figure: 422 (centre).
Berenson ID: 134175.
Subject: Aleppo. The courtyard of the Altunbugha Mosque.
Medium: gelatine silver print, 12×17 cm.
Date of creation: 1919-1920.
Handwritten notes on the back: 'Aleppo, Jami Altunbugha – sahn N/W corner — 718 (1318)' [Cres.].
Ashmolean negative: EA.CA.5753.

Figure: 423 (right)
Berenson ID: 134178.
Subject: Aleppo. Interior of the Altunbugha Mosque.
Medium: gelatine silver print, 12×17 cm.
Date of creation: 1919-1920.
Handwritten notes on the back: 'Aleppo, Jami Altunbugha – sanctuary — 718 (1318)' [Cres.].
Ashmolean negative: EA.CA.5754.

Figure: 424 (left).
Berenson ID: 134177.
Subject: Aleppo. Mihrab of the Altunbugha Mosque.
Medium: gelatine silver print, 12×17 cm.
Date of creation: 1919-1920.
Handwritten notes on the back: 'Aleppo, Jami Altunbugha – mihrab — 718 (1318)' [Cres.].
Ashmolean negative: EA.CA.5756.

Figure: 425 (right).
Berenson ID: 134179.
Subject: Aleppo. Entrance passage in the Altunbugha Mosque.
Medium: gelatine silver print, 12×17 cm.
Date of creation: 1919-1920.
Handwritten notes on the back: 'Aleppo, Jami Altunbugha – entrance passage — 718 (1318)' [Cres.].
Ashmolean negative: EA.CA.5752.

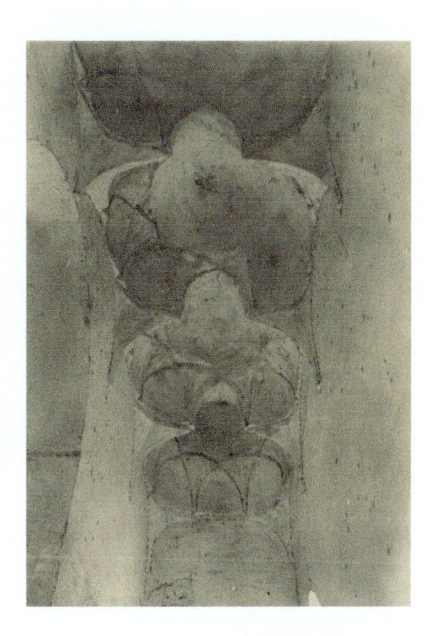

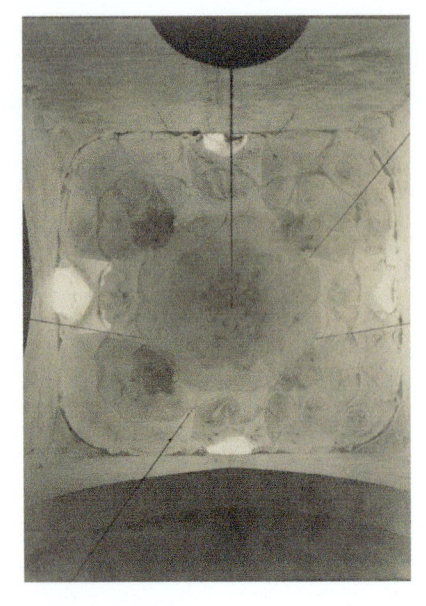

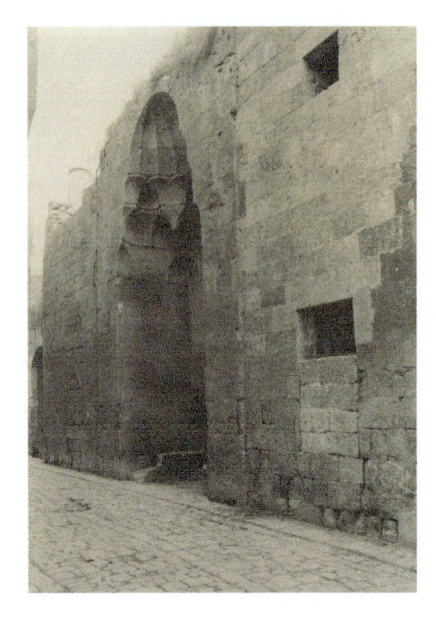

Figure: 426 (left).
Berenson ID: 134180.
Subject: Aleppo. Dome in the Altunbugha Mosque.
Medium: gelatine silver print, 12×17 cm.
Date of creation: 1919-1920.
Handwritten notes on the back: 'Aleppo, Jami Altunbugha – dome over mihrab — 718 (1318)' [Cres.].
Ashmolean negative: EA.CA.5755.

Figure: 427 (centre).
Berenson ID: 134193.
Subject: Aleppo. The entrance to the Arghun al-Kamili Bimaristan.
Medium: gelatine silver print, 12×17 cm.
Date of creation: 1919-1920.
Handwritten notes on the back: 'Aleppo, Munistan of Anghun Kamily – façade — 755 (1354)' [Cres.].
Ashmolean negative: EA.CA.5766.

Figure: 428 (right).
Berenson ID: 134192.
Subject: Aleppo. The entrance to the Arghun al-Kamili Bimaristan.
Medium: gelatine silver print, 12×17 cm.
Date of creation: 1919-1920.
Handwritten notes on the back: 'Aleppo, Munistan of Anghun Kamily – entrance — 755 (1354)' [Cres.].
Ashmolean negative: EA.CA.5767.

Figure: 429 (left).
Berenson ID: 134195.
Subject: Aleppo. Muqarnas of the Arghun al-Kamili Bimaristan.
Medium: gelatine silver print, 12×17 cm.
Date of creation: 1919-1920.
Handwritten notes on the back: Aleppo, Munistan [?] of Arghun Kamily – vault of entrance bay — 755 (1354)' [Cres.].
Ashmolean negative: EA.CA.5765.

Figure: 430 (right).
Berenson ID: 134194.
Subject: Aleppo. Vault at the entrance to the Arghun al-Kamili Bimaristan.
Medium: gelatine silver print, 12×17 cm.
Date of creation: 1919-1920.
Handwritten notes on the back: Aleppo, Munistan [?] of Arghun Kamily – vault of vestibule — 755 (1354)' [Cres.].
Ashmolean negative: EA.CA.5768.

THE SITES AND THE MONUMENTS – SYRIA

Figure: 431 (left).
Berenson ID: 134196.
Subject: Aleppo. The courtyard of the Arghun al-Kamili Bimaristan.
Medium: gelatine silver print, 12×17 cm.
Date of creation: 1919-1920.
Handwritten notes on the back: 'Aleppo, Munistan [?] of Arghun Kamily – courtyard — 755 (1354)' [Cres.].
Ashmolean negative: EA.CA.5769.

Figure: 432 (centre).
Berenson ID: 134198.
Subject: Aleppo. A secondary court of the Arghun al-Kamili Bimaristan.
Medium: gelatine silver print, 12×17 cm.
Date of creation: 1919-1920.
Handwritten notes on the back: 'Aleppo, Munistan [?] of Arghun Kamily – secondary court — 755 (1354)' [Cres.].
Ashmolean negative: EA.CA.5772.

Figure: 433 (right).
Berenson ID: 134199.
Subject: Aleppo. The courtyard of the Arghun al-Kamili Bimaristan.
Medium: gelatine silver print, 12×17 cm.
Date of creation: 1919-1920.
Handwritten notes on the back: 'Aleppo, Munistan [?] of Arghun Kamily – courtyard — 755 (1354)' [Cres.].
Ashmolean negative: EA.CA.5770.

Figure: 434 (left).
Berenson ID: 134200.
Subject: Aleppo. Interior of the Arghun al-Kamili Bimaristan
Medium: gelatine silver print, 12×17 cm.
Date of creation: 1919-1920.
Handwritten notes on the back: 'Aleppo, Munistan of Arghun Kamily – lower court 755 (1354)' [Cres.].
Ashmolean negative: EA.CA.5771.

Figure: 435 (right).
Berenson ID: 134304.
Subject: Aleppo. Mihrab of the Bahsita Mosque.
Medium: gelatine silver print, 12×17 cm
Date of creation: 1919-1920.
Handwritten notes on the back: 'Aleppo, Mosque in Bahsita – curious mihrab' [Cres.].
Ashmolean negative: EA.CA.5821

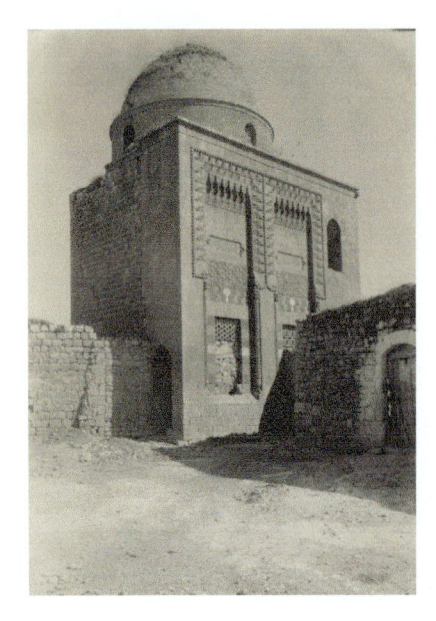

Figure: 436.
Subject: Aleppo. The Maqam Ughlulbak.
Berenson ID: 134300.
Medium: gelatine silver print, 12×17cm.
Date of creation: 1919-1920.
Handwritten notes on the back: 'Aleppo (Firdaus), Mausoleum of Osman bin Ahmad Oughlybey' [Cres.].
Ashmolean negative: EA.CA.5875.

Figure: 437.
Subject: Aleppo. The Musa Ibn Abdullah al-Nasiri Mausoleum.
Berenson ID: 134189.
Medium: gelatine silver print, 12×17cm.
Date of creation: 1919-1920.
Handwritten notes on the back: 'Aleppo (Firdaus), Mausoleum perhaps that of Musa ibn Abdullah ar-Nasriy – died 950 H' [Cres.].
Ashmolean negative: EA.CA.5862.

Figure: 438.
Subject: Aleppo. The Musa Ibn Abdullah al-Nasiri Mausoleum.
Berenson ID: 134190.
Medium: gelatine silver print, 12×17cm.
Date of creation: 1919-1920.
Handwritten notes on the back: 'Aleppo (Firdaus), Mausoleum perhaps that of Musa ibn Abdullah ar-Nasriy – N. side' [Cres.].
Ashmolean negative: EA.CA.5863.

Figure: 439.
Subject: Aleppo. The interior of the Musa Ibn Abdullah al-Nasiri Mausoleum.
Berenson ID: 134191.
Medium: gelatine silver print, 12×17cm.
Date of creation: 1919-1920.
Handwritten notes on the back: 'Aleppo (Firdaus), Mausoleum perhaps that of Musa ibn Abdullah ar-Nasriy – pendentive' [Cres.].
Ashmolean negative: EA.CA.5864.

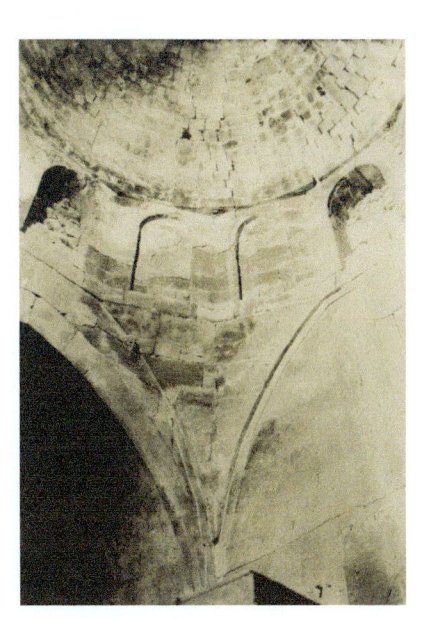

Figure: 440.
Subject: Aleppo. The Qubba Khayrbak.
Berenson ID: 134228.
Medium: gelatine silver print, 12×17cm.
Date of creation: 1919-1920.
Handwritten notes on the back: 'Aleppo, Mausoleum of Khaybak – from the S/W — 920 (1514)' [Cres.].
Ashmolean negative: EA.CA.5799.

Figure: 441.
Subject: Aleppo. The Qubba Khayrbak.
Berenson ID: 134226.
Medium: gelatine silver print, 12×17cm.
Date of creation: 1919-1920.
Handwritten notes on the back: 'Aleppo, Mausoleum of Khaybak – from the N/W — 920 (1514)' [Cres.].
Ashmolean negative: EA.CA.5798.

Figure: 442.
Subject: Aleppo. The Qubba Khayrbak.
Berenson ID: 134229.
Medium: gelatine silver print, 12×17cm.
Date of creation: 1919-1920.
Handwritten notes on the back: 'Aleppo, Mausoleum of Khaybak – S. side — 920 (1514)' [Cres.].
Ashmolean negative: EA.CA.5800.

Figure: 443.
Subject: Aleppo. The Qubba Khayrbak.
Berenson ID: 134227.
Medium: gelatine silver print, 12×17cm.
Date of creation: 1919-1920.
Handwritten notes on the back: 'Aleppo, Mausoleum of Khaybak — 920 (1514)' [Cres.]. 'Mausoleum in Cenetery. Kindness of Capt Creswell – p 229 photo 47' [Anon.]
Ashmolean negative: EA.CA.5797.

Figure: 444.
Subject: Aleppo. The Shihab al-Din Ahmad al-Adrai Mausoleum.
Berenson ID: 134214.
Medium: gelatine silver print, 12×17cm.
Date of creation: 1919-1920.
Handwritten notes on the back: 'Aleppo (Firdaus) Mausoleum of Shihab ad-Din Ahmad al-Arurayi — 807 (1404/5)' [Cres.].
Ashmolean negative: EA.CA.5876.

THE SITES AND THE MONUMENTS – SYRIA

Figure: 445.
Subject: Aleppo. Decorated windows of the Shihab al-Din Ahmad al-Adrai Mausoleum.
Berenson ID: 134215.
Medium: gelatine silver print, 12×17cm.
Date of creation: 1919-1920.
Handwritten notes on the back: 'Aleppo (Firdaus) Mausoleum of Shikab ad-Din al-Arurayi stone lattices — 807 (1404/5)' [Cres.].
Ashmolean negative: EA.CA.5877.

Figure: 446 (left).
Subject: Aleppo. Muqarnas of the Zawiya al-Bazzaziya.
Berenson ID: 134206.
Medium: gelatine silver print, 12×17cm.
Date of creation: 1919-1920.
Handwritten notes on the back: 'Aleppo, Zauriya of Sheykh Mohammad al-Bazazi al-Harapy, vault of entrance bay — 790 (1388)' [Cres.].
Ashmolean negative: EA.CA.5779.

Figure: 447 (centre).
Subject: Aleppo. The Zawiya al-Haidary.
Berenson ID: 134201.
Medium: gelatine silver print, 12×17cm.
Date of creation: 1919-1920.
Handwritten notes on the back: 'Zawiyya al-Haidary – entrance' [Cres.].
Ashmolean negative: EA.CA.5773.

Figure: 448 (right).
Subject: Aleppo. Detail of a decorated wall of the The Zawiya al-Haidary.
Berenson ID: 134298.
Medium: gelatine silver print, 12×17cm.
Date of creation: 1919-1920.
Handwritten notes on the back: 'Aleppo, animal carved over trough near Zawiyat al-Haidary' [Cres.].
Ashmolean negative: EA.CA.5820.

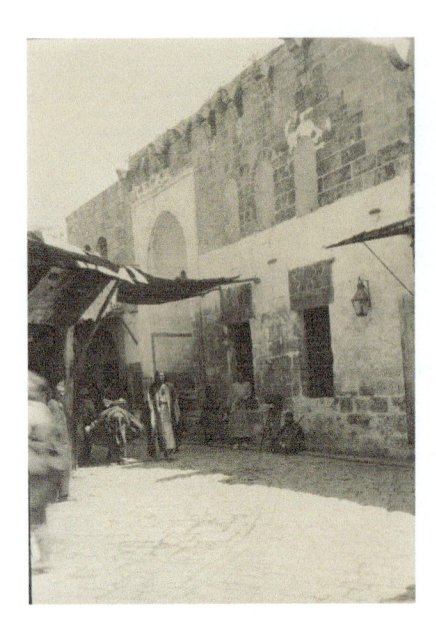

Figure: 449 (left).
Subject: Aleppo. The Zawiya al-Junashiya.
Berenson ID: 134183.
Medium: gelatine silver print, 12×17cm.
Date of creation: 1919-1920.
Handwritten notes on the back: 'Aleppo, Zauriyat al-Junashiya — 740 (1346/7)' [Cres.].
Ashmolean negative: EA.CA.5758.

Figure: 450 (right).
Subject: Aleppo. The Zawiya al-Junashiya.
Berenson ID: 134182.
Medium: gelatine silver print, 12×17cm.
Date of creation: 1919-1920.
Handwritten notes on the back: 'Aleppo, Zauriyat al-Junashiya – entrance — 740 (1346/7)' [Cres.].
Ashmolean negative: EA.CA.5759.

Figure: 451.
Subject: Aleppo. The decorated façade of the Khan al-Sabun.
Berenson ID: 134223.
Medium: gelatine silver print, 12×17cm.
Date of creation: 1919-1920.
Handwritten notes on the back: 'Aleppo, Khan as-Sabin – entrance — 910/922 (1504/10)' [Cres.].
Ashmolean negative: EA.CA.5793.

Figure: 452.
Subject: Aleppo. Interior of the Khan al-Sabun.
Berenson ID: 134297.
Medium: gelatine silver print, 12×17cm.
Date of creation: 1919-1920.
Handwritten notes on the back: 'Aleppo, Khan as-Sabin – interior' [Cres.].
Ashmolean negative: EA.CA.5794.

THE SITES AND THE MONUMENTS – SYRIA

Figure: 453 (left).
Subject: Aleppo. The Khan Qassabiya.
Berenson ID: 134225.
Medium: gelatine silver print, 12×17cm.
Date of creation: 1919-1920.
Handwritten notes on the back: 'Aleppo, Khan Khassabiya — 916 (1510/11)' [Cres.].
Ashmolean negative: EA.CA.5796.

Figure: 454 (centre).
Subject: Aleppo. The Khan Utchan.
Berenson ID: 134222.
Medium: gelatine silver print, 12×17cm.
Date of creation: 1919-1920.
Handwritten notes on the back: 'Aleppo. Khan Utchan — XVth cent.' [Cres.].
Ashmolean negative: EA.CA.5791.

Figure: 455 (right).
Subject: Aleppo. The Qastal Bab al-Maqam.
Berenson ID: 134220.
Medium: gelatine silver print, 12×17cm.
Date of creation: 1919-1920.
Handwritten notes on the back: 'Aleppo, Qatal Bab al-Maqam — 831 (1427/8)' [Cres.].
Ashmolean negative: EA.CA.5789.

Figure: 456 (left).
Subject: Aleppo. The Qastal Sahat Bizza.
Berenson ID: 134221.
Medium: gelatine silver print, 12×17cm.
Date of creation: 1919-1920.
Handwritten notes on the back: 'Aleppo, Qastal Sahet Bizeh — 910-922 (1504/16)' [Cres.].
Ashmolean negative: EA.CA.5795.

Figure: 457 (right).
Subject: Aleppo. The Qastal Sakakini.
Berenson ID: 134207.
Medium: gelatine silver print, 12×17cm.
Date of creation: 1919-1920.
Handwritten notes on the back: 'Aleppo, Qastal Sakakini — 776 (1374/5)' [Cres.].
Ashmolean negative: EA.CA.5778.

Figure: 458 (left).
Subject: Aleppo. The Qastal Shabariq.
Berenson ID: 134181.
Medium: gelatine silver print, 12×17cm.
Date of creation: 1919-1920.
Handwritten notes on the back: 'Aleppo, Qastal Shabaiak (drinking-trough) — 746 (1345/6)' [Cres.].
Ashmolean negative: EA.CA.5757.

Figure: 459 (centre).
Subject: Aleppo. The al-Khusrauriya Mosque.
Berenson ID: 134233.
Medium: gelatine silver print, 12×17cm.
Date of creation: 1919-1920.
Handwritten notes on the back: 'Aleppo, Jami al-Khusrauriya — 952 (1545)' [Cres.].
Ashmolean negative: EA.CA.5805.

Figure: 460 (right).
Subject: Aleppo. Mihrab of the al-Khusrauriya Mosque.
Berenson ID: 134235.
Medium: gelatine silver print, 12×17cm.
Date of creation: 1919-1920.
Handwritten notes on the back: 'Aleppo, Jami al-Khusrauriya – mihrab — 952 (1545)' [Cres.].
Ashmolean negative: EA.CA.5807.

Figure: 461 (left).
Subject: Aleppo. Interior of the al-Khusrauriya Mosque.
Berenson ID: 134234.
Medium: gelatine silver print, 12×17cm.
Date of creation: 1919-1920.
Handwritten notes on the back: 'Aleppo, Jami al-Khusrauriya – interior — 952 (1545)' [Cres.].
Ashmolean negative: EA.CA.5806.

Figure: 462 (right).
Subject: Aleppo. Interior of the Bahramiya Mosque.
Berenson ID: 134289.
Medium: gelatine silver print, 12×17cm.
Date of creation: 1919-1920.
Handwritten notes on the back: 'Aleppo, Jami Bahramiya – interior looking N' [Cres.].
Ashmolean negative: EA.CA.5817.

Figure: 463.
Subject: Aleppo. Interior of the Bahramiya Mosque.
Berenson ID: 134290.
Medium: gelatine silver print, 12×17cm.
Date of creation: 1919-1920.
Handwritten notes on the back: 'Aleppo, Jami Bahramiya – interior' [Cres.].
Ashmolean negative: EA.CA.5816.

Figure: 464.
Subject: Aleppo. The Takiya Shaykh Abu Bakr.
Berenson ID: 134237.
Medium: gelatine silver print, 12×17cm.
Date of creation: 1919-1920.
Handwritten notes on the back: 'Aleppo, Jekiyya of Sheykh Abu Bakr — Before 1041 (631)' [Cres.].
Ashmolean negative: EA.CA.5809.

Figure: 465.
Subject: Aleppo. Interior of the Takiya Shaykh Abu Bakr.
Berenson ID: 134238.
Medium: gelatine silver print, 12×17cm.
Date of creation: 1919-1920.
Handwritten notes on the back: 'Aleppo, Jekiyya of Sheykh Abu Bakr – pendentives of another chamber' [Cres.].
Ashmolean negative: EA.CA.5811.

Figure: 466.
Subject: Aleppo. Interior of the Takiya Shaykh Abu Bakr.
Berenson ID: 134239.
Medium: gelatine silver print, 12×17cm.
Date of creation: 1919-1920.
Handwritten notes on the back: 'Aleppo, Jekiyya of Sheykh Abu Bakr – pendentives of mausoleum — Before 1041 (1631)' [Cres.].

Figure: 467 (left).
Subject: Aleppo. Mihrab of the Takiya Shaykh Abu Bakr.
Berenson ID: 134240.
Medium: gelatine silver print, 12×17cm.
Date of creation: 1919-1920.
Handwritten notes on the back: 'Aleppo, Jekiyya of Sheykh Abu Bakr mihrab — Before 1041 (1631)' [Cres.].
Ashmolean negative: EA.CA.5810.

Figure: 468 (centre).
Subject: Aleppo. Blazon of a wall of the Khan al-Zait.
Berenson ID: 134299.
Medium: gelatine silver print, 12×17cm.
Date of creation: 1919-1920.
Handwritten notes on the back: 'Aleppo, Blazon on Khan az-Zait' [Cres.].
Ashmolean negative: EA.CA.5819.

Figure: 469 (right).
Subject: Aleppo. Interior of the Khan al-Jumruk.
Berenson ID: 134236.
Medium: gelatine silver print, 12×17cm.
Date of creation: 1919-1920.
Handwritten notes on the back: ' Aleppo, Khan al-Jumruk – entrance — 977 (1569/70)' [Cres.].
Ashmolean negative: EA.CA.5808.

THE SITES AND THE MONUMENTS – SYRIA

Figure: 470.
Subject: Aleppo. The entrance to the Khan al-Wazir.
Berenson ID: 134291.
Medium: gelatine silver print, 12×17cm.
Date of creation: 1919-1920.
Handwritten notes on the back: 'Aleppo, Khan al Wazir – inner side of entrance' [Cres.].
Ashmolean negative: EA.CA.5813.

Figure: 471 (left).
Subject: Aleppo. Inner side of the entrance to the Khan al-Wazir.
Berenson ID: 134292.
Medium: gelatine silver print, 12×17cm.
Date of creation: 1919-1920.
Handwritten notes on the back: 'Aleppo, Khan al-Wazir – inner side of entrance' [Cres.].
Ashmolean negative: EA.CA.5812.

Figure: 472 (centre).
Subject: Aleppo. House in Bahsita.
Berenson ID: 134295.
Medium: gelatine silver print, 12×17cm.
Date of creation: 1919-1920.
Handwritten notes on the back: 'Aleppo, Liwan of a house in Bahsita' [Cres.].
Ashmolean negative: EA.CA.5815.

Figure: 473 (right).
Subject: Aleppo. Private House.
Berenson ID: 134296.
Medium: gelatine silver print, 12×17cm.
Date of creation: 1919-1920.
Handwritten notes on the back: 'Aleppo, Private House' [Cres.].

179

Masyaf

Masyaf fortress lies about 45km from Hama, close to the eastern slopes of the Syrian coastal mountains, at an altitude of *c.* 450m asl. The Castle was built on a rocky promontory on the eastern border of the Old city of present-day Masyaf. The fortress, as well as the walls of the Old city, bear witness to a variety of building styles due to the site's long history, with traces of the earliest settlement dating back at least to the 1st millennium BCE.[334]

Figure: 474. Masyaf. The eastern front of the inner Castle a) in a Creswell's photo (below, Figure 479), and b) today (© Aga Khan Trust for Culture; photographer: Christian Richters).

The region was conquered by the Arab armies in 638 and Masyaf became strategically very important, especially from the second half of the 10th century. During this period, under the control of the Hamdanid dynasty, it became an outpost to control the routes threatened by Byzantine expansion attempts. It is likely that the first fortification structures date back to this period.

Its greatest flourishing occurred in the 12th century, when the Ismailis, a Shiite community from Iran, settled in northwestern Syria.[335] Much of what remains today dates back to this period of occupation, which lasted until the Mongol invasion in 1260.[336] In 1268, Masyaf was reconquered by the Mamluks, and remained under their control until 1516, when all the region came under Ottoman rule.

As a whole, the fortress measures 145m from north to south and about 60m in width from east to west. The natural rock of the promontory is integrated into its architectural structure. There was a single entrance to the fortress from the south, connected to the Old city to the east side by a stepped pathway. The major constructions belong to the building phase of the 12th-13th century, i.e., the Nizari-Ismaili period, such as the main entrance located in the south-western corner tower. The external walls that we see today, however, are the result of the massive construction works carried out during the Mamluk period.[337]

The fortress underwent extensive damage following riots in the city in 1808-1810, when groups of neighbourhoods attacked and occupied the city, before being expelled by the Ottoman army, after a long siege and bombing of the city and the fortress.[338] Between 2000 and 2004, the monument was the subject of a major restoration project funded by the Agha Khan Trust for Culture.[339]

The Berenson Collection contains six of Creswell's photographs dedicated to Masyaf. Since the same photographs are included in the collection of the Victoria & Albert Museum, where they were purchased by the Museum in 1926, they may possibly have been taken during a trip after Creswell's 1919-1920 visit, although it is not possible to date them with certainty. These are interesting photographs, especially those that portray architectural details of the structure. The photos show how the current structure has been modified in several points by the large amount of restoration works, such as in the case of the eastern front of the inner fortress of Figure 474.[340]

---

[334] Hasan H. 2007: 182-184.

[335] The myth of the Assassins is linked to the Ismailis and to the fortress of Masysf. Assassins was the term used in Europe to label the Ismaili fighters, corrupting the term 'hasisi' ('hashish-eater'), as they were called by their enemies (extensive literature is available on the Assassins, and the reasons for their name; recently, see Willey 2005).

[336] In fact, the Ismaili presence in the region also persisted afterwards. Hasan H. 2007: 188 recalls that Johan L. Burckhardt (1882: 149-154) mentions the presence of about 250 Ismaili families at the time of his trip to Syria in 1812.

[337] On the construction history of the fortress, see in particular Hasan H. 2007 and 2008, both enriched by a good number of diachronic figures.

[338] Haytham Hasan, *pers. com.*

[339] See AKTC 2006, Hasan H. 2007 and ARCHNET: site 6412. I would especially like to thank Lobna Monaster (Agha Khan Trust for Culture) and Haytham Hasan for providing assistance and photographs.

[340] Three photos in the collection (IDs 133964-133966) are labelled 'Crac des Chevaliers'. However, the calligraphy of the notes is not Creswell's and only one photograph actually portrays the Crac. Furthermore, none of them has a copy in the other archives, to my knowledge. Therefore, these three photographs have been removed from the list of Creswell's photographs and have been considered of doubtful origin.

Figure: 475.
Subject: Masyaf. The Castle, looking south.
Berenson ID: 133881.
Medium: gelatine silver print, 12×17cm.
Date of creation: 1919-1925.
Handwritten notes on the back: 'Masyaf – from the N' [Cres.].

Figure: 476.
Subject: Masyaf. The Castle, looking northwest.
Berenson ID: 133883.
Medium: gelatine silver print, 12×17cm.
Date of creation: 1919-1925.
Handwritten notes on the back: 'Masyaf – from the S/E' [Cres.].

Figure: 477.
Subject: Masyaf. The Castle, looking southwest.
Berenson ID: 133882.
Medium: gelatine silver print, 12×17cm.
Date of creation: 1919-1925.
Handwritten notes on the back: 'Masyaf – from the N/E' [Cres.].

Figure: 478.
Subject: Masyaf. The main entrance.
Berenson ID: 133880.
Medium: gelatine silver print, 12×17cm.
Date of creation: 1919-1925.
Handwritten notes on the back: 'Masyaf – entrance' [Cres.].

Figure: 479.
Subject: Masyaf. The eastern front of the inner Castle.
Berenson ID: 133879.
Medium: gelatine silver print, 12×17cm.
Date of creation: 1919-1925.
Handwritten notes on the back: 'Masyaf – interior looking west' [Cres.].

Figure: 480.
Subject: Masyaf. The entrance to the inner Castle, with an inscription on the doorway.
Berenson ID: 133878.
Medium: gelatine silver print, 12×17cm.
Date of creation: 1919-1925.
Handwritten notes on the back: 'Masyaf – doorway with inscription' [Cres.].

Hama

Hama is located in northwestern Syria, about 45km north of Homs, along the Orontes River.

Inhabited at least since the Neolithic, it has had a long history, which has been only partly reconstructed by archaeological research, the main results of which are still related to the excavations of the Danish archaeological expedition of the years 1931-1938 (Figure 481).[341]

In the 7th century Hama was conquered by the Arabs and became a very important provincial centre, especially for the transit of caravan routes that connected the inland with the Mediterranean coast and Syria with Anatolia.

The waters of the Orontes ensured a rich vegetation, allowing the prosperous city to thrive with gardens,[342] especially thanks to the irrigation provided by the famous norias (Figure 482). The first traces of these water wheels, characteristic of Hama, date back to the Ayyubid period, and their number increased in the Mamluk period.[343]

Creswell's photographs in Hama are probably datable to one of the trips made between 1920 and 1925 (some copies at the Victoria & Albert Museum belong to the group purchased in 1926) and depict three monuments: the Great Mosque of the Umayyads, the Mamluk Mosque of al-Nuri and the Ottoman Azm Palace.

The Great Mosque (Figures 483-486)[344] is one of the oldest in Syria and was built immediately after the Arab conquest of the city. It was built by the Umayyads in the 8th century, over the remains of a 6th century Byzantine church, which in turn had been built on the remains of a 3rd century Roman temple. It is quite a peculiar mosque from an architectural perspective, mainly because of the presence of two minarets: the first, the so-called 'South minaret', is square and made of white and black stone blocks forming a geometric decoration on the external surface. It is located at the southeastern corner of the prayer hall and can be dated back to the 12th century; the other, the so-called 'North minaret', has a square plan but based on an octagonal plan, and is adjacent to the northern wall, at the entrance. An inscription dates the minaret to 1422. Creswell discussed this mosque both his *Early Muslim architecture* and in an article, in response to a study by

---

[341] For a summary, with bibliography, of the Danish research, see Ingholt 1942. For a summary of the site's history, see ARCHNET site 644; Burns R. 1992: 125-126; Beattle 1996.

[342] Max van Berchem, who visited the city in 1895, described it as 'la plus pittoresque des villes syriennes du Nord' (van Berchem, Fatio 1914: 173). Due to its location and importance, it was visited and then photographed by many early European travellers visiting Syria; see for example the photos in Sachau 1883: pl. 9 and in Bell 1919: 221-235.

[343] Beattle 1996: 317-318.

[344] ARCHNET site 3497; Michell 1978: 234; Meinecke 1992: II/209.

Figure 481: Hama. View of the city, with a nouria on the left and the minaret of the al-Nuri Mosque on the right, in a watercolour of Ejnar Fugmann the architect of the 1931-1938 Danish archaeological expedition (courtesy of the National Museum of Denmark; photographer: Lennart Larsen; released under CC-BY-Sa license).

Figure 482: Hama. Waterwheel on Orontes River (date of creation: 1898-1914. Library of Congress, Prints & Photographs Division, nr. LC-DIG-matpc-06756; No known restrictions on publication: https://www.loc.gov/item/2019698140/).

Jean Sauvaget.[345] Creswell disputed Sauvaget's dating of some elements of the building to the Umayyad period, given that the mosque had undergone repeated rebuilding after the Umayyad period before reaching its current shape in the early 20th century.

A direct analysis of the monument is no longer feasible, since it was almost completely destroyed in 1982, following the riots of the 1982 Muslim Brotherhood revolt. What exists today is a modern reconstruction, which preserves little of the original.[346]

A minaret with black and white geometric decorations, probably just like the Great Mosque's, is also located

---

[345] Creswell 1932: 14, and 1959b. The question is extensively discussed and analysed in O'Kane 2009: 220-223.

[346] Bernard O'Kane, who visited and photographed it in 1988, before its reconstruction, described it as 'a mound of rubble' (O'Kane 2009: 219 and fig. 1).

Mesopotamia, Syria and Transjordan in the Creswell Collection

Figure: 486 (left).
Subject: Hama. Blazons and an inscription near the Great Mosque.
Berenson ID: 133627.
Medium: gelatine silver print, 12×17cm.
Handwritten notes on the back: 'Hama, inscriptions and blazons near Great Mosque' [Cres.].

Figure: 487 (right).
Subject: Hama. The minaret of the al-Nuri Mosque.
Berenson ID: 133629.
Medium: gelatine silver print, 12×17cm.
Date of creation: 1921-1925.
Handwritten notes on the back: 'Hama, Gami al-Nuri minaret' [Cres.].
Ashmolean negative: EA.CA.6084.

Figure: 488.
Subject: Hama. The setting of the dome of the al-Nuri Mosque.
Berenson ID: 133630.
Medium: gelatine silver print, 12×17cm.
Date of creation: 1921-1925.
Handwritten notes on the back: 'Hama, Gami al-Nuri – dome in the east riwaq' [Cres.].

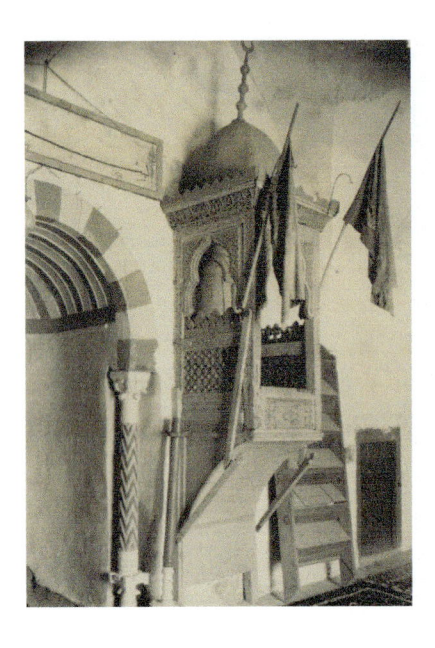

Figure: 489 (left).
Subject: Hama. The minbar of the al-Nuri Mosque.
Berenson ID: 133631.
Medium: gelatine silver print, 12×17cm.
Date of creation: 1921-1925.
Handwritten notes on the back: 'Hama, Gami al-Nuri – pulpit [Cres.].

Figure: 490 (right).
Subject: Hama. The minbar of the al-Nuri Mosque.
Berenson ID: 133632.
Medium: gelatine silver print, 12×17cm.
Date of creation: 1921-1925.
Handwritten notes on the back: 'Hama, Gami al-Nuri – pulpit' [Cres.].

THE SITES AND THE MONUMENTS – SYRIA

Figure: 491.
Subject: Hama. The lower court of the Azm Palace.
Berenson ID: 133613.
Medium: gelatine silver print, 12×17cm.
Date of creation: 1921-1925.
Handwritten notes on the back: 'Hama, Azm Palace – lower court' [Cres.].
Ashmolean negative: EA.CA.6091.

Figure: 492.
Subject: Hama. The portico of the main reception room of the Azm Palace.
Berenson ID: 133615.
Medium: gelatine silver print, 12×17cm.
Date of creation: 1921-1925.
Handwritten notes on the back: 'Hama, Azm Palace – portico of the main reception room' [Cres.].
Ashmolean negative: EA.CA.6093.

Figure: 493.
Subject: Hama. The upper court of the Azm Palace.
Berenson ID: 133614.
Medium: gelatine silver print, 12×17cm.
Date of creation: 1921-1925.
Handwritten notes on the back: 'Hama, Azm Palace – upper court' [Cres.].
Ashmolean negative: EA.CA.6092.

Mesopotamia, Syria and Transjordan in the Creswell Collection

Figure: 494 (left).
Subject: Hama. The main hall of the Azm Palace.
Berenson ID: 133626.
Medium: gelatine silver print, 12×17cm.
Date of creation: 1921-1925.
Handwritten notes on the back: 'Hama, Azm Palace – main hall' [Cres.].

Figure: 495 (centre).
Subject: Hama. The main hall of the Azm Palace.
Berenson ID: 133621.
Medium: gelatine silver print, 12×17cm.
Date of creation: 1921-1925.
Handwritten notes on the back: 'Hama, Azm Palace – main hall' [Cres.].
Ashmolean negative: EA.CA.5882.

Figure: 496 (right).
Subject: Hama. The main hall of the Azm Palace.
Berenson ID: 133619.
Medium: gelatine silver print, 12×17cm.
Date of creation: 1921-1925.
Handwritten notes on the back: 'Hama, Azm Palace – main hall' [Cres.].
Ashmolean negative: EA.CA.5881.

Figure: 497.
Subject: Hama. The main hall of the Azm Palace.
Berenson ID: 133618.
Medium: gelatine silver print, 12×17cm.
Date of creation: 1921-1925.
Handwritten notes on the back: 'Hama, Azm Palace – main hall' [Cres.].
Ashmolean negative: EA.CA.5880.

Figure: 498.
Subject: Hama. Room next to the main hall of the Azm Palace.
Berenson ID: 133617.
Medium: gelatine silver print, 12×17cm.
Date of creation: 1921-1925.
Handwritten notes on the back: 'Hama, Azm Palace – annexe of main hall' [Cres.].
Ashmolean negative: EA.CA.5879.

Figure: 499.
Subject: Hama. Three elaborated windows of the Azm Palace.
Berenson ID: 133616.
Medium: gelatine silver print, 12×17cm.
Date of creation: 1921-1925.
Handwritten notes on the back: 'Hama, Azm Palace – windows of main level' [Cres.].
Ashmolean negative: EA.CA.6094.

Figure: 500 (left).
Subject: Hama. The ceiling of the main hall of the Azm Palace.
Berenson ID: 133623.
Medium: gelatine silver print, 12×17cm.
Date of creation: 1921-1925.
Handwritten notes on the back: 'Hama, Azm Palace – ceiling of main hall' [Cres. N.B: along with the caption, there is the drawing of a map with the position of the photographed ceiling; see above, Figure 12].
Ashmolean negative: EA.CA.5887.

Figure: 501 (centre).
Subject: Hama. The ceiling of the main hall of the Azm Palace.
Berenson ID: 133624.
Medium: gelatine silver print, 12×17cm.
Date of creation: 1921-1925.
Handwritten notes on the back: 'Hama, Azm Palace – ceiling of Main Hall' [Cres. N.B: along with the caption, there is the drawing of a map with the position of the photographed ceiling].
Ashmolean negative: EA.CA.5885.

Figure: 502 (right).
Subject: Hama. a ceiling of the Azm Palace.
Berenson ID: 133625.
Medium: gelatine silver print, 12×17cm.
Date of creation: 1921-1925.
Handwritten notes on the back: 'Hama, Azm Palace main hall ceiling of recess' [Cres. N.B: along with the caption, there is the drawing of a map with the position of the photographed ceiling].
Ashmolean negative: EA.CA.5886.

Homs

Homs lies in central Syria, between Hama to the north and Damascus to the south, in a fertile plain irrigated from the nearby river Oronte.

The city was probably an important settlement already in the Hellenistic period, when its name was Emesa. Certain archaeological evidence, however, began in the Roman period and continued in the Byzantine period, when the city gained considerable prosperity and prestige: a remarkable number of churches were built in Homs, such as the Church of St. Helena (326) and the great church in which the head of St John the Baptist was buried. It was the largest Byzantine church in Syria. In the Islamic period, between the Arab conquest and the Mamluk period, it was repeatedly the subject of disputes between Arabs, Byzantines and Crusaders, and many historical monuments were destroyed.[349]

In Homs, Creswell photographed the Citadel, the Great Mosque and Bab al-Masdud. The date of the photographs is not certain, but the copies in the batch at the Victoria & Albert Museum belong to the purchase of 1926.

The Citadel is depicted in 6 photographs (Figures 505-510). It was built in the Ayyubid period, between the 12th and 13th century, opposite the southwestern corner of the city wall on a 32m high mound.

A photo by Louis or George Sabunji, taken before 1883 shows the citadel as being still in good condition.[350] Its dismantling probably began only at the time of the Ottoman domination and was massive especially during the period of the French Mandate, when the mound was used as a military post, maintaining that function until the 1980s. Excavations by the Syrian Department of Antiquities in the 1990s, which continued until the early 21st century, certainly yielded interesting data, but it is clear that the construction works between the mid-19th and mid-20th centuries greatly compromised the integrity of the archaeological levels.[351] A comparison between the views taken by Creswell and the current state clearly shows the differences, with a large number of modern installations especially on the central top (Figures 503 and 508).

The Great Mosque[352] was built on the remains of a Roman temple and is one of the most important monuments of Homs. Its current form mainly reflects the construction phase attributed to the Zanjid sultan al-Nuri (12th century), Creswell devoted a large group of photographs to this building (Figures 511-521), notably with a beautiful sequence of photographs depicting the entire façade. Finally, although represented in a single

Figure 503: Homs. The Citadel, in a photo taken in April 2007 (http://monumentsofsyria.com/places/homs-2/; courtesy of Ross Burns).

---

[349] On the history of Homs, see Abu Assaf 1997 and Burns R. 2009: 169-172. Early photos of Homs can be found in Sachau 1883: 62-64, pl. 8; van Berchem, Fatio 1914: 164-166; Bell 1919, fig. at p. 193; Dussaud 1927: 103-115.

[350] Sachau 1883, pl. 8. On George and Louis Sabounji, see Appendix 1: 269.

[351] King 2002.

[352] ARCHNET site 14952; Burns R. 1992: 171.

photo (Figure 522), Bab al-Masdud is one of the most interesting subjects of the Berenson Collection, since it was one of the two city gates of the Ayyubid period still existing at the time of Creswell's visit.

Figure 504: Homs. Aerial view taken on May 1932 by the French Armée de l'Air (https://hal.archives-ouvertes.fr/hal-02500959; Institut français du Proche-Orient; released under Licence Ouverte 1.0).

THE SITES AND THE MONUMENTS – SYRIA

Figure: 505.
Subject: Homs. The Citadel, looking south.
Berenson ID: 133732.
Medium: gelatine silver print, 12×17cm.
Date of creation: 1919-1925.
Handwritten notes on the back: 'Homs, The Citadel from the N' [Cres.].
Ashmolean negative: EA.CA.5909.

Figure: 506.
Subject: Homs. The Citadel, looking southeast.
Berenson ID: 133731.
Medium: gelatine silver print, 12×17cm.
Date of creation: 1919-1925.
Handwritten notes on the back: 'Homs, The Citadel, from the N/W' [Cres.].
Ashmolean negative: EA.CA.5910.

Figure: 507.
Subject: Homs. The northwestern corner of the Citadel.
Berenson ID: 133730.
Medium: gelatine silver print, 12×17cm.
Date of creation: 1919-1925.
Handwritten notes on the back: 'Homs, The Citadel – entrance (N.W. corner)' [Cres.].

Figure: 508.
Subject: Homs. The Citadel looking north.
Berenson ID: 133727.
Medium: gelatine silver print, 12×17cm.
Date of creation: 1919-1925.
Handwritten notes on the back: 'Homs, the Citadel – from the South' [Cres.].

Figure: 509.
Subject: Homs. Remains of the glacis of the Citadel.
Berenson ID: 133726.
Medium: gelatine silver print, 12×17cm.
Date of creation: 1919-1925.
Handwritten notes on the back: 'Homs, the Citadel – remains of glacis' [Cres.].

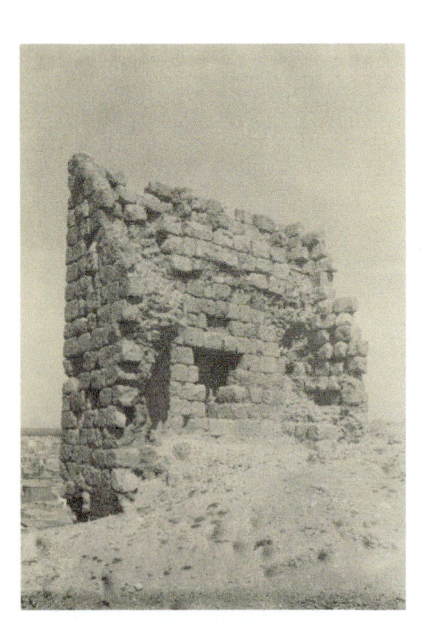

Figure: 510.
Subject: Homs. Remains of a tower on the Citadel.
Berenson ID: 133729.
Medium: gelatine silver print, 12×17cm.
Date of creation: 1919-1925.
Handwritten notes on the back: 'Homs, The Citadel – ruined tower' [Cres.].

THE SITES AND THE MONUMENTS – SYRIA

Figure: 511.
Subject: Homs. The façade of the Great Mosque of al-Nuri.
Berenson ID: 133734.
Medium: gelatine silver print, 12×17cm.
Date of creation: 1919-1925.
Handwritten notes on the back: 'Homs, Great Mosque' [Cres.].
Ashmolean negative: EA.CA.5896.

Figure: 512.
Subject: Homs. The façade of the Great Mosque of al-Nuri.
Berenson ID: 133735.
Medium: gelatine silver print, 12×17cm.
Date of creation: 1919-1925.
Handwritten notes on the back: 'Homs, Great Mosque – façade of sanctuary' [Cres.].
Ashmolean negative: EA.CA.5897.

Figure: 513.
Subject: Homs. The façade of the Great Mosque of al-Nuri.
Berenson ID: 133736.
Medium: gelatine silver print, 12×17cm.
Date of creation: 1919-1925.
Handwritten notes on the back: 'Homs, Great Mosque – façade of sanctuary' [Cres.].
Ashmolean negative: EA.CA.5898.

Mesopotamia, Syria and Transjordan in the Creswell Collection

Figure: 514.
Subject: Homs. The façade of the Great Mosque of al-Nuri.
Berenson ID: 133737.
Medium: gelatine silver print, 12×17cm.
Date of creation: 1919-1925.
Handwritten notes on the back: 'Homs, Great Mosque – façade of sanctuary' [Cres.].
Ashmolean negative: EA.CA.5899.

Figure: 515.
Subject: Homs. The façade of the Great Mosque of al-Nuri.
Berenson ID: 133738.
Medium: gelatine silver print, 12×17cm.
Date of creation: 1919-1925.
Handwritten notes on the back: 'Homs, Great Mosque – façade of sanctuary' [Cres.].
Ashmolean negative: EA.CA.5900.

Figure: 516.
Subject: Homs. The rear façade of the Great Mosque of al-Nuri.
Berenson ID: 133725.
Medium: gelatine silver print, 12×17cm.
Date of creation: 1919-1925.
Handwritten notes on the back: 'Homs, Great Mosque – rear façade (S.)' [Cres.].
Ashmolean negative: EA.CA.5901.

THE SITES AND THE MONUMENTS – SYRIA

Figure: 517.
Subject: Homs. The southern entrance of the Great Mosque of al-Nuri.
Berenson ID: 133739.
Medium: gelatine silver print, 12×17cm.
Date of creation: 1919-1925.
Handwritten notes on the back: 'Homs, Great Mosque – S. entrance' [Cres.].
Ashmolean negative: EA.CA.5894.

Figure: 518.
Subject: Homs. Detail of a door-post in the Great Mosque of al-Nuri.
Berenson ID: 133740.
Medium: gelatine silver print, 12×17cm.
Date of creation: 1919-1925.
Handwritten notes on the back: 'Homs, Great Mosque – door post of pulpit with fleur-de-lis' [Cres.].
Ashmolean negative: EA.CA.5906.

Figure: 519.
Subject: Homs. the minbar of the Great Mosque of al-Nuri.
Berenson ID: 133741.
Medium: gelatine silver print, 12×17cm.
Date of creation: 1919-1925.
Handwritten notes on the back: 'Homs, Great Mosque' [Cres.].
Ashmolean negative: EA.CA.5904.

Figure: 520 (left).
Subject: Homs. The mirhab of the Great Mosque of al-Nuri.
Berenson ID: 133742.
Medium: gelatine silver print, 12×17cm.
Date of creation: 1919-1925.
Handwritten notes on the back: 'Homs, Great Mosque – mihrab' [Cres.].
Ashmolean negative: EA.CA.5903.

Figure: 521 (right).
Subject: Homs. a balzon on the southeastern minaret of the Great Mosque of al-Nuri.
Berenson ID: 133743.
Medium: gelatine silver print, 12×17cm.
Date of creation: 1919-1925.
Handwritten notes on the back: 'Homs, Great Mosque – S/E minaret' [Cres.].
Ashmolean negative: EA.CA.6076.

Figure: 522.
Subject: Homs. The Bab al-Masdud.
Berenson ID: 133744.
Medium: gelatine silver print, 12×17cm.
Date of creation: 1919-1925.
Handwritten notes on the back: 'Homs, Bab Masdud' [Cres.].
Ashmolean negative: EA.CA.5908.

Damascus

The Syrian capital is located on a plateau in inner Syria, about 80km from the Mediterranean coast and at about 680m asl, and is crossed by the Barada river. It is located in a crossroads area on the routes that connect Anatolia to Palestine and Egypt on the north-south axis and Mesopotamia and the Mediterranean on the east-west.[353]

The city probably rose around the nucleus that developed near a sanctuary of the god Hadad, in the 1st millennium BCE. It has been speculated that it was founded in the area where the Umayyad mosque is presently located and was built by the caliph al-Walid in 705 reusing part of the western and southern perimeter walls of the temenos of a Roman temple, first built in the 1st century BCE and completed in the 4th century, after the cell of the temple had already been used as a church between the 5th and 6th centuries.[354] The city was taken by the Arabs in 635 and in 656 it became the seat of the Umayyad caliphate, until its fall in 750. The Abbasid conquest caused the destruction of much of its architecture and also led to a decline in the city's prestige. It has been observed that it was probably at this stage that the fragmentation in neighbourhoods increased and the large number of mosques that characterise the city's urban fabric grew.[355] A new moment of prosperity and architectural development came to pass under the Zanjid Caliphate of Nur-al Din, in the 12th century, and then with the Ayyubid and Mamluk dominations, when the city's prestige again increased, as witnessed by the construction of new important buildings. In particular, after a pause due to the destruction brought by the Mongol invasion in the middle of the 13th century, the Mamluk phase was particularly significant for the city's architectural history. The reason for this was that the city was chosen as the main residence of Malik al-Zahir Baibars during his reign, between 1260 and 1277, becoming a 'second capital' of the Mamluk empire. In 1516, Syria became part of the Ottoman Empire, and Damascus experienced moments of notable architectural and urban vigour in the 18th century due to the resourcefulness of various governors belonging to the powerful Azm family.

Figure 523: Damascus. Engraving of a late 19th century view of the city, taken from the Christian quarter (Reclus 1876, fig. 182).

Finally, starting from the 19th century, the marked building expansion in the areas outside the city walls is certainly worth highlighting. The defensive function of the walls had ceased because the city now belonged to the Ottoman Empire, similar to what has been seen for Aleppo (see pp. 116-117).

The city now occupies a vast area of over 100 square kilometres, partly developed also on the slopes of the Jebel Qassiun, and therefore covering an area enormously greater than the ancient city. Initially, the city had developed only south of the course of the Barada, with an area fortified by walls. Around these walls, residential neighbourhoods had already developed along the streets leading from the fortified city to sanctuaries in the surrounding areas. The urban development of the late 19th century particularly spread west of the Barada, in an area destined to become soon vital to the history of the city, with important administrative buildings, the railway station and the 'European' residential district. From the beginning of the 20th century, urban development mainly concerned the now northern part of the city.

Based on the comparison with the collection of the Victoria & Albert Museum, we can say that the photos of the Berenson Collection belong to several trips made by Creswell, at least until 1926. The largest group includes photographs taken during his 1919-1920 trip, when the city was already one of the main and most densely populated of the entire Syrian region[356] and before the significant urban transformation bringing it to its current appearance. Some of the monuments that were then standing and visitable, no longer exist today. It is also important to point out that Creswell's survey predates the leading publications for the study of the architecture of Damascus: the first accurate survey was conducted in 1917 by Karl Wulzinger and Carl Watzinger. Their work was published shortly

---

[353] About Damascus in general and its history: Sack 1985 and 1989; Burns R. 1992: 94-99; Meinecke 1992: I/131, 188-194, 206-208; Moaz 1998; Keenan, Beddow 2000; Weber 2009; in particular, for the ancient city through the tales of early photography, El-Hage 2000 is a fundamental work. Among the many photographers who have portrayed ancient Damascus, particular mention deserves Gertrude Bell, since many of her photographs date back to the same period as those taken by Creswell (Bell 1919: 134-158). See also the card in ARCHNET site 3603, and the notes below for references to specific works on the topography of the Old City and the history of individual monuments.

[354] Sobczak 2015.

[355] https://www.archnet.org/authorities/3603

[356] The 1912 *Baedeker Guide* counts about 300,000 inhabitants (Baedeker 1912: 299).

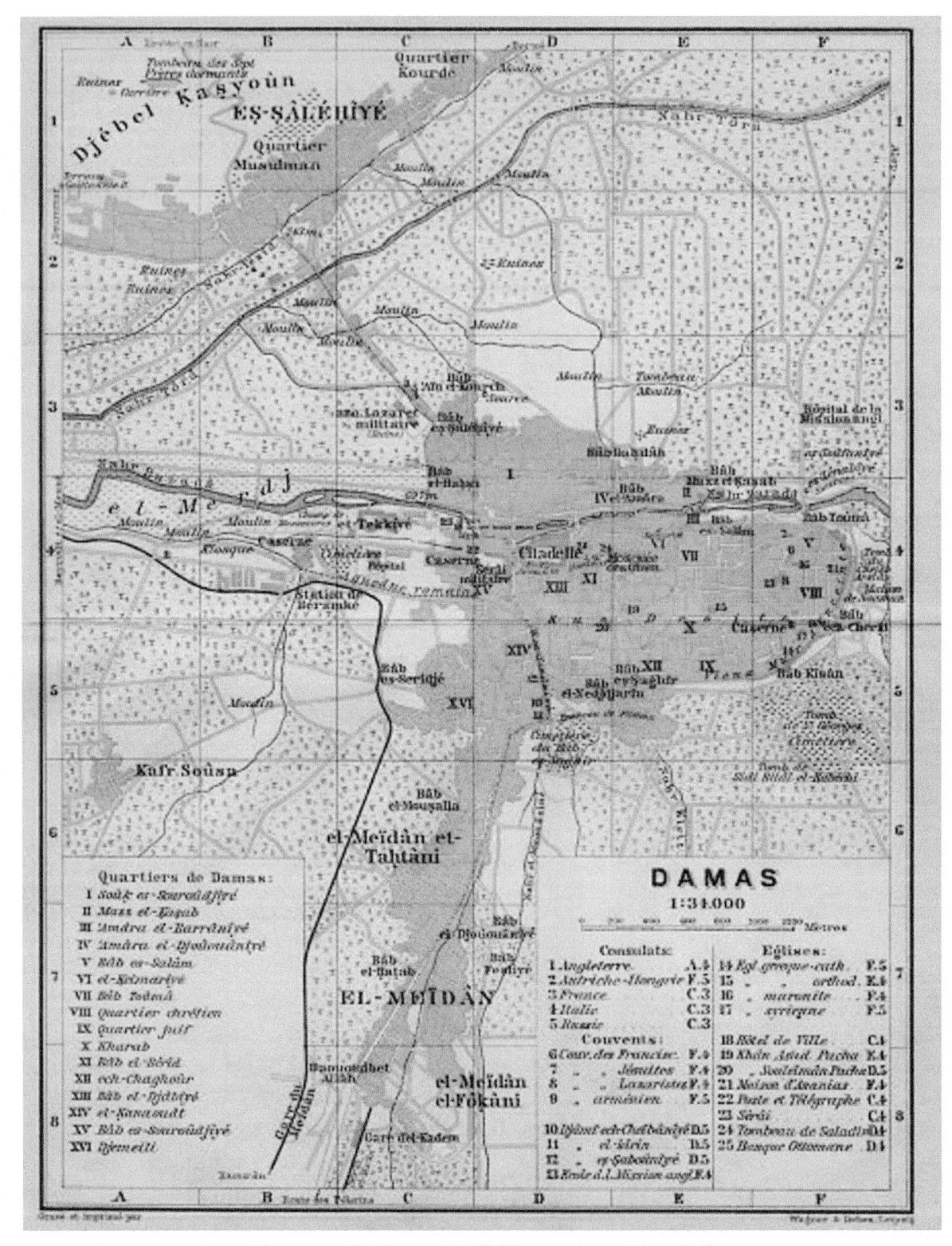

Figure 524: Damascus. City map by Wagner & Debes, c. 1912 (folding map in Baedeker 1912).

after Creswell's visit.[357] More recent are the important research and publications of Jean Sauvaget,[358] who conducted an in-depth study on the history of the city (and of Aleppo), gathering information from different sources. Finally, some works published by Ernst Herzfeld in the 1940s are worth remembering, which are also essential for the reconstruction of the architectural history of the city.[359]

With regard to photography, Creswell photographed the city when it had already been the subject of many

---

[357] Wulzinger, Watzinger 1921 e 1924.
[358] Sauvaget 1932, 1938, 1940, 1948, 1949.
[359] Herzfeld 1942, 1943, 1946, 1948a.

early photographs: the first daguerreotype of the city is dated 19 January 1840 and is the work of Frédéric Goupil Fesquet,[360] whose photos are unfortunately largely lost, but were soon followed by those of many other photographers.[361]

Creswell's photographic documentation has deserved a place in the photographic history of Damascus: his photos portray, with the expertise of an architecture historian, important buildings at a time when Damascus had not yet expanded and modified several existing neighbourhoods to adapt their structures to those of the new capital.

As mentioned about Aleppo, it is interesting to note that even in the case of Damascus, the photographs portray monuments that Creswell does not always consider in his publications. An exception is the Umayyad Mosque: in this case, many of the photographs were used in *Early Muslim architecture*. The area represented is mainly that of the neighbourhoods to the west of the Umayyad Mosque, with a remarkable group of photographs concerning the district of Salihiya (Figure 524).

Listed below are the monuments photographed and illustrated in the catalogue (Figures 525-661), organised chronologically. For details on building chronology and location of individual monuments, see Appendix 4 directly.

A total of 164 photos are dedicated to Damascus. Of these, 54 concern the Ummayad Mosque (Figures 525-578), which also occupies an important place in Creswell's *Early Muslim architecture*.[362] The photographs well reflect the attention that Creswell paid to this monument. The number of photographs that focus on the marble and mosaic decorations is indeed remarkable (in particular, Figures 556-578). These latter photos are particularly noteworthy for the photographic method and technique used: scaffolds were specifically built to take these shots, earning our admiration because they clearly show Creswell's commitment and pursuit of perfection (Figure 542).

The Zanjid period is testified by the photographs of two of the city gates, Bab al-Salam (Figure 579)[363] and Bab al-Faraj (Figure 580)[364], and various other monuments: those captured in the greatest number of photographs are the Nur al-Din Madrasa and Bimaristan (Figures 581-585)[365] and the al-Adiliya Madrasa (Figures 586-594).[366] Creswell considered the latter monument as a useful example to support his thesis on the origin of the cruciform plant of the madrasas in the aforementioned study on this topic.[367] Finally, one photo concerns the al-Nuriya al-Kubra Madrasa (Figure 595).[368]

The period most represented in the photographs is the Ayyubid period, with no less than 19 monuments photographed, although in all cases only one or two photographs were taken. In detail, these monuments were the following: Abd al-Rahman ibn Abdallah al-Tashtadar Madrasa (Figure 596),[369] Abu Abdallah Hasan ibn Salama Mausoleum (Figures 597-598),[370] al-Maridaniya Mosque (Figures 599-600),[371] al-Qaymari Maristan and Mausoleum (Figures 601-604),[372] al-Rihaniya Madrasa (Figure 605),[373] al-Sahiba Madrasa (Figure 606),[374] al-Shamiya al-Kubra Madrasa (Figures 607-608),[375] Ali al-Faranti Mausoleum (Figures 609-611),[376] Amat al-Latif Mausoleum (Figures 612-613),[377] Atabektya Mosque (Figure 614),[378] Dar al-Hadith al-Ashrafiya al-Muqaddasiya (Figure 615),[379] Hanabila

---

[360] El-Hage 2000: 18. See also below, p. 264
[361] The 1912 *Baedeker Guide* mentions Araqtinji, Harentz, and Bonfils as active photographic studios in the city (Baedeker 1912: 295). Damascus, however, is a particularly well-documented case as regards its photographic history, and the aforementioned volume of Badr El-Hage offers a comprehensive and well-documented picture of the period between 1840 and 1918 (El-Hage 2000; see the chapter 'Damas à travers la phptographie, 1840-1918', pp. 17-50, in particular).
[362] Creswell 1932: 100-252, with a chapter on mosaics, by Marguerite van Berchem, pp. 149-228. Previously, see also Creswell 1926: 7, and 1958: 44-80. Further bibliography: Wulzinger, Watzinger 1921: 3-42, 77-79, 1924: 143-147; Sauvaget 1932: 15-29; Herzfeld 1948; Michell 1978: 232; Meinecke 1992: I/37, II/37; Sobczak 2015; Daiber 2022d; ARCHNET site 31.

[363] Wulzinger, Watzinger 1924: 184; Sauvaget 1932: 30; Burns R. 1992: 109; Meinecke 1992: I/188-195; Allen 1999, chapter 10; Mouton, Guilhot, Piaton 2018.
[364] Wulzinger, Watzinger 1924: 184; Sauvaget 1932: 30; Burns R. 1992: 109; Meinecke 1992: I/188-195; Mouton, Guilhot, Piaton 2018.
[365] Wulzinger, Watzinger 1924: 70; Herzfeld 1942: 2-14; Burns R. 1992: 111; Allen 1999, chapter 2; ARCHNET site 3548.
[366] Sauvaget 1932: 42, 1940: 77-91; Herzfeld 1942: 46-49; Burns R. 1992: 113; Meinecke 1992: I/37, 52, 91, 94; Allen 1999, chapter 2; Moaz, Takieddine 2022b; ARCHNET site 3723.
[367] Creswell 1922: 6.
[368] Herzfeld 1942: 40-46.
[369] Wulzinger, Watzinger 1924: 133-134.
[370] Herzfeld 1946: 52.
[371] Sauvaget 1932: 16, 1948: 119-130.
[372] Sauvaget 1932: 67; Herzfeld 1946: 34; Meinecke 1992: II/373; Allen, chapter 10; Moaz, Takieddine 2022a; ARCHNET site 3078.
[373] Possibly referring to a madrasa in the Amara district (according to Herzfeld's map at https://libmma.contentdm.oclc.org/digital/collection/p16028coll11/id/6368).
[374] Sauvaget 1932: 65-66; Herzfeld 1946: 9-12; Burns R. 1992: 137; Moaz 2022c.
[375] Herzfeld 1942: 40-46.
[376] Sauvaget 1932: 63; Herzfeld 1946: 56-57; Burns R. 1992: 134.
[377] Burns R. 1992: 134; Meinecke 1992: I/31; Allen 1999, chapter 9.
[378] Sauvaget 1932: 65; Herzfeld 1946: 12; Burns R. 1992: 134; Meinecke 1992: I/31; Allen 1999, chapter 9.
[379] Herzfeld 1946: 58; Burns R. 1992: 134; Meinecke 1992: II/92; Allen 1999, chapter 2. For this monument, there is some uncertainty about the possible attribution of some additional photographs, for which copies also exist in other archives

Mosque (Figures 616-618),[380] Izz al-Din Madrasa (Figures 619-622),[381] Jaharkasiya Madrasa (Figure 623),[382] Khatuniya Mausoleum (Figure 624),[383] Raihan Mausoleum (Figure 625),[384] Rukn al-Din Mausoleum (Figure 626),[385] Saladin Mausoleum (Figures 627-628),[386] and a not identified Shaykh Muhammad ibn Ali ibn Nadif Mausoleum (Figure 629).

The number of Mamluk monuments photographed is smaller (3), but the documentation is certainly interesting: in the case of the al-Zahiriya Madrasa, the number of photographs (Figures 630-635)[387] dedicated to internal and external architecture elements is remarkable, while in the case of the Amir Tankiz Mosque and Mausoleum (Figures 636-640)[388] it is interesting that the Ottoman phase of the building is documented, although it had been converted into barracks and military academy. A photograph of the Amir Kujkun al-Mansuri Mausoleum (Figure 641)[389] and the detail of a lintel with blazon embedded in a house in the quarter of Salihiya (Figure 642)[390] complete the repertoire.

As mentioned, the Ottoman period is marked by the construction of several important buildings in Damascus, and Creswell photographed some of them: the greatest number of photographs is dedicated to Takiya al-Sulaymaniya, otherwise called Sultan Selim Mosque, currently a large complex including a mosque, hospital, madrasa, and takiya with a suq (Figures 643-649);[391] followed by two other religious buildings — the al-Sibaiyah Madrasa (Figures 650-651)[392] and the Sinan Pasha Mosque (Figures 652-655)[393] —, the Azm Palace (Figures 656-658)[394] and two khans, i.e., the Khan Asad Pasha (Figures 659-660),[395] deeply renovated in the 1980s, and the Khan Sulayman Pasha (Figure 661).[396] Compared to other major cities, such as Aleppo or Hama, Damascus has suffered minor damage following the recent Civil War. However, there have been some cases of considerable damage, including to important monuments photographed by Creswell, such as the Umayyad Mosque and the Madrasa al-Adiliya. This circumstance, as with almost all the cases dealt with above, makes the photographic documentation of the photograph collection of the Biblioteca Berenson particularly important for the future safeguarding and conservation of monuments.[397]

---

but with different captions and, to my knowledge, it is not possible to identify exactly the individual subjects. They are not included in this catalogue and are: IDs 133518, 133519, 133520, accessible on Hollis Images.

[380] Wulzinger, Watzinger 1924: 128-131.
[381] Sauvaget 1940: 65-75.
[382] Sauvaget 1932: 62, 1938: 41-50; Herzfeld 1946: 50-52; Burns R. 1992: 134-135.
[383] Wulzinger, Watzinger 1924: 116-118; Sauvaget 1932: 61-62; Burns R. 1992: 135.
[384] Sauvaget 1940: 51-56; Herzfeld 1946: 62; Burns R. 1992: 134.
[385] Wulzinger, Watzinger 1924: 135-138; Herzfeld 1942: 20-26.
[386] Wulzinger, Watzinger 1924: 63; Burns R. 1992: 113; Moaz 1989; Moaz, Takieddine 2022d.
[387] Sauvaget 1932: 45-46; Michell 1978: 232-233; Daiber 2022a.
[388] Sauvaget 1932: 46; Meinecke 1992: I/97, II/181; Kenney 2009, 2012.
[389] Burns R. 1992: 134.
[390] The central blazon probably corresponds to the coat of arms with fleur-de-lis published in Herzfeld 1942, fig. 8.

[391] Sauvaget 1932: 52-54; Michell 1978: 233; Burns R. 1992: 129-131; Daiber 2022c.
[392] Sauvaget 1932: 52; Burns R. 1992: 124.
[393] Sauvaget 1932: 56; Burns R. 1992: 124.
[394] Michell 1978: 233; Burns R. 1992: 116-117; Daiber 2022b.
[395] Wulzinger, Watzinger 1924: 81-86; Sauvaget 1932: 57-58; Michell 1978: 234; Burns R. 1992: 118.
[396] Wulzinger, Watzinger 1924: 86; Sauvaget 1932: 57; Burns R. 1992: 118.
[397] UNESCO 2016: 22. See also a map with aerial photo and indication of the damaged structures in *SOC Report by the State Party 2015*, p. 8 (https:///whc.unesco.org/en/soc/3183).

Figure: 525.
Subject: Damascus. Umayyad Mosque, remains of the Roman temple.
Berenson ID: 133446.
Medium: gelatine silver print, 12×17cm.
Date of creation: 1919-1920.
Handwritten notes on the back: 'Damascus, Great Mosque – remains of prophylae' [Cres.].
Ashmolean negative: EA.CA.5459.

Figure: 526.
Subject: Damascus. Umayyad Mosque, remains of the Roman temple.
Berenson ID: 133487.
Medium: gelatine silver print, 12×17cm.
Date of creation: 1919-1920.
Handwritten notes on the back: 'Damascus, Great Mosque. West façade' [Cres.].
Published in Creswell 1932, pl. 33.a.

Figure: 527.
Subject: Damascus. Umayyad Mosque, remains of the Roman temple.
Berenson ID: 133450.
Medium: gelatine silver print, 12×17cm.
Date of creation: 1919-1920.
Handwritten notes on the back: 'Damascus, Great Mosque – classical doorway in S. facade' [Cres.]
Ashmolean negative: EA.CA.5467.
Published in Creswell 1932, pl. 34.a.

Figure: 528 (left).
Subject: Damascus. The southwestern minaret of the Umayyad Mosque.
Berenson ID: 133448.
Medium: gelatine silver print, 12×17cm.
Date of creation: 1919-1920.
Handwritten notes on the back: 'Damascus, Great Mosque – S/W minaret (Qayt-Bay)' [Cres.].
Ashmolean negative: EA.CA.5462.

Figure: 529 (centre).
Subject: Damascus. The southwestern minaret of the Umayyad Mosque.
Berenson ID: 133447.
Medium: gelatine silver print, 12×17cm.
Date of creation: 1919-1920.
Handwritten notes on the back: 'Damascus, Great Mosque – S/W minaret' [Cres.].
Ashmolean negative: EA.CA.5464.

Figure: 530 (right).
Subject: Damascus. The southern façade of the Umayyad Mosque.
Berenson ID: 133449.
Medium: gelatine silver print, 12×17cm.
Date of creation: 1919-1920.
Handwritten notes on the back: 'Damascus, Great Mosque – S. façade' [Cres.].
Ashmolean negative: EA.CA.714.
Published in Creswell 1932, pl. 33.d.

Figure: 531 (left).
Subject: Damascus. The southern façade of the Umayyad Mosque.
Berenson ID: 133451.
Medium: gelatine silver print, 12×17cm.
Date of creation: 1919-1920.
Handwritten notes on the back: 'Damascus, Great Mosque – S. facade' [Cres.]

Figure: 532 (right).
Subject: Damascus. The southeastern minaret of the Umayyad Mosque.
Berenson ID: 133586.
Medium: gelatine silver print, 12×17cm.
Date of creation: 1919-1925.
Handwritten notes on the back: 'Damascus, Great Mosque – S.E. minaret' [Cres.].
Ashmolean negative: EA.CA.717.
Published in Creswell 1932, pl. 34.c.

THE SITES AND THE MONUMENTS – SYRIA

Figure: 533.
Subject: Damascus. The southern façade of the Umayyad Mosque.
Berenson ID: 133587.
Medium: gelatine silver print, 12×17cm.
Date of creation: 1919-1925.
Handwritten notes on the back: 'Damascus, Great Mosque – S. façade' [Cres.].
Ashmolean negative: EA.CA.719.

Figure: 534 (left).
Subject: Damascus. The southwestern minaret of the Umayyad Mosque.
Berenson ID: 133588.
Medium: gelatine silver print, 12×17cm.
Date of creation: 1919-1925.
Handwritten notes on the back: 'Damascus, Great Mosque – S.W. minaret' [Cres.].
Ashmolean negative: EA.CA.5465.
Published in Creswell 1932, pl. 33.c.

Figure: 535 (centre).
Subject: Damascus. The western façade of the Umayyad Mosque.
Berenson ID: 133488.
Medium: gelatine silver print, 12×17cm.
Date of creation: c. 1919-1925.
Handwritten notes on the back: 'Damascus, Great Mosque – west façade' [Cres.].

Figure: 536 (right).
Subject: Damascus. The northern entrance of the Umayyad Mosque.
Berenson ID: 133456.
Medium: gelatine silver print, 12×17cm.
Date of creation: 1919-1920.
Handwritten notes on the back: 'Damascus, Great Mosque – bronze doors in north side – c. 1400 A.D.' [Cres.].
Ashmolean negative: EA.CA.5475.

Figure: 537.
Subject: Damascus. The western entrance of the Umayyad Mosque.
Berenson ID: 133499.
Medium: gelatine silver print, 12×17cm.
Date of creation: 1919-1920.
Handwritten notes on the back: 'Damascus, Great Mosque – west door' [Cres.].

Figure: 538.
Subject: Damascus. The main façade of the sanctuary of the Umayyad Mosque.
Berenson ID: 133452.
Medium: gelatine silver print, 12×17cm.
Date of creation: 1919-1920.
Handwritten notes on the back: 'Damascus, Great Mosque – facade of sanctuary' [Cres.].
Ashmolean negative: EA.CA.5491.
Published in Creswell 1932, pl. 38.c; Creswell 1958, fig. 15.

Figure: 539 (left).
Subject: Damascus. The main main façade of the sanctuary of the Umayyad Mosque.
Berenson ID: 133457.
Medium: gelatine silver print, 12×17cm.
Date of creation: 1919-1920.
Handwritten notes on the back: 'Damascus, Great Mosque – entrance to transept' [Cres.].
Ashmolean negative: EA.CA.5482.

Figure: 540 (right).
Subject: Damascus. Mosaics over the entrance to the sanctuary of the Umayyad Mosque.
Berenson ID: 133575.
Medium: gelatine silver print, 12×17cm.
Date of creation: 1919-1925.
Handwritten notes on the back: 'Damascus, Great Mosque – mosaics on gable' [Cres.].

Figure: 541 (left).
Subject: Damascus. Mosaics over the entrance to the sanctuary of the Umayyad Mosque.
Berenson ID: 133576.
Medium: gelatine silver print, 12×17cm.
Date of creation: 1919-1925.
Handwritten notes on the back: 'Damascus, Great Mosque – mosaics on gable' [Cres.].
Ashmolean negative: EA.CA.102.

Figure: 542 (centre).
Subject: Damascus. The platform used for photographing the mosaics of the Umayyad Mosque.
Berenson ID: 133577.
Medium: gelatine silver print, 12×17cm.
Date of creation: 1919-1925.
Handwritten notes on the back: 'Damascus, Great Mosque – platform employed for photographing mosaics' [Cres.].
Ashmolean negative: EA.CA.5481.

Figure: 543 (right).
Subject: Damascus. The northern side of the main courtyard of the Umayyad Mosque.
Berenson ID: 133573.
Medium: gelatine silver print, 12×17cm.
Date of creation: 1919-1925.
Handwritten notes on the back: 'Damascus, Great Mosque – mosaics on N. side of sahn' [Cres.].
Ashmolean negative: EA.CA.396.

Figure: 544.
Subject: Damascus. The western side of the main courtyard of the Umayyad Mosque.
Berenson ID: 133589.
Medium: gelatine silver print, 12×17cm.
Date of creation: 1919-1925.
Handwritten notes on the back: 'Damascus, Great Mosque – W. side of sahn' [Cres.].
Ashmolean negative: EA.CA.5479.
Published in Creswell 1932, pl. 35.a; Creswell 1958, fig. 18.

MESOPOTAMIA, SYRIA AND TRANSJORDAN IN THE CRESWELL COLLECTION

Figure: 545 (left).
Subject: Damascus. The northern side of he main courtyard of the Umayyad Mosque.
Berenson ID: 133453.
Medium: gelatine silver print, 12×17cm.
Date of creation: 1919-1920.
Handwritten notes on the back: 'Damascus, Great Mosque – sahn – N. side' [Cres.].
Ashmolean negative: EA.CA.5476.

Figure: 546 (right).
Subject: Damascus. The southwestern corner of the main courtyard of the Umayyad Mosque.
Berenson ID: 133454.
Medium: gelatine silver print, 12×17cm.
Date of creation: 1919-1920.
Handwritten notes on the back: 'Damascus, Great Mosque – S/W corner of sahn' [Cres.].
Ashmolean negative: EA.CA.5480.
Published in Creswell 1932, pl. 34.d.

Figure: 547.
Subject: Damascus. Detail of the Qubba al-Khazn in the Umayyad Mosque.
Berenson ID: 133533.
Medium: gelatine silver print, 12×17cm.
Date of creation: 1919-1925.
Handwritten notes on the back: 'Damascus, Qubbat al-Khazna' [Cres.].
Ashmolean negative: EA.CA.5478.

Figure: 548 (left).
Subject: Damascus. The dome of the Umayyad Mosque.
Berenson ID: 133459.
Medium: gelatine silver print, 12×17cm.
Date of creation: 1919-1920.
Handwritten notes on the back: 'Damascus, Great Mosque – squinch of dome' [Cres.].
Ashmolean negative: EA.CA.5494.

Figure: 549 (right).
Subject: Damascus. Stucco grilles of the Umayyad Mosque.
Berenson ID: 133591.
Medium: gelatine silver print, 12×17cm.
Date of creation: 1919-1925.
Handwritten notes on the back: 'Damascus, Great Mosque: stucco grilles' [Cres.].

The Sites and the Monuments – Syria

Figure: 550 (left).
Subject: Damascus. Stucco grilles of the Umayyad Mosque.
Berenson ID: 133592.
Medium: gelatine silver print, 12×17cm.
Date of creation: 1919-1925.
Handwritten notes on the back: 'Damascus, Great Mosque – stucco grilles' [Cres.].
Ashmolean negative: EA.CA.5486.

Figure: 551 (centre).
Subject: Damascus. Stucco grilles of the Umayyad Mosque.
Berenson ID: 133593.
Medium: gelatine silver print, 12×17cm.
Date of creation: 1919-1925.
Handwritten notes on the back: 'Damascus, Great Mosque – stucco grilles' [Cres.].
Ashmolean negative: EA.CA.5488.

Figure: 552 (right).
Subject: Damascus. Stucco grilles of the Umayyad Mosque.
Berenson ID: 133594.
Medium: gelatine silver print, 12×17cm.
Date of creation: 1919-1925.
Handwritten notes on the back: 'Damascus, Great Mosque – stucco grilles' [Cres.].
Ashmolean negative: EA.CA.5487.

Figure: 553 (left).
Subject: Damascus. Mihrab of the Umayyad Mosque.
Berenson ID: 133595.
Medium: gelatine silver print, 12×17cm.
Date of creation: 1919-1925.
Handwritten notes on the back: 'Damascus, Great Mosque – Tulunide mihrab' [Cres.].
Ashmolean negative: EA.CA.5485.

Figure: 554 (right).
Subject: Damascus. Window in the northern minaret of the Umayyad Mosque.
Berenson ID: 133590.
Medium: gelatine silver print, 12×17cm.
Date of creation: 1919-1925.
Handwritten notes on the back: 'Damascus, Great Mosque – window in N. minaret – from within' [Cres.].
Ashmolean negative: EA.CA.5495.

Figure: 555 (left).
Subject: Damascus. Interior of the Umayyad Mosque.
Berenson ID: 133458.
Medium: gelatine silver print, 12×17cm.
Date of creation: 1919-1920.
Handwritten notes on the back: 'Damascus, Great Mosque – transept looking N' [Cres.].
Ashmolean negative: EA.CA.5493.

Figure: 556 (centre).
Subject: Damascus. Marble paneling at the eastern entrance of the Umayyad Mosque.
Berenson ID: 133574.
Medium: gelatine silver print, 12×17cm.
Date of creation: 1919-1925.
Handwritten notes on the back: 'Damascus, Great Mosque – marble panelling in E. entrance' [Cres.].
Ashmolean negative: EA.CA.107.
Published in Creswell 1932, pl. 39.b; Creswell 1958, fig. 21.

Figure: 557 (right).
Subject: Damascus. The southwestern corner of the courtyard of the Umayyad Mosque.
Berenson ID: 133455.
Medium: gelatine silver print, 12×17cm.
Date of creation: 1919-1920.
Handwritten notes on the back: 'Damascus, Great Mosque – S/W corner of sahn' [Cres.].
Ashmolean negative: EA.CA.5492.

Figure: 558 (left).
Subject: Damascus. Mosaics of the Umayyad Mosque.
Berenson ID: 133460.
Medium: gelatine silver print, 12×17cm.
Date of creation: 1919-1920.
Handwritten notes on the back: 'Damascus, Great Mosque – remains of gold mosaic' [Cres.].

Figure: 559 (right).
Subject: Damascus. Mosaics of the Umayyad Mosque.
Berenson ID: 133507.
Medium: gelatine silver print, 12×17cm.
Date of creation: c. 1919-1925.
Handwritten notes on the back: 'Damascus, Great Mosque – mosaic over W. entrance' [Cres.].
Ashmolean negative: EA.CA.108.

Figure: 560 (left).
Subject: Damascus. Mosaics of the Umayyad Mosque.
Berenson ID: 133443.
Medium: gelatine silver print, 12×17cm.
Date of creation: c. 1919-1925.
Handwritten notes on the back: 'Damascus, Grand Mosque – Mosaics over W entrance' [Cres.]. 'Photo Creswell pp. 164-165 photo 32 + Great Mosque Damascus' [Anon.].
Ashmolean negative: EA.CA.613. Published in Creswell 1932, pl. 36.

Figure: 561 (centre).
Subject: Damascus. Mosaics of the Umayyad Mosque.
Berenson ID: 133598.
Medium: gelatine silver print, 12×17cm.
Date of creation: c. 1919-1925.
Handwritten notes on the back: 'Damascus, Great Mosque – mosaics on soffits of gable windows' [Cres.].
Ashmolean negative: EA.CA.606. Published in Creswell 1932, pl. 40.c.

Figure: 562 (right).
Subject: Damascus. Mosaics of the Umayyad Mosque.
Berenson ID: 133600.
Medium: gelatine silver print, 12×17cm.
Date of creation: c. 1919-1925.
Handwritten notes on the back: 'Damascus, Great Mosque – mosaics on soffits of gable windows' [Cres.].
Ashmolean negative: EA.CA.607. Published in Creswell 1932, pl. 40.d.

Figure: 563 (left).
Subject: Damascus. Mosaics of the Umayyad Mosque.
Berenson ID: 133601.
Medium: gelatine silver print, 12×17cm.
Date of creation: c. 1919-1925.
Handwritten notes on the back: 'Damascus, Great Mosque – mosaics on soffits of gable window' [Cres.].
Ashmolean negative: EA.CA.608.
Published in Creswell 1932, pl. 40.b.

Figure: 564 (right).
Subject: Damascus. Mosaics of the Umayyad Mosque.
Berenson ID: 133605.
Medium: gelatine silver print, 12×17cm.
Date of creation: 1925 [above, p. 15].
Handwritten notes on the back: 'Damascus, Great Mosque – mosaics on inner side of gable' [Cres.].
Ashmolean negative: EA.CA.626.
Published in Creswell 1932, pl. 42.c.

Figure: 565.
Subject: Damascus. Mosaics of the Umayyad Mosque.
Berenson ID: 133596.
Medium: gelatine silver print, 12×17cm.
Date of creation: c. 1919-1925.
Handwritten notes on the back: 'Telephoto – Damascus, Great Mosque – mosaics on gable' [Cres.].
Ashmolean negative: EA.CA.604.

Figure: 566.
Subject: Damascus. Mosaics of the Umayyad Mosque.
Berenson ID: 133599.
Medium: gelatine silver print, 12×17cm.
Date of creation: c. 1919-1925.
Handwritten notes on the back: 'Telephoto – Damascus, Great Mosque – mosaics on gable' [Cres.].
Ashmolean negative: EA.CA.605.

Figure: 567 (left).
Subject: Damascus. Mosaics of the Umayyad Mosque.
Berenson ID: 133603.
Medium: gelatine silver print, 12×17cm.
Date of creation: c. 1919-1925.
Handwritten notes on the back: 'Damascus, Great Mosque – mosaic on N.W pier of dome' [Cres.].
Ashmolean negative: EA.CA.625.

Figure: 568 (right).
Subject: Damascus. Mosaics of the Umayyad Mosque.
Berenson ID: 133606.
Medium: gelatine silver print, 12×17cm.
Date of creation: c. 1919-1925.
Handwritten notes on the back: 'Damascus, Great Mosque – mosaic on N.E. pier of dome' [Cres.].
Ashmolean negative: EA.CA.627.
Published in Creswell 1932, pl. 41.b.

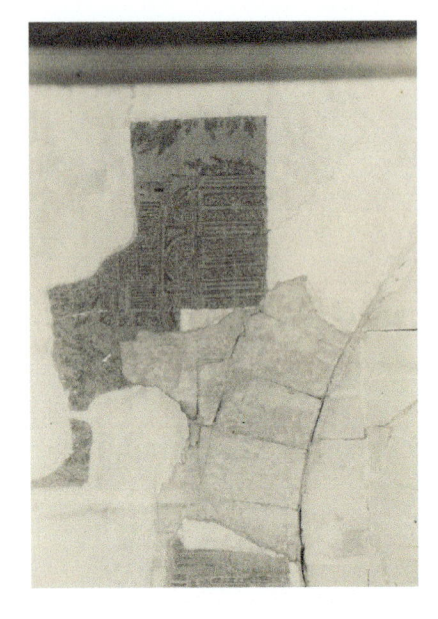

The Sites and the Monuments – Syria

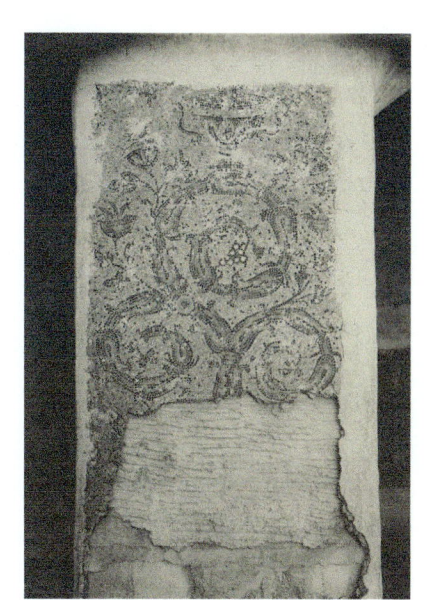

Figure: 569 (left).
Subject: Damascus. Mosaics of the Umayyad Mosque.
Berenson ID: 133578.
Medium: gelatine silver print, 12×17cm.
Date of creation: c. 1919-1925.
Handwritten notes on the back: 'Damascus, Great Mosque – mosaics on W. Side of sahn' [Cres.].
Ashmolean negative: EA.CA.110.
Published in Creswell 1932, pl. 37.a.

Figure: 570 (centre).
Subject: Damascus. Mosaics of the Umayyad Mosque.
Berenson ID: 133597.
Medium: gelatine silver print, 12×17cm.
Date of creation: c. 1919-1925.
Handwritten notes on the back: 'Damascus, Great Mosque – mosaics on W. side of sahn' [Cres.].
Ashmolean negative: EA.CA.1478.

Figure: 571 (right).
Subject: Damascus. Mosaics of the Umayyad Mosque.
Berenson ID: 133604.
Medium: gelatine silver print, 12×17cm.
Date of creation: c. 1919-1925.
Handwritten notes on the back: 'Damascus, Great Mosque – mosaics on W. side of sahn' [Cres.].
Ashmolean negative: EA.CA.623.
Published in Creswell 1932, pl. 34.b.

Figure: 572 (left).
Subject: Damascus. Mosaics of the Umayyad Mosque.
Berenson ID: 133579.
Medium: gelatine silver print, 12×17cm.
Date of creation: c. 1919-1925.
Handwritten notes on the back: 'Damascus, Great Mosque – mosaics on W. side of sahn' [Cres.].
Published in Creswell 1932, pl. 37.b.

Figure: 573 (right).
Subject: Damascus. Mosaics of the Umayyad Mosque.
Berenson ID: 133580.
Medium: gelatine silver print, 12×17cm.
Date of creation: c. 1919-1925.
Handwritten notes on the back: 'Damascus, Great Mosque – mosaics in W. Vestibule' [Cres.].
Ashmolean negative: EA.CA.1479.

Figure: 574 (left).
Subject: Damascus. Mosaics of the Umayyad Mosque.
Berenson ID: 133581.
Medium: gelatine silver print, 12×17cm.
Date of creation: c. 1919-1925.
Handwritten notes on the back: 'Damascus, Great Mosque – mosaics in W. Vestibule' [Cres.].
Ashmolean negative: EA.CA.614.
Published in Creswell 1932, pl. 36.a; Creswell 1958, fig. 25.

Figure: 575 (centre).
Subject: Damascus. Mosaics of the Umayyad Mosque.
Berenson ID: 133582.
Medium: gelatine silver print, 12×17cm.
Date of creation: c. 1919-1925.
Handwritten notes on the back: 'Damascus, Great Mosque – mosaics in W. Vestibule' [Cres.].
Ashmolean negative: EA.CA.617.
Published in Creswell 1932, pl. 37.c.

Figure: 576 (right).
Subject: Damascus. Mosaics of the Umayyad Mosque.
Berenson ID: 133583.
Medium: gelatine silver print, 12×17cm.
Date of creation: c. 1919-1925.
Handwritten notes on the back: 'Damascus, Great Mosque – mosaics in W. Vestibule' [Cres.].
Ashmolean negative: EA.CA.88.

Figure: 577 (left).
Subject: Damascus. Mosaics of the Umayyad Mosque.
Berenson ID: 133584.
Medium: gelatine silver print, 12×17cm.
Date of creation: c. 1919-1925.
Handwritten notes on the back: 'Damascus, Great Mosque – mosaics in W. Vestibule' [Cres.].
Ashmolean negative: EA.CA.624.
Published in Creswell 1932, pl. 37.d.

Figure: 578 (right).
Subject: Damascus. Mosaics of the Umayyad Mosque.
Berenson ID: 133585.
Medium: gelatine silver print, 12×17cm.
Date of creation: c. 1919-1925.
Handwritten notes on the back: 'Damascus, Great Mosque – mosaics in W. Vestibule' [Cres.].
Ashmolean negative: EA.CA.615.
Published in Creswell 1932, pl. 36.b.

Figure: 579 (left).
Subject: Damascus. The Bab al-Salam.
Berenson ID: 133515.
Medium: gelatine silver print, 12×17cm.
Date of creation: 1919-1925.
Handwritten notes on the back: 'Damascus, Bab as-Salam — 641 (1243/4)' [Cres.].
Ashmolean negative: EA.CA.5550.

Figure: 580 (centre).
Subject: Damascus. Bab al-Faraj.
Berenson ID: 133516.
Medium: gelatine silver print, 12×17cm.
Date of creation: 1919-1925.
Handwritten notes on the back: 'Damascus, Bab al-Farag — 637 (1239/40)' [Cres.].
Ashmolean negative: EA.CA.5547.

Figure: 581 (right).
Subject: Damascus. The entrance of the Nur al-Din Madrasa and Bimaristan.
Berenson ID: 133572.
Medium: gelatine silver print, 12×17cm.
Date of creation: 1919-1925.
Handwritten notes on the back: 'Damascus, Maristan of Nur ad-Din, entrance' [Cres.].
Ashmolean negative: EA.CA.5497.

Figure: 582 (left).
Subject: Damascus. Muqarnas in the Nur al-Din Madrasa and Bimaristan.
Berenson ID: 133563.
Medium: gelatine silver print, 12×17cm.
Date of creation: 1919-1925.
Handwritten notes on the back: 'Damascus, Maristan of Nur ad-Din stalactite bay of vestibule — 549 (1154/5)' [Cres.].
Ashmolean negative: EA.CA.5498.

Figure: 583 (right).
Subject: Damascus. Western iwan of the Nur al-Din Madrasa and Bimaristan.
Berenson ID: 133570.
Medium: gelatine silver print, 12×17cm.
Date of creation: 1919-1925.
Handwritten notes on the back: 'Damascus, Maristan of Nur ad-Din – W. liwan' [Cres.].
Ashmolean negative: EA.CA.5499.

Figure: 584.
Subject: Damascus. The dome of the vestibule of the Nur al-Din Madrasa and Bimaristan.
Berenson ID: 133571.
Medium: gelatine silver print, 12×17cm.
Date of creation: 1919-1925.
Handwritten notes on the back: 'Damascus, Maristan of Nur ad-Din, dome of vestibule' [Cres.].
Ashmolean negative: EA.CA.7997.

Figure: 585 (left).
Subject: Damascus. Mihrab of the Nur al-Din Madrasa and Bimaristan.
Berenson ID: 133567.
Medium: gelatine silver print, 12×17cm.
Date of creation: 1919-1925.
Handwritten notes on the back: 'Damascus, Maristan of Nur ad-Din mihrab' [Cres.].

Figure: 586 (right).
Subject: Damascus. architectural decoration in the al-Adiliya Madrasa.
Berenson ID: 133497.
Medium: gelatine silver print, 12×17cm.
Date of creation: 1919-1920.
Handwritten notes on the back: 'Damascus, Adeliya Madrasa – sahn, east side — finished 1220' [Cres.].
Ashmolean negative: EA.CA.5523.

Figure: 587.
Subject: Damascus. Façade of the sanctuary of the al-Adiliya Madrasa.
Berenson ID: 133491.
Medium: gelatine silver print, 12×17cm.
Date of creation: 1919-1920.
Handwritten notes on the back: 'Damascus, Adeliya Madrasa – façade of sanctuary — finished 1220' [Cres.].
Ashmolean negative: EA.CA.5525.

The Sites and the Monuments – Syria

Figure: 588.
Subject: Damascus. Interior of the sanctuary of the al-Adiliya Madrasa.
Berenson ID: 133493.
Medium: gelatine silver print, 12×17cm.
Date of creation: 1919-1920.
Handwritten notes on the back: 'Damascus, Adeliya Madrasa – interior of sanctuary — finished 1220' [Cres.].
Ashmolean negative: EA.CA.5527.

Figure: 589.
Subject: Damascus. Interior of the sanctuary of the al-Adiliya Madrasa.
Berenson ID: 133494.
Medium: gelatine silver print, 12×17cm.
Date of creation: 1919-1920.
Handwritten notes on the back: 'Damascus, Adeliya Madrasa – interior of sanctuary — finished 1220' [Cres.].
Ashmolean negative: EA.CA.5528.

Figure: 590.
Subject: Damascus. The al-Adiliya Madrasa.
Berenson ID: 133498.
Medium: gelatine silver print, 12×17cm.
Date of creation: 1919-1920.
Handwritten notes on the back: 'Damascus, Adeliya Madrasa – sahn, east side — finished 1220' [Cres.].
Ashmolean negative: EA.CA.5524.

Figure: 591.
Subject: Damascus. The entrance of the al-Adiliya Madrasa.
Berenson ID: 133486.
Medium: gelatine silver print, 12×17cm.
Date of creation: 1919-1920.
Handwritten notes on the back: 'Damascus, Adiliya Madrasa – entrance — finished 1220' [Cres.].
Ashmolean negative: EA.CA.5520.

Figure: 592.
Subject: Damascus. Vaulting of the entrance of the al-Adiliya Madrasa.
Berenson ID: 133490.
Medium: gelatine silver print, 12×17cm.
Date of creation: 1919-1920.
Handwritten notes on the back: 'Damascus, Adeliya Madrasa – vaulting of entrance bay — finished 1220' [Cres.].
Ashmolean negative: EA.CA.5522.

Figure: 593.
Subject: Damascus. Restored façade of the al-Adiliya Madrasa.
Berenson ID: 133492.
Medium: gelatine silver print, 12×17cm.
Date of creation: 1919-1920.
Handwritten notes on the back: 'Damascus, Adeliya Madrasa – façade of sanctuary after (so-called) restoration — c. 1220' [Cres.].
Ashmolean negative: EA.CA.5526.

THE SITES AND THE MONUMENTS – SYRIA

Figure: 594.
Subject: Damascus. The western side of the al-Adiliya Madrasa.
Berenson ID: 133495.
Medium: gelatine silver print, 12×17cm.
Date of creation: 1919-1920.
Handwritten notes on the back: 'Damascus, Adeliya Madrasa – west side of sahn (modern) — finished 1220' [Cres.].
Ashmolean negative: EA.CA.5529.

Figure: 595.
Subject: Damascus. The dome of the al-Nuriya al-Kubra Madrasa.
Berenson ID: 133562.
Medium: gelatine silver print, 12×17cm.
Date of creation: 1919-1925.
Handwritten notes on the back: 'Damascus, Mausoleum of Nur ad-Din dome — 561 (1171/2)' [Cres.].
Ashmolean negative: EA.CA.5502.

Figure: 596 (left).
Subject: Damascus. The mihrab of the Abd al-Rahman ibn Abdallah al-Tashtadar Madrasa.
Berenson ID: 133517.
Medium: gelatine silver print, 12×17cm.
Date of creation: 1919-1925.
Handwritten notes on the back: 'Damascus, Madrasa of 'abd ar-Rahman ibn 'Abdallah at-Tashtadar – mihrab — 637 (1239/40)' [Cres.].
Ashmolean negative: EA.CA.5548.

Figure: 597 (right).
Subject: Damascus. The Abu Abdallah Hasan ibn Salama Mausoleum.
Berenson ID: 133550.
Medium: gelatine silver print, 12×17cm.
Date of creation: 1919-1925.
Handwritten notes on the back: 'Damascus, Mausoleum of 'Abu 'Abdallah Hasan as-Salami — 620 (1223)' [Cres.].
Ashmolean negative: EA.CA.5531.

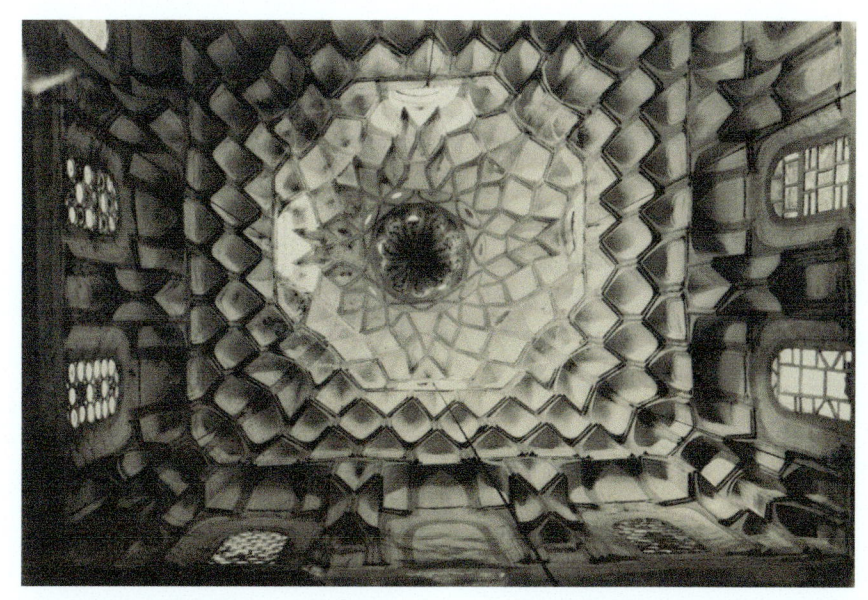

Figure: 598.
Subject: Damascus. The setting of the dome of the Abu Abdallah Hasan ibn Salama Mausoleum.
Berenson ID: 133551.
Medium: gelatine silver print, 12×17cm.
Date of creation: 1919-1925.
Handwritten notes on the back: 'Damascus, Mausoleum of 'Abu 'Abdallah Hasan as-Salami – pendentive' [Cres.].
Ashmolean negative: EA.CA.5530.

Figure: 599.
Subject: Damascus. The al-Maridaniya Mosque.
Berenson ID: 133553.
Medium: gelatine silver print, 12×17cm.
Date of creation: 1919-1925.
Handwritten notes on the back: 'Damascus, Madrasa Mardaniya — barely 610 (1213)' [Cres.].
Ashmolean negative: EA.CA.5517.

Figure: 600.
Subject: Damascus. The interior of the al-Maridaniya Mosque.
Berenson ID: 133552.
Medium: gelatine silver print, 12×17cm.
Date of creation: 1919-1925.
Handwritten notes on the back: 'Damascus, Mardaniya Madrasa – pendentives' [Cres.].
Ashmolean negative: EA.CA.5519.

THE SITES AND THE MONUMENTS – SYRIA

Figure: 601 (left).
Subject: Damascus. The al-Qaymari Maristan and Mausoleum.
Berenson ID: 133510.
Medium: gelatine silver print, 12×17cm.
Date of creation: 1919-1925.
Handwritten notes on the back: 'Damascus, Mausoleum of Qaymari — 654 (1256)' [Cres.].
Ashmolean negative: EA.CA.5566.

Figure: 602 (right).
Subject: Damascus. The entrance of the al-Qaymari Maristan and Mausoleum.
Berenson ID: 133511.
Medium: gelatine silver print, 12×17cm.
Date of creation: 1919-1925.
Handwritten notes on the back: 'Damascus, Maristan of Qaymari, entrance — 646 (1245/9)' [Cres.].
Ashmolean negative: EA.CA.5553.

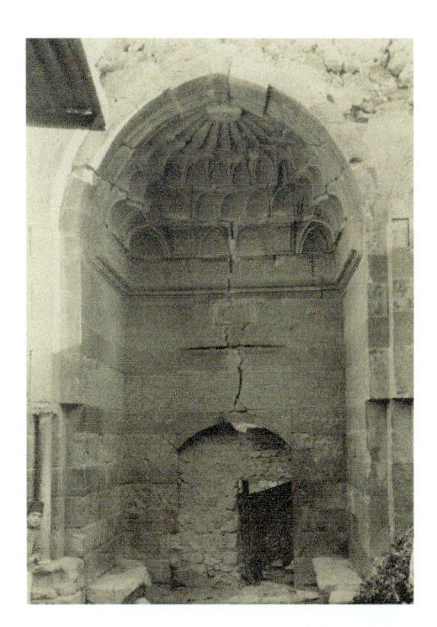

Figure: 603.
Subject: Damascus. The al-Qaymari Maristan and Mausoleum.
Berenson ID: 133512.
Medium: gelatine silver print, 12×17cm.
Date of creation: 1919-1925.
Handwritten notes on the back: 'Damascus, Maristan of Qaymari – sahn – IV – side' [Cres.].
Ashmolean negative: EA.CA.5555.

Figure: 604.
Subject: Damascus. The al-Qaymari Maristan and Mausoleum.
Berenson ID: 133514.
Medium: gelatine silver print, 12×17cm.
Date of creation: 1919-1925.
Handwritten notes on the back: 'Damascus, Maristan of Qaymari – sahn – looking S/W' [Cres.].
Ashmolean negative: EA.CA.5557.

Figure: 605 (left).
Subject: Damascus. The al-Rihaniya Madrasa.
Berenson ID: 133561.
Medium: gelatine silver print, 12×17cm.
Date of creation: 1919-1925.
Handwritten notes on the back: 'Damascus, Madrasa ar-Rihaniya — 575 (1179/80)' [Cres.].
Ashmolean negative: EA.CA.5504.

Figure: 606 (right).
Subject: Damascus. The entrance of the al-Sahiba Madrasa.
Berenson ID: 133537.
Medium: gelatine silver print, 12×17cm.
Date of creation: 1919-1925.
Handwritten notes on the back: 'Damascus, Madrasa al Salihiya' [Cres.].

Figure: 607.
Subject: Damascus. The interior of the al-Shamiya al-Kubra Madrasa.
Berenson ID: 133560.
Medium: gelatine silver print, 12×17cm.
Date of creation: 1919-1925.
Handwritten notes on the back: 'Damascus, Madrasa ash-Shamiya – interior' [Cres.].
Ashmolean negative: EA.CA.2371.

Figure: 608.
Subject: Damascus. The mihrab of the al-Shamiya al-Kubra Madrasa.
Berenson ID: 133444.
Medium: gelatine silver print, 12×17cm.
Date of creation: c. 1919-1925.
Handwritten notes on the back: 'Damascus, Madrasah ash-Shamiya – mihrab — 582 (1186/7)' [Cres.].
Ashmolean negative: EA.CA.5506.

THE SITES AND THE MONUMENTS – SYRIA

Figure: 609.
Subject: Damascus. The Ali-Faranti Mausoleum.
Berenson ID: 133531.
Medium: gelatine silver print, 12×17cm.
Date of creation: 1919-1925.
Handwritten notes on the back: 'Damascus, (D.N.V.G.), Mausoleum of Shaeykh Ali (to right) — (621/1224)' [Cres.].
Ashmolean negative: EA.CA.5563.

Figure: 610 (left).
Subject: Damascus. The Ali-Faranti Mausoleum.
Berenson ID: 133528.
Medium: gelatine silver print, 12×17cm.
Date of creation: 1919-1925.
Handwritten notes on the back: 'Damascus, Mausoleum of Sheykh 'Ali — 621 (1226)' [Cres.].
Ashmolean negative: EA.CA.5534

Figure: 611.
Subject: Damascus. The Ali-Faranti Mausoleum.
Berenson ID: 133530.
Medium: gelatine silver print, 12×17cm.
Date of creation: 1919-1925.
Handwritten notes on the back: 'Damascus, Mausoleum of Sheykh 'Ali – pendentive — 621 (1226)' [Cres.].
Ashmolean negative: EA.CA.5533.

Figure: 612.
Subject: Damascus. The Amat al-Latif Mausoleum.
Berenson ID: 133541.
Medium: gelatine silver print, 12×17cm.
Date of creation: 1919-1925.
Handwritten notes on the back: 'Damascus, Mausoleum of Salihiya — 620 (1223)' [Cres.].
Ashmolean negative: EA.CA.5580.

Figure: 613.
Subject: Damascus. The interior of the Amat al-Latif Mausoleum (probable).
Berenson ID: 133539.
Medium: gelatine silver print, 12×17cm.
Date of creation: 1919-1925.
Handwritten notes on the back: 'Damascus, (Salihiyya), Mausoleum – opposite Wulzinger, Watzinger's D.N.TTC' [Cres.].
Ashmolean negative: EA.CA.5589.

Figure: 614.
Subject: Damascus. The entrance of the Atabektya Mosque.
Berenson ID: 133532.
Medium: gelatine silver print, 12×17cm.
Date of creation: 1919-1925.
Handwritten notes on the back: 'Damascus, Atabektiya Mosque, entrance' [Cres.].
Ashmolean negative: EA.CA.5595.

THE SITES AND THE MONUMENTS – SYRIA

Figure: 615.
Subject: Damascus. The Dar al-Hadith al-Ashrafiya al-Muqaddasiya.
Berenson ID: 133521.
Medium: gelatine silver print, 12×17cm.
Date of creation: c. 1919-1925.
Handwritten notes on the back: 'Damascus, Ashrafiya Muqaddasiya — 634 (1236)' [Cres.].

Figure: 616.
Subject: Damascus. The Hanabila Mosque, from above.
Berenson ID: 133556.
Medium: gelatine silver print, 12×17cm.
Date of creation: 1919-1925.
Handwritten notes on the back: 'Damascus, Hanabila Mosque — 599 (1202/3)' [Cres.].
Ashmolean negative: EA.CA.5510.

Figure: 617.
Subject: Damascus. The Hanabila Mosque.
Berenson ID: 133555.
Medium: gelatine silver print, 12×17cm.
Date of creation: 1919-1925.
Handwritten notes on the back: 'Damascus, Hanabila Mosque – sahn' [Cres.].
Ashmolean negative: EA.CA.5513.

Figure: 618 (left).
Subject: Damascus. Stucco on the façade of the Hanabila Mosque.
Berenson ID: 133445.
Medium: gelatine silver print, 12×17cm.
Date of creation: 1919-1925.
Handwritten notes on the back: 'Damascus, Hanabila Mosque – stucco ornament on facade of sanctuary' [Cres.].
Ashmolean negative: EA.CA.5511.

Figure: 619 (centre).
Subject: Damascus. The Izz al-Din Madrasa.
Berenson ID: 133526.
Medium: gelatine silver print, 12×17cm.
Date of creation: 1919-1925.
Handwritten notes on the back: 'Damascus, Madrasa/Mausoleum of 'Izz ad-Din' [Cres.].
Ashmolean negative: EA.CA.5539.

Figure: 620 (right).
Subject: Damascus. The Izz al-Din Madrasa.
Berenson ID: 133524.
Medium: gelatine silver print, 12×17cm.
Date of creation: 1919-1925.
Handwritten notes on the back: 'Damascus, Madrasa/Mausoleum of 'Izz ad-Din – entrance in enclosure — 626 (1228)' [Cres.].
Ashmolean negative: EA.CA.5537.

Figure: 621.
Subject: Damascus. The detting of the dome of the Izz al-Din Madrasa.
Berenson ID: 133523.
Medium: gelatine silver print, 12×17cm.
Date of creation: 1919-1925.
Handwritten notes on the back: 'Damascus, Madrasa-Mausoleum of 'Izz ad-Din – pendentive' [Cres.].
Ashmolean negative: EA.CA.5541.

Figure: 622 (left).
Subject: Damascus. architectural decoration of the Izz al-Din Madrasa.
Berenson ID: 133522.
Medium: gelatine silver print, 12×17cm.
Date of creation: 1919-1925.
Handwritten notes on the back: 'Damascus, Madrasa/Mausoleum of 'Izz ad-Din – ornament in mausoleum' [Cres.].
Ashmolean negative: EA.CA.5540.

Figure: 623 (right).
Subject: Damascus. The Jaharkasiya Madrasa.
Berenson ID: 133554.
Medium: gelatine silver print, 12×17cm.
Date of creation: 1919-1925.
Handwritten notes on the back: 'Damascus, Malik Seraksi' [Cres.].
Ashmolean negative: EA.CA.5516.

Figure: 624 (left).
Subject: Damascus. The mihrab of the Khatuniya Mausoleum.
Berenson ID: 133536.
Medium: gelatine silver print, 12×17cm.
Date of creation: c. 1919-1925.
Handwritten notes on the back: 'Damascus, Khatuniya Madrasa + mausoleum – mihrab in mausoleum — 650 (1252/3)' [Cres.].
Ashmolean negative: EA.CA.5564.

Figure: 625 (right).
Subject: Damascus. The Raihan Mausoleum.
Berenson ID: 133542.
Medium: gelatine silver print, 12×17cm.
Date of creation: c. 1919-1925.
Handwritten notes on the back: 'Damascus, Mausoleum of Sheykh Rihan — 641 (1242)' [Cres.].
Ashmolean negative: EA.CA.5552.

Figure: 626.
Subject: Damascus. The interior of the Rukn al-Din Mausoleum.
Berenson ID: 133549.
Medium: gelatine silver print, 12×17cm.
Date of creation: 1919-1925.
Handwritten notes on the back: 'Damascus, Mosque/Mausoleum of Rukn ad-Din — 620 (1223)' [Cres.].
Ashmolean negative: EA.CA.5532.

Figure: 627.
Subject: Damascus. The dome of the Saladin Mausoleum.
Berenson ID: 133557.
Medium: gelatine silver print, 12×17cm.
Date of creation: 1919-1925.
Handwritten notes on the back: 'Damascus, Mausoleum of Saladin – pendentives — 592 (1195)' [Cres.].
Ashmolean negative: EA.CA.5508.

Figure: 628 (left).
Subject: Damascus. The cenotaph of Imad ad-Din in the Saladin Mausoleum.
Berenson ID: 133558.
Medium: gelatine silver print, 12×17cm.
Date of creation: 1919-1925.
Handwritten notes on the back: 'Damascus, Mausoleum of Saladin, cenotaph of Imad ad-Din' [Cres.].
Ashmolean negative: EA.CA.5509

Figure: 629.
Subject: Damascus. Shaykh Muhammad ibn Ali ibn Nadif Mausoleum.
Berenson ID: 133527.
Medium: gelatine silver print, 12×17cm.
Date of creation: 1919-1925.
Handwritten notes on the back: 'Damascus, Mausoleum of Sheykh Muh. Ibn 'Ali ibn Nadif — 622 (1225)' [Cres.].
Ashmolean negative: EA.CA.5536.

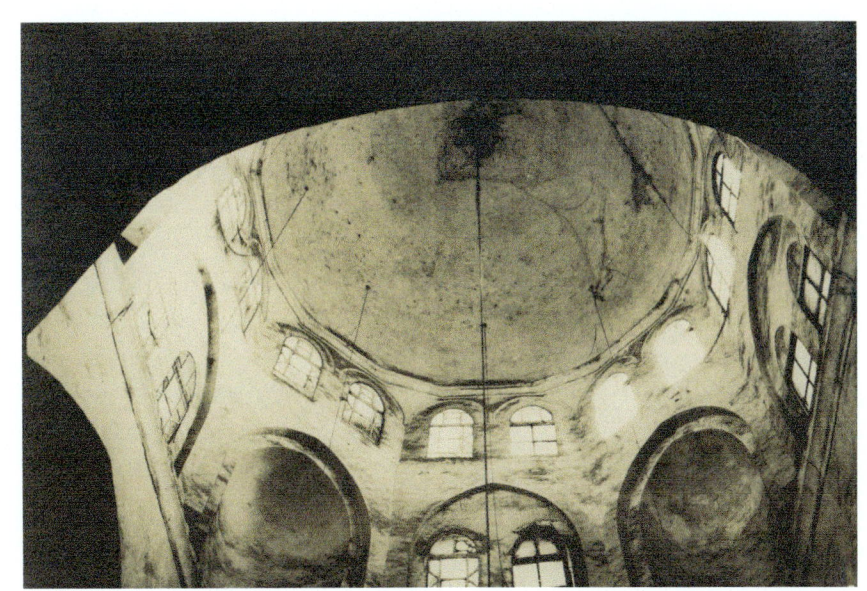

The Sites and the Monuments – Syria

Figure: 630.
Subject: Damascus. The dome of the al-Zahiriya Madrasa.
Berenson ID: 133464.
Medium: gelatine silver print, 12×17cm.
Date of creation: 1919-1920.
Handwritten notes on the back: 'Damascus, Zaheriya Madrasa – squinches of mausoleum' [Cres.].
Ashmolean negative: EA.CA.5571.

Figure: 631(right).
Subject: Damascus. The entrance of the al-Zahiriya Madrasa.
Berenson ID: 133461.
Medium: gelatine silver print, 12×17cm.
Date of creation: 1919-1920.
Handwritten notes on the back: 'Damascus, Zaheriya Madrasa – entrance — c. 1270' [Cres.].
Ashmolean negative: EA.CA.5569.

Figure: 632 (left).
Subject: Damascus. architectural decoration of the interior of the al-Zahiriya Madrasa.
Berenson ID: 133463.
Medium: gelatine silver print, 12×17cm.
Date of creation: 1919-1920.
Handwritten notes on the back: 'Damascus, Zaheriya Madrasa – panelling of mausoleum — c. 1270' [Cres.].
Ashmolean negative: EA.CA.5570.

Figure: 633 (centre).
Subject: Damascus. a detail of the al-Zahiriya Madrasa.
Berenson ID: 133482.
Medium: gelatine silver print, 12×17cm.
Date of creation: 1919-1920.
Handwritten notes on the back: 'Damascus, Zaheriya Madrasa – mausoleum — c. 1270' [Cres.].
Ashmolean negative: EA.CA.5573.

Figure: 634 (right).
Subject: Damascus. The mhrab of the al-Zahiriya Madrasa.
Berenson ID: 133484.
Medium: gelatine silver print, 12×17cm.
Date of creation: 1919-1920.
Handwritten notes on the back: 'Damascus, Zaheriya Madrasa – mihrab in mausoleum' [Cres.].
Ashmolean negative: EA.CA.5575.

Figure: 635.
Subject: Damascus. Remains of iwan of the al-Zahiriya Madrasa.
Berenson ID: 133485.
Medium: gelatine silver print, 12×17cm.
Date of creation: 1919-1920.
Handwritten notes on the back: 'Damascus, Zaheriya Madrasa – remains of S. Iiwan' [Cres.].
Ashmolean negative: EA.CA.5576.

Figure: 636.
Subject: Damascus. The façade of the Amir Tankiz Mosque and Mausoleum.
Berenson ID: 133544.
Medium: gelatine silver print, 12×17cm.
Date of creation: 1919-1925.
Handwritten notes on the back: 'Damascus, Mosque/Mausoleum of the Emir Tenkiz façade — 717 (1317)' [Cres.].
Ashmolean negative: EA.CA.5583.

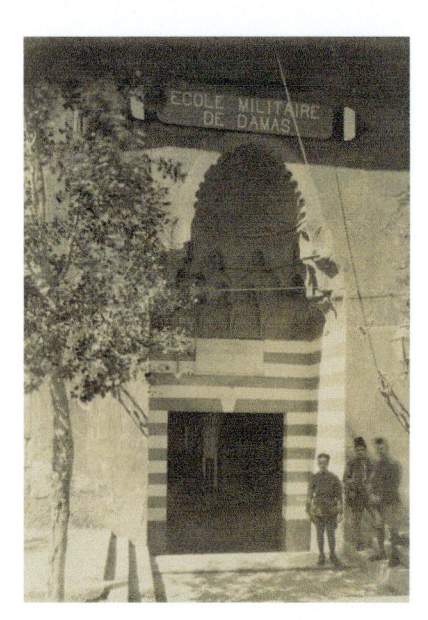

Figure: 637 (left).
Subject: Damascus. The eastern entrance of the Amir Tankiz Mosque and Mausoleum.
Berenson ID: 133545.
Medium: gelatine silver print, 12×17cm.
Date of creation: 1919-1925.
Handwritten notes on the back: 'Damascus, Mosque/Mausoleum of the Emir Tenkiz – E entrance' [Cres.].
Ashmolean negative: EA.CA.5585.

Figure: 638 (centre).
Subject: Damascus. The western entrance of the Amir Tankiz Mosque and Mausoleum.
Berenson ID: 133546.
Medium: gelatine silver print, 12×17cm.
Date of creation: 1919-1925.
Handwritten notes on the back: 'Damascus, Mosque/Mausoleum of the Emir Tenkiz – W ent.' [Cres.].
Ashmolean negative: EA.CA.5584.

Figure: 639.
Subject: Damascus. The middle entrance of the Amir Tankiz Mosque and Mausoleum.
Berenson ID: 133547.
Medium: gelatine silver print, 12×17cm.
Date of creation: 1919-1925.
Handwritten notes on the back: 'Damascus, Mosque/Mausoleum of the Emir Tenkiz – middle entrance' [Cres.].
Ashmolean negative: EA.CA.5586.

Figure: 640.
Subject: Damascus. Façade of the Amir Tankiz Mosque and Mausoleum.
Berenson ID: 133548.
Medium: gelatine silver print, 12×17cm.
Date of creation: 1919-1925.
Handwritten notes on the back: 'Damascus, Mosque/Mausoleum of the Emir Tenkiz – façade of sanctuary' [Cres.].
Ashmolean negative: EA.CA.5587.

Figure: 641.
Subject: Damascus. The Amir Kujkun al-Mansuri Mausoleum.
Berenson ID: 133540.
Medium: gelatine silver print, 12×17cm.
Date of creation: c. 1919-1925.
Handwritten notes on the back: 'Damascus, Mausoleum of Salihiya opposite Wulzinger + Watzinger's D.N.TT' [Cres.].
Ashmolean negative: EA.CA.5590.

Figure: 642.
Subject: Damascus. Blazons on the lintel of a house in Salihiya.
Berenson ID: 133508.
Medium: gelatine silver print, 12×17cm.
Date of creation: 1919-1925.
Handwritten notes on the back: 'Damascus, Lintel with blason embedded in a house at Salihiya' [Cres.].

Figure: 643.
Subject: Damascus. The Takiya al-Sulaymaniya.
Berenson ID: 133465.
Medium: gelatine silver print, 12×17cm.
Date of creation: 1919-1920.
Handwritten notes on the back: 'Tekiyya of Sultan Selim' [Cres.].
Ashmolean negative: EA.CA.5597.

Figure: 644.
Subject: Damascus. The Takiya al-Sulaymaniya.
Berenson ID: 133505.
Medium: gelatine silver print, 12×17cm.
Date of creation: 1919-1920.
No Handwritten notes on the back.
Ashmolean negative: EA.CA.5598.

THE SITES AND THE MONUMENTS – SYRIA

Figure: 645.
Subject: Damascus. The portico of the mosque of the Takiya al-Sulaymaniya.
Berenson ID: 133466.
Medium: gelatine silver print, 12×17cm.
Date of creation: 1919-1920.
Handwritten notes on the back: 'Damascus, Tekiyya of Sultan Selim – portico of mosque — 1516 aD' [Cres.]
Ashmolean negative: EA.CA.5599.

Figure: 646 (left).
Subject: Damascus. The entrance to the mosque of the Takiya al-Sulaymaniya.
Berenson ID: 133468.
Medium: gelatine silver print, 12×17cm.
Date of creation: 1919-1920.
Handwritten notes on the back: 'Damascus, Tekiyya of Sultan Selim – entrance to mosque — 1516' [Cres.].
Ashmolean negative: EA.CA.5601.

Figure: 647 (cebtre).
Subject: Damascus. The mihrab of the mosque of the Takiya al-Sulaymaniya.
Berenson ID: 133471.
Medium: gelatine silver print, 12×17cm.
Date of creation: 1919-1920.
Handwritten notes on the back: 'Damascus, Tekiyya of Sultan Selim – mihrab of mosque — 1516' [Cres.].
Ashmolean negative: EA.CA.5604.

Figure: 648.
Subject: Damascus. a tile panel in the mosque of the Takiya al-Sulaymaniya.
Berenson ID: 133470.
Medium: gelatine silver print, 12×17cm.
Date of creation: c. 1919-1925.
Handwritten notes on the back: 'Damascus, Tekiyya of Sultan Selim – tile panel in mosque — 1516' [Cres.].
Ashmolean negative: EA.CA.5603.

Figure: 649 (left).
Subject: Damascus. an opening of the Takiya al-Sulaymaniya.
Berenson ID: 133472.
Medium: gelatine silver print, 12×17cm.
Date of creation: 1919-1920.
Handwritten notes on the back: 'Damascus, Tekiyya of Sultan Selim – window of tekiyya' [Cres.].
Ashmolean negative: EA.CA.5605.

Figure: 650 (centre).
Subject: Damascus. The façade of the al-Sibaiya Madrasa.
Berenson ID: 133489.
Medium: gelatine silver print, 12×17cm.
Date of creation: 1919-1920.
Handwritten notes on the back: 'Damascus, Jami al-Kharratin – façade' [Cres.].
Ashmolean negative: EA.CA.5612.

Figure: 651 (right).
Subject: Damascus. The entrance of the al-Sibaiya Madrasa.
Berenson ID: 133480.
Medium: gelatine silver print, 12×17cm.
Date of creation: 1919-1920.
Handwritten notes on the back: 'Damascus, Jami al-Kharratin – entrance' [Cres.].
Ashmolean negative: EA.CA.5613.

Figure: 652 (left).
Subject: Damascus. The Sinan Pasha Mosque.
Berenson ID: 133506.
Medium: gelatine silver print, 12×17cm.
Date of creation: 1919-1920.
Handwritten notes on the back: 'Damascus, Mosque of Sinan Pasha — c. 990 (1582)' [Cres.].
Ashmolean negative: EA.CA.5606.

Figure: 653 (right).
Subject: Damascus. The entrance of the Sinan Pasha Mosque.
Berenson ID: 133503.
Medium: gelatine silver print, 12×17cm.
Date of creation: 1919-1920.
Handwritten notes on the back: 'Damascus, Mosque of Sinan Pasha – entrance — c. 990 (1582)' [Cres.].
Ashmolean negative: EA.CA.5607.

Figure: 654 (left).
Subject: Damascus. The interior of the Sinan Pasha Mosque.
Berenson ID: 133479.
Medium: gelatine silver print, 12×17cm.
Date of creation: 1919-1920.
Handwritten notes on the back: 'Damascus, Mosque of Sinan Pasha – interior — c. 990 (1582)' [Cres.].
Ashmolean negative: EA.CA.5608.

Figure: 655 (right).
Subject: Damascus. The mihrab of the Sinan Pasha Mosque.
Berenson ID: 133478.
Medium: gelatine silver print, 12×17cm.
Date of creation: 1919-1920.
Handwritten notes on the back: 'Damascus, Mosque of Sinan Pasha – mihrab' [Cres.].
Ashmolean negative: EA.CA.5609.

Figure: 656.
Subject: Damascus. The Azm Palace.
Berenson ID: 133476.
Medium: gelatine silver print, 12×17cm.
Date of creation: 1919-1920.
Handwritten notes on the back: 'Damascus, House of Asad Pasha' [Cres.].
Ashmolean negative: EA.CA.5619.

Figure: 657 (left).
Subject: Damascus. The interior of the Azm Palace.
Berenson ID: 133477.
Medium: gelatine silver print, 12×17cm.
Date of creation: 1919-1920.
Handwritten notes on the back: 'Damascus, House of Asad Pasha' [Cres.].
Ashmolean negative: EA.CA.5622.

Figure: 658 (right).
Subject: Damascus. The interior of the Azm Palace.
Berenson ID: 133504.
Medium: gelatine silver print, 12×17cm.
Handwritten notes on the back: 'Damascus, House of Asad Pasha' [Cres.].
Date of creation: 1919-1920.
Ashmolean negative: EA.CA.5621.

Figure: 659 (left).
Subject: Damascus. The entrance of the Khan Asad Pasha.
Berenson ID: 133473.
Medium: gelatine silver print, 12×17cm.
Date of creation: 1919-1920.
Handwritten notes on the back: 'Damascus, Khan of Asad Pasha – entrance' [Cres.].
Ashmolean negative: EA.CA.5614.

Figure: 660 (right).
Subject: Damascus. The interior of the Khan Asad Pasha.
Berenson ID: 133474.
Medium: gelatine silver print, 12×17cm.
Date of creation: 1919-1920.
Handwritten notes on the back: 'Damascus, Khan of Asad Pasha – interior' [Cres.].
Ashmolean negative: EA.CA.5615.

Figure: 661.
Subject: Damascus. The interior of the Khan Sulayman Pasha (Khan al-Jumruk in Creswell's caption).
Berenson ID: 133502.
Medium: gelatine silver print, 12×17cm.
Date of creation: 1919-1920.
Handwritten notes on the back: 'Damascus, Khan al-Gumruk, interior' [Cres.].
Ashmolean negative: EA.CA.5618.

Transjordan

Amman

Creswell visited Amman immediately before Emir Abdallah turned it into the new capital of the Hashemite kingdom. Compared to al-Salt, which had been the regional capital during the Ottoman rule, Amman was located more centrally and was one of the stations of the Hejaz railway which connected Damascus to Medina: two factors that certainly contributed to Emir Abdallah's decision.[398]

However, even at the time of proclamation of the capital — and therefore of Creswell's visit — Amman was little more than a village. It had developed around the ruins of the Roman settlement and in 1876 the Circassians fleeing from the Russian persecution sought refuge here. The fact that Amman was positioned along the route of the Hajaz railway gave new impetus to its development at the end of the 19th century, but the real growth of the city came only after World War I, as confirmed in the descriptions of travellers and western residents in slightly more recent years: interesting information in this regard can be found in the writings of Renato Bartoccini, who began the excavations of the Italian archaeological expedition to Transjordan in 1928,[399] and those of Gerald L. Harding. Bartoccini, in particular, reports that at the end of the 1920s the population had already reached 20,000 inhabitants.[400] This growth was also due to the massive arrival of Arabs from Palestine and other regions, making the population an amalgam of very different groups. The colourful report given by Bartoccini about the beginning of the 1933 excavation campaign is very interesting in this regard: 'In this campaign, as never before, the entire Muslim world was represented on the acropolis of Amman: Javaneses, Zanzibarians, Somalians, Eritreans, Yemenis, Iraqis, Druzes, Syrians, Circassians, Tripolitans, Tunisians, Egyptians, a small Tower of Babel, complicated by natives who had previously immigrated to South America and feared that their companions would consider them almost to be …Italians, because they spoke Spanish or Portuguese to us!'[401]. Serving as Director of the Department of Antiquities of Jordan between 1936 and 1956, Harding published a guide to Jordanian antiquities in 1959 which contains the news and information he collected

Figure 662: Amman. The northern façade of the Umayyad Congregational Mosque (a: from the inside; b: from the outside. Courtesy of Special Collections, Fine Arts Library, Harvard University).

since his first visit to Jordan in 1932.[402] Harding goes into great detail when recalling that the settlement was 'little more than an overgrown village' at the time of his first visit in 1932, and that 'the war brought great prosperity to the town, and residential areas began to spread farther and farther out from the center'[403].

Creswell's photographs are therefore particularly interesting because they were taken at a time immediately preceding the start of the great urban transformations in Amman, and they concern almost all the monuments known and visible at that time, which had been previously photographed only partially.[404]

---

[398] Nicholson 2005.

[399] Bartoccini 1930 and 1941. For a summary on the research of the Italian expedition, see Anastasio, Botarelli 2015. The expedition had actually begun as early as 1927, with a first campaign directed by Giacomo Guidi. Unfortunately, no written document has been kept, to my knowledge, apart from a letter with scanty information on the excavation (Anastasio, Botarelli 2015: 32).

[400] Bartoccini 1941: 51.

[401] Translated from the Italian original text in Bartoccini 1933-1934: 10.

[402] Harding 1959: 45-54.

[403] Harding 1959: 45-46.

[404] Among the main photographic surveys of Amman, prior to Creswell's visit, of note are those carried out in the following archaeological expeditions: the Palestine Exploration Fund (P.E.F.) expeditions in 1867-1970 (Warren Ch. 1880; photographer: Corporal H. Phillips) and in 1875 (Moulton J. 1928); the British expedition led by Major Claude R. Conder in 1881 (Conder 1889: 38, 44, 55, 64; photographer: Liutenant A.M. Mantell); the Russian expedition led by Nikodim P. Kondakov in 1891 (Adashinskaya, A. 2020; Kondakov 1904; photographer: Ivan Fedorovich Barshchevsky); the expedition of Rudolf-Ernst

Mesopotamia, Syria and Transjordan in the Creswell Collection

The arrival of colonies of Circassians in 1878 was certainly significant for the fate of the monuments, which were partly dismantled to obtain building material already before the visit of Creswell. A vivid picture of the situation is given in the account of the American archaeologist Frederick J. Bliss, who visited Amman in 1893:[405] 'Amman has much changed since the Circassians came in 1880. They now number 10,000 souls. Their houses are built of old materials as well as of mud brick. The town has a neat, thrifty appearance. Every room has its chimney; every house its porch or balcony. The yards are nicely swept. The people have a free and independent air. At first the destruction of the monuments, consequent on the establishment of this colony, was great; the Basilica has disappeared, and one apse of the interesting Thermae; but the Mukhtar told me that they now have orders to leave the ruins alone. Fortunately, they appear not to have touched the theatre'. However, it must be said that many of the monuments subsequently excavated were in areas difficult to reach and already covered with rubble scattered on the surface, or they were still buried; the spoliation, therefore, was probably less invasive than Bliss's story suggests.

In all, the photographs of the Berenson Collection dedicated to Amman are 27. It is easy to understand the state of visibility and accessibility of the monuments at the time of Creswell's visit by reading a volume of the 1912 *Baedeker Guide* dedicated to Syria and Palestine.[406] The Guide offers a brief description of Amman, listing all the monuments that could be visited. Creswell visited and photographed four of them, namely the Umayyad Congregational Mosque, the Roman Theatre and the Nymphaeum, and the so-called Audience Hall.[407]

A monument catalogued by Creswell referring to a different location can also be added: Qusayr al-Nuwaijis. In the 1920s, it was actually outside Amman, about 4km north of the Citadel. However, it is now fully incorporated into modern Amman. It is a Roman mausoleum of the 2nd/3rd century, which intrigued Creswell especially for its dome, supported by pendentives (Figure 666).[408]

The Umayyad Congregational Mosque is curiously not included among the monuments photographed in

Figure 663: Amman. Early photographs of the Roman Nimphaeum; a: 1904 (Butler 1907-1930, vol.II.a.I, Ammonitis: ill. 35); b: 1919-1920 (Creswell, below Figure 669); c: 1929 (Bartoccini 1935: 808).

Brünnow and Alfred von Domaszewski in 1897-1898 (Brünnow, Domaszewski 1904-1909); the German Baalbeck expedition in 1902 (Puchstein *et al.* 1902; Schulz-Strzygowski 1904; photographer: Bruno Schulz); the Princeton Archaeological Expedition to Syria (Butler *et al.* 1907-1930; photographer: G.D. Cavalcanty); the P.E.F. expedition of 1910 (Mackenzie 1911a, 1911b). Outside the archaeological expeditions, the photographs taken in 1850s-1860s by Rev. William M. Thomson, during his travels as a missionary, are noteworthy (Thomson 1886). The work of the Bonfils studio is also worth mentioning, which took many photographs in the 1890s (most recently: Abujaber, Cobbing 2005: 226), and that of the American Colony Photo Department, since 1898 (Bair 2011). Mention should also be made of the photos taken by Hermann Thiersch (Thiersch, Hölscher 1904), and those taken in 1900s-1910s by Gertrude Bell (Lukitz 2004).

[405] Bliss 1895: 234.
[406] Baedeker 1912: 145-147. The guide also reproduces a map of the citadel area, drawn by G. Armstrong.
[407] In the Baedeker guide, the Roman Nymphaeum corresponds to the 'Basilica', while the Audience Hall is referred to as 'an interesting specimen of Arab architecture (El-Kasr; hardly a mosque)' (Baedeker 1912: 146).
[408] Creswell 1932: 313-314, fig. 382. On the mausoleum see Yoshitake 2013: 2389-2391. Further views of the structure, not preserved in the Berenson Collection, are those of the Ashmolean's negatives EA.CA.5410 and EA.CA.5411. It should be noted that the negative EA.CA.5409, attributed to the mausoleum, actually represents the small nymphaeum at the top of the Roman theatre discussed above.

Figure 664: Amman. The restored right flank of north iwan of the Audience Hall; a: Creswell's time (see below, Figure 688); b: The Restoration carried out by the Italian expedition (Bartoccini 1933-1934, pl. 6/24); c: the current state (photo: 2014).

the Berenson Collection, while two views of the main facade, from inside and outside, are found in other archives (Figure 662).[409]

The Roman Theatre lies south of the Citadel, in the lower town, and it was minted in 169-177. There are only two photographs of this monument in the Berenson Collection: a large panorama and a photograph dedicated to the small nymphaeum that is still well preserved at the top of the cavea (Figures 667-668). It may seem strange that Creswell took just these photos of this monument which until then had certainly been the most photographed in Amman by all previous travellers, thanks to the excellent state of conservation of the cavea and its good accessibility at the foot of the Citadel. However, its dating to the Roman period probably meant that the monument was of less interest for Creswell's selection, except for the small decorated nymphaeum.[410]

The most interesting subjects of Creswell's photographs are undoubtedly the Roman Nymphaeum and the Audience Hall.

In the case of the Nymphaeum, although Creswell captured it in a single shot, the photograph is quite meaningful. The monument lies at a short distance from the theatre, on the edge of a stream, and it is generally credited to the 2nd century. It has a half octagonal plan, with a still standing wall with three large apsidal recesses, flanked by small niches. The wall is viewed from the northeast in Creswell's photograph, which is the opposite viewpoint compared to most of the other early photos of the monuments (Figure 663).[411] The visible masonry details make it possible to link all the photos, despite differences in perspective and in the date of the shots. Creswell's photograph shows an intermediate state of preservation of the structure, if we consider the condition illustrated in Butler's photo (1904) and Bartoccini's photo (1929): the higher part of the wall is still preserved in Butler's photo, and completely lost at the time of Bartoccini's excavation in 1929. The photo taken by Creswell shows us that the wall had already collapsed, but not to the extent shown in Bartoccini's photo.

The other monument photographed is known as the Audience Hall (Figures 670-691).[412] It was most likely a sort of waiting lounge before entering the Umayyad palace, which lies immediately to the north. There has been a long debate about its chronology, but it is generally agreed today that it dates back to the very early Islamic occupation of the site, in the 8th century, even though the building was also reused after the end of the Umayyad period. It has an almost square plan, 24×26m, with a square court in the middle and four large niches (iwans), on each side, to form a sort of Greek cross plan. The eastern and western iwans are semi-domed, while the northern and southern are tunnel-vaulted. In modern times, a wooden dome was reconstructed by a Spanish archaeological mission, but the original roofing, if any, was lost at the time of Creswell's visit. Creswell photographed the monument both from the outside and the inside, and he recorded several details of the carved decorations that are inside

---

[409] Corresponding to the Ashmolean's negatives EA.CA.5438 and EA.CA.543. On the mosque, see Northedge 1992: 64-69.

[410] On the Roman Theatre and its representation in early photos see Anastasio, Botarelli 2015: 163-175; a photograph and a drawing of the little nymphaeum are shown in figs 301 and 315.

[411] For a list of early photographs of the Roman Nymphaeum, see Anastasio, Botarelli 2015: 183.

[412] Creswell 1940: 113-114. The monument is mentioned in literature with other names: Reception Hall, Monumental Gateway, Vestibule, just to quote the most common.

MESOPOTAMIA, SYRIA AND TRANSJORDAN IN THE CRESWELL COLLECTION

Figure: 669.
Subject: Amman. The outer wall of the Roman Nymphaeum.
Berenson ID: 133300.
Medium: gelatine silver print, 12×17.5cm.
Date of creation: 1919-1920.
Handwritten notes on the back: "Amman. Back wall of the Nymphaeum (?)' [Cres.].

Figure: 670.
Subject: Amman. The Audience Hall, looking east.
Berenson ID: 133304.
Medium: gelatine silver print, 12×17.5cm.
Date of creation: 1919-1920.
Handwritten notes on the back: "Amman. Palace (?) from the West' [Cres.].
Ashmolean negative: EA.CA.5436.

Figure: 671.
Subject: Amman. the Audience Hall, looking north-west.
Berenson ID: 133303.
Medium: gelatine silver print, 12×17.5cm.
Date of creation: 1919-1920.
Handwritten notes on the back: "Amman. Entrance to palace' [Cres.].
Ashmolean negative: EA.CA.5418.

Figure: 672.
Subject: Amman. Detail of the southern iwan of the Audience Hall.
Berenson ID: 133305.
Medium: gelatine silver print, 12×17.5cm.
Date of creation: 1919-1920.
Handwritten notes on the back: "Amman. Palace (?) Interior looking S' [Cres.].
Ashmolean negative: EA.CA.5435.

Figure: 673.
Subject: Amman. Detail of the southern iwan of the Audience Hall.
Berenson ID: 133306.
Medium: gelatine silver print, 12×17.5cm.
Date of creation: 1919-1920.
Handwritten notes on the back: "Amman. Palace (?) Interior looking S' [Cres.].
Ashmolean negative: EA.CA.1552.

Figure: 674.
Subject: Amman. Detail of the western iwan of the Audience Hall.
Berenson ID: 133308.
Medium: gelatine silver print, 12×17.5cm.
Date of creation: 1919-1920.
Handwritten notes on the back: "Amman. Palace (?) - Interior - West side' [Cres.].
Ashmolean negative: EA.CA.5433.

Figure: 675.
Subject: Amman. Detail of the eastern iwan of the Audience Hall.
Berenson ID: 133321.
Medium: gelatine silver print, 12×17.5cm.
Date of creation: 1919-1920.
Handwritten notes on the back: "Amman. Palace (?). East liwan' [Cres.].
Ashmolean negative: EA.CA.5420.

Figure: 676.
Subject: Amman. Detail of the northern iwan of the Audience Hall.
Berenson ID: 133315.
Medium: gelatine silver print, 12×17.5cm.
Date of creation: 1919-1920.
Handwritten notes on the back: "Amman. Palace (?). Interior looking N' [Cres.].
Ashmolean negative: EA.CA.5424.

Figure: 677.
Subject: Amman. Detail of the eastern iwan of the Audience Hall.
Berenson ID: 133319.
Medium: gelatine silver print, 12×17.5cm.
Date of creation: 1919-1920.
Handwritten notes on the back: "Amman. Palace (?). East liwan' [Cres.].
Ashmolean negative: EA.CA.5421.

THE SITES AND THE MONUMENTS – TRANSJORDAN

Figure: 678.
Subject: Amman. Detail of the western iwan of the Audience Hall.
Berenson ID: 133320.
Medium: gelatine silver print, 12×17.5cm.
Date of creation: 1919-1920.
Handwritten notes on the back: "Amman. Palace (?). Interior, west side' [Cres.]. 'Kindness of Capt. Creswell. Amman, Sasanian Ommayad ruins photo 13 p. 102' [Anon. N.B: 'Sasanian' is crossed out and corrected in 'Ommayad'].
Ashmolean negative: EA.CA.5432.

Figure: 679 (left).
Subject: Amman. The western side of the southern iwan of the Audience Hall.
Berenson ID: 133307.
Medium: gelatine silver print, 12×17.5cm.
Date of creation: 1919-1920.
Handwritten notes on the back: "Amman. Palace (?) Interior S/W corner' [Cres.].
Ashmolean negative: EA.CA.5434.

Figure: 680 (right).
Subject: Amman. The eastern side of the northern iwan of the Audience Hall.
Berenson ID: 133312.
Medium: gelatine silver print, 12×17.5cm.
Date of creation: 1919-1920.
Handwritten notes on the back: "Amman. Palace (?). Interior. South side to left' [Cres.].
Ashmolean negative: EA.CA.5428.

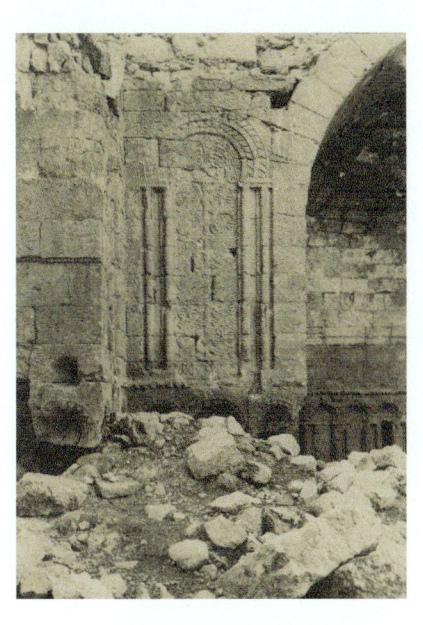

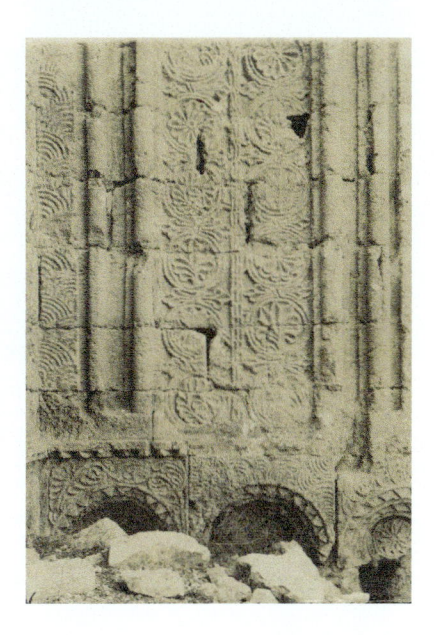

Figure: 681 (left).
Subject: Amman. The southern side of the western iwan of the Audience Hall.
Berenson ID: 133309.
Medium: gelatine silver print, 12×17.5cm.
Date of creation: 1919-1920.
Handwritten notes on the back: "Amman. Palace (?). Interior. West side' [Cres.].
Ashmolean negative: EA.CA.5431.

Figure: 682 (right).
Subject: Amman. Detail of the southern side of the western iwan of the Audience Hall.
Berenson ID: 133310.
Medium: gelatine silver print, 12×17.5cm.
Date of creation: 1919-1920.
Handwritten notes on the back: "Amman. Palace (?). Interior. West side to left' [Cres.].
Ashmolean negative: EA.CA.5430.

Figure: 683 (left).
Subject: Amman. Detail of the carved blind niches of the eastern iwan of the Audience Hall.
Berenson ID: 133322.
Medium: gelatine silver print, 12×17.5cm.
Date of creation: 1919-1920.
Handwritten notes on the back: "Amman. Palace (?). Panels at back of E Iiwan' [Cres.].
Ashmolean negative: EA.CA.5419.

Figure: 684 (centre).
Subject: Amman. Detail of the carved blind niches of the eastern iwan of the Audience Hall.
Berenson ID: 133323.
Medium: gelatine silver print, 12×17.5cm.
Date of creation: 1919-1920.
Handwritten notes on the back: "Amman. Palace (?). Panels at back of E Iiwan' [Cres.].
Ashmolean negative: EA.CA.5417.

Figure: 685 (right).
Subject: Amman. Detail of the carved blind niches on the southern side of the western iwan of the Audience Hall.
Berenson ID: 133311.
Medium: gelatine silver print, 12×17.5cm.
Date of creation: 1919-1920.
Handwritten notes on the back: "Amman. Palace (?). Interior. East Iiwan N side' [Cres.].
Ashmolean negative: EA.CA.5429.

Figure: 686.
Subject: Amman. Detail of the of the blind niches on on the eastern side of the northern iwan of the Audience Hall.
Berenson ID: 133318.
Medium: gelatine silver print, 12×17.5cm.
Date of creation: 1919-1920.
Handwritten notes on the back: "Amman. Palace (?). Interior' [Cres.].
Ashmolean negative: EA.CA.5427.

Figure: 687.
Subject: Amman. Detail of the carved blind niches on the southern side of the western iwan of the Audience Hall.
Berenson ID: 133316.
Medium: gelatine silver print, 12×17.5cm.
Date of creation: 1919-1920.
Handwritten notes on the back: "Amman. Palace (?). S liwan, east side' [Cres.].
Ashmolean negative: EA.CA.5423.

Figure: 688.
Subject: Amman. Detail of the carved blind niches on the northern side of the western iwan of the Audience Hall.
Berenson ID: 133313.
Medium: gelatine silver print, 12×17.5cm.
Date of creation: 1919-1920.
Handwritten notes on the back: "Amman. Palace (?). West liwan, south side' [Cres.].
Ashmolean negative: EA.CA.5426.

Figure: 689.
Subject: Amman. Detail of the carved blind niches on the northern side of the western iwan of the Audience Hall.
Berenson ID: 133314.
Medium: gelatine silver print, 12×17.5cm.
Date of creation: 1919-1920.
Handwritten notes on the back: "Amman. Palace (?). West liwan, south side' [Cres.].
Ashmolean negative: EA.CA.5425.

Figure: 690.
Subject: Amman. a decorated stone fragment, possibly re-used from the Hellenistic or Roman period, inside the northeastern room of the Audience Hall.
Berenson ID: 133324.
Medium: gelatine silver print, 12×17.5cm.
Date of creation: 1919-1920.
Handwritten notes on the back: "Amman. Palace (?). Classical fragment built into side of N/E room' [Cres.].
Ashmolean negative: EA.CA.5416.

Figure: 691.
Subject: Amman. an arch inside the Audience Hall.
Berenson ID: 133325.
Medium: gelatine silver print, 12×17.5cm.
Date of creation: 1919-1920.
Handwritten notes on the back: "Amman. Palace (?). S/E room – west side' [Cres.].
Ashmolean negative: EA.CA.5415.

Iraq al-Amir

Iraq al-Amir is one of the most famous and best-preserved Hellenistic monuments in Transjordan. It is located 17km south-east of Amman, in the Wadi al-Sir valley, a region renowned since ancient times for its wealth of springs and the cultivation of fruit and olive trees, and it benefits from a particularly favourable climate thanks also to the remarkable altitude above sea level (c. 500m asl). It is an important destination for trips and visits by both locals and tourists, favoured by its proximity to Amman. At the time of Creswell's visit, however, the situation was quite different and the monument could only be reached after a fairly challenging hike.

A good idea of the monument's transformation is given by the initial words of Nancy Lapp, in the introduction to the report of the American excavations that were conducted at the site in the early 1960s:[419] 'Today Araq el-Emir is approached by a paved road from the village of Wadi Sir, now almost a suburb of Amman. For the 1961 and 1962 excavations a roadbed had to be cleared, "bridges" constructed over the wadi, and only with a Landrover would one attempt the trip. Today the excavators and architects commute from Amman: in the '60s the excavators made the trip in on Sunday evening, hopefully before dark, and except for village messengers, police, or occasional adventurous visitors they were isolated from the world until they returned to Jerusalem at the end of the week'. At the time of Creswell, the region must have been even more isolated, almost completely uninhabited, given that its cultivation began in the 1920s.[420]

The monument itself, known as Qasr al-Abd, literally 'Palace of the Servant', is a rectangular building measuring 37.5×19m. It originally consisted of at least two floors. The lower storey is very massive, built in very large limestone blocks, with reliefs of lions and lionesses in the corners; the upper storey featured several openings and intercolumnia. The entire complex was designed to rise inside a sort of artificial lake, although the construction was probably never completed. Actually, it is not certain whether the building was a palace or a temple, although the prevailing opinion is that it was a sort of 'sommer residence'.[421] Flavius Josephus talks about it, at the end of the 1st century, and says, among other things, that Hyrcanus of the Tobiads' dynasty 'built a strong fortress which was constructed entirely of white marble up to the very roof, and had beasts of gigantic size carved on it, and he enclosed it with a wide and deep moat' (*Jewish Antiquities* XII/229-236.).

The monument had already been visited and described by Charles L. Irby and James Mangles in 1817, and then by all major late-nineteenth-century expeditions[422] until the 1904 reconnaissance of Princeton University, conducted by Howard C. Butler, who spent six days to take over the site.[423] Butler's documentation is the most interesting for the study of Creswell's photographs. We can assume that Creswell was familiar with Butler's publication; in any case, he took some shots that can be compared exactly with some of the photographs published by Butler.[424] First of all, they show that the state of the monument was practically the same 15 years after Butler's visit. Although the images are panoramic, i.e., taken from a certain distance, and show no particular details, they are nevertheless important because they provide evidence of the state of the monument before the excavations and restoration.

The site, in fact, was subsequently investigated by an American expedition between 1961 and 1963 and a Franco-Jordanian expedition between 1975 and 1980.[425] The latter, after having detected all the scattered materials on the surface, also carried out significant restoration work. Although this work certainly improved the state of the monument and made it more legible, it most certainly altered the state that had reached us from antiquity, which is instead testified in Creswell's photographs.

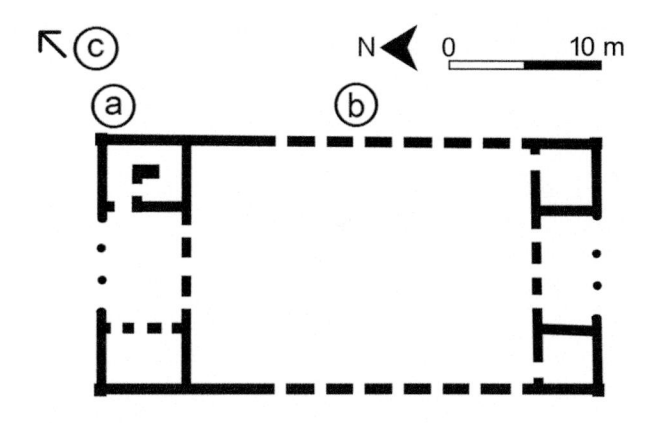

Figure 692: Iraq al-Amir. Map of Creswell's photographs of the Qasr al-Abd; a: Figure 694; b: Figure 693; c: Figure 695.

---

[419] Lapp 1980: 1.
[420] Borel 2006: 291; Gentelle 2003: 105.
[421] Schmid S.G. 2008: 357-358.

[422] For a history of site exploration see Lapp 1980: 3-4, and Borel 2006: 294-295. In particular, the photographs taken in 1864 by Louis Vigne are worth mentioning (Luynes 1871-1874: pls 30-33). See also the report given by Melchior de Vogüé (1864).
[423] Butler *et al.* 1907-1930: vol.I2A.I/1-28.
[424] Cf. Figures 698, 699, and 700 with those in Butler *et al.* 1907-1930: vol. I2A.I, ill. 2, pl. 3, and ill. 9 respectively.
[425] Will, Larché 1991; Larché 2005.

Figure: 693.
Subject: Iraq al-Amir. The eastern side of the Qasr al-Abd.
Berenson ID: 133746.
Physical description: gelatine silver print, 12×17cm.
Date of creation: 1919-1920.
Handwritten notes on the back: 'Araq al Emir, remains of Palace' [Cres.].

Figure: 694.
Subject: Iraq al-Amir. The northern end of the eastern wall of the Qasr al-Abd.
Berenson ID: 133747.
Physical description: gelatine silver print, 12×17cm.
Date of creation: 1919-1920.
Handwritten notes on the back: 'Araq al Emir, remains of Palace' [Cres.]. 'or Arak-el-Emir' [Anon.].

Figure: 695.
Subject: Iraq al-Amir. Main entrance on the northern side of the Qasr al-Abd.
Berenson ID: 133745.
Physical description: gelatine silver print, 12×17cm.
Date of creation: 1919-1920.
Handwritten notes on the back: 'Araq al Emir – entrance of enclosure' [Cres.].

Qusayr Amra

Qusayr Amra is located 85km east of Amman, in the Jordan steppe, and is one of the most famous Jordanian archaeological monuments, *World Heritage Site UNESCO* since 1985.[426] It is a small rural compound characterised by the presence of a bath house decorated with frescoes, representing a 'one of its kind' in ancient Islamic production.

From an architectural point of view, it is a single complex, but composed of several units: the bath house, which is the main element, at the east end; a structure with cistern and a well for water; a triangular-shaped yard, bounded by a low wall enclosure, northwest of the bath house. A little further north of the bath house is a residential structure, built around a courtyard, and a small mosque.

The monument's fame is mainly linked to the remains of the bath house which consists of a rectangular 'Main Hall' divided into three main bays by a triple barrel vault. The entrance is from north, in the central axis, and lighting is guaranteed by windows. A recessed alcove can be found at the opposite side of the entrance, with two small apsidal side chambers. The actual bath is east of the Main Hall, with three sequential rooms that can be interpreted as *apodyterium*, *calidarium* and *tepidarium* (Figure 696). The entire structure is decorated internally with extraordinary frescoes depicting various scenes: hunting, mythology, astronomy, daily work and life, as well as the representation of historical figures. The depiction of some 'kings', including the Visigot Roderick, killed in the war against the Umayyads in 711, was among the reasons for attributing the complex to the time of the Umayyad caliph Walid I, who reigned between 705 and 715. Today, based on the analysis of the frescoes and particularly of an inscription discovered in 2012, the construction of the complex is attributed to Walid Ibn Yazid, or Walid II, while he was still a prince, which means between 723 and 743.[427]

In his *Early Muslim architecture*, after examining the building from an architectural perspective, Creswell devotes a great deal of attention to the paintings. The reason for this is probably not only due to the evident importance of the paintings, but also to their precarious state and the inadequate documentation available. Actually, Creswell visited and photographed the site somewhere between 1919 and 1925, when it was already well known, thanks to Alois Musil's publications.[428] Musil first described the frescoes and then restored

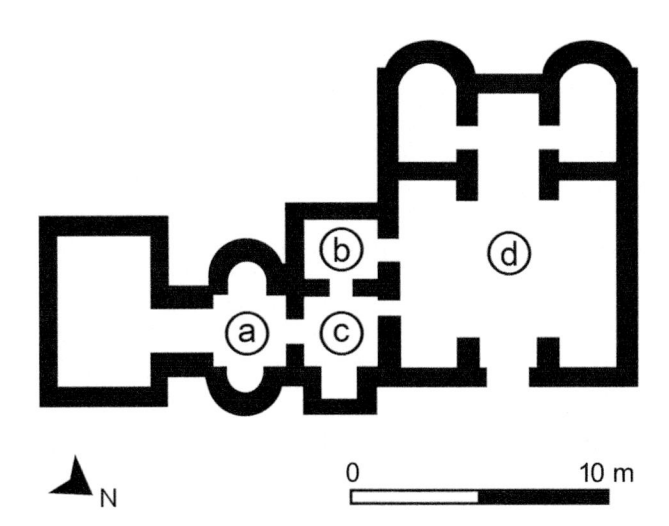

Figure 696: Qusayr Amra. Map of the photographed rooms; a: the calidarium (Figure 701); b: the apodyterium (Figures 702-703); c: the tepidarium (Figures 704-705); d: the Main Hall (Figures 699-700).

them and reproduced them in his publication with copies made by Alphons L. Mielich, an Austrian painter who had accompanied him on site.[429] The copies were made only later after the end of the work on site, and Creswell emphasised this circumstance as a criticality for evaluating the quality of the paintings.[430]

After Musil, however, apart from some visits by Antonin Jaussen and Raphaël Savignac of the École Biblique de Jerusalem between 1909 and 1912,[431] the site does not appear to have been subject to any particular surveys. The monument underwent significant excavation and restoration after Creswell's visit: by the Department of Antiquities of Jordan in the 1950s and 1960s, then by joint missions of the same Department with Spanish (1971-194 and 1996), French (1989-1996) and Italian (2010) teams.[432] These restorations, in addition to guaranteeing their much needed conservation, certainly made the paintings more legible, since appearing already strongly compromised at the time of Musil.

The Berenson Collection includes eight photos of the monument, four of which are dedicated to the frescoes. The latter are particularly significant because, although limited in number, they give us a good view of the actual state of conservation before restoration, showing a condition that is radically different from the one we see today. We must also consider the fact that taking photographs inside the monument, especially if during a short visit and without sophisticated equipment to improve lighting, is a challenging task

---

[426] https://whc.unesco.org/en/list/327/

[427] Imbert 2015. For a discussion on the theory regarding the chronology of the monument, see Fowden 2004: 19-21, with bibliography.

[428] Musil 1907. The site had been briefly described earlier by travellers such as Ulrich J. Seetzen (c. 1805) Johann L. Burckhardt (1822), and Gray Hill (1896); see Musil 1907: 168, for a detailed list, with bibliography.

[429] Regarding Musil's activity in Qusayr Amra, see Fowden 2004: 1-12 in particular.

[430] Creswell 1932: 253-272 (including a contribution authored by F. Saxl, on the Zodiac of Qusayr 'Amra, at pp. 289-303). See also Creswell 1958: 84-106.

[431] Jaussen, Savignac 1922.

[432] Palumbo, Atzori 2014: 29.

MESOPOTAMIA, SYRIA AND TRANSJORDAN IN THE CRESWELL COLLECTION

today as it certainly was at Creswell's time: for this reason, the choice of subjects was probably limited to those that were most visible with natural light only, avoiding the many dark blotches on the walls. The result is a small number of shots, but which are actually quite legible, with many details. Specifically, Creswell's photos depict the exterior and the architectural details of the interior of the Main Hall and the vault of the *calidarium*, and details of the frescoes of the *apodyterium* and the *tepidarium*. In the latter case, Creswell's photo is particularly worthy of attention (Figure 705) because it shows a detail of the northern side room of the tepedarium in a representation among the least documented of the whole complex.[433]

Figure 697: Qusayr Amra. Details of the frescoes in the apodyterium, in Creswell's photos (a, c: see below, Figures 704 and 702), and today (b, d: courtesy of Daniel C. Waugh, photos taken in 2010).

---

[433] Prior to Creswell's photo, to my knowledge this detail may be found only in a reproduction by Mielich published in Musil 1907, pl. 39. Most recently, it can be appreciated in the work of Vibert-Gigue, Bisheh 2007, pl. 135b.

THE SITES AND THE MONUMENTS – TRANSJORDAN

Figure: 698.
Subject: Qusayr Amra, looking north.
Berenson ID: 133921.
Physical description: gelatine silver print, 12 × 17 cm.
Date of creation: 1919-1925.
Creswell's handwritten notes on the back: 'Qusair Amra – Syria' [Cres.].
Ashmolean negative: EA.CA.5443.
Published in Creswell 1932, pl. 47.c.

Figure: 699.
Subject: The main hall inside Qusayr Amra.
Berenson ID: 133922.
Physical description: gelatine silver print, 12 × 17 cm.
Date of creation: 1919-1925.
Creswell's handwritten notes on the back: 'Qusair Amra, main hall' [Cres.].
Ashmolean negative: EA.CA.5444.

Figure: 700.
Subject: The main hall inside Qusayr Amra.
Berenson ID: 133923.
Physical description: gelatine silver print, 12 × 17 cm.
Date of creation: 1919-1925.
Creswell's handwritten notes on the back: 'Qusair Amra, main hall' [Cres.].
Published in Creswell 1932, pl. 48.d; Creswell 1958, fig. 29.

Figure: 701.
Subject: The dome of the calidarium of Qusayr Amra.
Berenson ID: 133924.
Physical description: gelatine silver print, 12 × 17 cm.
Date of creation: 1919-1925.
Creswell's handwritten notes on the back: 'Qusair Amra – wall paintings' [Cres.].
Published in Creswell 1932, pl. 51.a.

Figure: 702.
Subject: Detail of the fresco in the apodyterium of Qusayr Amra.
Berenson ID: 133926.
Physical description: gelatine silver print, 12 × 17 cm.
Date of creation: 1919-1925.
Creswell's handwritten notes on the back: 'Qusair Amra – wall paintings' [Cres.].
Published in Creswell 1932, pl. 49.a; Creswell 1958, fig. 30.

Figure: 703.
Subject: Detail of the fresco in the apodyterium of the Qusayr Amra.
Berenson ID: 133928.
Physical description: gelatine silver print, 12 × 17 cm.
Date of creation: 1919-1925.
Creswell's handwritten notes on the back: 'Qusair Amra, wall paintings' [Cres.].
Published in Creswell 1932, pl. 49.b.

THE SITES AND THE MONUMENTS – TRANSJORDAN

Figure: 704 (above).
Subject: detail of the fresco on the southern lunette of the tepidarium of Qusayr Amra.
Berenson ID: 133925.
Physical description: gelatine silver print, 12 × 17 cm.
Date of creation: 1919-1925.
Creswell's handwritten notes on the back: 'Qusair Amra – wall paintings' [Cres.].
Published in Creswell 1932, pl. 50.a.

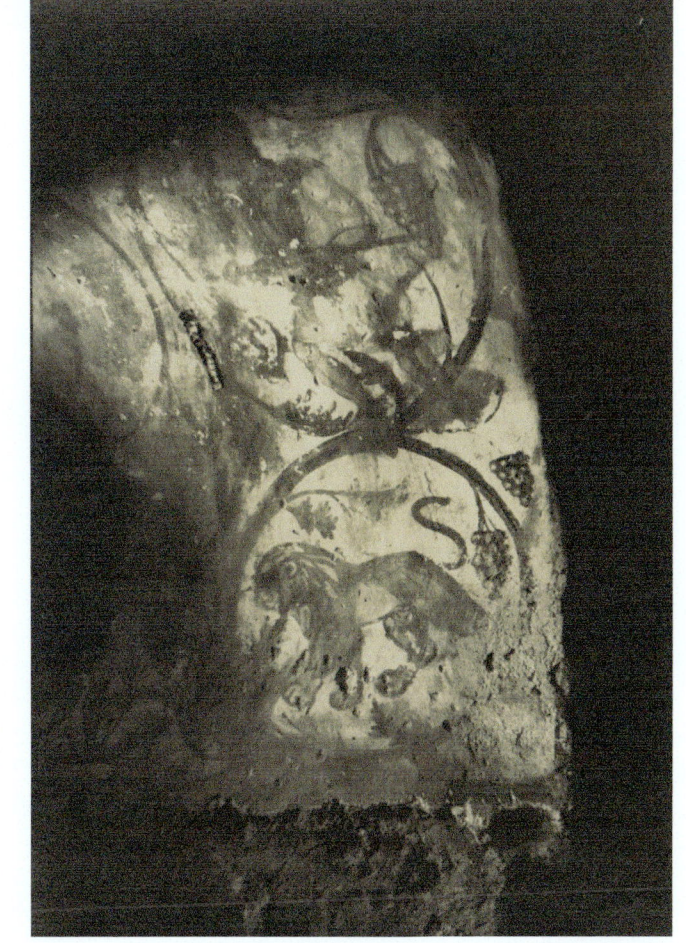

Figure: 705 (right).
Subject: Detail of the fresco on the vault over the window niche on the north side of the tepedarium of Qusayr Amra.
Berenson ID: 133927.
Physical description: gelatine silver print, 12 × 17 cm.
Date of creation: 1919-1925.
Creswell's handwritten notes on the back: 'Qusair Amra – wall paintings' [Cres.].
Published in Creswell 1932, pl. 50.b.

Conclusions

The Middle East photographed by Creswell no longer exists.

Any architectural monument, by nature, is destined to have a long and uninterrupted building history, which is actually what allows it to survive throughout the centuries. 'Life is like riding a bicycle. To keep your balance, you must keep moving',[434] applies to people as well as buildings. More or less substantial changes, functional modifications, conservative restorations, destructive episodes and reconstructions are inevitable, although obviously with different outcomes depending on individual cases. All this is of special relevance in the region considered here.

Creswell photographed a world in which part of its ancient monumental buildings was still intact and functioning, and discovered others that had been forgotten, following the nascent interest in archaeological research. At the same time, it was a world that had not yet entered, or was just entering, a time when the rural and urban landscape would have radically changed, following the political and social changes caused by World War I. These changes continued with even greater impetus after World War II and, more recently, after yet another destruction — in this case it is useless to speak of generic 'changes' — following the events of these first twenty years of the 21st century.

If I think of a possible epitome of this work, I believe it is the photographs of the monuments of Aleppo, especially in the area immediately at the foot of the Citadel, and their projection on the satellite photos of the last ten years: a pitiless but instructive experiment! Yet we must think that this will not all last forever. Fortunately, some situations have already partly improved and there are reports of projects for the restoration and recovery of many damaged monuments. Therefore, the value of early photographs like those taken by Creswell is indeed extraordinary, because they can help guide the development of philologically accurate restoration projects.

The general question of how to intervene in cases such as these is an open issue. In the Middle East in particular, perhaps more than in other regions, alongside conservative restoration there is often an actual work of *anastylosis*, with many examples that could be cited. In cases like these, where conservation is accompanied by reconstruction, as a rule, each project is accompanied by a wide debate, with the archaeological community often deeply divided between those who are in favour and those who are not. This is all well and truly justified since there are indeed many factors to consider when evaluating such projects, which always need to be viewed individually. This is not the place to discuss this issue in detail, and the list of pros and cons of the different approaches would be very long. Nonetheless, today more than ever, every single project related to the recovery of an ancient building demands great attention, to avoid exaggerated confidence in the 'rebuilding approach'.[435]

The hope is that in the near future increasingly more effort will be put into recovering the Syrian and Iraqi cultural heritage. This could lead to countless cases for potential application of *anastylosis*. It is essential to make sure that documentation on the building history of the monuments is fully available so as to effectively steer both the design and the implementation of the interventions. In this scenario, a fundamental role is played by early photos and films (the latter still too little used, although there are many, starting from the beginning of the 20th century, that offer an invaluable wealth of information). For this reason, the development of better shared standards and common practices for the publication of data would help in comparing information from different projects.

In this sense, the Creswell Collection has an undoubtedly extraordinary value, both for the wealth of its data and for the opportunity it brings to have a consistent picture of such a far-reaching cultural heritage, spanning from Turkey to North Africa. The picture presented here is just a piece of the puzzle, consisting simply of a collection and a restricted area, but it is a piece that hopefully will contribute to the overall mosaic of the history of early photography in the Middle East, offering rich opportunities for researchers wishing to devote attention to this research topic.

---

[434] Albert Einstein, in a letter of 1930 to his son Eduard: 'Beim Menschen ist es wie beim Velo. Nur wenn er faehrt, kann er bequem die Balance halten' (see Isaacson 2007: 565).

[435] I had already expressed my comments on this aspect in Anastasio 2017.

Appendix 1. Register of photographers in Mesopotamia, Syria and Transjordan between the 1840s and the 1930s

A list is provided below of the photographers known to have worked in the regions considered in this volume – Mesopotamia, Syria and Transjordan –, from the beginning of the history of photography to the years of Creswell's photographs, i.e., 1840s-1930s.

The list of course is not exhaustive, nor does it claim to be so. However, the photographers listed below are all those regarding whom I have found information in the course of my studies on the subject, which includes not only documented photographs in archives, but also simple mention of their work in specialised literature. The latter is indeed very extensive; the main works I have referred to and from which I have drawn a large amount of data and information are the publications by Perez 1988, Jarrar, Riedlmayer, Spurr 1994: 239-252, El-Hage 2000, Abujaber, Cobbing 2005, Hannavy 2008, as well as the section 'photographers' of *Luminous-lint*.

Also worthy of consideration is the subject of 'excavation photography'. From the mid-1870s onwards, photographers were included among the staff of the majority of archaeological expeditions. However, when gathering the data to compile this list, I was surprised to see how often the information published is not sufficient to determine who was actually in charge of the photographic documentation of the excavations. This list only mentions the names of photographers whose work on the excavations was explicitly mentioned, concerned sites/monuments connected with those photographed by Creswell, or was particularly important for the history of photography and for documenting the cultural heritage of the region in which they worked. An accurate and exhaustive analysis on this topic would certainly be useful, to gain a more accurate picture of the history of excavation photography and to recover information about many archives and files that could probably be of great interest for research.

The progress of the online publication of photographic repertoires allows access to many of the photographs taken by these authors (or to the engravings and lithographs derived from the photographs, especially in the 1840s-1880s). The entry 'web repositories' indicates only those where complete or at least large selections dedicated to individual photographers may be accessed. As far as citizenship is concerned, in the case of British photographers, English, Scottish and Welsh nationality is specified when known, otherwise it is referred to as British. In the case of photographers born in the Ottoman Empire, their ethnic-religious identity (Jew, Armenian...), as well as their birth in a well-defined region, which later became independent (Syrian, Iraqi...), is mentioned when known.

Photographers are listed alphabetically, and two tables at the end allow them to be grouped by chronology and geography.

Any suggestions and corrections to update this list, in view of possible future publications of similar repertoires, are welcome (stefano.anastasio@cultura.gov.it).

Al-Azm, Mahmoud
Syrian, dates unknown, active in the 1870s (Syria). To my knowledge, the first Syrian professional photographer in Damascus, in the 1870s.
Bibliography: El-Hage 2000: 47.

Altman, Charles Bramman
American, 1903-1988, active in the 1930s (Mesopotamia). He was an architect and archaeologist who worked on the Khorsabad Expedition, taking care of photography in the 1933-1934 campaign.
Bibliography: Loud 1938: vii; Green : 14.

American Colony Photo Department
Active in the 1890s-1930s (Mesopotamia, Syria, Transjordan). The Department was composed of religious pilgrims who emigrated in the 1880s from the USA and Sweden to Jerusalem. Many photographers worked in ACPD, including Elijah Meyers, Lewis Larsson, Eric and Edith Matson, Furman Baldwin. In 1940, the business was taken over by 'The Matson Photo Service'.
Bibliography: El-Hage 2000: 46; Bair 2011.

Web repositories:
https://www.loc.gov/pictures/collection/matpc/colony.html#department

Araqtinji, Philippe and Michel
Nationality and dates unknown, active in the 1910s (Syria). Professional photographers in Damascus, quoted in the *Baedeker Guide*.
Bibliography: Baedeker 1912: 295; El-Hage 2000: 46.

Bain, Robert Edward Mather
American, 1858-1932, active in the 1890s (Syria). He participated in an expedition to the Levant (1894), with the purpose of publishing a volume on the life of Jesus Christ and the Apostoles. A collection of his photos, entitled *Scenes of the Holy Land, incl. Egypt; also places in Italy, Greece, and Turkey which were visited by St. Paul* is held at the Library of Congress (Washington D.C.).
Bibliography: Lee, Bain, Vincent 1894. El-Hage 2000: 41-42.
Web repository:
https://www.loc.gov/item/2005688257/

Baker, Nathan Flint
See below: Hunt, Leavitt.

Baldwin, Furman
See above: American Colony Photo Department.

Ban, H. Major
French, name and dates unknown, active in the 1850s (Mesopotamia). He took part in an expedition to the Persian Gulf area (1856-1857), taking photographs, none of which have reached us, to my knowledge.
Bibliography: Anonymous 1857; Perez 1988: 128.

Banks, Edgard James
American, 1866-1945, active in the 1900s (Mesopotamia). American consul in Baghdad at the end of the 19th century, he excavated the ancient site of Bismaya in 1903-1904, taking most of the photos of the expedition.
Bibliography: Banks 1912; Wilson *et al.* 2021: 8.

Banse, Ewald
German, 1883-1953, active in the 1910s-1920s (Mesopotamia, Syria). German geographer, who travelled extensively in Turkey, Armenia, Syria, and Mesopotamia, taking photographs that were in part published in his books.
Bibliography: Banse 1919; Lammers 2015.

Barry, Maximillien-Étienne-Émile
French, 1843-1910, active in the 1880s (Mesopotamia). Photographer of Ernest Chantre's scientific mission to the Caucasus, Kurdistan and Mesopotamia, conducted in 1881.
Bibliography: Barry 1881; Perez 1988: 129.
Web repository:
https://gallica.bnf.fr/ark:/12148/btv1b8451574s.item

Barshchevsky, Ivan Fedorovich
Russian, 1851-1946, active in the 1890s (Syria, Transjordan). The photographer of the 1891 expedition led by Nikodim Pavlovich Kondakov in Jordan, Palestine and Southern Syria.
Bibliography: Kondakov 1904; Chmyreva 2010: 538; Adashinskaya 2020.

Bartoccini, Renato
Italian, 1893-1963, active in the late 1920s-1930s (Syria, Transjordan). Director of the first Italian archaeological expedition to Transjordan, between 1928 and 1938. His photo archive consists of *c.* 2,000 photographs of archaeological sites in Jordan, Syria, Lebanon, Palestine and Turkey.
Bibliography: Bartoccini 1941; Anastasio, Botarelli 2015.

Beato, Felice and Antonio
Italian born, naturalised British, 1832-1909 (Felice) and 1835-1906 (Antonio), active in the 1850s (Syria). Felice Beato is one of the most notorious pioneers of photography, who worked mainly in the Far East (Japan, Korea). However, we know that he also worked for a while in Turkey, Syria and Palestine during the 1850s. His younger brother Antonio worked with him, sometimes sharing the same signature and so leading to problems in identifying the actual author of some photographs. For the same reason, it is not entirely clear whether both or just one of the brothers entered into the partnership with James Robertson (known by the signature 'Robertson & Beato').
Bibliography: Zannier 1986; Perez 1988: 131-132; Hannavy 2008: 128-130; Jacobson 2016: 70-71.

Bedford, Francis
British, 1816-1894, active in the 1860s (Syria). In 1862, he accompanied the Prince of Wales, as the official photographer of the Prince's tour of the Near East. He took photographs of sites that had never been accessed before by other European photographers.
Bibliography: Bedford, Thompson 1867; Perez 1988: 134; El-Hage 2000: 33; Hannavy 2008: 134-136; Gordon, el-Hage 2014; Jacobson 2016: 67-68.
Web repositories:
https://www.rct.uk/collection/themes/exhibitions/cairo-to-constantinople/the-queens-gallery-buckingham-palace/francis-bedford-photographer-to-the-prince-of-wales
https://www.flickr.com/photos/palestineexplorationfund/albums/72157625407163433
https://www.getty.edu/art/collection/objects/33249/francis-bedford-wm-thompson-the-holy-land-egypt-etc-photographs-taken-for-hrh-the-prince-of-wales-english-about-1863-1867/

Beke, Emily
English, dates unknown, active in the 1860s (Syria). Wife of the traveller Charles Tilstone Beke, she accompanied him in his travels to Syria and Palestine in 1861-1862, dedicating herself to photography.
Bibliography: Beke 1865; El-Hage 2000: 31.

Bell, Getrude
English, 1868-1926, active in the 1900s-1910s (Mesopotamia, Syria, Transjordan). One of the most renowned explorers and photographers of the Near East. Her legacy of photos concern many of the monuments photographed by Creswell.
Bibliography: Bell 1911, 1914, 1919 (just to quote the most relevant titles); El-Hage 2000: 50; Lenzen 2003; Lukitz 2004 (with references to bibliography).
Web repository:
http://www.gerty.ncl.ac.uk/photos.php

Benecke, Ernst
German, 1817-1894, active in the 1850s (Syria). One of the first photographers in the Near East, who travelled

in Syria in 1852. Unfortunately, only a few of the photographs taken by him are known. He portrayed mainly people and their costumes.
Bibliography: Howe 1997: 24; Perez 1988: 134-135; El-Hage 2000: 23; Hannavy 2008: 146-148.
Web repository:
http://www.getty.edu/art/collection/ (search 'Ernest Benecke').

Bergheim, Melville Peter
Jew, emigrated from Poland to England, 1813-1895, active in the 1850s-1880s (Syria, Transjordan). Jewish photographer who emigrated to England. Active in Jerusalem from the late 1850s, he travelled and photographed several sites also beyond Palestine, particularly in Syria and in Transjordan (Petra).
Bibliography: El-Hage 2000: 26-27; Perez 1988: 135-136; Zuckerman 2000.

Bishof, Th.
Name, nationality and dates unknown, active in the 1880s (Syria). 'Th. Bishof' is known as a photographer working in Aleppo in 1879. To my knowledge, no photographs taken by him have reached us.
Bibliography: Perez 1988: 138.

Bliss, Frederick Jones
American, 1859-1937, active in the 1890s (Transjordan). He directed several Palestine Exploration Fund expeditions in Palestine, excavating at Jerusalem in the 1890s. In 1895 he also made a trip to explore Transjordan, taking photos of Madaba, Mushatta and Qasr Bshir. He probably knew Creswell, because he was also an advisor of General Allenby.
Bibliography: Bliss 1895; Blakely 1997; Abujaber, Cobbing 2005: 226.

Bonfils (Maison)
Félix Bonfils: French, 1931-1885. Studio active in the 1860s-1930s (Syria, Transjordan). In 1867, Félix Bonfils opened the 'Maison Bonfils' photography studio in Beirut, and photographed many sites in the Middle East during the 1870s. His photos were used by many travellers to illustrate their books (e.g., Lucien Gautier). After Félix Bonfils' death in 1885, the firm was run by his heirs, until the studio officially closed in 1938.
Bibliography: Bonfils, A. 1876, 1877-1878; Sobieszek, Gavin 1980; Chevedden 1981; Perez 1988: 141; Aubenas, Lacarrière 1999; El-Hage 2000: 36-37; Abujaber, Cobbing 2005: 226; Hannavy 2008: 173-175; Jacobson 2016: 68; Vârtejanu-Joubert 2019.
Web repositories:
https://www.europeana.eu/ (search 'Felix Bonfils').
http://hdl.handle.net/10020/2008r3a19
https://archnet.org/authorities/2256
http://www.artandarchitecture.org.uk/
https://eap.bl.uk/collection/EAP644-1

Bowman, H.T.
British, name and dates unknown, active in the 1860s (Syria, Transjordan). In 1864, he travelled with Harry B. Tristram, visiting Palestine, Syria and Transjordan. To my knowledge, all of Bowman's known photos concern sites in Palestine.
Bibliography: Tristram 1865: vii; Perez 1988: 141; El-Hage 2000: 34.

Bridges, Rev. George Wilson
English, 1788-1863, active in the 1840s-1850s (Syria). An Anglican cleric, who was introduced to photography by William Henry Fox Talbot, and who travelled around the Mediterranean (including Syria) in 1846-1952, taking several photographs.
Bibliography: Perez 1988: 142-143; El-Hage 2000: 21-22; Hannavy 2008: 211-212.

Brünnow, Rudolf-Ernst
German born, naturalised American, 1858-1917, active in the 1890s (Syria, Transjordan). In 1895, 1897 and 1898, Rudolf-Ernst Brünnow, Professor of Semitic philology and languages at the University of Heidelberg, and his colleague Alfred von Domaszewski explored the former Roman provinces in the area that today comprises parts of Syria, Jordan, and Lebanon, taking several photographs of the visited monuments.
Bibliography: Brünnow, Domaszewski 1904-1909; Kenfield 2010.
Web repository:
https://researchphotographs.princeton.edu/brunnow-and-domaszewski/

Burchardt, Hermann
German, 1857-1909, active in the 1890s (Mesopotamia, Syria, Transjordan). German explorer, who began to travel in the Near East in 1890. He took and collected many photographs during his expeditions, which were then exhibited at the Berlin University Library.
Bibliography: Sader, Scheffler, Neuwirth 1998: 183-186; Nippa 1994; El-Hage 2000: 46-47.
Web repository:
https://recherche.smb.museum/?language=de&limit=15&controls=none (search 'Hermann Burchardt').

Buxton, C. Louis
British, dates unknown, active in the 1870s (Transjordan). Harry B. Tristram quotes C. Louis Buxton as a photographer who participated in his expedition to the land of Moab in 1872. To my knowledge, no existing photograph taken by him is known.
Bibliography: Tristram 1873: v; Perez 1988: 145.

Byron, Robert
British, 1905-1945, active in the 1930s (Syria). The well known British travel writer, author of *The Road to Oxiana*, was an excellent photographer, particularly interested

in Islamic architecture.
Bibliography: Knox 2003.
Web repositories:
http://www.artandarchitecture.org.uk/ (search: 'Robert Byron').
https://www.archnet.org/collections/18

Cahun, Léon
French, 1841-1900, active in the late 1860s-1880s (Mesopotamia, Syria). He travelled in Syria and Mesopotamia between 1864 and 1880. To my knowledge, no existing photograph taken by him is known.
Bibliography: Cahun 1884; Singer, Kahn 1901-1906; Perez 1988: 145-146.

Cavalcanty, George D.
Nationality and dates unknown, active in the 1899-1900s (Syria, Transjordan). Photographer, based in Jerusalem, who worked during Howard C. Butler's expedition to Syria during 1899-1909. More than 1500 photographs were taken during the surveys.
Bibliography: Butler 1903: xxv; Kenfield 2010; Gilento 2022: 44.
Web repositories:
https://researchphotographs.princeton.edu/butler/
https://digi.ub.uni-heidelberg.de/diglit/syria

Chadirji, Kamil
Iraqi, 1897-1968, active in the 1920s (Mesopotamia, Syria). He was an active leftist politician in Iraq in the first half of the 20th century. He took several photographs in Iraq and elsewhere in the Near East.
Web repository:
https://www.archnet.org/collections/1427/details

Charlier-Béziès, Jean-Baptiste
French, 1822-1907, active in the 1860s (Syria). Amateur photographer, resident in Beirut and active in Lebanon, Palestine and Syria in the 1860s.
Bibliography: Perez 1988: 148; El-Hage 2000: 35.

Clapp, Frederick G.
American, 1879-1944, active in the 1920s-1930s (Syria, Transjordan). American geologist, who worked and travelled extensively in the Near East in the 1920s-1930s, taking several photographs.
Bibliography: Anonymous 1945.
Web repository:
https://uwm.edu/lib-collections/asia-middle-east/

Cooke, M. George-Albert
British, dates unknown, active in the 1890s (Mesopotamia, Syria, Transjordan). Fellow of the Oxford University who accompanied Lucien Gautier in his trip in Transjordan in 1894, taking several photos.
Bibliography: Gautier 1896: 6.

Cotton, Rev. Arthur B.
British, dates unknown, active in the 1850s (Syria). He travelled extensively in Egypt, Palestine and Syria, taking several photos that were used as lithographs to illustrate various publications. To my knowledge, no existing photograph taken by him is known.
Bibliography: Perez 1988: 150-151.

de Beylié, Léon
French, 1849-1910, active in the 1900s (Mesopotamia, Syria). General of the French Army and archaeologist. In 1907, he made a long trip to Birmania, Mesopotamia, Syria and Palestine, taking several photos that were published in his travel report. In particular, he carried out the first archeological survey of Samarra.
Bibliography: de Beylié 1907.

de Campigneulles, François Joseph Edouard
French, 1826-1879, active in the 1850s (Syria). He travelled in Egypt and the Levant in 1858, and exhibited his photographs at the Société Française de Photographie in 1859.
Bibliography: Perez 1988: 147; El-Hage 2000: 25.

de Champlouis, Baron Albert Victor Nau
French, 1833-1868, active in the 1860s (Mesopotamia, Syria, Transjordan). Captain of the French Army during the 1860-1861 military expedition in Syria. He exhibited his photographs in various European cities in the 1860s.
Bibliography: Perez 1988: 147, El-Hage 2000: 29.

de Chartre, Duc Robert-Philippe
French, 1840-1910, active in 1859-1860 (Syria). He toured Egypt and the Levant between 1859 e 1860, taking photographs.
Bibliography: Perez 1988: 148.

de Clerq, Louis-Constantin
French, 1836-1901, active in the 1850s (Syria). In August 1859, he accompanied Emmanuel-Guillaume Rey on an expedition to the crusader castles of Syria and Asia Minor, taking several photographs that he used to illustrate his publications.
Bibliography: de Clercq 1859, 1860; El-Hage 2000: 27-28; Hannavy 2008: 393-394; Perez 1988: 148; Howe 1997: 28.
Web repository:
https://gallica.bnf.fr/ark:/12148/btv1b53192910s

de Genouillac, Henri
French, 1881-1940, active in the 1910-1930s (Mesopotamia). One of the pioneers of archaeological research and director of the excavations at Kish and Tello. He was the author of most of the photos published in his works.
Bibliography: Parrot 1941.

APPENDIX 1 – REGISTER OF PHOTOGRAPHERS

de Rumine, Gabriel
French, 1841-1871, active in the 1850s (Syria). He was the photographer who accompanied the Great Duke Constantine on his trip around the Mediterranean, between 1858 and 1859. He took several photographs that were greatly appreciated for their high technical quality.
Bibliography: Perez 1988: 213; El-Hage 2000: 25.

de Saulcy, Félicien
French, 1807-1880, active in the 1850s-1860s (Syria, Transjordan). He travelled through Syria, Palestine and the region of the Dead Sea in 1850-1851, 1863, and 1869. Unfortunately, no photographs taken by him have reached us, to my knowledge.
Bibliography: de Saulcy 1865: 105; Northedge 1992: 17.

de Vorys, Jules
French, 1838-1928, active in the 1860s (Syria). French poet who travelled to Syria in 1865, taking photographs. The photographs he took during the trip no longer exist, to my knowledge.
Bibliography: El-Hage 2000: 32.

Derounian, Vartan
Armenian, 1888-1954, active in the 1910-1930s (Syria). He began his activity as a photographer with the Sarrafian brothers (below). He opened a studio in Aleppo, before moving to Beirut in 1926.
Bibliography: Terunean 2010.

Dickie, Archibald Campbell
British, 1868-1941, active in the 1900s (Transjordan). In 1907-1908, he travelled in Palestine but also toured Petra.
Bibliography: Abujaber, Cobbing 2005: 226.

Dieulafoy, Jean
French, dates unknown, active in the 1890s (Mesopotamia). She travelled in Mesopotamia and Persia along with her husband, Marcel Dieulafoy, who used her photos in his publications. The photos of the Taq Kisra are of particular interest for comparison with Creswell's photos.
Bibliography: Dieulafoy 1885, pls 3-6; Gran-Aymerich 2006.

du Camp, Maxime
French, 1822-1894, active in the 1840s-1850s (Syria). One of the major photographers of the mid-19th century. He travelled in Egypt, Syria and Palestine, taking photographs that were published and well known in Europe.
Bibliography: du Camp 1852; Perez 1988: 159-160; Hannavy 2008: 441-442.
Web repository:
https://digitalcollections.nypl.org/ (search 'du Camp, Maxime').

Dumas, Tàncrede
Italian, 1830-1905, active in 1870s (Syria, Transjordan). One of the most active photographers in the Near East in the second half of the 19th century. In 1866, he opened a studio in Beirut. As for the regions concerned in this study, worthy of mention is his participation in the 1875 Expedition of the American Palestine Exploration Society (A.P.E.S.) directed by Selah Merrill.
Bibliography: Merrill 1877, 1881; Moulton J. 1926-1927; Perez 1988: 160; El-Hage 2000: 35; Abujaber, Cobbing 2005: 227; Hannavy 2008: 452; Frecker n.d.

Egerton, G.H.
British, names and dates unknown, active in the 1870s (Syria). Amateur photographer, who toured Lebanon, Palestine, and Syria in 1877, taking photographs that were in part published in his travel accounts (*Letters from the East*).
Bibliography: Perez 1988: 160; El-Hage 2000: 40-41.

Enlart, Camille
French, 1862-1927, active in the 1920s (Syria). French art historian and archaeologist, who traveled in Syria between 1921 and 1922 to study and photograph the architecture of the crusader castles.
Bibliography: Paul-Célimon 2009.

Ferrier, Claude-Marie
French, 1811-1889, active in the 1860s (Syria). French photographer, who probably took the first stereoscopies in Syria, during a trip in 1860-1861.
Bibliography: El-Hage 2000: 49.

Frankfort, Henri
Dutch, 1897-1954, active in the 1930s (Mesopotamia). One of the most renowned archaeologists of Egypt and the Near East, field director of the 'Oriental Institute (OIP) of Chicago expedition to Iraq' between 1929 and 1937. He took care of the photography in some campaigns of the expedition.
Bibliography: Loud 1936: 1; Lloyd 1954.

Frith, Francis
English, 1822-1898, active in the 1850s (Syria). One of the best-known photographers of the Near East, he worked mainly in Egypt and Palestine. He also travelled to Syria leaving several photos, in particular of Damascus.
Bibliography: Frith 1858; Chevedden 1984; Perez 1988: 163-165; El-Hage 2000: 25; Hannavy 2008: 560-562.
Web repositories:
https://www.metmuseum.org/art/collection (search 'Francis Frith').

Germer-Durand, Joseph
French, 1845-1917, active in the 1880s (Syria, Transjordan). He was an Assumptionist Father who

travelled throughout the Levant, including Syria and Transjordan, taking photographs today held at the École Biblique in Jerusalem.
Bibliography: Abujaber, Cobbing 2005: 227; de Tarragon 2919 (on the archive of the École Biblique).

Gervais-Courtellemont, Jules
French, 1863-1931, active in the 1890s (Syria). French photographer who travelled in several countries of the Near East. In 1894, converted to Islam, he made a pilgrimage to Mecca.
Bibliography: Courtellemont 1994; El-Hage 2000: 44.

Girault de Prangey, Joseh-Philibert
French, 1804-1892, active in the 1840s (Syria). Between 1842 and 1844, he travelled in Greece, the Near East and Egypt, taking several daguerrotypes. He was particularly interested in Islamic architecture.
Bibliography: Girault de Prangey 1846; Perez 1988: 167-168; Howe 1997: 23; Hannavy 2008: 397-398, 1034.
Web repository:
https://gallica.bnf.fr/ (search 'Girault de Prangey Philibert-Joseph').

Glubb, John
British, 1897-1986, active in the 1920s (Mesopotamia). British soldier, also known as 'Glubb Pasha', commanding general of the Arab Legion of Transjordan between 1939 and 1956. The Middle East Centre in Oxford holds several photos taken by him.
Web repository:
http://www.sant.ox.ac.uk/mec/mecaphotos-john-glubb.html

Good, Frank Mason
British, 1839-1928, active in the 1860s-1870s (Syria, Transjordan). He completed four tours in the Levant, between 1866 and 1875, taking several photographs in Syria and Transjordan (Petra in particular), some of them highly excellent from a technical point of view.
Bibliography: Perez 1988: 169; El-Hage 2000: 32-33; Abujaber, Cobbing 2005: 227; Hannavy 2008: 598-599; Jacobson 2016: 69.
Web repository:
http://www.getty.edu/art/collection (search 'Frank Mason Good').

Goupil-Fesquet, Frédéric Auguste Antoine
French, 1817-1878, active in 1839-1840 (Syria). He toured the Near East together with the painter Horace Vernet, taking several daguerrotypes. In his photographs, he portrayed mainly Egyptian monuments, but he also travelled in Syria. It is worth noting that he was probably the first to photograph Jerusalem, in December 1839.
Bibliography: Goupil-Fesquet 1843; Perez 1988: 169-171; Howe 1997: 23; El-Hage 2000: 18; Hannavy 2008: 1034.

Web repositories:
https://eng.travelogues.gr/collection.php?view=30
https://gallica.bnf.fr/ark:/12148/bpt6k317008s

Graham, James
British, 1806-1869, active in the 1850s (Syria). Lay secretary of the London Society for Promoting Christianity among the Jews, he visited Egypt and the Levant between 1853 and 1857. Many of his photographs were used to produce the drawn illustrations of some books published in those years.
Bibliography: Perez 1988: 171-172; El-Hage 2000: 23-24; Hannavy 2008: 605-606; Jacobson 2016: 70.

Hakim, Suleiman
Nationality and dates unknown, active in the 1880s-1890s (Syria). Photographer known from the *Baedeker Guide* as working in Damascus.
Bibliography: Baedeker 1898: 340; Perez 1988: 174; El-Hage 2000: 47.
Web repositories:
https://lib-webarchive.aub.edu.lb/BorreLudvigsen/
https://almashriq.hiof.no/ddc/projects/jafet/blatchford/html/index.html

Hallajan, Jean
Nationality and dates unknown, active in the 1890s-1900s (Syria). Photographer resident in Haifa, who photographed the works for the construction of the Hejaz railway.
Bibliography: El-Hage 2000: 44.

Hammerschmidt, Wilhelm
German, dates unknown, active in the 1860s (Syria). Professional photographer operating both in Egypt and in Syria in the 1860s.
Bibliography: Perez 1988: 174; En-Hage 2000: 32; Hannavy 2008: 633.

Harentz, G. and Sarkis
Nationality and dates unknown, active in the 1910s (Syria). Photographers quoted in the *Baedeker Guide* as being active in Damascus.
Bibliography: Baedeker 1912: El-Hage 2000: 47.

Hart, Ludovico Woolfgang
English, 1836-1912, active in the 1860s (Syria). English photographer who travelled in Syria in 1864-1865, taking several photographs, mainly of traditional costumes and landscapes.
Bibliography: Perez 1988: 174-175.

Hawawiri, Habib Mitri
Syrian, 1872-1922, active in the 1900s-1910s (Syria). Photographer who was active in Damascus in the first twenty years of the 20th century.
Bibliography: El-Hage 2000: 47.

Haynes, John Henry

American, 1849-1910, active in the 1880s-1890s (Mesopotamia, Syria). Archaeologist and photographer, especially known for his participation as official photographer in the 1884 Wolfe expedition to Syria and the 1889 expedition to Nippur. He also travelled elsewhere in the Near East.
Bibliography: Ward 1885: 56; Bohrer 2011: 50-51; Ousterhout 2016.
Web repositories:
https://digital.library.cornell.edu/ (search: 'Sitlington Sterret Collection')
https://antiquities.library.cornell.edu/photos/haynes
http://www.luminous-lint.com/app/photographer (search 'Haynes, John Henry').

Herford, Wilhelm

German, 1814-1866, active in 1850s-1860s (Syria). Prussian diplomat, consular officer in Beirut, Cairo and Trabzon between 1855 and 1866. He travelled in the Near East, taking many photographs, especially dedicated to archaeological monuments.
Bibliography: Perez 1988: 176; El-Hage 2000: 24-25; Hannavy 2008: 1458.

Herzfeld, Ernst

German, 1879-1948, active in the 1900s-1910s (Mesopotamia). One of the major archaeologists of the first half of the 20th century. Between 1903 and 1913 in particular, he intensively visited, mapped, photographed and drew many archaeological sites, notably Samarra, Baghdad and Ctesiphon.
Bibliography: Hauser 2003; Gunter, Hauser 2005; Bohrer 2011: 17.
Web repository:
https://asia.si.edu/research/archives/herzfeld/

Hogarth, David George

English, 1862-1967, active in the 1910s (Syria). In the first half of the 1910s he carried out the excavations at the site of Karkemish. He was interested in photography and toke several photographs during his expeditions.
Bibliography: Lock 1990.

Hornstein, Charles Alexander

Born in Jerusalem from German-Jews immigrants, active in the 1890s. Photographer for the Palestine Exploration Fund. In 1896, he took photographs in Transjordan, which were donated to the Palestine Exploration Fund.
Bibliography: Hornstein 1898; Abujaber, Cobbing 2005: 227.

Hoskins, Franklin

American, 1858-1920, active in the 1900s (Transjordan). At the beginning of the 20th century, together with William Libbey (American, 1855-1927), he visited Petra and the Jordan Valley, taking many photographs that were reproduced in the publication of the survey. To my knowledge, it is not possible to attribute the photographs to one photographer or the other.
Bibliography: Libbey, Hoskins 1905.

Hull, E. Gordon

Irish, dates unknown, active in the 1880s (Transjordan). He was the photographer of the Palestine Exploration Fund expedition to the Wadi Arabah, directed by Capt. Horatio H. Kitchener in 1883-1884.
Bibliography: Hull, Kitchener 1885; Abujaber, Cobbing 2005: 228.

Hunt, Leavitt and Morriss

American, 1831-1907 (Leavitt) and 1831-1907 (Morriss), active in the 1850s (Syria, Transjordan). Leavitt Hunt and Nathan Felix Baker (American, c. 1822-1891) went on a 'Grand Tour' of Greece, Egypt and the Levant in 1851-1852, taking several photos (those of Petra are of particular interest). Leavitt's brother Morris repeated the same tour in 1852-1853, taking and purchasing photographs.
Bibliography: Perez 1988: 178; El-Hage 2000: 22-23; Hannavy 2008: 729-731; Stapp 2008; Saunders 2019.

Hyslop, James McAdam

British, 1822-1897, active in the 1840-1860s (Mesopotamia). Residency surgeon at Baghdad, he assisted Commander James Felix Jones in his Iraqi survey, taking the photographs used for some lithographed views of Baghdad, then published in the survey report.
Bibliography: Jones 1857: 311.

Indiveri, Francesco

Italian, dates unknown, active in the 1890s (Syria). Italian photographer, known to have been active in Damascus between 1896 and 1908.
Bibliography: El-Hage 2000: 47.
Web repository:
https://sites.google.com/view/adriano-silingardi-fotografia/fototeca/impero-ottomano/francesco-indiveri

Jacobson, Rigmor

Danish, ?-1947, active in the 1930s (Mesopotamia). She participated in several excavations of the Oriental Institute of Chicago (Jerwan, Tell Asmar, Ishtschali), being in charge of the photography
Bibliography: Jacobsen, Lloyd 1935: vii.; Frankfort 1936: viii; Green, Teeter, Larson 2012:56.

Jardin, ?

Name, nationality and dates unknown, active in the 1860s (Transjordan). Unknown photographer, mentioned as a participant in the expedition to the

Dead Sea led in 1864 by the Duke of Luynes, in addition to Louis Vignes (below).
Bibliography: Perez 1988: 180.

Johnson, R.C.
British, name and dates unknown, active in the 1870s (Transjordan). Photographer who participated in the trip led by Horatio B. Tristram in Moab in 1872.
Bibliography: Tristram 1873: v; Perez 1988: 181.

Joly de Lotbinière, Pierre Gaspard Gustave
Swiss born, naturalised Canadian, 1798-1865, active in the 1839-1840 (Syria). One of the pioneers in the use of daguerreotypes, he travelled in the Levant, including Syria, in 1839-1840. The daguerreotypes were copied as engravings in order to be printed. No original plate by him is preserved, to my knowledge.
Bibliography: Perez 1988: 181-182; Howe 1997: 23; Brown 1999; El-Hage 2000: 18-20; Hannavy 2008: 779; Desautels, Aubin, Blanchet 2011.

Keith, George Skene
Scottish, 1819-1910, active in the 1840s (Transjordan). He travelled with his father, Alexander, taking daguerroptypes of biblical landscapes that were reproduced and turned into steel engravings.
Bibliography: Perez 1988: 182; Howe 1997: 23; Mortensen 2018: 174.
Web repository:
https://wellcomecollection.org/works/mvt4t5k2/items?canvas=1&langCode=eng&sierraId=b22027580

Kerim, Abdul (also: Abdulkarim)
Nationality and dates unknown, active in the 1920s (Mesopotamia). Photographer, quoted as the author of a series of ethnographic photos published by the Hasso Brothers in Baghdad around 1923.
Web repository:
https://archnet.org/collections/14

Kitchener, Horatio Herbert
Irish, 1850-1916, active in the 1870s-1880s (Transjordan). Photographer for the Palestine Exploration Fund in the 1870s-1880s. To my knowledge, all known photos by him concern his expedition in Western Palestine, but he may have taken photographs also later (in 1883-1884 he participated in the survey of the Wadi Arabah).
Bibliography: Perez 1988: 183-184; Howe 1997: 38-39; Abujaber, Cobbing 2005: 228.

Krikorian, Garabed
Armenian, 1847-1920, active in the 1890s (Syria). One of the first Armenian professional photographers, who worked with Georges Sabunji (below) and was an official photographer of the visit of Kaiser Wilhelm II to Jerusalem in 1898.
Bibliography: Perez 1988: 186-188; El-Hage 2000: 45.

Lallemand, Charles
French, 1826-1904, active in the 1860s (Syria). French journalist, who toured the Near East in 1863 together with Jules Gervais-Courtellemont (above), and in 1864 together with Ludovico Wolfgang Hart (above), taking several photographs, mainly dedicated to the people and their costumes.
Bibliography: Lallemand 1866; El-Hage 2000: 32.

Larsson, Lewis
See above: American Colony Photo Department.

Lawrence, Thomas Edward
Welsh, 1888-1935, active in the 1910s (Mesopotamia, Syria). The famous 'Lawrence of Arabia' was also a talented photographer. Because of his skills in archaeology, and his collaboration with David G. Hogarth and Leonard Woolley, his photographs are often dedicated to archaeological subjects.
Bibliography: Lawrence 1939; Gibson, Chapman 1996; Abujaber, Cobbing 2005: 228.

Le Bon, Gustave
French, 1841-1931, active in the 1860s-1880s (Syria). Anthropologist and ethnographer, he travelled extensively in the Near East between the 1860s and 1880s, taking many photographs that were reproduced in his publications.
Bibliography: Le Bon 1889; Perez 1988: 189-190.

Le Gray, Jean Baptiste Gustave
French, 1820-1882, active in the 1860s (Syria, Transjordan). He was one of the most technically skilled photographers of the 19th century. In 1860-1862 he toured Egypt and the Levant, taking several photographs that were later shown in various European exhibitions.
Bibliography: Parry Janis 1987; Perez 1988: 190-191; El-Hage 2000: 29; Hannavy 2008: 832-836.

Lees, George Robinson
English, 1860-1944, active in the 1890s (Syria). In 1893, Rev. G. Robinson Lees left Jerusalem and travelled in Palestine, Syria and Jordan, taking several photographs, in part published in his works.
Bibliography: Lees 1895, 1909; El-Hage 2000: 43.

Leeuw, Honoré
French, dates unknown, active in the 1880s (Syria). Son of the photographer Théodore Leeuw, he opened a photo studio in Damascus in the early 1880s. To my knowledge, none of his photographs are known.
Bibliography: El-Haage 2000: 22.

Leon, Moyse and Lévy, Isac George
French, dates unknown, active in the 1870s (Syria). In 1864, L. Moyse and I.G. Lévy took over the Ferrier &

Soulier firm and photo-studio. They published at least two catalogues with many photogaphs of the Levant. Unfortunately, the photographs are not signed as a rule, so it is often difficult to identify their author. I.G. Lévy was commercially known as J. Lévy.
Bibliography: Perez 1988: 192; Hannavy 2008: 850-852.

Levi, Teodoro (Doro)
Italian, 1898-1991, active in the 1930s (Mesopotamia). One of the major Italian archaeologists of the 20th century, he participated in the first Italian expedition to Mesopotamia (1930-1933)- He took photographs both during a survey in southern Iraq and during an excavation campaign in Assyria.
Bibliography: Anastasio 2012, 2013.

Libbey, William
See above: Hoskins, Franklin.

Lorent, Jacob August
German born, naturalised American, 1813-1884, active in the 1840s and 1860s (Syria). He travelled in the Levant in 1842-1843, and then in 1863, taking several photos, only a small amount of which has survived. He most probably visited Syria too, taking photographs, despite none of them have survived, to my knowledge.
Bibliography: Lorent 1845; Waller 1982; Perez 1988: 192-193; El-Hage 2000: 21; Hannavy 2008: 872-874.

Lottin, Pierre René Victorien
French, 1810-1903, active in 1840s-1850s (Mesopotamia). A skilled photographer, who invented the process called Lottinoplastie. He travelled in Mesopotamia in 1844, and then in Sinai, Egypt and the Arabian peninsula, until 1859. Some of the photographs he took there still exist, so it is possible that he also took photographs during his first journey to Mesopotamia, although there is no evidence yet, to my knowledge.
Bibliography: Perez 1988: 193.

Loud, Gordon
American, 1900-1971, active in the 1930s (Mesopotamia). In the 1930s, he excavated the Assyrian site of Khorsabad, taking photographs on the excavation.
Bibliography: Loud 1936: 1.

Mackenzie, Duncan
Scottish, 1861-1934, active in the 1910s (Transjordan). In 1910, he visited Petra and the surrounding region, together with Francis G. Newton, on behalf of the Palestine Exploration Fund, taking several photographs.
Bibliography: Mackenzie 1911a, 1911b. Abujaber, Cobbing 2005: 229; Momigliano 2013.
Web repository:
https://hdl.handle.net/2027/coo.31924011395831

Mackie, Rev. George M.
British, 1854-1922, active in the 1880s (Syria). Missionary resident in Beirut, who travelled in Syria, around 1880, taking several photographs.
Bibliography: El-Hage 2000: 44.

Mantell, Lt A.M.
Name, nationality and dates unknown, active in the 1880s (Transjordan). Lt. A.M. Mantell is quoted in Conder's Survey of the Eastern Palestine as a photographer of the monuments surveyed in 1881-1882.
Bibliography: Conder 1889: 38, 44, 55, 64; Perez 1988: 193; Abujaber, Cobbing 2005: 229.

Matson, Eric and Edith
See above: American Colony Photo Department.

Meyers, Elijah
See above: American Colony Photo Department.

Missirliyan, ?
Name, nationality (Armenian?) and dates unknown, active in the 1910s (Syria). Photographer quoted as active in Aleppo in the *Baedeker Guide* of 1912.
Bibliography: Baedeker 1912: 370.

Monckton, Reginald Francis Percy
English, 1896-1975, active in the 1920s (Transjordan). British officer active in Jordan after 1920.
Web repository:
https://www.sant.ox.ac.uk/mec/mecaphotos-monckton.html

Monneret de Villard, Ugo
Italian, 1881-1954, active in the 1920s-1930s (Mesopotamia, Syria, Transjordan). One of the most renowned Italian Orientalists in the first half of the 20th century. He photographed several sites in Egypt and the Near East, especially between 1920 and 1938.
Bibliography: Armando 2011.
Web repository:
https://www.inasaroma.org/patrimonio/fototeca-6/fondo-monneret/

Moritz, Bernhard
German, 1859–1939, active in the 1900s-1910s (Transjordan). German archaeologist and orientalist, who created an album of 105 photographs of various sites in the Near East, taken between 1905 and 1915, including some views of Petra.
Bibliography: Moritz 1916; Bobzin 1997.
Web repository:
https://www.loc.gov/photos/?q=Moritz,+Bernhard

Mouterde, René
French, 1880-1961, active in the 1900s-1950s (Syria). French Jesuit, archaeologist. He collected a great

number of photographs dedicated to the archaeology of Lebanon and Syria.
Bibliography: Seyrig 1963; El-Hage 2000: 42.

Musil, Alois
Czech, 1868-1944, active in the 1890s-1910s (Transjordan). One of the most famous early explorers of the Near East, which he toured between 1897 and 1917, taking photographs of the surveyed monuments. His discovery of Qusayr Amra is worth noting.
Bibliography: Musil 1907; 1907-1908; Veselá 2012.

Oppenheim, Max Freiherr von
German, 1860-1946, active in 1900s-1930s (Mesopotamia, Syria). The famous German archaeologist, who excavated Tell Halaf in Syria, was also a collector of photographs and a photographer himself, particularly interested in archaeological photography. His photo collection, created between 1899 and 1939, comprises *c.* 13.000 photographs.
Bibliography: El-Hage 2000: 50.
Web repositories:
https://max-von-oppenheim.foundation/collections/the-photographic-collection/
https://arachne.uni-koeln.de/drupal/?q=de_DE/node/197 (search 'Fotosammlung Max von Oppenheim)

Ostheim, Othon von
Austrian, dates unknown, active in the 1860s (Syria). Former officer of the Austrian cavalry, he accompanied the Comte de Chambord in his travels in the Near East in 1861. In the 1860s, he was resident in Beirut.
Bibliograhy: Perez 1988: 201-203; El-Hage 2000. 30-31.

Persons, Victor Smith
American, 1878-1940, active in the 1900s (Mesopotamia). He took part in the Bismaya excavations, taking some photographs during the expedition.
Bibliography: Wilson et al. 2012: 20-21.

Peters, John Punnet
American, 1852-1921, active in the 1880s-1890s (Syria, Transjordan). He conducted excavations at Nippur, whose official photographer was John Henry Haynes (above), between 1888 and 1895. He toured the Near East, notably between 1889-1809, when he travelled along the route from Philadelphia (Amman) to Jerash, as well as from Beirut to Baghdad, taking several photographs.
Bibliography: Peters 1893.

Phillips, Corporal Henry
English, 1830-1905/6, active in the 1860s (Transjordan). Photographer for the Palestine Exploration Fund, he participated in the expeditions in Transjordan led by Capt. Wilson (in 1865-1866) and by Lt. Charles Warren (in 1867-1869).
Bibliography: Warren Ch. 1870; 1880; Perez 1988: 204-205; El-Hage 2000: 34; Abujaber, Cobbing 2005: 229; Jacobson 2016: 71.

Poche, Albert
French, 1842-1930, active in the 1860s (Syria). He was an artist and a photographer. He took several photographs in Aleppo and the surrounding region, including Qalat Siman. His photos were used for various publications by other travellers.
Bibliography: Perez 1988: 205.
Web repository:
https://rosettaapp.getty.edu/delivery/DeliveryManagerServlet?dps_pid=IE4474505

Pognon, Paul Pascal Henri
French, 1853-1921, active in the 1890s-1900s (Mesopotamia, Syria). Engineer and archaeologist, he was appointed French Consul in Baghdad and later in Aleppo, between 1887 and 1914. It is worth noting that he was the author of some of the earliest photographs of Samarra, published in the report by Léon de Beylié.
Bibliography: Basset 1921.

Poidebard, Antoine
French, 1878-1955, active in the 1920s-1940s (Syria). French Jesuit, archaeologist and aviator. He pioneered aerial archaeology in the Near East.
Bibliography: Poidebard 1934.; El-Hage 2000: 42; Helbig 2016.
Web repository:
https://www.usj.edu.lb/poidebard/muse.htm

Purinton, Carl E.
American, 1900-1982, active in the 1920s (Transjordan). As a recipient of a Ph.D. in religion from Yale University, he participated in a trip lead by William F. Albright to the Hawran, taking the photos that were published in Albright's report.
Bibliography: Albright 1925.

Puttrich-Reignard, Oswin
German, 1906-1942, active in the 1930s (Mesopotamia). Photographer of the 1931-1932 German expedition at Ctesiphon, directed by Ernst Kühnel.
Bibliography: Upton 1932.

Raad, Khalil
Nationality unknown, 1869-1957, active in the 1890s-1940s (Syria, Transjordan). Photographer active in Syria and Transjordan (and other sites) in the 1890s and the first half of the 20th century.
Bibliography: El-Hage 2000: 45.

Raboisson, Antoine (Abbé)
French, dates unknown, active in the 1880s (Syria) In 1882, he visited Egypt and Syria, taking photographs

that were published in 1886. Despite his signature on the photos, it is possible that at least part of them were taken by different photographers.
Bibliography: Raboisson 1886, Perez 1988: 207; El-Hage 2000: 42.

Rambeau, ?
Name, nationality and dates unknown, active in the 1880s (Syria). Photographer, probably of French origins, active in Damascus in the 1880s. No detailed information or existing photographs are known to my knowledge.
Bibliography: Perez 1988: 207.

Raphael (Père)
Name, nationality and dates unknown, active in the 1900s (Mesopotamia). Capuchin friar and author of a series of gelatin aristotypes collected in a dedicated album, depicting some monuments in northern Mesopotamia (Urfa, Mardin, Malatya).
Bibliography: Raphael (Père) 1904.
Web repository:
https://gallica.bnf.fr/ark:/12148/btv1b531680094

Rassam, Hormuzd
Assyrian-Iraqi, 1826-1910, active in the 1850s-1870s (Mesopotamia). Assyrian archaeologist, who took photographs during his trips to the Near East between 1851 and 1876. However, no photograph has been surely identified as taken by him, to my knowledge.
Bibliography: Perez 1988: 208.

Rau, William Herman
American, 1855-1920, active in the 1880s (Syria, Transjordan). American photographer. He travelled to the Near East in 1882, taking several photos (Petra, especially).
Bibliography: Brey 1984; Perez 1988: 209; El-Hage 2000: 48; Hannavy 2008: 1184.

Reid, A.
Name, nationality and dates unknown, active in the 1910s-1920s (Syria, Transjordan). An almost unknown photographer, despite his significant activity in the Near East, documented between 1914 and 1920.
Bibliography: Abujaber, Cobbing 2005: 230.

Rey, Emmanuel Guillaume
French, 1837-1916, active in the 1850s-1860s (Syria, Transjordan). French geographer and explorer who toured the Levant between the late 1850s and 1860s, taking several photographs.
Bibliography: Perez 1988: 209.

Roberts, Lieutenant A.H.
British, name and dates unknown, active in the 1910s-1920s (Mesopotamia). It is likely that he was the author of a box containing a collection of 65 projectable lantern slides relating to the Arab Revolt of 1916-1918, today at the Qatar National Library.
Web repository:
https://www.wdl.org/en/item/18812/#collection=lt-roberts-middle-eastern-magic-lantern-slides-collection

Robertson, James
English, 1813-1888, active in the 1850s (Syria). In 1857, Robertson and one or both the Beato brothers (above) travelled to the Near East, where they produced a number of topographical photographs of Egypt, Syria and Palestine. For a while, they also worked together with the signature 'Robertson & Beato'.
Bibliography: Perez 1988: 210-211; Oztunçay 1992; El-Hage 2000: 24-25; Jacobson 2016: 70-71.

Rombau, Henri
Nationality and dates unknown, active in the 1870s (Syria). Collaborator of the Maison Bonfils (above), resident in Damascus around the mid-1870s.
Bibliography: Apostolou 2013: 7.

Rovier, Jules
French, dates unknown, active in the 1890s (Syria). Franciscan friar, resident in Syria, who published a photo album titled *Syria, Chypre et Egypte* (c. 1893).
Bibliography: El-Hage 2000: 43.

Sabunji, Louis and George
Arab Ottoman, 1833-1931 (Louis) and 1840-1910 (George), active in the 1850s-1860s (Syria). Georges Sabounji was one of the first professional photographers resident in Beirut. He was introduced to photography by his brother Louis, a professional photographer and owner of a company that sold photographs. Louis also took photographs in Syria, especially those used by the archaeologist Edward Sachau for his publications. 'Sabounji' was mentioned as being active in Damascus in the *Baedeker Guide* of 1912.
Bibliography: Baedeker 1912: 295; El-Hage 2000: 37-39; Perez 1988: 214; Sheehi *et al.* 2017.

Saint-Elme, Gautier
French, 1849-1903, active in the 1860s (Syria). He travelled in the Levant in 1868, together with Jean-Léon Gérome, taking photos that did not reach us, to my knowledge.
Bibliography: Perez 1988: 215.

Salzmann, Auguste
French, 1842-1872, active in the 1860s (Syria?, Transjordan). Archaeologist, painter and photographer. He travelled in the Holy Land in the 1850s-1860s. In particular, in 1863 he visited the Jordan Valley, taking photographs. He paid great attention to architecture.
Bibliography: Solomon-Godeau 1981; Perez 1988: 215-216; Hannavy 2008: 1239-1240; Brossard-Gabastou 2013.

Web repositories:
https://www.alinari.it/it/esplora-immagini (search: 'Auguste Salzman').
https://www.metmuseum.org/art/collection (search: 'Auguste Salzmann').

Sarrafian, Abraham
Armenian, 1875-1926, active in 1890s (Mesopotamia, Syria). In 1894, he made a trip to Mesopotamia, taking several photographs in the region of Mosul. In 1895, together with his two brothers, he set up the photo studio Sarrafian Brothers, which was very successful not only in Lebanon but also elsewhere in the Near East, especially Syria.
Bibliography: El-Hage 2000: 37; Toubia 2008.

Sauvaire, Henry-Joseph
French, 1831-1896, active in the 1860s-1870s (Syria, Transjordan). He toured the Levant in the 1860s and 1870s. In particular, he participated as a photographer in the 1864 expedition led by the Duc de Luynes. In Damascus, he documented the civil conflicts of 1860, working as a sort of modern photo-reporter.
Bibliography: Sauvaire 1894-1896; Luynes 1871-1874: pl. 13; Perez 1988: 216-217; El-Hage 2000: 29-30; Hannavy 2008: 1244-1245.
Web repository:
https://www.getty.edu/research/special_collections/notable/duc_du_luynes.html

Schmidt, Erich
German born, naturalised American 1897-1964, active in the 1930s (Mesopotamia). Renowned German archaeologist who worked in Turkey, Iraq and Iran. He made extensive use of photography on excavations.
Bibliography: Bohrer 2011: 124.

Schulz, Bruno
German, 1865-1932, active in the 1890s-1900s (Mesopotamia, Syria, Transjordan). German architect, who travelled in Mesopotamia, Syria and Transjordan between 1897 and 1904, taking several photos of architectural interest, especially those concerning Mushatta in Jordan.
Bibliography: Puchstein *et al.* 1902; Schulz, Strzygowsky 1904; Anastasio, Botarelli 2015: 18.

Scölik, Charles
Austrian, 1853-1928, active in the 1890s (Syria). One of the most renowned Austrian photographers, who visited Syria in 1894.
Bibliography: El-Hage 2000: 34.

Sebah & Joailler Studio
Studio active in the 1890-1940s (Syria). Jean Sebah (Syrian-Armenian, 1872-1947) and Polycarpe Joailler (French, 1848-1904) opened a photo studio in Istanbul. They became the official photographers to the Sultan, taking photographs in various regions of the Ottoman empire, Syria included.
Bibliography: Perez 1988: 221-222; El-Hage 2000: 39-49; Hannavy 2008: 1260-1261.
Web repository:
http://katalog.istanbul.edu.tr/client/en_US/defaulteng/ (search under 'II.Abdülhamid Han Fotoğraf Albümleri', subject: 'Birecik').

Smith, Arthur Lionel Forster
British, 1880-1972, active in the 1920s-1930s (Mesopotamia). He served as Director of Education, Mesopotamia, in 1920-1921 and then as Adviser of Education, Iraq, in 1921-1931.
Bibliography: Anonymous 1973.
Web repository:
http://www.sant.ox.ac.uk/mec/mecaphotos-alf-smith.html

Smith, John Shaw
Irish, 1811-1873, active in the 1850s (Syria, Transjordan). In 1850-1852 he travelled extensively throughout the Levant, including Syria and Transjordan, taking several photographs of great technical and artistic value.
Bibliography: Perez 1988: 222; El-Hage 2000: 22; Abujaber, Cobbing 2005: 230-231; Hannavy 2008: 1273-1274.
Web repository:
https://norman.hrc.utexas.edu/photopublic/fullDisplay.cfm?CollID=15669

Spranger, John Alfred
English, 1889-1968, active in the 1930s (Mesopotamia). Both archaeologist and photographer, as well as engineer and topographer, he was the author of an archaeological photo reportage in southern Iraq, in 1936.
Bibliography: Anastasio, Arbeid 2015; Koutsoumpos 2019; Harlan 2022.

Stark, Freya
British, 1893-1993, active in the 1920s-1940s (Mesopotamia, Syria, Transjordan). Famous traveller, author and photographer, who travelled extensively throughout the Near East in the 1920s-1940s. She is the author of c. 6,000 photographs held at the Middle East Centre, St. Antony's College, Oxford.
Bibliography: Hansen 2004 (with bibliography).
Web repository:
https://www.sant.ox.ac.uk/mec/MEChandlists/Freya-Stark-Photo-Albums-Catalogue.pdf

Svoboda, Alexander
Most likely Russian, dates unknown, active in the 1850s (Mesopotamia, Syria). Photographer resident in Smyrne. His studio produced several travel albums with photos of Biblical sites.
Bibliography: Perez 1988: 225.

Sykes, M.
Name, nationality and dates unknown, active in the 1890s (Transjordan). A little-known clergyman, who accompanied Lucien Gautier in his trip in Transjordan in 1894, taking several photos.
Bibliograhy: Gautier 1896: 6.

Tchalenko, George
Russian, 1905–1987, active in 1930s-1980s (Syria). Graduated in Architecture and Engineering in Germany, he fled the country when Hitler seized power and spent the rest of his life in Syria and Lebanon, studying the ancient architecture of Northern Syria. Up to 20,000 photographs are held in the *Georges Tchalenko Archive*, housed in Oxford's Institute of Archaeology.
Bibliography: Tchalenko G. 1953; Tchalenko J. 2019.
Web repository:
https://www.ocla.ox.ac.uk/tchalenko-archive-project

Thevénet, Clovis
French, dates unknown, active in the 1910s (Syria). Photographer mentioned as active in Aleppo in the *Baedeker Guide*.
Bibliography: Baedeker 1912: 370.

Thiersch, Hermann
German, 1874-1939, active in the 1900s (Syria, Transjordan). Archaeologist who toured the Levant between 1902 and 1903 as fellow of the German Archaeological institute, taking several photographs of archeological sites and monuments.
Bibliography: Thiersch-Holscher 1904, Anastasio, Botarelli 2015: 18.

Thompson, Elizabeth Bowen
British, 1812/13-1869, active in the 1860s-1870s (Syria). British Protestant missionary, who founded a school in Damascus in 1868. She took several photographs during her stay in Syria.
Bibliography: Bowen Thompson 1872; El-Hage 2000: 43.

Thomson, Rev. William McClure
American, 1806-1894, active in the 1850s-1860s (Syria, Transjordan). American Protestant missionary, who travelled to the Near East in the 1850s-1860s, taking several photographs that were reproduced, drawn and engraved, in his publications.
Bibliography: Thomson 1886: iv; Abujaber, Cobbing 2005: 34.
Web repository:
https://archive.org/details/landbookorbiblic00thom

Tobler, Arthur John
American, dates unknown, active in the 1930s (Mesopotamia). Archaeologist, who participated in the Tepe Gawra end Tell Billa excavations, taking care of the photographic documentation.
Bibliography: Speiser 1935: 8.

Tranchand, Gabriel
French, dates unknown, active in the 1850s (Mesopotamia). French engineer who used photography for the first time to record an archaeological excavation in the Near East, in 1852 at the site of Khorsabad.
Bibliography: Place 1867: vi; Perez 1988: 227; Bohrer 2011: 37-38.
Web repository:
https://salamandre.college-de-france.fr/ (in 'Fonds Pillet' search: 'Tranchand, Gabriel').

Tyrwhitt-Drake, Charles Frederick
British, 1846-1874, active in the 1870s (Syria). He travelled in the Near East between 1869 and 1874. Together with Richard Burton, he was co-author of *Unexplored Syria*, published in 1872. He operated mainly in Palestine and Sinai, but he also travelled and took pictures in Hama, Aleppo and other sites in Syria.
Bibliography: Burton, Tyrwhitt-Drake 1872: 334; Perez 1988: 159; Jacobson 2016: 68.

Underwood & Underwood
Studio active in the 1880s-1940s (Mesopotamia). It was an America producer and distributor of stereoscopies and photographs, founded by two brothers, Elmer and Bert Elias Underwood. Several professional photographers worked for this company, both full-time and freelance, and many photos concern Iraq.
Bibliography: Hannavy 2008: 1417-1420.
Web repository:
https://www.loc.gov/search/?fa=location:iraq&q=Underwood+%26+underwood

van Berchem, Max
Swiss, 1863-1921, active in the 1890s (Syria). Renowned orientalist, specialist in Islamic archaeology and skilled photographer, who travelled in the Near East between 1886 and 1921 (visiting Syria in 1894 and 1895).
Bibliography: Herzfeld 1922; El-Hage 2000: 50.

Vignes, Louis
French, 1831-1896, active in the 1860s (Transjordan). Photographer of the expedition organised by the Duke of Luynes to the Dead Sea basin and inner Transjordan (1864). Most of his photos were reproduced in photogravure in the book on the results of the expedition.
Bibliography: Luynes 1871-1874; Perez 1988: 229; Hannavy 2008: 1454.
Web repositories:
https://gallica.bnf.fr/ark:/12148/bpt6k3193389/f1.double
http://www.luminous-lint.com/app/photographer/Louis_Vignes/C/

Viollet, Henri
French, 1880-1955, active in the 1900s (Mesopotamia). Architect and archaeologist, he carried out excavations

Wade, Harry Llewellyn
British, 1908-1983, active the 1920s (Mesopotamia). Officer of the Royal Air Force. In 1928-1930, he took several photographs during his posting to Iraq.
Web repository:
http://www.sant.ox.ac.uk/mec/mecaphotos-wade.html

Wheelhouse, Claudius Galen
English, 1826-1909, active in the 1850s (Syria). Surgeon, who worked as attendant doctor on a cruise ship touring the Mediterranean in 1851. He was probably the first to use the calotype in Syria. Unfortunately, most of his photos went lost in a fire at the end of the 1870s.
Bibliography: Perez 1988: 232; El-Hage 2000: 22; Hannavy 2008: 1493-1494; Wheelhouse 2006.

Woolley, Leonard
English, 1880-1960, active in the 1910s-1940s (Mesopotamia, Syria). One of the major archaeologists in the history of Ancient Near Eastern archaeology, he was also a talented photographer.
Bibliography: Gibson, Chapman 1996; Mallowan 1960.

At Samarra between 1907 and 1910. Some of his photographs were published in his excavation reports.
Bibliography: Viollet 1909, 1913; Rose 2017.

Table a. Chronological order

1840s	Bridges • Du Camp • Girault de Prangey • Goupil-Fesquet • Hyslop • Joly de Lotbinière • Keith • Lorent • Lottin.
1850s	Baker • Ban • Beato • Benecke • Bergheim • Bridges • Cotton • de Campigneulles • de Chartre • de Clerq • de Rumine • de Saulcy • Du Camp • Frith • Graham • Herford • Hunt • Hyslop • Lottin • Rassam • Rey • Robertson • Sabunji • Smith, J.A. • Svoboda • Thomson • Tranchand • Wheelhouse.
1860s	Bedford • Beke • Bergheim • Bonfils (Maison) • Bowman • Cahun • Charlier-Béziès • de Champlouis • de Chartre • de Saulcy • de Vorys • Ferrier • Good • Hammerschmidt • Hart • Herford • Hyslop • Jardin • Lallemand • Le Bon • Le Gray • Lorent • Ostheim • Phillips • Poche • Rassam • Rey • Sabunji • Saint-Elme • Salzmann • Sauvaire • Thompson • Thomson • Vignes.
1870s	Al-Azm • Bergheim • Bonfils (Maison) • Buxton • Cahun • Dumas • Egerton • Good • Johnson • Kitchener • Le Bon • Leon & Lévy • Rassam • Rombau • Sauvaire • Thompson • Tyrwhitt-Drake.
1880s	Barry • Bishof • Bonfils (Maison) • Cahun • Germer-Durand • Hakim • Haynes • Hull • Kitchener • Le Bon • Leeuw • Mackie • Mantell • Peters • Raboisson • Rambeau • Rau • Underwood & Underwood.
1890s	American Colony Photo Dept. • Bain • Barshchevsky • Bliss • Bonfils (Maison) • Brünnow • Burchardt • Cooke • Dieulafoy • Gervais-Courtellemont • Hakim • Hallajan • Haynes • Hornstein • Indiveri • Krikorian • Lees • Musil • Peters • Pognon • Raad • Rovier • Sarrafian • Schulz • Scölik • Sebah & Joailler Studio • Sykes • Underwood & Underwood • van Berchem.
1900s	American Colony Photo Dept. • Banks • Bell, G. • Bonfils (Maison) • Cavalcanty • de Beylié • Dickie • Hallajan • Hawawiri • Herzfeld • Hoskins • Libbey • Moritz • Mouterde • Musil • Oppenheim • Persons • Pognon • Raad • Raphael • Schulz • Sebah & Joailler Studio • Thiersch • Underwood & Underwood • Viollet
1910s	American Colony Photo Dept. • Araqtinji • Banse • Bell • Bonfils (Maison) • de Genouillac • Derounian • Harentz • Hawawiri • Herzfeld • Hogarth • Lawrence • Mackenzie • Missirliyan • Moritz • Mouterde • Musil • Oppenheim • Raad • Reid • Roberts • Sebah & Joailler Studio • Thévenet • Underwood & Underwood • Woolley.
1920s	American Colony Photo Dept. • Banse • Banse • Bartoccini • Bonfils (Maison) • Chadirji • Clapp • de Genouillac • Derounian • Enlart • Glubb • Kerim • Monckton • Monneret de Villard • Mouterde • Oppenheim • Poidebard • Purinton • Raad • Reid • Roberts • Sebah & Joailler Studio • Smith, A.L.F. • Stark • Underwood & Underwood • Wade • Woolley.
1930s	Altman • American Colony Photo Dept. • Bartoccini • Bonfils (Maison) • Byron • Clapp • de Genouillac • Derounian • Frankfort • Jacobson • Levi • Loud • Monneret de Villard • Mouterde • Oppenheim • Poidebard • Puttrich-Reignard • Raad • Schmidt • Sebah & Joailler Studio • Smith, A.L.F. • Spranger • Stark • Tchalenko • Tobler • Underwood & Underwood • Woolley • Zu Eltz.

Table b. Geographical order

Mesopotamia	Altman • American Colony Photo Dept. • Ban • Banks • Banse • Barry • Bell • Burchardt • Cahun • Chadirji • Cooke • de Beylié • de Champlouis • de Genouillac • Dieulafoy • Frankfort • Glubb • Haynes • Herzfeld • Hyslop • Jacobson • Kerim • Lawrence • Levi • Lottin • Loud • Monneret de Villard • Oppenheim • Persons • Pognon, • Puttrich-Reignard • Raphael • Rassam • Roberts • Sarrafian • Schmidt • Schulz • Smith, A.L.F. • Spranger • Stark • Svoboda • Tobler • Tranchand • Underwood & Underwood • Viollet • Wade • Woolley • Zu Eltz.
Syria	Al-Azm • American Colony Photo Dept. • Araqtinji • Bain • Baker • Banse • Barshchevsky • Bartoccini • Beato • Bedford • Beke • Bell • Benecke • Bergheim • Bishof • Bonfils (Maison) • Bowman • Bridges • Brünnow • Burchardt • Byron • Cahun • Cavalcanty • Chadirji • Charlier-Béziès • Clapp • Cooke • Cotton • de Beylié • de Campigneulles • de Champlouis • de Chartre • de Clerq • de Rumine • de Saulcy • de Vorys • Derounian • Du Camp • Dumas • Egerton • Enlart • Ferrier • Frith • Germer-Durand • Gervais-Courtellemont • Girault de Prangey • Good • Goupil-Fesquet • Graham • Hakim • Hallajan • Hammerschmidt • Harentz • Hart • Hawawiri • Haynes • Herford • Hogarth • Hunt • Indiveri • Joly de Lotbinière • Krikorian • Lallemand • Lawrence • Le Bon • Le Gray • Lees • Leeuw • Leon & Lévy • Lorent • Mackie • Missirliyan • Monneret de Villard • Mouterde • Ostheim • Peters • Poche • Pognon • Poidebard • Raad • Raboisson • Rambeau • Rau • Reid • Rey • Robertson • Rombau • Rovier • Sabunji • Saint-Elme • Salzmann (?) • Sarrafian • Sauvaire • Schulz • Scölik • Sebah & Joailler Studio • Smith, J.A. • Stark • Svoboda • Tchalenko • Thevénet • Thiersch • Thompson • Thomson • Tyrwhitt-Drake • van Berchem • Wheelhouse • Woolley.
Transjordan	American Colony Photo Dept. • Barshchevsky • Bartoccini • Bell • Bergheim • Bliss • Bonfils (Maison) • Bowman • Brünnow • Burchardt • Buxton • Cavalcanty • Clapp • Cooke • de Champlouis • de Saulcy • Dickie • Dumas • Germer-Durand • Good • Hornstein • Hoskins • Hull • Hunt • Jardin • Johnson • Keith • Kitchener • Le Gray • Libbey • Mackenzie • Mantell • Monckton • Monneret de Villard • Moritz • Musil • Peters • Phillips • Purinton • Raad • Rau • Reid • Rey • Salzmann • Sauvaire • Schulz • Smith, J.A. • Stark • Sykes • Thiersch • Thomson • Vignes.

Appendix 2. Register of Creswell's photographs of the Biblioteca Berenson

The following list contains the IDs of all the photographs concerning Mesopotamia, Syria and Transjordan, which are available on Hollis Images (https://images.hollis.harvard.edu/; search 'Creswell', within 'Berenson, Fototeca'). The list is sorted according to the alphabetical list of monuments.

The images were digitised between December 2018 and April 2019 by Daniele Fratini, imaging service assistant at I Tatti, using a scanner Epson Expression 11000XL and the SilverFast software Ai Studio Version 8.8 (settings: *.tiff, 600 DPI, 24 bit depth, 8 bits per channel, colour profile: Adobe RGB 1998, color target used for scanner calibration: IT8 calibration target). The front of each photograph was digitised and uploaded on Hollis Images, labelled with '_1'. (therefore, to search for an ID, '_1' needs to be added; e.g., to search for the ID 133146, search for 133146_1).

Monuments' names — The figure captions written in Creswell's calligraphy are essential to recognise and interpret the subject of many photos, especially those portraying details or monuments that have disappeared. However, in some cases they can be misleading: apart from some errors in the translation of Arabic names, even the annotations on the identification of monuments are sometimes inconsistent when making cross-checks between the captions written in Creswell's calligraphy on the Berenson photos and those held at the other archives. I tried, as far as possible, to verify all the contents of the captions (this is the reason why, in some cases, the 'subject' in the captions of the figures of the catalogue differs slightly from what is reported under 'handwritten notes').

Site	Monument	Figures in the volume	IDs in Hollis Images and not in the volume
Mesopotamia			
Al-Madain	Taq Kisra	200-205	/
Al-Ukhaidir	Al-Ukhaidir Fortress	208-244	/
Baghdad	Al-Khulafa Minaret	183-185	/
Baghdad	Al-Mirjaniya Madrasa	186-189	/
Baghdad	Al-Mustansiriya Madrasa	170-177	133176, 133179
Baghdad	Bab al-Wastani	166-169	/
Baghdad	Khan Mirjan	190-195	/
Baghdad	Mihrab of al-Khassaki Mosque	144-148	/
Baghdad	Qasr al-Abbasi	152-161	133147, 133150, 133153
Baghdad	Shaykh Aquli Tomb	196-197	/
Baghdad	Shaykh Maruf al-Kharkhi Mausoleum	178-182	133168
Baghdad	Suhrawardi Mosque and Mausoleum	162-165	/
Baghdad	Zumurrud Khatun Mosque	149-151	/
Birecik	Citadel	18-52	133358, 133366-133367, 133383
Harran	Citadel	60-71	/
Harran	City Walls	56-59	/
Harran	Great Mosque	72-87	133637, 133644, 133646, 133648, 133650, 133656-133658
Harran	Mazar of Shaikh Yahia	88-91	/
Qantarat Harba	Bridge	137-139	/
Samarra	Abu Dulaf Mosque	119-126	133240, 133244

Samarra	Al-Askari Shrine	134-135	/
Samarra	Dar al-Khalifa	96-104	133235
Samarra	Great Mosque (or Jami al-Mutawakil)	105-118	/
Samarra	Qasr al-Ashiq	129-133	/
Samarra	Qubba al-Sulaibiya	127-128	/
	Syria			
Aleppo	Al-Atrush Mosque	393-397	/
Aleppo	Al-Bayada Mosque	398-399	/
Aleppo	Al-Firdaws Madrasa	339-350	134067-134069, 134138, 134141-134142, 134149-134150
Aleppo	Al-Halawiya Madrasa	320-323	134271
Aleppo	Al-Kamiliya Madrasa	363-368	134277, 134279, 134281, 134284
Aleppo	Al-Karimiya Mosque	369	/
Aleppo	Al-Khusrauriya Mosque	459-461	/
Aleppo	Al-Maqam Mosque	400-401	/
Aleppo	Al-Muqaddamiya Madrasa	324-327	/
Aleppo	Al-Qadi al-Mahmandar Mosque	402	/
Aleppo	Al-Qiqan Mosque	403-404	/
Aleppo	Al-Rumi Mosque	405-408	/
Aleppo	Al-Safahiya Mosque	409-411	/
Aleppo	Al-Sahibiya Madrasa	412-416	/
Aleppo	Al-Shadhbakhtiya Madrasa	351-356	/
Aleppo	Al-Sharafiya Madrasa	370-377	134161, 134164
Aleppo	al-Shuaybiya Mosque	312-315	/
Aleppo	Al-Sultaniya Madrasa	357-362	134059
Aleppo	Al-Tawashy Mosque	417-418	/
Aleppo	Al-Zahiriya Madrasa	378-385	134045, 134047, 134051-134053
Aleppo	Al-Zaki Mosque	419	/
Aleppo	Altunbugha Mosque	420-426	134174
Aleppo	Arghun al-Kamili Bimaristan	427-434	/
Aleppo	Bab al-Hadid	297	/
Aleppo	Bab al-Jinan	287	/
Aleppo	Bab al-Maqam	296	/
Aleppo	Bab Antakya	288-290	/
Aleppo	Bab Qinnasrin	291-295	/
Aleppo	Bahramiya Mosque	462-463	/
Aleppo	Bahsita Mosque	435	/

Aleppo	Citadel	254-273	133989, 134019
Aleppo	Citadel Mosque	274	/
Aleppo	City Walls	278-296	/
Aleppo	Great Mosque	298-307	/
Aleppo	Khan al-Jumruk	469	/
Aleppo	Khan al-Sabun	451-452	134224
Aleppo	Khan al-Wazir	470-471	/
Aleppo	Khan al-Zait	468	/
Aleppo	Khan Qassabiya	453	/
Aleppo	Khan Utchan	454	/
Aleppo	Khanqah al-Farafra	386-388	134152-134154
Aleppo	Maqam Ibrahim al-Sulfi Mosque	275-277	/
Aleppo	Maqam Ibrahim fi al-Salihin	311	/
Aleppo	Maqam Ughulbak	436	/
Aleppo	Mashhad al-Husayn	328-338	134020, 134022-134023
Aleppo	Mashhad al-Muhassin	308-310	134036, 134039, 134041
Aleppo	Masjid Yusuf	391-392	/
Aleppo	Musa Ibn Abdullah al-Nasiri Mausoleum	437-439	/
Aleppo	Nur al-Din Maristan	316-319	/
Aleppo	Private house / House in Bahsita	472-473	/
Aleppo	Qastal Bab al-Maqam	455	/
Aleppo	Qastal Sahat Bizza	456	/
Aleppo	Qastal Sakakini	457	/
Aleppo	Qastal Shabariq	458	/
Aleppo	Qubba Khayrbak	440-443	/
Aleppo	Shihab al-Din Ahmad al-Adrai Mausoleum	444-445	/
Aleppo	Takiya Shaykh Abu Bakr	464-467	/
Aleppo	Umm Malik al-Afdal Mausoleum	389-390	/
Aleppo	Zawiya al-Bazzaziya	446	/
Aleppo	Zawiya al-Haidary	447-448	/
Aleppo	Zawiya al-Junashiya	449-450	/
Damascus	Abd al-Rahman ibn Abdallah al-Tashtadar Madrasa	596	/
Damascus	Abu Abdallah Hasan ibn Salama Mausoleum	597-598	/
Damascus	Al-Adiliya Madrasa	586-594	/
Damascus	Al-Maridaniya Mosque	599-600	/

Damascus	Al-Nuriya al-Kubra Madrasa	595	/
Damascus	Al-Qaymari Maristan and Mausoleum	601-604	133509, 133513
Damascus	Al-Rihaniya Madrasa	605	/
Damascus	Al-Sahiba Madrasa	606	133538
Damascus	Al-Shamiya al-Kubra Madrasa	607-608	133559
Damascus	Al-Sibaiya Madrasa	650-651	/
Damascus	Al-Zahiriya Madrasa	630-635	133462, 133481, 133483
Damascus	Ali al-Faranti Mausoleum	609-611	/
Damascus	Amat al-Latif Mausoleum	612-613	/
Damascus	Amir Kujkun al-Mansuri Mausoleum	641	/
Damascus	Amir Tankiz Mosque and Mausoleum	636-640	/
Damascus	Atabektya Mosque	614	/
Damascus	Azm Palace	656-658	133475
Damascus	Bab al-Faraj	580	/
Damascus	Bab al-Salam	579	/
Damascus	Dar al-Hadith al-Ashrafiya al-Muqaddasiya	615	/
Damascus	Hanabila Mosque	616-618	/
Damascus	Izz al-Din Madrasa	619-622	133525
Damascus	Jaharkasiya Madrasa	623	/
Damascus	Khan Asad Pasha	659-660	133500
Damascus	Khan Sulayman Pasha	661	/
Damascus	Khatuniya Mausoleum	624	133534, 133535
Damascus	Nur al-Din Madrasa and Bimaristan	581-585	133564-133566, 133568-133569
Damascus	Raihan Mausoleum	625	133529, 133543
Damascus	Rukn al-Din Mausoleum	626	/
Damascus	Saladin Mausoleum	627-628	/
Damascus	Salihiya (not specified)	642	/
Damascus	Shaykh Muhammad ibn Ali ibn Nadif Mausoleum	629	/
Damascus	Sinan Pasha Mosque	652-655	/
Damascus	Takiya al-Sulaymaniya	643-649	133467, 133469
Damascus	Umayyad Mosque	525-578	133602
Damascus	Uncertain		133496, 133518-133521, 133534, 133501
Hama	Al-Nuri Mosque	487-490	/
Hama	Azm Palace	491-502	/
Hama	Great Mosque	483-486	/

Homs	Bab al-Masdud	522	/
Homs	Citadel	505-510	133728
Homs	Great Mosque of al-Nuri	511-521	133733
Masyaf	Masyaf Fortress	475-480	/
Qalat Siman	Church of Saint Simeon Stylites	245-248	/
Qalb Lawzah	Basilica	249	/
Ruweiha	Bizzos Mausoleum	250	/
Transjordan			
Amman	Roman Nymphaeum	669	/
Amman	Qusayr al-Nuwaijis	666	/
Amman	Roman Theatre	667-668	/
Amman	Umayyad Palace (Audience Hall)	670-691	133317
Iraq al-Amir	Qasr al-Abd	693-695	/
Qusayr Amra	Qusayr Amra	698-705	/

Appendix 3. Synopsis of Creswell's photographs in the different archives

Below is a synopsis between the IDs of the collection at the Biblioteca Berenson and those of the other archives already mentioned in the text. The list is not exhaustive, because it is only based on a cross-check between the data available in the online catalogues (Ashmolean Museum, Victoria & Albert Museum) and in some work-sheets. The symbol — means that there is no photo available or that no photo was found when checking the catalogues. Further IDs will probably be able to be recorded in the future, thanks to the ongoing work for the general, unified cataloguing of the various collections.

Berenson ID	Ashmolean ID	V&A ID	Fine Arts Lib. ID	AUC ID	ARCHNET ID	Site
133146	EA.CA.6277	2870-1930	156 B 146 3ab C Iw 2	—	ICR2170	Baghdad
133147	EA.CA.6277	2870-1930	156 B 146 3ab C Iw 2	—	ICR2170	Baghdad
133149	EA.CA.6275	2874-1930	156 B 146 3ab C Iw 2a	—	ICR2171	Baghdad
133150	EA.CA.6276	2873-1930	156 B 146 3ab C Iw 2b	—	ICR2172	Baghdad
133151	EA.CA.6279	2869-1930	156 B 146 3ab C Iw 3a	—	ICR2173	Baghdad
133152	EA.CA.6280	2871-1930	156 B 146 3ab C Iw 3b	—	ICR2174	Baghdad
133153	EA.CA.6289	2872-1930	156 B 146 3ab C Iw 3d	—	ICR2175	Baghdad
133154	EA.CA.6281	2878-1930	156 B 146 3ab C 2	—	ICR2169	Baghdad
133155	EA.CA.6283	2880-1930	156 B 146 3ab (i) 2	—	ICR2177	Baghdad
133156	EA.CA.6282	2879-1930	156 B 146 3ab (i) 1	—	ICR2176	Baghdad
133157	EA.CA.6285	2876-1930	156 B 146 3ab (i) Re 1	—	ICR2178	Baghdad
133158	EA.CA.6286	2875-1930	156 B 146 3ab (i) Re 2	—	ICR2179	Baghdad
133159	EA.CA.6288	2877-1930	156 B 146 3ab (i) Re 3	—	ICR2180	Baghdad
133160	EA.CA.6264	2888-1930	156 B 146 2M (i) Mr 1	—	ICR2161	Baghdad
133161	EA.CA.6268	2889-1930	156 B 146 2M (i) Mr 2	—	ICR2163	Baghdad
133162	EA.CA.6265	2892-1930	156 B 146 2M (i) Mr 1	—	ICR2162	Baghdad
133163	EA.CA.6267	2890-1930	156 B 146 2M (i) Mr 3	—	ICR2164	Baghdad
133164	EA.CA.6266	2891-1930	156 B 146 2M (i) Mr 3	—	ICR2165	Baghdad
133165	EA.CA.6269	—	156 B 146 9Ma 1	—	ICR2201	Baghdad
133166	EA.CA.6270	2884-1930	156 B 146 9Ma 1	—	ICR2202	Baghdad
133167	EA.CA.6272	—	156 B 146 9Ma Mi 1	—	ICR2203	Baghdad
133168	EA.CA.6271	—	156 B 146 9Ma Mi 1	—	ICR2204	Baghdad
133169	EA.CA.6273	—	156 B 146 9Ma Mi 2	—	ICR2205	Baghdad
133170	EA.CA.6274	—	156 B 146 9Ma Mi 2	—	ICR2206	Baghdad
133171	EA.CA.6328	2834-1930	156 B 146 13Wa 1	—	ICR2157	Baghdad
133172	EA.CA.6327	2835-1930	156 B 146 13Wa 1	—	ICR2158	Baghdad
133173	EA.CA.6326	2836-1930	156 B 146 13Wa (i) 1	—	ICR2160	Baghdad
133174	EA.CA.6325	2837-1930	156 B 146 13Wa 2	—	ICR2159	Baghdad
133175	EA.CA.6294	2847-1930	156 B 146 5Mu C(a) 1	—	ICR2188	Baghdad
133176	EA.CA.6293	2846-1930	156 B 146 5Mu C(a) 1	—	ICR2189	Baghdad
133177	EA.CA.6296	2845-1930	156 B 146 5Mu C(a) 2b	—	ICR2194	Baghdad
133178	EA.CA.6295	2844-1930	156 B 146 5Mu C(a) 2	—	ICR2190	Baghdad
133179	EA.CA.6297	2841-1930	156 B 146 5Mu C(a) 2	—	ICR2191	Baghdad
133180	EA.CA.6298	2842-1930	156 B 146 5Mu C(a) 2a	—	ICR2192	Baghdad
133181	EA.CA.6299	2843-1930	156 B 146 5Mu C(a) 2a	—	ICR2193	Baghdad
133182	EA.CA.6300	2848-1930	156 B 146 5Mu 1	—	ICR2186	Baghdad

Berenson ID	Ashmolean ID	V&A ID	Fine Arts Lib. ID	AUC ID	ARCHNET ID	Site
133183	EA.CA.6301	2849-1930	156 B 146 5Mu 1	—	ICR2185	Baghdad
133184	EA.CA.6302	2850-1930	156 B 146 5Mu 1	—	ICR2187	Baghdad
133185	EA.CA.6320	2864-1930	156 B 146 5Mir C 1	—	ICR2184	Baghdad
133186	EA.CA.6321	2866-1930	156 B 146 5Mir 2	—	ICR2182	Baghdad
133187	EA.CA.6318	2865-1930	156 B 146 5Mir 2	—	ICR2181	Baghdad
133188	EA.CA.6319	2863-1930	156 B 146 5Mir C 1	—	ICR2183	Baghdad
133189	EA.CA.6290	2838-1930	156 B 146 9Zu 1	—	ICR2211	Baghdad
133190	EA.CA.6291	2839-1930	156 B 146 9Zu 1	—	ICR2212	Baghdad
133191	EA.CA.6292	2840-1930	156 B 146 9Zu (i) 1	—	ICR2213	Baghdad
133192	EA.CA.6306	2853-1930	156 B 146 9Um 1	—	ICR2207	Baghdad
133193	EA.CA.6308	2854-1930	156 B 146 9Um C 1	—	ICR2209	Baghdad
133194	EA.CA.6307	2855-1930	156 B 146 9Um 2	—	ICR2208	Baghdad
133195	EA.CA.6309	2856-1930	156 B 146 9Um (i) 1	—	ICR2210	Baghdad
133196	EA.CA.6310	2857-1930	156 B 146 8Mir 1	—	ICR2195	Baghdad
133197	EA.CA.6314	2860-1930	156 B 146 8Mir (i) 2	—	ICR2198	Baghdad
133198	EA.CA.6315	2859-1930	156 B 146 8Mir (i) 2	—	ICR2197	Baghdad
133199	EA.CA.6313	2858-1930	156 B 146 8Mir (i) 1	—	ICR2196	Baghdad
133200	EA.CA.6316	2861-1930	156 B 146 8Mir (i) 3	—	ICR2199	Baghdad
133201	EA.CA.6317	2862-1930	156 B 146 8Mir (i) 4	—	ICR2200	Baghdad
133202	EA.CA.6304	2852-1930	156 B 146 2Suq 1	—	ICR2167	Baghdad
133203	EA.CA.6303	2851-1930	156 B 146 2Suq 1	—	ICR2166	Baghdad
133204	EA.CA.6305	2887-1930	156 B 146 2Suq 1	—	ICR2168	Baghdad
133205	EA.CA.6322	2867-1930	—	—	—	Baghdad
133206	EA.CA.6324	2868-1930	—	—	—	Baghdad
133207	EA.CA.6262	2745-1930	—	—	—	Madain
133208	EA.CA.6261	2748-1930	—	—	Iwan Kisra	Madain
133209	EA.CA.6258	2750-1930	—	—	Iwan Kisra	Madain
133210	EA.CA.6257	2746-1930	—	—	Iwan Kisra	Madain
133211	EA.CA.6330	2747-1930	—	—	Iwan Kisra	Madain
133212	EA.CA.6329	2749-1930	—	—	Iwan Kisra	Madain
133213	EA.CA.6331	2801-1930	—	—	—	Samarra
133214	—	2804-1930	156 Sa 43 2Mu (b) 3	—	ICR2233	Samarra
133215	EA.CA.6353	2809-1930	156 Sa 43 2Mu (b) 2	—	ICR2232	Samarra
133216	EA.CA.6347	2806-1930	156 Sa 43 2Mu (b) 3b 1	—	ICR2236	Samarra
133217	EA.CA.6333	2791-1930	156 Sa 43 3Dar B 1	—	ICR2248	Samarra
133218	EA.CA.6348	2811-1930	156 Sa 43 2Mu (C) 2	—	ICR2239	Samarra
133219	EA.CA.6363	2812-1930	156 Sa 43 2Mu (C) 1	—	ICR2238	Samarra
133220	EA.CA.6346	2808-1930	156 Sa 43 2Mu (b) 3a	—	ICR2234	Samarra
133221	EA.CA.6349	2807-1930	156 Sa 43 2Mu (b) 1a	—	ICR2230	Samarra
133222	EA.CA.6345	2805-1930	156 Sa 43 2Mu (b) 3b	—	ICR2235	Samarra
133223	EA.CA.6350	2803-1930	156 Sa 43 2Mu (b) 2	—	ICR2231	Samarra
133224	EA.CA.6355	2816-1930	156 Sa 43 2Mu (b) 1	—	ICR2229	Samarra
133225	EA.CA.6356	2813-1930	156 Sa 43 2Mu Mi 1	—	ICR2241	Samarra

Appendix 3 – Synopsis of Creswell's Photographs in Different Archives

Berenson ID	Ashmolean ID	V&A ID	Fine Arts Lib. ID	AUC ID	ARCHNET ID	Site
133226	EA.CA.6358	2814-1930	156 Sa 43 2Mu Mi 1	—	ICR2240	Samarra
133227	EA.CA.6354	2810-1930	156 Sa 43 2Mu (b) 4	—	ICR2237	Samarra
133228	EA.CA.6359	2815-1930	156 Sa 43 2Mu Mi 2	—	ICR2242	Samarra
133229	EA.CA.6334	2792-1930	156 Sa 43 3Dar B 1	—	ICR2249	Samarra
133230	EA.CA.6335	2793-1930	156 Sa 43 3Dar B 2	—	ICR2251	Samarra
133231	EA.CA.6339	2796-1930	156 Sa 43 3Dar B 3	—	ICR2255	Samarra
133232	EA.CA.6336	2794-1930	156 Sa 43 3Dar B 3	—	ICR2254	Samarra
133233	EA.CA.6337	—	156 Sa 43 3Dar B 2	—	ICR2252	Samarra
133234	EA.CA.6338	2795-1930	156 Sa 43 3Dar B 2a	—	ICR2253	Samarra
133235	EA.CA.6344	2799-1930	156 Sa 43 3Dar (z)	—	ICR2258	Samarra
133236	EA.CA.6342	2798-1930	156 Sa 43 3Dar Pava 1	—	ICR2257	Samarra
133237	EA.CA.6343	2797-1930	156 Sa 43 3Dar CG 1	—	ICR2256	Samarra
133238	EA.CA.6369	2817-1930	156 Sa 43 2Abu (b) 1b	—	ICR2219	Samarra
133239	EA.CA.6368	2818-1930	155 Sa 43 2Abu (b) 1a	—	ICR2218	Samarra
133240	EA.CA.6382	2821-1930	156 Sa 43 2Abu (b) 2a	—	ICR2220	Samarra
133241	EA.CA.6380	2820-1930	156 Sa 43 2Abu (b) 4a	—	ICR2227	Samarra
133242	EA.CA.6381	2819-1930	156 Sa 43 2Abu (b) 4	—	ICR2226	Samarra
133243	EA.CA.6370	2822-1930	156 Sa 43 2Abu (b) 3	—	ICR2221	Samarra
133244	EA.CA.6371	2823-1930	156 Sa 43 2Abu (b) 3a	—	ICR2222	Samarra
133245	EA.CA.6373	2824-1930	156 Sa 43 2Abu (b) 3a	—	ICR2223	Samarra
133246	EA.CA.6378	2826-1930	156 Sa 43 2Abu Mi 1	—	ICR2228	Samarra
133247	EA.CA.6375	2825-1930	156 Sa 43 2Abu (b) 3b	—	ICR2224	Samarra
133248	EA.CA.6394	2827-1930	156 Sa 43 3Ash 2	—	ICR2245	Samarra
133249	EA.CA.6395	2829-1930	156 Sa 43 3Ash 1	—	ICR2243	Samarra
133250	EA.CA.6398	2828-1930	156 Sa 43 3Ash 3b	—	ICR2247	Samarra
133251	EA.CA.6391	2830-1930	156 Sa 43 3Ash 1	—	ICR2244	Samarra
133252	EA.CA.6388	2831-1930	156 Sa 43 3Ash 3a	—	ICR2246	Samarra
133253	EA.CA.6384	2832-1930	156 Sa 43 9Su 1	—	ICR2261	Samarra
133254	EA.CA.6383	2833-1930	156 Sa 43 9Su 1	—	ICR2260	Samarra
133255	EA.CA.6332	2802-1930	156 Sa 43 9Ma(b) 1	—	ICR2259	Samarra
133256	EA.CA.6406	—	156 Sa 43 12Ha 1	—	ICR2215	Qantarat Harba
133257	EA.CA.6407	—	156 Sa 43 12Ha 1	—	ICR2216	Qantarat Harba
133258	EA.CA.6408	—	156 Sa 43 12Ha 1a	—	ICR2217	Qantarat Harba
133259	EA.CA.6438	2754-1930	156 Uk 4 3Pl (b) 1	—	ICR2262	Al-Ukhaidir
133260	EA.CA.6530	2756-1930	156 Uk 4 3Pl Ano 1	—	ICR2271	Al-Ukhaidir
133261	EA.CA.6529	2757-1930	156 Uk 4 3Pl Ano 2	—	ICR2272	Al-Ukhaidir
133262	EA.CA.6533	2758-1930	156 Uk 4 3Pl Ano 3	—	ICR2273	Al-Ukhaidir
133263	EA.CA.6439	2788-1930	156 Uk 4 3Pl (C) 1	—	ICR2264	Al-Ukhaidir
133264	EA.CA.6414	2755-1930	156 Uk 4 3Pl (b) 2	—	ICR2263	Al-Ukhaidir
133265	EA.CA.6431	2762-1930	156 Uk 4 3Pl BW 1	—	ICR2274	Al-Ukhaidir
133266	EA.CA.6420	2760-1930	156 Uk 4 3Pl (C) 2	—	ICR2265	Al-Ukhaidir
133267	EA.CA.6421	2759-1930	156 Uk 4 3Pl (C) 2	—	ICR2266	Al-Ukhaidir
133268	EA.CA.6433	2763-1930	156 Uk 4 3Pl BW 2	—	ICR2275	Al-Ukhaidir

Berenson ID	Ashmolean ID	V&A ID	Fine Arts Lib. ID	AUC ID	ARCHNET ID	Site
133269	EA.CA.6419	2762-1930	156 Uk 4 3Pl (C) 3	—	ICR2267	Al-Ukhaidir
133270	EA.CA.6436	2764-1930	156 Uk 4 3Pl (d) 2	—	ICR2269	Al-Ukhaidir
133271	—	2765-1930	156 Uk 4 3Pl (d) 1	—	ICR2268	Al-Ukhaidir
133272	EA.CA.6496	2787-1930	156 Uk 4 3Pl Cm 1	—	ICR2284	Al-Ukhaidir
133273	EA.CA.6526	2789-1930	156 Uk 4 3Pl Ani 1	—	ICR2270	Al-Ukhaidir
133274	—	2774-1930	156 Uk 4 3Pl (I) GH 1	—	ICR2297	Al-Ukhaidir
133275	EA.CA.6445	2776-1930	156 Uk 4 3Pl (I) 2	—	ICR2293	Al-Ukhaidir
133276	EA.CA.6443	2775-1930	156 Uk 4 3Pl (I) 1	—	ICR2292	Al-Ukhaidir
133277	EA.CA.6456	2773-1930	156 Uk 4 3Pl (I) GH 1	—	ICR2298	Al-Ukhaidir
133278	EA.CA.296	2771-1930	156 Uk 4 3Pl CH 1a	—	ICR2277	Al-Ukhaidir
133279	EA.CA.6470	2770-1930	156 Uk 4 3Pl CH 4	—	ICR2283	Al-Ukhaidir
133280	EA.CA.6480	2768-1930	156 Uk 4 3Pl CH 2	—	ICR2279	Al-Ukhaidir
133281	EA.CA.6479	2767-1930	156 Uk 4 3Pl CH 2	—	ICR2278	Al-Ukhaidir
133282	EA.CA.6478	2790-1930	156 Uk 4 3Pl CH 3a	—	ICR2282	Al-Ukhaidir
133283	EA.CA.6472	2772-1930	156 Uk 4 3Pl CH 3a	—	ICR2281	Al-Ukhaidir
133284	EA.CA.6468	2769-1930	156 Uk 4 3Pl CH 3	—	ICR2280	Al-Ukhaidir
133285	EA.CA.6504	2779-1930	156 Uk 4 3Pl M 1	—	ICR2285	Al-Ukhaidir
133286	EA.CA.6495	2784-1930	156 Uk 4 3Pl (I) 4	—	ICR2296	Al-Ukhaidir
133287	EA.CA.6507	2779-1930	156 Uk 4 3Pl M 1	—	ICR2286	Al-Ukhaidir
133288	EA.CA.6488	2785-1930	156 Uk 4 3Pl (I) 3	—	ICR2295	Al-Ukhaidir
133289	EA.CA.6484	2783-1930	156 Uk 4 3Pl (I) 3	—	ICR2294	Al-Ukhaidir
133290	EA.CA.293	2763-1930	156 Uk 4 3Pl CH 1	—	ICR2276	Al-Ukhaidir
133291	EA.CA.6512	2786-1930	156 Uk 4 3Pl M 4	—	ICR2291	Al-Ukhaidir
133292	—	2778-1930	156 Uk 4 3Pl M 3	—	ICR2290	Al-Ukhaidir
133293	EA.CA.6513	2782-1930	156 Uk 4 3Pl M 2	—	ICR2288	Al-Ukhaidir
133294	EA.CA.6503	277-1930	156 Uk 4 3Pl M 3	—	ICR2289	Al-Ukhaidir
133295	EA.CA.6511	2782-1930	156 Uk 4 3Pl M 2	—	ICR2287	Al-Ukhaidir
133300	—	2570-1921	—	B15 pl. 25 C/3	—	Amman
133301	—	2569-1921	—	B15 pl. 25 A/3	—	Amman
133302	EA.CA.5409	2574-1921	—	B15 pl. 25 B/3	—	Amman
133303	EA.CA.5418	2578-1921	158 Am 61 13Q 2	B15 pl. 26 A/3	ICR2643	Amman
133304	EA.CA.5436	2577-1921	158 Am 61 13Q 1	B15 pl. 26 B/3	ICR2641	Amman
133305	EA.CA.5435	2579-1921	158 Am 61 13Q (i) 3a	B15 pl. 26 C/3	ICR2662	Amman
133306	EA.CA.1552	2580-1921	158 Am 61 13Q (i) 3a	B15 pl. 27 A/4	ICR2661	Amman
133307	EA.CA.5434	2583-1921	—	B15 pl. 27 B/4	—	Amman
133308	EA.CA.5433	2581-1921	158 Am 61 13Q (i) 1a	B15 pl. 27 C/4	ICR2648	Amman
133309	EA.CA.5431	2591-1921	158 Am 61 13Q (i) 1a	B15 pl. 28 A/4	ICR2647	Amman
133310	EA.CA.5430	2592-1921	158 Am 61 13Q (i) 1	B15 pl. 28 B/4	ICR2646	Amman
133311	EA.CA.5429	2590-1921	158 Am 61 13Q (i) 3a	B15 pl. 28 C/4	ICR2663	Amman
133312	EA.CA.5428	2584-1921	158 Am 61 13Q (i) 1d	B15 pl. 30 B/4	ICR2655	Amman
133313	EA.CA.5426	2593-1921	158 Am 61 13Q (i) 1b	B15 pl. 28 D/4	ICR2649	Amman
133314	EA.CA.5425	2594-1921	158 Am 61 13Q (i) 1b	B15 pl. 29 A/3	ICR2650	Amman
133315	EA.CA.5424	2585-1921	158 Am 61 13Q 1	B15 pl. 29 B/3	ICR2642	Amman

Appendix 3 – Synopsis of Creswell's Photographs in Different Archives

Berenson ID	Ashmolean ID	V&A ID	Fine Arts Lib. ID	AUC ID	ARCHNET ID	Site
133316	EA.CA.5423	2595-1921	158 Am 61 13Q (i) 1c	B15 pl. 29 C/3	ICR2651	Amman
133317	EA.CA.5422	2596-1921	158 Am 61 13Q (i) 1c	B15 pl. 30 A/4	ICR2652	Amman
133318	EA.CA.5427	2597-1921	158 Am 61 13Q (i) 2b	B15 pl. 30 C/4	ICR2658	Amman
133319	EA.CA.5421	2599-1921	158 Am 61 13Q (i) 2a	B15 pl. 30 D/4	ICR2656	Amman
133320	EA.CA.5432	2686-1921	158 Am 61 13Q (i) 1	B15 pl. 27 D/4	ICR2645	Amman
133321	EA.CA.5420	2582-1921	158 Am 61 13Q (i) 2a	B15 pl. 31 A/4	ICR2657	Amman
133322	EA.CA.5419	2587-1921	158 Am 61 13Q (i) 2b	B15 pl. 31 B/4	ICR2659	Amman
133323	EA.CA.5417	2588-1921	158 Am 61 13Q (i) 2b	B15 pl. 31 C/4	ICR2660	Amman
133324	EA.CA.5416	2598-1921	158 Am 61 13Q (i) 1d	B15 pl. 32 A/4	ICR2654	Amman
133325	EA.CA.5415	2600-1921	158 Am 61 13Q 2	B15 pl. 32 B/4	ICR2644	Amman
133326	EA.CA.1514	2531-1926	158 Am 61 1(b) 1	B15 pl. 24 B/3	ICR2640	Amman
133347	EA.CA.6553	3082-1921	159 B 533 1(b) 1	—	ICR1506	Birecik
133348	EA.CA.6554	3095-1921	159 B 533 1(b) 3	—	ICR1512	Birecik
133349	EA.CA.6555	3081-1921	159 B 533 1(b) 1	—	ICR1507	Birecik
133350	EA.CA.6556	3084-1921	159 B 533 1(b) 3	—	ICR1511	Birecik
133351	EA.CA.6557	3083-1921	159 B 533 1(b) 3	—	ICR1510	Birecik
133352	EA.CA.6558	3085-1921	159 B 533 1(b) 2	—	ICR1508	Birecik
133353	EA.CA.6559	3086-1921	159 B 533 1(b) 2	—	ICR1509	Birecik
133354	EA.CA.6560	3087-1921	159 B 533 1(b)	—	ICR1505	Birecik
133355	EA.CA.6561	3089-1921	159 B 533 1 (C) 1	—	ICR1513	Birecik
133356	EA.CA.6562	3090-1921	159 B 533 1 (C) 1	—	ICR1514	Birecik
133357	EA.CA.6563	3091-1921	159 B 533 1 (C) 3	—	ICR1518	Birecik
133358	EA.CA.6564	—	159 B 533 1 (C) 2	—	ICR1516	Birecik
133359	EA.CA.6566	3094-1921	159 B 533 1 (C) 2	—	ICR1517	Birecik
133360	EA.CA.6568	3088-1921	—	—	—	Birecik
133361	EA.CA.6569	3101-1921	159 B 533 1 (d) 7	—	ICR1534	Birecik
133362	EA.CA.6570	3100-1921	159 B 533 1 (d) 7	—	ICR1535	Birecik
133363	EA.CA.6571	3103-1921	159 B 533 1 (d) 6	—	ICR1532	Birecik
133364	EA.CA.6572	3099-1921	159 B 533 1 (d) 1	—	ICR1523	Birecik
133365	EA.CA.6565	3093-1921	159 B 533 1 (C) 2	—	ICR1515	Birecik
133366	EA.CA.6573	3097-1921	159 B 533 1 (d) 4	—	ICR1529	Birecik
133367	EA.CA.6574	3098-1921	159 B 533 1 (d) 3	—	ICR1528	Birecik
133368	EA.CA.6575	3104-1921	159 B 533 1 (d) 7	—	ICR1536	Birecik
133369	EA.CA.6576	3102-1921	159 B 533 1 (d) 6	—	ICR1533	Birecik
133370	EA.CA.6577	3096-1921	159 B 533 1 (d) 4	—	ICR1530	Birecik
133371	EA.CA.6578	3106-1921	159 B 533 1 (d) 1	—	ICR1521	Birecik
133372	EA.CA.6579	3107-1921	159 B 533 1 (d) 1	—	ICR1522	Birecik
133373	EA.CA.6580	3111-1921	159 B 533 1 (d) 3	—	ICR1527	Birecik
133374	EA.CA.6581	3110-1921	159 B 533 1 (d) 2	—	ICR1525	Birecik
133375	EA.CA.6582	3109-1921	159 B 533 1 (d) 2	—	ICR1526	Birecik
133376	EA.CA.6583	3108-1921	159 B 533 1 (d) 5	—	ICR1531	Birecik
133377	EA.CA.6584	3105-1921	159 B 533 1 (d) 2	—	ICR1524	Birecik
133378	EA.CA.6586	3112-1921	159 B 533 1 (d)	—	ICR1519	Birecik

Berenson ID	Ashmolean ID	V&A ID	Fine Arts Lib. ID	AUC ID	ARCHNET ID	Site
133379	EA.CA.6587	3113-1921	159 B 533 1 (d)	—	ICR1520	Birecik
133380	EA.CA.6588	3114-1921	159 B 533 2M 2	—	ICR1538	Birecik
133381	EA.CA.6589	3115-1921	159 B 533 2M (i) 2	—	ICR1541	Birecik
133382	EA.CA.6591	3117-1921	159 B 533 2M (i) 1	—	ICR1539	Birecik
133383	EA.CA.6590	3116-1921	159 B 533 2M (i) 1	—	ICR1540	Birecik
133384	EA.CA.6592	3118-1921	159 B 533 2G 2	—	ICR1537	Birecik
133443	EA.CA.613	—	—	—	—	Damascus
133444	EA.CA.5506	—	—	—	—	Damascus
133445	EA.CA.5511	2548-1926	—	—	—	Damascus
133446	EA.CA.5459	2508-1921	158 D 18 2U 1	—	ICR2530	Damascus
133447	EA.CA.5464	2528-1921	158 D 18 2U M 1	—	ICR2549	Damascus
133448	EA.CA.5462	2527-1921	158 D 18 2U M 1	—	ICR2548	Damascus
133449	EA.CA.714	2526-1921	158 D 18 2U 3	—	ICR2535	Damascus
133450	EA.CA.5467	2508-1921	158 D 18 2U 3	—	ICR2536	Damascus
133451	—	2525-1921	—	—	—	Damascus
133452	EA.CA.5491	2524-1921	158 D 18 2U C 2	—	ICR2538	Damascus
133453	EA.CA.5476	2538-1921	158 D 18 2U C 3b	—	ICR2540	Damascus
133454	EA.CA.5480	2532-1921	158 D 18 2U C 4b	—	ICR2542	Damascus
133455	EA.CA.5492	2531-1921	158 D 18 2U C 4b	—	ICR2541	Damascus
133456	EA.CA.5475	2536-1921	158 D 18 2U 4a	—	ICR2537	Damascus
133457	EA.CA.5482	2529-1921	158 D 18 2U C 2	—	ICR2539	Damascus
133458	EA.CA.5493	2530-1921	158 D 18 2U (i) 2	—	ICR2551	Damascus
133459	EA.CA.5494	2534-1921	158 D 18 2U (i) 4	—	ICR2552	Damascus
133460	—	2535-1921	158 D 18 2U (i) 5	—	ICR2553	Damascus
133461	EA.CA.5569	2515-1921	158 D 18 5B 1	—	ICR2572	Damascus
133462	EA.CA.5568	2516-1921	158 D 18 5B 1	—	ICR2573	Damascus
133463	EA.CA.5570	2520-19210	158 D 18 5B (i) 3	—	ICR2578	Damascus
133464	EA.CA.5571	2517-1921	158 D 18 5B (i) 1	—	ICR2575	Damascus
133465	EA.CA.5597	2543-1921	158 D 18 5S 2	—	ICR2585	Damascus
133466	EA.CA.5599	2508-1921	158 D 18 5S 4	—	ICR2588	Damascus
133467	EA.CA.5600	2545-1921	158 D 18 5S 1a	—	ICR2583	Damascus
133468	EA.CA.5601	2546-1921	158 D 18 5S 1a	—	ICR2584	Damascus
133469	EA.CA.5602	2544-1921	158 D 18 5S (i) 1	—	ICR2589	Damascus
133470	EA.CA.5603	—	158 D 18 5S (i) 3	—	ICR2591	Damascus
133471	EA.CA.5604	2547-1921	158 D 18 5S (i) 2	—	ICR2590	Damascus
133472	EA.CA.5605	2548-1921	158 D 18 5S (i) 4	—	ICR2592	Damascus
133473	EA.CA.5614	2552-1921	158 D 18 8A 1	—	ICR2593	Damascus
133474	EA.CA.5615	2553-1921	158 D 18 8A (i) 1	—	ICR2595	Damascus
133475	EA.CA.5620	2512-1921	158 D 18 3A (i) 1	—	ICR2559	Damascus
133476	EA.CA.5619	2509-1921	158 D 18 3A C2	—	ICR2558	Damascus
133477	EA.CA.5622	2510-1921	158 D 18 3A (i) 2	—	ICR2560	Damascus
133478	EA.CA.5609	2568-1921	158 D 18 2S (i) 2	—	ICR2529	Damascus
133479	EA.CA.5608	2567-1921	158 D 18 2S (i) 1	—	ICR2528	Damascus

APPENDIX 3 – SYNOPSIS OF CRESWELL'S PHOTOGRAPHS IN DIFFERENT ARCHIVES

Berenson ID	Ashmolean ID	V&A ID	Fine Arts Lib. ID	AUC ID	ARCHNET ID	Site
133480	EA.CA.5613	2551-1921	158 D 18 2D 1	—	ICR2696	Damascus
133481	EA.CA.5572	2523-1921	158 D 18 5B (i) 5	—	ICR2580	Damascus
133482	EA.CA.5573	2522-1921	158 D 18 5B (i) 4	—	ICR2579	Damascus
133483	EA.CA.5574	2519-1921	158 D 18 5B (i) 2	—	ICR2577	Damascus
133484	EA.CA.5575	2518-1921	158 D 18 5B (i) 2	—	ICR2576	Damascus
133485	EA.CA.5576	2521-1921	158 D 18 5B 3	—	ICR2574	Damascus
133486	EA.CA.5520	2556-1921	158 D 18 5A 1	—	ICR2562	Damascus
133487	EA.CA.718	2533-1921	158 D 18 2U 1a	—	ICR2531	Damascus
133488	—	—	—	—	—	Damascus
133489	EA.CA.5612	2550-1921	158 D 18 2D 1	—	ICR2695	Damascus
133490	EA.CA.5522	2564-1921	158 D 18 5A 1	—	ICR2563	Damascus
133491	EA.CA.5525	2560-1921	158 D 18 5A 3a	—	ICR2566	Damascus
133492	EA.CA.5526	2558-1921	158 D 18 5A 3a R	—	ICR2564	Damascus
133493	EA.CA.5527	2563-1921	158 D 18 5A (i) 1	—	ICR2570	Damascus
133494	EA.CA.5528	2562-1921	158 D 18 5A (i) 1	—	ICR2569	Damascus
133495	EA.CA.5529	2559-1921	158 D 18 5A 3c R	—	ICR2568	Damascus
133496	—	—	—	—	—	Damascus
133497	EA.CA.5523	2557-1921	158 D 18 5A (i) 2	—	ICR2571	Damascus
133498	EA.CA.5524	2561-1921	158 D 18 5A 3b	—	ICR2567	Damascus
133499	—	2537-1921	—	—	—	Damascus
133500	EA.CA.5616	2554-1921	158 D 18 8A (i) 1	—	ICR2594	Damascus
133501	EA.CA.5617	2513-1921	158 D 18 8G 1	—	ICR2596	Damascus
133502	EA.CA.5618	2508-1921	158 D 18 8G (i) 1	—	ICR2597	Damascus
133503	EA.CA.5607	2566-1921	158 D 18 2S 1	—	ICR2527	Damascus
133504	EA.CA.5621	2510-1921	158 D 18 3A (i) 2	—	ICR2561	Damascus
133505	EA.CA.5598	2541-1921	158 D 18 5S 4	—	ICR2587	Damascus
133506	EA.CA.5606	2565-1921	158 D 18 2S 1	—	ICR2526	Damascus
133507	EA.CA.108	—	—	—	—	Damascus
133508	—	2623-1926	—	—	—	Damascus
133509	EA.CA.5567	2558-1926	—	—	—	Damascus
133510	EA.CA.5566	2610-1926	—	—	—	Damascus
133511	EA.CA.5553	2612-1926	—	—	—	Damascus
133512	EA.CA.5555	2607-1926	—	—	—	Damascus
133513	EA.CA.5556	2609-1926	—	—	—	Damascus
133514	EA.CA.5557	2608-1926	—	—	—	Damascus
133515	EA.CA.5550	2545-1926	—	—	—	Damascus
133516	EA.CA.5547	2544-1926	—	—	—	Damascus
133517	EA.CA.5548	2532-1926	—	—	—	Damascus
133518	EA.CA.5545	2542-1926	—	—	—	Damascus
133519	EA.CA.5546	2539-1926	—	—	—	Damascus
133520	—	2541-1926	—	—	—	Damascus
133521	—	2540-1926	—	—	—	Damascus
133522	EA.CA.5540	2552-1926	—	—	—	Damascus

Berenson ID	Ashmolean ID	V&A ID	Fine Arts Lib. ID	AUC ID	ARCHNET ID	Site
133523	EA.CA.5541	2553-1926	—	—	—	Damascus
133524	EA.CA.5537	2551-1926	—	—	—	Damascus
133525	EA.CA.5538	2550-1926	—	—	—	Damascus
133526	EA.CA.5539	2549-1926	—	—	—	Damascus
133527	EA.CA.5536	2559-1926	—	—	—	Damascus
133528	EA.CA.5534	2535-1926	—	—	—	Damascus
133529	EA.CA.5535	2538-1926	—	—	—	Damascus
133530	EA.CA.5533	2536-1926	—	—	—	Damascus
133531	EA.CA.5563	2537-1926	—	—	—	Damascus
133532	EA.CA.5595	2543-1926	—	—	—	Damascus
133533	EA.CA.5478	2606-1926	—	—	—	Damascus
133534	EA.CA.5565	2555-1926	—	—	—	Damascus
133535	EA.CA.5562	—	—	—	—	Damascus
133536	EA.CA.5564	—	—	—	—	Damascus
133537	—	2620-1926	—	—	—	Damascus
133538	—	2622-1926	—	—	—	Damascus
133539	EA.CA.5589	2621-1926	—	—	—	Damascus
133540	EA.CA.5590	—	—	—	—	Damascus
133541	EA.CA.5580	2619-1926	—	—	—	Damascus
133542	EA.CA.5552	—	—	—	—	Damascus
133543	EA.CA.5551	—	—	—	—	Damascus
133544	EA.CA.5583	2629-1926	—	—	—	Damascus
133545	EA.CA.5585	2628-1926	—	—	—	Damascus
133546	EA.CA.5584	2627-1926	—	—	—	Damascus
133547	EA.CA.5586	2631-1926	—	—	—	Damascus
133548	EA.CA.5587	2630-1926	—	—	—	Damascus
133549	EA.CA.5532	2616-1926	—	—	—	Damascus
133550	EA.CA.5531	2533-1926	—	—	—	Damascus
133551	EA.CA.5530	2534-1926	—	—	—	Damascus
133552	EA.CA.5519	2558-1926	—	—	—	Damascus
133553	EA.CA.5517	2557-1926	—	—	—	Damascus
133554	EA.CA.5516	2624-1926	—	—	—	Damascus
133555	EA.CA.5513	2546-1926	—	—	—	Damascus
133556	EA.CA.5510	2547-1926	—	—	—	Damascus
133557	EA.CA.5508	2617-1926	—	—	—	Damascus
133558	EA.CA.5509	2618-1926	—	—	—	Damascus
133559	EA.CA.5507	2626-1926	—	—	—	Damascus
133560	EA.CA.2371	2625-1926	—	—	—	Damascus
133561	EA.CA.5504	2615-1926	—	—	—	Damascus
133562	EA.CA.5502	2568-1926	158 D 18 5N (i) 1	—	ICR2581	Damascus
133563	EA.CA.5498	2565-1926	158 D 18 8N (i) 1	—	ICR2600	Damascus
133564	—	2562-1926	158 D 18 8N (i) 3	—	ICR2602	Damascus
133565	—	2567-1926	—	—	—	Damascus

Appendix 3 – Synopsis of Creswell's Photographs in Different Archives

Berenson ID	Ashmolean ID	V&A ID	Fine Arts Lib. ID	AUC ID	ARCHNET ID	Site
133566	EA.CA.5500	—	—	—	—	Damascus
133567	—	2566-1926	158 D 18 8N (i) 2	—	ICR2601	Damascus
133568	EA.CA.5501	2569-1926	—	—	—	Damascus
133569	EA.CA.5503	2563-1926	—	—	—	Damascus
133570	EA.CA.5499	2561-1926	—	—	—	Damascus
133571	EA.CA.7997	2564-1926	158 D 18 8N (i) 4	—	ICR2603	Damascus
133572	EA.CA.5497	2560-1926	158 D 18 8N 1	—	ICR2598	Damascus
133573	EA.CA.396	2593-1926	—	—	—	Damascus
133574	EA.CA.107	2601-1926	—	—	—	Damascus
133575	—	2592-1926	—	—	—	Damascus
133576	EA.CA.102	2591-1926	—	—	—	Damascus
133577	EA.CA.5481	2594-1926	—	—	—	Damascus
133578	EA.CA.110	—	—	—	—	Damascus
133579	—	—	—	—	—	Damascus
133580	EA.CA.1479	—	—	—	—	Damascus
133581	EA.CA.614	—	—	—	—	Damascus
133582	EA.CA.617	—	—	—	—	Damascus
133583	EA.CA.88	—	—	—	—	Damascus
133584	EA.CA.624	—	—	—	—	Damascus
133585	EA.CA.615	—	—	—	—	Damascus
133586	EA.CA.717	2595-1926	—	—	—	Damascus
133587	EA.CA.719	2599-1926	—	—	—	Damascus
133588	EA.CA.5465	2596-1926	—	—	—	Damascus
133589	EA.CA.5479	2600-1926	—	—	—	Damascus
133590	EA.CA.5495	2605-1926	—	—	—	Damascus
133591	—	2604-1926	—	—	—	Damascus
133592	EA.CA.5486	2598-1926	—	—	—	Damascus
133593	EA.CA.5488	2603-1926	—	—	—	Damascus
133594	EA.CA.5487	2597-1926	—	—	—	Damascus
133595	EA.CA.5485	2602-1926	158 D 18 2U C 5b	—	ICR2547	Damascus
133596	EA.CA.604	—	—	—	—	Damascus
133597	EA.CA.1478	—	—	—	—	Damascus
133598	EA.CA.606	—	—	—	—	Damascus
133599	EA.CA.605	—	—	—	—	Damascus
133600	EA.CA.607	—	—	—	—	Damascus
133601	EA.CA.608	—	—	—	—	Damascus
133602	EA.CA.611	—	158 D 18 2U C Mo W(C) 1	—	ICR2550	Damascus
133603	EA.CA.625	—	—	—	—	Damascus
133604	EA.CA.623	—	—	—	—	Damascus
133605	EA.CA.626	—	—	—	—	Damascus
133606	EA.CA.627	—	—	—	—	Damascus
133613	EA.CA.6091	2643-1926	—	—	—	Hama

Berenson ID	Ashmolean ID	V&A ID	Fine Arts Lib. ID	AUC ID	ARCHNET ID	Site
133614	EA.CA.6092	2642-1926	—	—	—	Hama
133615	EA.CA.6093	2641-1926	—	—	—	Hama
133616	EA.CA.6094	2652-1926	—	—	—	Hama
133617	EA.CA.5879	2651-1926	—	—	—	Hama
133618	EA.CA.5880	2648-1926	—	—	—	Hama
133619	EA.CA.5881	2644-1926	—	—	—	Hama
133620	EA.CA.6072	2632-1926	—	—	—	Hama
133621	EA.CA.5882	2646-1926	—	—	—	Hama
133622	EA.CA.6077	2634-1926	—	—	—	Hama
133623	EA.CA.5887	2649-1926	—	—	—	Hama
133624	EA.CA.5885	2647-1926	—	—	—	Hama
133625	EA.CA.5886	2650-1926	—	—	—	Hama
133626	—	2645-1926	—	—	—	Hama
133627	—	2636-1926	—	—	—	Hama
133628	—	2633-1926	—	—	—	Hama
133629	EA.CA.6084	2637-1926	158 H 17 9A 1	—	ICR1767	Hama
133630	—	2638-1926	—	—	—	Hama
133631	—	2639-1926	—	—	—	Hama
133632	—	2640-1926	—	—	—	Hama
133633	EA.CA.6618	3119-1921	159 H 235 1 (C) 1	—	ICR1555	Harran
133634	EA.CA.6619	3120-1921	159 H 235 1 (C) 1	—	ICR1556	Harran
133635	EA.CA.6621	3122-1921	159 H 235 2M 2a 1	—	ICR1558	Harran
133636	EA.CA.674	3124-1921	159 H 235 2M 2a 2	—	ICR1559	Harran
133637	EA.CA.6620	3127-1921	159 H 235 2M 2a 3	—	ICR1561	Harran
133638	—	3126-1921	159 H 235 2M 2a 3	—	ICR1562	Harran
133639	EA.CA.676	3125-1921	159 H 235 2M 2a 2	—	ICR1560	Harran
133640	EA.CA.673	3123-1921	159 H 235 2M 2b 1	—	ICR1563	Harran
133641	EA.CA.6622	3121-1921	159 H 235 2M 1	—	ICR1557	Harran
133642	EA.CA.6623	3138-1921	159 H 235 2M 2b 2	—	ICR1564	Harran
133643	EA.CA.6624	3128-1921	159 H 235 2M 2b 2	—	ICR1565	Harran
133644	EA.CA.672	3129-1921	159 H 235 2M 2b 3	—	ICR1566	Harran
133645	EA.CA.6630	3130-1921	159 H 235 2M 4b	—	ICR1569	Harran
133646	EA.CA.6626	3132-1921	159 H 235 2M 4b 1	—	ICR1571	Harran
133647	EA.CA.6625	3131-1921	159 H 235 2M 4a	—	ICR1568	Harran
133648	EA.CA.6627	3133-1921	159 H 235 2M 4b 1	—	ICR1572	Harran
133649	EA.CA.6628	3137-1921	159 H 235 2M 3	—	ICR1567	Harran
133650	EA.CA.6629	3136-1921	159 H 235 2M 4b 1	—	ICR1570	Harran
133651	EA.CA.675	3134-1921	159 H 235 2M 5a	—	ICR1573	Harran
133652	EA.CA.678	3139-1921	159 H 235 2M Mi 1	—	ICR1580	Harran
133653	EA.CA.6632	3135-1921	159 H 235 2M 5b	—	ICR1574	Harran
133654	EA.CA.6633	3140-1921	159 H 235 2M 6	—	ICR1575	Harran
133655	EA.CA.6634	3141-1921	159 H 235 2M 7b	—	ICR1576	Harran
133656	EA.CA.6631	3142-1921	159 H 235 2M 7b	—	ICR1577	Harran

Appendix 3 – Synopsis of Creswell's Photographs in Different Archives

Berenson ID	Ashmolean ID	V&A ID	Fine Arts Lib. ID	AUC ID	ARCHNET ID	Site
133657	EA.CA.6636	3144-1921	159 H 235 2M 7b	—	ICR1578	Harran
133658	EA.CA.6635	3143-1921	159 H 235 2M 7b	—	ICR1579	Harran
133659	EA.CA.6637	3145-1921	159 H 235 1 (a) 2	—	ICR1543	Harran
133660	EA.CA.6638	3146-1921	159 H 235 1 (a) 3	—	ICR1544	Harran
133661	EA.CA.6639	3147-1921	159 H 235 1 (a) 4	—	ICR1545	Harran
133662	EA.CA.6640	3149-1921	159 H 235 1 (a) 4	—	ICR1546	Harran
133663	EA.CA.6641	3150-1921	—	—	—	Harran
133664	EA.CA.6642	3148-1921	159 H 235 1 (a) 1	—	ICR1542	Harran
133665	EA.CA.6643	3155-1921	159 H 235 1 (a) 5c	—	ICR1551	Harran
133666	EA.CA.6644	3156-1921	159 H 235 1 (a) 5d	—	ICR1552	Harran
133667	EA.CA.6645	3154-1921	159 H 235 1 (a) 5a	—	ICR1547	Harran
133668	EA.CA.6646	3137-1921	159 H 235 1 (a) 5a	—	ICR1548	Harran
133669	EA.CA.6647	3151-1921	159 H 235 1 (a) 5b	—	ICR1550	Harran
133670	EA.CA.6649	3152-1921	159 H 235 1 (a) 5a	—	ICR1549	Harran
133671	EA.CA.6648	3161-1921	159 H 235 1 (b) 1	—	ICR1553	Harran
133672	EA.CA.6650	3162-1921	159 H 235 1 (b) 2a	—	ICR1554	Harran
133673	EA.CA.6651	3159-1921	159 H 235 9Y 1	—	ICR1581	Harran
133674	EA.CA.6652	3160-1921	159 H 235 9Y 1a	—	ICR1582	Harran
133675	EA.CA.6653	3157-1921	159 H 235 9Y 2	—	ICR1583	Harran
133676	EA.CA.6654	3158-1921	159 H 235 9Y 3	—	ICR1584	Harran
133725	EA.CA.5901	2659-1926	—	—	—	Homs
133726	—	2670-1926	—	—	—	Homs
133727	—	2667-1926	—	—	—	Homs
133728	—	2659-1926	—	—	—	Homs
133729	—	2669-1926	—	—	—	Homs
133730	—	2666-1926	—	—	—	Homs
133731	EA.CA.5910	2665-1926	—	—	—	Homs
133732	EA.CA.5909	2664-1926	—	—	—	Homs
133733	EA.CA.5895	2653-1926	—	—	—	Homs
133734	EA.CA.5896	2658-1926	—	—	—	Homs
133735	EA.CA.5897	2655-1926	—	—	—	Homs
133736	EA.CA.5898	2656-1926	—	—	—	Homs
133737	EA.CA.5899	2657-1926	—	—	—	Homs
133738	EA.CA.5900	2654-1926	—	—	—	Homs
133739	EA.CA.5894	2661-1926	—	—	—	Homs
133740	EA.CA.5906	2662-1926	—	—	—	Homs
133741	EA.CA.5904	2660-1926	—	—	—	Homs
133742	EA.CA.5903	2663-1926	—	—	—	Homs
133743	EA.CA.6076	2635-1926	—	—	—	Homs
133744	EA.CA.5908	2671-1926	—	—	—	Homs
133745	—	2613-1921	—	—	—	Iraq al-Amir
133746	—	2612-1921	—	—	—	Iraq al-Amir
133747	—	2614-1921	—	—	—	Iraq al-Amir

Berenson ID	Ashmolean ID	V&A ID	Fine Arts Lib. ID	AUC ID	ARCHNET ID	Site
133878	—	2713-1926	—	—	—	Masyaf
133879	—	2711-1926	—	—	—	Masyaf
133880	—	2712-1926	—	—	—	Masyaf
133881	—	2710-1926	—	—	—	Masyaf
133882	—	2708-1926	—	—	—	Masyaf
133883	—	2709-1926	—	—	—	Masyaf
133907	EA.CA.6009	2622-1921	158 Q 1145 2S (z) 1	—	ICR2148	Qalat Siman
133908	EA.CA.6010	2621-1921	158 Q 1145 2SBS 6a	—	ICR2145	Qalat Siman
133909	EA.CA.6011	2619-1921	158 Q 1145 2SO (i) 2a 1	—	ICR2147	Qalat Siman
133916	EA.CA.6023	2618-1921	158 K 527 2C (i) 7a	—	ICR2097	Qalb Lawzah
133920	EA.CA.6012	2620-1921	158 Q 1145 2SD (i) 1a	—	ICR2146	Qalat Siman
133921	EA.CA.5443	2714-1926	—	—	—	Qusayr Amra
133922	EA.CA.5444	—	—	—	—	Qusayr Amra
133923	—	—	—	—	—	Qusayr Amra
133924	—	2715-1926	—	—	—	Qusayr Amra
133925	—	—	—	—	—	Qusayr Amra
133926	—	—	—	—	—	Qusayr Amra
133927	—	—	—	—	—	Qusayr Amra
133928	—	—	—	—	—	Qusayr Amra
133948	EA.CA.6030	—	158 R 941 9(a) 2a	B15 pl. 24 A/3	ICR1496	Ruweiha
133980	EA.CA.5683	2331-1921	158 AL 25 13Ct 2	—	ICR2305	Aleppo
133981	EA.CA.5681	2329-1921	158 AL 25 13Ct 3	—	ICR2307	Aleppo
133982	EA.CA.5682	2328-1921	158 AL 25 13Ct 2	—	ICR2304	Aleppo
133983	EA.CA.5680	2330-1921	158 AL 25 13Ct 3	—	ICR2306	Aleppo
133984	EA.CA.5696	2332-1921	—	—		Aleppo
133985	EA.CA.5688	2339-1921	158 AL 25 13Ct Bo 2	—	ICR2320	Aleppo
133986	EA.CA.5684	2334-1921	158 AL 25 13Ct GL 1	—	ICR2323	Aleppo
133987	EA.CA.5693	2341-1921	158 AL 25 13Ct BM 1	—	ICR2310	Aleppo
133988	EA.CA.5690	2340-1921	158 AL 25 13Ct Bo 1	—	ICR2318	Aleppo
133989	EA.CA.5689	2338-1921	158 AL 25 13Ct Bo 1	—	ICR2317	Aleppo
133990	EA.CA.5629	2327-1921	158 AL 25 13W 4	—	ICR2341	Aleppo
133991	EA.CA.5692	2333-1921	158 AL 25 13Ct Br 1	—	ICR2321	Aleppo
133992	EA.CA.5662	2472-1921	158 AL 25 2Sh 1	—	ICR2426	Aleppo
133993	EA.CA.5663	2473-1921	158 AL 25 2Sh 1	—	ICR2425	Aleppo
133994	EA.CA.5666	2476-1921	158 AL 25 2Sh 2	—	ICR2428	Aleppo
133995	EA.CA.5664	2475-1921	158 AL 25 2Sh 2	—	ICR2427	Aleppo
133996	EA.CA.5668	2455-1921	158 AL 25 2Qa (i) 1	—	ICR2410	Aleppo
133997	EA.CA.5667	—	158 AL 25 2Sh (i)	—	ICR2429	Aleppo
133998	—	2454-1921	158 AL 25 2Qa (i) 1	—	ICR2411	Aleppo
133999	—	2497-1921	158 AL 25 5K 1	—	ICR2449	Aleppo
134000	EA.CA.5671	2500-1921	158 AL 25 5K (i) 1	—	ICR2452	Aleppo
134001	EA.CA.5669	2498-1921	158 AL 25 5K 1	—	ICR2450	Aleppo
134002	EA.CA.5679	2440-1921	158 AL 25 5M 2	—	ICR2464	Aleppo

Appendix 3 – Synopsis of Creswell's Photographs in Different Archives

Berenson ID	Ashmolean ID	V&A ID	Fine Arts Lib. ID	AUC ID	ARCHNET ID	Site
134003	EA.CA.5670	2499-1921	158 AL 25 5K (i) 1	—	ICR2451	Aleppo
134004	—	2439-1921	158 AL 25 5M 1	—	ICR2462	Aleppo
134005	EA.CA.5677	2441-1921	158 AL 25 5M 1	—	ICR2463	Aleppo
134006	EA.CA.5676	2438-1921	158 AL 25 5M (i) 1	—	ICR2466	Aleppo
134007	EA.CA.7984	2437-1921	158 AL 25 5M (i) 1	—	ICR2467	Aleppo
134008	EA.CA.5678	2436-1921	158 AL 25 5M 2	—	ICR2465	Aleppo
134009	EA.CA.5699	2348-1921	158 AL 25 13Ct BM Th(I) 1	—	ICR2316	Aleppo
134010	EA.CA.5697	2344-1921	158 AL 25 13Ct BM Th B 1	—	ICR2314	Aleppo
134011	EA.CA.5698	2345-1921	158 AL 25 13Ct BM Th(I) 1	—	ICR2315	Aleppo
134012	EA.CA.5687	2342-1921	158 AL 25 13Ct Bars 1	—	ICR2309	Aleppo
134013	EA.CA.5694	2346-1921	158 AL 25 13Ct BM (I) 1	—	ICR2311	Aleppo
134014	EA.CA.7985	2337-1921	158 AL 25 13Ct BM (I) L1	—	ICR2313	Aleppo
134015	EA.CA.5695	2336-1921	158 AL 25 13Ct BM (I) L1	—	ICR2312	Aleppo
134016	EA.CA.5685	2343-1921	158 AL 25 13Ct Barn 1	—	ICR2308	Aleppo
134017	EA.CA.5686	2335-1921	158 AL 25 13Ct GL 1	—	ICR2322	Aleppo
134018	EA.CA.5691	2350-1921	158 AL 25 13Ct Bo 2	—	ICR2319	Aleppo
134019	EA.CA.5814	2347-1921	158 AL 25 13Ct PL B1	—	ICR2325	Aleppo
134020	EA.CA.5713	—	158 AL 25 9Hus (i) 3	—	ICR2617	Aleppo
134021	EA.CA.5720	2349-1921	158 AL 25 13Ct MG Mi 1	—	ICR2324	Aleppo
134022	EA.CA.5711	2403-1921	158 AL 25 9Hus (i) 2	—	ICR2616	Aleppo
134023	EA.CA.5710	2405-1921	158 AL 25 9Hus (i) 2	—	ICR2615	Aleppo
134024	EA.CA.5701	2394-1921	158 AL 25 9Hus 1	—	ICR2606	Aleppo
134025	EA.CA.5700	2392-1921	158 AL 25 9Hus 1	—	ICR2605	Aleppo
134026	—	2395-1921	158 AL 25 9Hus 2	—	ICR2607	Aleppo
134027	EA.CA.5703	2393-1921	158 AL 25 9Hus 2	—	ICR2608	Aleppo
134028	EA.CA.5704	2396-1921	158 AL 25 9Hus C 1	—	ICR2610	Aleppo
134029	EA.CA.5705	2397-1921	158 AL 25 9Hus C 1	—	ICR2609	Aleppo
134030	—	2398-1921	158 AL 25 9Hus C 1	—	ICR2611	Aleppo
134031	EA.CA.5706	2401-1921	158 AL 25 9Hus (i) 1	—	ICR2612	Aleppo
134032	EA.CA.5707	2400-1921	158 AL 25 9Hus (i) 1	—	ICR2614	Aleppo
134033	—	2402-1921	158 AL 25 9Hus (i) 1	—	ICR2613	Aleppo
134034	EA.CA.5714	2444-1921	158 AL 25 2C 1	—	ICR2361	Aleppo
134035	EA.CA.5708	2404-1921	158 AL 25 9Hus (i) 3	—	ICR2618	Aleppo
134036	EA.CA.5716	2445-1921	158 AL 25 2C 2	—	ICR2364	Aleppo
134037	EA.CA.5715	2446-1921	158 AL 25 2C 1	—	ICR2362	Aleppo
134038	EA.CA.5718	2443-1921	158 AL 25 2C (i) 1	—	ICR2365	Aleppo
134039	EA.CA.5814	2442-1921	158 AL 25 13Ct PL B1	—	ICR2325	Aleppo
134040	—	2295-1921	158 AL 25 5Z 2a	—	ICR2490	Aleppo

Berenson ID	Ashmolean ID	V&A ID	Fine Arts Lib. ID	AUC ID	ARCHNET ID	Site
134041	EA.CA.5717	2447-1921	158 AL 25 2C 2	—	ICR2363	Aleppo
134042	EA.CA.5829	2293-1921	158 AL 25 5Z 2	—	ICR2488	Aleppo
134043	EA.CA.5834	2296-1921	158 AL 25 5Z 1	—	ICR2486	Aleppo
134044	EA.CA.5830	2301-1921	158 AL 25 5Z 1	—	ICR2487	Aleppo
134045	EA.CA.5828	2297-1921	158 AL 25 5Z 1	—	ICR2485	Aleppo
134046	EA.CA.5824	2305-1921	158 AL 25 5Z (i) 2	—	ICR2497	Aleppo
134047	EA.CA.5831	2302-1921	158 AL 25 5Z (i) 1	—	ICR2492	Aleppo
134048	EA.CA.5825	2294-1921	158 AL 25 5Z 2	—	ICR2489	Aleppo
134049	—	2303-1921	158 AL 25 5Z (i) 1	—	ICR2493	Aleppo
134050	EA.CA.5833	2298-1921	158 AL 25 5Z 2a	—	ICR2491	Aleppo
134051	EA.CA.5826	2300-1921	158 AL 25 5Z (i) 2	—	ICR2495	Aleppo
134052	EA.CA.5827	2299-1921	158 AL 25 5Z (i) 2	—	ICR2496	Aleppo
134053	EA.CA.5832	2304-1921	158 AL 25 2Ma 1	—	ICR2394	Aleppo
134054	EA.CA.5721	2489-1921	158 AL 25 5S 1	—	ICR2469	Aleppo
134055	EA.CA.5722	2490-1921	158 AL 25 5S 1	—	ICR2468	Aleppo
134056	EA.CA.5723	2491-1921	158 AL 25 5S 2	—	ICR2471	Aleppo
134057	EA.CA.5724	2487-1921	158 AL 25 5S 2	—	ICR2472	Aleppo
134058	—	2492-1921	158 AL 25 5S 2	—	ICR2470	Aleppo
134059	EA.CA.5725	2488-1921	158 AL 25 5S (i) 1	—	ICR2473	Aleppo
134060	—	2493-1921	158 AL 25 5S (i) 1	—	ICR2474	Aleppo
134061	EA.CA.5835	2251-1921	158 AL 25 9M 1	—	ICR2626	Aleppo
134062	—	2252-1921	158 AL 25 13j 1	—	ICR2327	Aleppo
134063	EA.CA.5837	2254-1921	158 AL 25 2F 1	—	ICR2366	Aleppo
134064	EA.CA.5844	2253-1921	158 AL 25 2F 1	—	ICR2367	Aleppo
134065	EA.CA.5843	2255-1921	158 AL 25 2F 1	—	ICR2368	Aleppo
134066	EA.CA.5839	2258-1921	158 AL 25 2F 2	—	ICR2370	Aleppo
134067	EA.CA.5838	2257-1921	158 AL 25 2F 2	—	ICR2369	Aleppo
134068	EA.CA.5858	2256-1921	158 AL 25 2F 2	—	ICR2371	Aleppo
134069	EA.CA.5841	2260-1921	158 AL 25 2F 3	—	ICR2372	Aleppo
134070	EA.CA.5840	2259-1921	158 AL 25 2F 3	—	ICR2373	Aleppo
134071	EA.CA.5850	2261-1921	158 AL 25 2F (i) 3	—	ICR2384	Aleppo
134138	EA.CA.5852	—	158 AL 25 2F (i) 3	—	ICR2383	Aleppo
134139	EA.CA.5851	2266-1921	158 AL 25 2F (i) 3	—	ICR2382	Aleppo
134140	EA.CA.5849	2264-1921	158 AL 25 2F (i) 2	—	ICR2380	Aleppo
134141	EA.CA.5845	2267-1921	158 AL 25 2F (i) 4	—	ICR2385	Aleppo
134142	EA.CA.5853	2262-1921	158 AL 25 2F (i) 2	—	ICR2378	Aleppo
134143	EA.CA.5847	2262-1921	158 AL 25 2F (i) 2	—	ICR2379	Aleppo
134144	EA.CA.5859	2272-1921	158 AL 25 2F (i) 4	—	ICR2386	Aleppo
134145	EA.CA.5848	2263-1921	158 AL 25 2F (i) 2a	—	ICR2381	Aleppo
134146	EA.CA.5846	2268-1921	158 AL 25 2F (i) 1	—	ICR2377	Aleppo
134147	EA.CA.5857	2269-1921	158 AL 25 2F (i) 4	—	ICR2387	Aleppo
134148	EA.CA.5856	2270-1921	158 AL 25 2F (i) 1	—	ICR2375	Aleppo
134149	EA.CA.5854	2271-1921	158 AL 25 2F (i) 1	—	ICR2376	Aleppo

Berenson ID	Ashmolean ID	V&A ID	Fine Arts Lib. ID	AUC ID	ARCHNET ID	Site
134150	EA.CA.5842	2265-1921	158 AL 25 2F 3	—	ICR2374	Aleppo
134151	EA.CA.5730	2419-1921	158 AL 25 2RK 1	—	ICR2414	Aleppo
134152	EA.CA.5729	—	158 AL 25 2RK 1	—	ICR2415	Aleppo
134153	EA.CA.5727	2420-1921	158 AL 25 2RK 1	—	ICR2416	Aleppo
134154	—	2421-1921	158 AL 25 2RK (i) 1	—	ICR2417	Aleppo
134155	EA.CA.5732	2423-1921	158 AL 25 2RK (i) 1	—	ICR2419	Aleppo
134156	EA.CA.5731	2422-1921	158 AL 25 2RK (i) 1	—	ICR2418	Aleppo
134157	EA.CA.5735	2482-1921	158 AL 25 5Sh 1	—	ICR2475	Aleppo
134158	EA.CA.5741	2480-1921	158 AL 25 5Sh 1	—	ICR2477	Aleppo
134159	EA.CA.5738	2478-1921	158 AL 25 5Sh 2	—	ICR2479	Aleppo
134160	EA.CA.5740	2479-1921	158 AL 25 5Sh 2	—	ICR2478	Aleppo
134161	EA.CA.5742	2484-1921	158 AL 25 5Sh (i) 1	—	ICR2481	Aleppo
134162	EA.CA.5739	2477-1921	158 AL 25 5Sh 2	—	ICR2480	Aleppo
134163	EA.CA.5736	2483-1921	158 AL 25 5Sh 1	—	ICR2476	Aleppo
134164	EA.CA.5744	2481-1921	158 AL 25 5Sh (i) 1	—	ICR2482	Aleppo
134165	EA.CA.5737	2485-1921	158 AL 25 5Sh (i) 1a	—	ICR2484	Aleppo
134166	EA.CA.5743	2486-1921	158 AL 25 5Sh (i) 1a	—	ICR2483	Aleppo
134167	EA.CA.5733	2504-1921	158 AL 25 2Y 1	—	ICR2439	Aleppo
134168	EA.CA.5745	2418-1921	158 AL 25 2Ka 1	—	ICR2391	Aleppo
134169	EA.CA.5860	2273-1921	158 AL 25 2Maq 1	—	ICR2397	Aleppo
134170	EA.CA.5861	2274-1921	158 AL 25 16 Ma 1	—	ICR2345	Aleppo
134171	EA.CA.5747	2383-1921	158 AL 25 2B 1	—	ICR2356	Aleppo
134172	EA.CA.5748	2382-1921	158 AL 25 2B 1	—	ICR2357	Aleppo
134173	EA.CA.5749	2365-1921	158 AL 25 2A 1	—	ICR2348	Aleppo
134174	EA.CA.5751	2367-1921	158 AL 25 2A 2	—	ICR2350	Aleppo
134175	EA.CA.5753	2372-1921	158 AL 25 2A 1	—	ICR2349	Aleppo
134176	EA.CA.5750	2366-1921	158 AL 25 2A 2	—	ICR2351	Aleppo
134177	EA.CA.5756	2371-1921	158 AL 25 2A (i) 1	—	ICR2353	Aleppo
134178	EA.CA.5754	2370-1921	158 AL 25 2A (i) 1	—	ICR2352	Aleppo
134179	EA.CA.5752	2369-1921	158 AL 25 2A (i) 1	—	ICR2355	Aleppo
134180	EA.CA.5755	2368-1921	158 AL 25 2A (i) 1	—	ICR2354	Aleppo
134181	EA.CA.5757	2466-1921	158 AL 25 16 Ch 1	—	ICR2343	Aleppo
134182	EA.CA.5759	2407-1921	—	—	—	Aleppo
134183	EA.CA.5758	2406-1921	—	—	—	Aleppo
134184	EA.CA.5764	2467-1921	158 AL 25 9 Sa 1	—	ICR2635	Aleppo
134185	EA.CA.5760	2468-1921	158 AL 25 9 Sa 1	—	ICR2634	Aleppo
134186	EA.CA.5762	2471-1921	158 AL 25 9 Sa (i) 1	—	ICR2636	Aleppo
134187	EA.CA.5763	2470-1921	158 AL 25 9 Sa (i) 1	—	ICR2637	Aleppo
134188	EA.CA.5761	2469-1921	158 AL 25 9 Sa 1	—	ICR2633	Aleppo
134189	EA.CA.5862	2285-1921	158 AL 25 9Ma 1	—	ICR2628	Aleppo
134190	EA.CA.5863	2286-1921	158 AL 25 9Ma 1	—	ICR2629	Aleppo
134191	EA.CA.5864	2287-1921	158 AL 25 9Ma 1	—	ICR2630	Aleppo
134192	EA.CA.5767	2412-1921	158 AL 25 8A 1	—	ICR2499	Aleppo

Berenson ID	Ashmolean ID	V&A ID	Fine Arts Lib. ID	AUC ID	ARCHNET ID	Site
134193	EA.CA.5766	2413-1921	158 AL 25 8A 1	—	ICR2498	Aleppo
134194	EA.CA.5768	2414-1921	158 AL 25 8A (i) 3	—	ICR2506	Aleppo
134195	EA.CA.5765	2411-1921	158 AL 25 8A 1	—	ICR2500	Aleppo
134196	EA.CA.5769	2410-1921	158 AL 25 8A (i) 1	—	ICR2502	Aleppo
134197	—	2410-1921	158 AL 25 8A (i) 1	—	ICR2501	Aleppo
134198	EA.CA.5772	2417-1921	158 AL 25 8A (i) 2	—	ICR2505	Aleppo
134199	EA.CA.5770	2415-1921	158 AL 25 8A (i) 1	—	ICR2503	Aleppo
134200	EA.CA.5771	2416-1921	158 AL 25 8A (i) 2	—	ICR2504	Aleppo
134201	EA.CA.5773	2385-1921	158 AL 25 9H 1	—	ICR2604	Aleppo
134202	EA.CA.5775	2434-1921	158 AL 25 2Ma 2	—	ICR2395	Aleppo
134203	EA.CA.5774	2433-1921	158 AL 25 2Ma 1	—	ICR2393	Aleppo
134204	EA.CA.5777	2432-1921	158 AL 25 2Ma 1	—	ICR2394	Aleppo
134205	EA.CA.5776	2435-1921	158 AL 25 2Ma 2	—	ICR2396	Aleppo
134206	EA.CA.5779	2448-1921	—	—	ICR2632	Aleppo
134207	EA.CA.5778	2465-1921	158 AL 25 16 Sak 1	—	ICR2347	Aleppo
134208	EA.CA.5780	2373-1921	158 AL 25 2U 1	—	ICR2433	Aleppo
134209	EA.CA.5781	2378-1921	158 AL 25 2U 1	—	ICR2434	Aleppo
134210	EA.CA.5783	2374-1921	158 AL 25 2U 2	—	ICR2436	Aleppo
134212	EA.CA.5785	2377-1921	158 AL 25 2U (i) 1	—	ICR2437	Aleppo
134213	EA.CA.5784	2376-1921	158 AL 25 2U (i) 1	—	ICR2438	Aleppo
134214	EA.CA.5876	2291-1921	158 AL 25 9C 1	—	ICR2524	Aleppo
134215	EA.CA.5877	2292-1921	158 AL 25 9C 1	—	ICR2523	Aleppo
134216	EA.CA.5787	2462-1921	158 AL 25 2S 1	—	ICR2421	Aleppo
134217	EA.CA.5786	2461-1921	158 AL 25 2S 1	—	ICR2420	Aleppo
134218	EA.CA.5788	2463-1921	158 AL 25 2S 1	—	ICR2422	Aleppo
134219	EA.CA.5790	2506-1921	158 AL 25 2Z 1	—	ICR2441	Aleppo
134220	EA.CA.5789	2325-1921	158 AL 25 16 Bab M1	—	ICR2342	Aleppo
134221	EA.CA.5795	2464-1921	158 AL 25 16 Sah 1	—	ICR2346	Aleppo
134222	EA.CA.5791	2501-1921	—	—	—	Aleppo
134223	EA.CA.5793	2459-1921	158 AL 25 8S 1	—	ICR2519	Aleppo
134224	EA.CA.5792	2460-1921	158 AL 25 8S 1	—	ICR2520	Aleppo
134225	EA.CA.5796	2424-1921	158 AL 25 8Q 1	—	ICR2517	Aleppo
134226	EA.CA.5798	2431-1921	158 AL 25 9K 1	—	ICR2623	Aleppo
134227	EA.CA.5797	2429-1921	158 AL 25 9K 2	—	ICR2624	Aleppo
134228	EA.CA.5799	2430-1921	158 AL 25 9K 1	—	ICR2622	Aleppo
134229	EA.CA.5800	2428-1921	158 AL 25 9K 2	—	ICR2625	Aleppo
134230	EA.CA.5801	2494-1921	158 AL 25 2T 1	—	ICR2432	Aleppo
134231	EA.CA.5802	2496-1921	158 AL 25 2T 1	—	ICR2430	Aleppo
134233	EA.CA.5805	2425-1921	158 AL 25 2K 1	—	ICR2388	Aleppo
134234	EA.CA.5806	2426-1921	158 AL 25 2K (i) 1	—	ICR2389	Aleppo
134235	EA.CA.5807	2427-1921	158 AL 25 2K (i) 1	—	ICR2390	Aleppo
134236	EA.CA.5808	2384-1921	158 AL 25 8G 1	—	ICR2511	Aleppo
134237	EA.CA.5809	2361-1921	158 AL 25 8C 1	—	ICR2507	Aleppo

Appendix 3 – Synopsis of Creswell's Photographs in Different Archives

Berenson ID	Ashmolean ID	V&A ID	Fine Arts Lib. ID	AUC ID	ARCHNET ID	Site
134238	EA.CA.5811	2363-1921	158 AL 25 8C (i) 1	—	ICR2509	Aleppo
134239	—	2362-1921	—	—	—	Aleppo
134240	EA.CA.5810	2364-1921	158 AL 25 8C (i) 1	—	ICR2508	Aleppo
134241	EA.CA.5645	2359-1921	158 AL 25 2Mo 2	—	ICR2403	Aleppo
134242	EA.CA.5646	2357-1921	158 AL 25 2Mo 2	—	ICR2402	Aleppo
134243	EA.CA.5653	2351-1921	158 AL 25 2Mo 1	—	ICR2399	Aleppo
134244	EA.CA.5654	2352-1921	158 AL 25 2Mo 1	—	ICR2400	Aleppo
134245	EA.CA.5647	2355-1921	158 AL 25 2Mo 1	—	ICR2398	Aleppo
134246	EA.CA.5648	2356-1921	158 AL 25 2Mo (i) 1	—	ICR2404	Aleppo
134247	EA.CA.5649	2354-1921	158 AL 25 2Mo (i) 1	—	ICR2405	Aleppo
134248	EA.CA.5650	2353-1921	158 AL 25 2Mo (i) 2	—	ICR2406	Aleppo
134249	EA.CA.5651	2358-1921	158 AL 25 2Mo (i) 2	—	ICR2407	Aleppo
134250	EA.CA.5652	2360-1921	158 AL 25 2Mo (i) 2	—	ICR2408	Aleppo
134251	EA.CA.5626	2310-1921	158 AL 25 13j 1	—	ICR2328	Aleppo
134252	EA.CA.5627	2312-1921	158 AL 25 13A 1	—	ICR2300	Aleppo
134253	EA.CA.5628	2319-1921	158 AL 25 13W 4	—	ICR2340	Aleppo
134254	EA.CA.5630	2318-1921	158 AL 25 13A 1	—	ICR2299	Aleppo
134255	EA.CA.5631	2321-1921	158 AL 25 13W 2	—	ICR2336	Aleppo
134256	EA.CA.5632	2309-1921	158 AL 25 13W 2	—	ICR2337	Aleppo
134257	EA.CA.5634	2308-1921	158 AL 25 13W 3	—	ICR2338	Aleppo
134258	EA.CA.5635	2320-1921	158 AL 25 13W 1	—	ICR2335	Aleppo
134259	EA.CA.5636	—	158 AL 25 13A 2	—	ICR2302	Aleppo
134260	EA.CA.5637	2313-1921	158 AL 25 13A 2	—	ICR2301	Aleppo
134261	EA.CA.5638	2317-1921	158 AL 25 13A 3	—	ICR2303	Aleppo
134262	EA.CA.5639	2322-1921	158 AL 25 13Q 1	—	ICR2330	Aleppo
134263	EA.CA.5640	2323-19	158 AL 25 13Q 1	—	ICR2331	Aleppo
134264	—	2314-1921	158 AL 25 13Q 2	—	ICR2332	Aleppo
134265	EA.CA.5641	2316-1921	158 AL 25 13Q 2	—	ICR2333	Aleppo
134266	EA.CA.5642	2315-1921	158 AL 25 13Q 2	—	ICR2334	Aleppo
134267	EA.CA.5644	2326-1921	158 AL 25 13M	—	ICR2329	Aleppo
134268	EA.CA.5625	2311-1921	—	—	ICR2327	Aleppo
134269	EA.CA.5643	2324-1921	158 AL 25 13H	—	ICR2326	Aleppo
134270	EA.CA.5655	2390-1921	158 AL 25 5H (i) 1	—	ICR2447	Aleppo
134271	EA.CA.5656	2388-1921	158 AL 25 5H 1	—	ICR2444	Aleppo
134272	EA.CA.5658	2387-1921	158 AL 25 5H 1	—	ICR2445	Aleppo
134273	EA.CA.5657	2389-1921	158 AL 25 5H (i) 1	—	ICR2446	Aleppo
134274	EA.CA.5659	2391-1921	158 AL 25 5H (i) 1	—	ICR2448	Aleppo
134275	EA.CA.5865	2275-1921	158 AL 25 5Ka 1	—	ICR2453	Aleppo
134276	EA.CA.5866	2280-1921	158 AL 25 5Ka 2	—	ICR2456	Aleppo
134277	EA.CA.5865	2277-1921	158 AL 25 5Ka 1	—	ICR2453	Aleppo
134278	EA.CA.5868	2278-1921	158 AL 25 5Ka 2	—	ICR2458	Aleppo
134279	EA.CA.5869	2279-1921	158 AL 25 5Ka 2	—	ICR2457	Aleppo
134280	EA.CA.5870	2276-1921	158 AL 25 5Ka 1	—	ICR2454	Aleppo

Berenson ID	Ashmolean ID	V&A ID	Fine Arts Lib. ID	AUC ID	ARCHNET ID	Site
134281	EA.CA.5871	2284-1921	158 AL 25 5Ka 1	—	ICR2455	Aleppo
134282	EA.CA.5872	2281-1921	158 AL 25 5Ka (i) 1	—	ICR2460	Aleppo
134283	EA.CA.5873	2283-1921	158 AL 25 5Ka (i) 1	—	ICR2459	Aleppo
134284	EA.CA.5874	2282-1921	158 AL 25 5Ka (i) 1	—	ICR2461	Aleppo
134285	EA.CA.5674	2450-1921	158 AL 25 8N (i) 1	—	ICR2515	Aleppo
134286	EA.CA.5675	2449-1921	158 AL 25 8N (i) 1	—	ICR2514	Aleppo
134287	EA.CA.5672	2451-1921	158 AL 25 8N 1	—	ICR2512	Aleppo
134288	EA.CA.5673	2452-1921	158 AL 25 8N 1	—	ICR2513	Aleppo
134289	EA.CA.5817	2380-1921	158 AL 25 2Ba (i) 1	—	ICR2358	Aleppo
134290	EA.CA.5816	2379-1921	158 AL 25 2Ba (i) 1	—	ICR2359	Aleppo
134291	EA.CA.5813	2502-1921	158 AL 25 8W 1	—	ICR2522	Aleppo
134292	EA.CA.5812	2503-1921	158 AL 25 8W 1	—	ICR2521	Aleppo
134293	EA.CA.5660	2456-1921	158 AL 25 2Qi 1	—	ICR2412	Aleppo
134294	EA.CA.5661	2457-1921	158 AL 25 2Qi 1	—	ICR2413	Aleppo
134295	EA.CA.5815	2307-1921	158 AL 25 4(a)	—	ICR2443	Aleppo
134296	—	2306-1921	158 AL 25 4(a)	—	ICR2442	Aleppo
134297	EA.CA.5794	2458-1921	158 AL 25 8S 1	—	ICR2518	Aleppo
134298	EA.CA.5820	2386-1921	158 AL 25 16 Ha 1	—	ICR2344	Aleppo
134299	EA.CA.5819	2507-1921	—	—	—	Aleppo
134300	EA.CA.5875	2288-1921	158 AL 25 9 o 1	—	ICR2631	Aleppo
134301	EA.CA.5746	2453-1921	158 AL 25 2Q 1	—	ICR2409	Aleppo
134302	EA.CA.5823	2289-1921	158 AL 25 2Sai (i) 1	—	ICR2424	Aleppo
134303	EA.CA.5734	2505-1921	158 AL 25 2Y 1	—	ICR2440	Aleppo
134304	EA.CA.5821	2381-1921	158 AL 25 2Bh (i) 1	—	ICR2360	Aleppo
402895	—	—	—	—	—	Birecik

Appendix 4. Sites and monuments geolocation
by Francesco Saliola

Since the Antiquity and the Middle Ages, a need for locating peoples, events, roads and mythological creatures too, has inspired humans to draw maps. In our age of Global Navigation Satellite Systems and always-connected smart devices, that need is even more compelling.

Today, almost any newly created digital information is natively geolocated; the same is not true for old documentation. Therefore, digitising analogue pictures should take their relevant geolocation into consideration, especially when that position adds more value to the provided data, as in Archaeology or Architecture.

Several buildings that had been photographed by K.A.C. Creswell are still standing, and their geolocation was clearly known. Some other monuments, however, have been difficult to locate, since they were poorly documented or because they have gone ruined or destroyed since Creswell's time. When the proposed geolocation is not completely certain, their position is labelled as "Approximate". Some monuments could not be located at all, and they are listed as such. UTM metric coordinates (Easting, Northing) are provided with the relevant UTM grid zones, as referred to the WGS84 datum.

In order to provide users with an easy visual tool, we have decided to create a Google My Maps map: simple, usable, effective. The map will provide the same user experience many users are already familiar with. Furthermore, it will be quite easy for the author to update and make corrections to the data, so that information can be enhanced.

The map is available at:
https://t.ly/DJpnK

Mesopotamia

Al-Madain, Taq Kisra: Remains of a Sasanian palace, built in the middle of the 6th cent. *UTM coordinates:* 38S 460882 3661754.

Al-Ukhaidir, Fortress: Abbasid fortified residence, built in the second half of the 8th cent. *UTM coordinates:* 38S 368645 3590112.

Baghdad, al-Khulafa Minaret: The earliest mosque was probably built in the Abbasid period (10th cent.). It underwent numerous restorations and reconstructions. The minaret was built during the Ilkhanid period (13th cent.). *UTM coordinates:* 38S 443957 3689023.

Baghdad, al-Mirjaniya Madrasa: Madrasa built in the Jalayirid period (14th cent.). It was restored in the Ottoman period (18th cent.), and then in 1926, shortly before Creswell's visit. *UTM coordinates:* 38S 443544 3689029.

Baghdad, al-Mustansiriya Madrasa: Theological school commissioned by the Abbasid caliph al-Mustansir Billah in the 13th cent. *UTM coordinates:* 38S 443215 3688993.

Baghdad, Bab al-Wastani: One of the gates of the Abbasid city, built in the 13th cent. *UTM coordinates:* 38S 444550 3690445.

Baghdad, Khan Mirjan: Khan built during the Jalayrid period (14th cent.). *UTM coordinates:* 38S 443466 3688992.

Baghdad, Qasr al-Abbasi: Large brick building, whose functional interpretation is still discussed, built in the Abbasid period, probably during the caliphate of al-Mustansir (12th-13th cent.). *UTM coordinates:* 38S 442620 3689484.

Baghdad, Shaykh Maruf al-Kharkhi Mausoleum: Mausoleum dedicated to the Sufi Maruf al-Kharqi, who died in 816. The mausoleum was rebuilt and restored several times. The minaret can be dated to the Abbasid period (13th cent.). while the dome was built later, at some time during the Ottoman period. *UTM coordinates:* 38S 441742 3688429.

Baghdad, Suhrawardi Mosque and Mausoleum: Complex including mosque and shrine of Shaykh Umar Suhrawardi, built in the Abbasid period in the 13th cent. It has been restored many times, to such an extent that what we see today is essentially an Ottoman structure. *UTM coordinates:* 38S 444369 3690286.

Baghdad, Zumurrud Khatun Mosque: Abbasid mausoleum, built by the caliph al-Nasir li-Din Allah for his mother, at the end of the 12th cent. *UTM coordinates:* 38S 441643 3688228.

Birecik, Castle: The standing architectural remains date for the most part to the Mamluk and Ottoman periods (13th-15th cent.). *UTM coordinates:* 37S 409209 4098844.

Harran, Castle: The visible remains mainly belong to the 11th/12th centuries. Recently, two Greek inscriptions dating back to the 4th-6th centuries have been found in this building. *UTM coordinates:* 37S 503146 4079299.

Harran, Great Mosque: One of the earliest mosques of the Umayyad period (8th cent.) although most of the standing remains date back to the Ayyubid period (12th cent.). *UTM coordinates:* 37S 502786 4079869.

Harran, Mazar of Shaikh Yahia: Shaikh Yahia was an ascetic of the 12th cent., and the mausoleum was probably added to an already existing mosque of the 10th/11th cent. *UTM coordinates:* 37S 502201 4080036.

Qantarat Harba, Bridge: The Abbasid bridge was built in the 13th cent., to connect the two banks of the old Dujail canal. *UTM coordinates:* 38S 416354 3761081.

Samarra, Abu Dulaf Mosque: Mosque built by the Abbasid caliph al-Mutawakil in the 9th cent. *UTM coordinates:* 38S 389787 3802819.

Samarra, al-Askari Shrine: It was built during the Hamdanid period, and expanded significantly during the Buyid dynasty (10th cent.). The two minarets and the golden dome were built in 1905. *UTM coordinates:* 38S 396196 3784777.

Samarra, Dar al-Khalifa: Residence of the Abbasid caliph al-Mutasim, built in the 9th cent. *UTM coordinates:* 38S 395980 3788258.

Samarra, Great Mosque (or Jami al-Mutawakil): Mosque built by the Abbasid caliph al-Mutawakil in the 9th cent. *UTM coordinates:* 38S 396782 3785538.

Samarra, Qasr al-Ashiq: The last large Abbasid palace of Samarra, built by caliph al-Mutamid in the second half of the 9th cent. *UTM coordinates:* 38S 390303 3789564.

Samarra, Qubba al-Sulaibiya: Abbasid mausoleum with octagonal plan built in the second half of the 9th cent. *UTM coordinates:* 38S 389380 3788080.

Syria

Aleppo, al-Atrush Mosque: Mosque built during the Mamluk period, at some time between the very end of the 14th cent. and the early 15th cent. *UTM coordinates:* 37S 334884 4007292.

Aleppo, al-Bayada Mosque: Mosque built during the Mamluk period (14th cent.), with later additions. *UTM coordinates:* 37S 335118 4007820.

Aleppo, al-Firdaws Madrasa: Mosque built during the Ayyubid period (13th cent.), outside the Medieval city walls. *UTM coordinates:* 37S 334136 4006210.

Aleppo, al-Halawiya Madrasa: The madrasa was founded in the Zanjid period (12th cent.), converting an existing Byzantine cathedral of the 5th cent. *UTM coordinates:* 37S 334220 4007652.

Aleppo, al-Kamiliya Madrasa: Madrasa built in the Ayyubid period (13th cent.). *UTM coordinates:* 37S 334530 4006458.

Aleppo, al-Karimiya Mosque: Mosque built in the Ayyubid period (13th cent.). *UTM coordinates:* 37S 334254 4007259.

Aleppo, al-Khusrauriya Mosque: It is the first Ottoman monument of the city, built in the 16th cent. by architect Mimar Sinan. It was almost completely destroyed in 2014-2015, during the Syrian Civil War. *UTM coordinates:* 37S 334663 4007343.

Aleppo, al-Maqam Mosque: Mosque built in the Mamluk period (14th cent.). *UTM coordinates:* 37S 334457 4006463.

Aleppo, al-Muqaddamiya Madrasa: Mosque built in the Zanjid period (12th cent.) on the remains of an earlier Byzantine church. *UTM coordinates:* 37S 334057 4007522(approximate).

Aleppo, al-Qadi al-Mahmandar Mosque: Mosque built in the Mamluk period (14th cent.). *UTM coordinates:* 37S 334568 4007961.

Aleppo, al-Qiqan Mosque: Mosque probably built in the late Mamluk period. Among the building stones, one contains a Hittite relief of the late 2nd millennium BCE. It was restored in 1996. *UTM coordinates:* 37S 333850 4007659.

Aleppo, al-Rumi Mosque: Mosque built in the Mamluk period (14th cent.). *UTM coordinates:* 37S 334122 4007572.

Aleppo, al-Safahiya Mosque: Mosque built in the Mamluk period (15th cent.). *UTM coordinates:* 37S 334424 4007360.

Aleppo, al-Sahibiya Madrasa: Madrasa built in the Mamluk period (14th cent.). *UTM coordinates:* 37S 334454 4007667.

Aleppo, al-Shadhbakhtiya Madrasa: One of the earliest existing Ayyubid madrasas, built in the 12th cent. In part demolished in the 19th cent. due to the enlargement of an adjacent bazar. *UTM coordinates:* 37S 334530 4007557.

APPENDIX 4 – SITES AND MONUMENTS GEOLOCATION

Aleppo, al-Sharafiya Madrasa: Ayyubid madrasa built in the 13th cent., today largely disappeared (only the entrance and the vaulted prayer hall still exist). *UTM coordinates: 37S 334369.38 4007688.*

Aleppo, al-Shuaybiya Mosque: Madrasa built in the Zanjid period (12th cent.) on the site where a former Umayyad mosque stood. It was remodelled several times and has recently been restored. *UTM coordinates: 37S 333870 4007569.*

Aleppo, al-Sultaniya Madrasa: Madrasa built in the Ayyubid period (13th cent.). *UTM coordinates: 37S 334737 4007382.*

Aleppo, al-Tawashy Mosque: Mosque built in the Mamluk period (14th cent.), and restored in the Ottoman period (16th cent.). *UTM coordinates: 37S 334740 4007122.*

Aleppo, al-Zahiriya Madrasa: Madrasa built in the Ayyubid period (13th cent.). *UTM coordinates: 37S 334356 4006344.*

Aleppo, al-Zaki Mosque: Mosque built in the Mamluk period (14th cent.). *UTM coordinates: 37S 334680 4008229.*

Aleppo, Altunbugha Mosque: Mosque built in the Mamluk period (14th cent.). *UTM coordinates: 37S 335155 4007301.*

Aleppo, Arghun al-Kamili Bimaristan: One of the most important historical Islamic hospitals, built in the Mamluk period (14th cent.). *UTM coordinates: 37S 334284 4007326.*

Aleppo, Bab al-Hadid: Also known as the Iron Gate, it was first built in the Ayyubid period (13th cent.), but it reached modern times in its current form due to the Mamluk reconstruction (16th cent.). Damaged during the Syrian Civil War, it has recently been restored. *UTM coordinates: 37S 335231 4008063.*

Aleppo, Bab al-Jinan: Firstly built in the Hamdanid period (10th cent.) and then remodelled in the Mamluk period (early 16th cent.). Demolished in the early 20th cent. to broaden a street. There are still remains of one tower. *UTM coordinates: 37S 333844 4007975 (approximate).*

Aleppo, Bab al-Maqam: City gate built in the Ayyubid period (13th cent.). *UTM coordinates: 37S 334617 4006804.*

Aleppo, Bab Antakya: City gate built in the Ayyubid period (13th cent.), with later repairs and restorations (14th-15th cent.). *UTM coordinates: 37S 333831 4007596.*

Aleppo, Bab Qinnasrin: Originally built in the Hamdanid period (10th cent.) and then rebuilt in the Ayyubid period (13th cent.). It was damaged during the recent Syrian Civil War. *UTM coordinates: 37S 334193 4007101.*

Aleppo, Bahramiya: Mosque: Mosque built in the Ottoman period (16th cent.). *UTM coordinates: 37S 334091 4007532.*

Aleppo, Bahsita Mosque: Mosque built in the Mamluk period (14th cent.). *UTM coordinates: 37S 334032 4008148.*

Aleppo, Citadel: Most of the visible remains belong to the Hamdanid, Ayyubid, and Mamluk periods (10th-15th cent.). *UTM coordinates: 37S 334819 4007591.*

Aleppo, Citadel Mosque: Mosque built in the Ayyubid period (13th cent.). Also known as the Great Mosque of the Citadel. *UTM coordinates: 37S 334789 4007682.*

Aleppo, Great Mosque: The largest mosque in Aleppo, whose main building periods were Umayyad, Zangid, Mamluk, Seljuk (8th-13th cent.). *UTM coordinates: 37S 334291 4007634.*

Aleppo, Khan al-Jumruk: Khan built in the Ottoman period (16th cent.). *UTM coordinates: 37S 334210 4007507.*

Aleppo, Khan al-Sabun: Khan built in the Mamluk period (15th cent.). *UTM coordinates: 37S 334406 4007697.*

Aleppo, Khan al-Wazir: Khan built in the Ottoman period (17th cent.), in part demolished during the French Mandate. *UTM coordinates: 37S 334511 4007680.*

Aleppo, Khan Khassabiya: Khan built in the Mamluk period (16th cent.). *UTM coordinates: 37S 334136 4007610*

Aleppo, Khan Utchan: The oldest khan outside the city walls, built in the Mamluk period (16th cent.). *UTM coordinates: 37S 334721 4008216 (approximate).*

Aleppo, Khanqah al-Farafra: Sufi monument built in the Ayyubid period (13th cent.). *UTM coordinates: 37S334678 4007878.*

Aleppo, Maqam Ibrahim al-Sulfi Mosque: Mosque located on the Citadel of Aleppo dedicated to the prophet Abraham. It was built in the Zanjid period (12th cent.) and restored, probably after the Mongol conquest of the city in 1260. *UTM coordinates: 37S 334774 4007623.*

Aleppo, Maqam Ibrahim fi al-Salihin: Its foundation dates back to the Seljuk period (11th cent.). The minaret was probably built during the Ayyubid period (12th cent.). *UTM coordinates: 37S 334533 4005918.*

Aleppo, Maqam Ughulbak: Mausoleum built in the Mamluk period (15th cent.). *UTM coordinates:* 37S 334385 4006441.

Aleppo, Mashhad al-Husayn: A Shiite sanctuary and a mosque built in the Ayyubid period (12th cent.). Destroyed in 1919 or 1920, it was reconstructed after World War II. *UTM coordinates:* 37S 332142 4007228.

Aleppo, Mashhad al-Muhassin: Its first construction dates back to the Abbasid period (10th cent.), but the standing remains belong to the Zanjid and Ayyubid periods (12th cent.). *UTM coordinates:* 37S 332101 4006890.

Aleppo, Musa Ibn Abdullah al-Nasiri Mausoleum: Mausoleum built in the Mamluk period (14th cent.). *UTM coordinates:* 37S 334219 4006490.

Aleppo, Nur al-Din Maristan: Hospital built in the Zanjid period (12th cent.). Only the entrance is still preserved. *UTM coordinates:* 37S 334102 4007474.

Aleppo, Qastal Sahat Bizza: Fountain built in the Mamluk period (15th cent.). *UTM coordinates:* 37S 334489 4007015 (approximate).

Aleppo, Qastal Sakakini: Fountain built in the Mamluk period (14th cent.). *UTM coordinates:* 37S 334946 4007103 (approximate).

Aleppo, Qubba Khayrbak: Mausoleum built in the Mamluk period (16th cent.). *UTM coordinates:* 37S 334566 4006702.

Aleppo, Shihab al-Din Ahmad al-Adrai Mausoleum: Mausoleum built in the Mamluk period (15th cent.). *UTM coordinates:* 37S 334432 4006475.

Aleppo, Takiya Shaykh Abu Bakr: Mausoleum built in the Ottoman period (16th cent.). *UTM coordinates:* 37S 335326 4009283.

Aleppo, Umm Malik al-Afdal Mausoleum: Ayyubid mausoleum, built in the 13th cent. *UTM coordinates:* 37S 334035 4005916.

Aleppo, Zawiya al-Bazzaziya: Worship place (zawiya) built in the Mamluk period (14th cent.). *UTM coordinates:* 37S 333917 4007501 (approximate).

Damascus, Abd al-Rahman ibn Abdallah al-Tashtadar Madrasa: Madrasa built in the Ayyubid period (13th cent.). *UTM coordinates:* 37S 248369 3713455 (approximate).

Damascus, Abu Abdallah Hasan ibn Salama Mausoleum: Mausoleum built in the Ayyubid period (13th cent.). *UTM coordinates:* 37S 248460 3713483.

Damascus, al-Adiliya Madrasa: Madrasa built in the Zanjid period (13th cent.). *UTM coordinates:* 37S 249659 3711354.

Damascus, al-Maridaniya Mosque: Mosque built in the Ayyubid period (13th cent.). *UTM coordinates:* 37S 248127 3712773.

Damascus, al-Nuriya al-Kubra Madrasa: Madrasa built in the Zanjid period (12th cent.). *UTM coordinates:* 37S 249674 3711058.

Damascus, al-Qaymari Maristan and Mausoleum: Hospital and mausoleum built in the Ayyubid period (13th cent.). *UTM coordinates:* 37S 248118 3713247.

Damascus, al-Sahiba Madrasa: Madrasa built in the Ayyubid period (13th cent.). *UTM coordinates:* 37S 248546 3713547.

Damascus, al-Sibaiya Madrasa: Madrasa built in the Ottoman period (16th cent.). *UTM coordinates:* 37S 249292 3710927.

Damascus, al-Zahiriya Madrasa: Originally a residential building, it was transformed into a tomb-madrasa in the Mamluk period (13th cent.). *UTM coordinates:* 37S 249701 3711351.

Damascus, Ali al-Faranti Mausoleum: Mausoleum built in the Ayyubid period (13th cent.). *UTM coordinates:* 37S 247830 3713021.

Damascus, Amat al-Latif Mausoleum: Mausoleum built in the Ayyubid period (13th cent.). *UTM coordinates:* 37S 247785 3712909.

Damascus, Amir Kujkun al-Mansuri Mausoleum: Mausoleum built in the Mamluk period (14th cent.). *UTM coordinates:* 37S 247804 3712928.

Damascus, Amir Tankiz Mosque and Mausoleum: Mosque built in the Mamluk period (14th cent.), then converted into barracks and military academy during the late Ottoman period (19th cent.). *UTM coordinates:* 37S 248951 3711262.

Damascus, Atabektya Mosque: Ayyubid mosque, built in the 13th cent. *UTM coordinates:* 37S 247884 3713066.

Damascus, Azm Palace: Palace built in the Ottoman period (18th cent.). *UTM coordinates:* 37S 249859 3711101.

Damascus, Bab al-Faraj: City gate built in the Zanjid period (12th cent.). *UTM coordinates:* 37S 249554 3711433.

Damascus, Bab al-Salam: City gate built in the Zanjid period (12th cent.) on the remains of a Roman gate. *UTM coordinates:* 37S 250168 3711529.

Damascus, Dar al-Hadith al-Ashrafiya al-Muqaddasiya: Mausoleum built in the Ayyubid period (13th cent.). *UTM coordinates:* 37S 247872 3713058.

Damascus, Hanabila Mosque: Mosque built in the Ayyubid period (13th cent.). *UTM coordinates:* 37S 248267 3713479.

Damascus, Izz al-Din Madrasa: Madrasa built in the Ayyubid period (13th cent.). *UTM coordinates:* 37S 248592 3711596 (approximate).

Damascus, Jaharkasiya Madrasa: Madrasa built in the Ayyubid period (13th cent.). *UTM coordinates:* 37S 248006 371317.

Damascus, Khan Asad Pasha: Khan built in the Ottoman period (18th cent.), restored in the 1980s. *UTM coordinates:* 37S 249820 3710998.

Damascus, Khan Sulayman Pasha: Khan built in the Ottoman period (18th cent.). *UTM coordinates:* 37S 249726 371090.

Damascus, Khatuniya Mausoleum: Mausoleum built in the Ayyubid period (late 12th cent CE), incorporated in the al-Jadid mosque in the 14th cent. *UTM coordinates:* 37S 247993 3713130.

Damascus, Nur al-Din Bimaristan: Hospital built in the Zanjid period, with two main building phases, in the 12th and the 13th cent. The Tomb/Madrasa of Nur al-Din is a separate building. *UTM coordinates:* 37S 249527 3711103.

Damascus, Raihan Mausoleum: Mausoleum built in the Ayyubid period (13th cent.). *UTM coordinates:* 37S 247772 3712917.

Damascus, Rukn al-Din Mausoleum: Mausoleum built in the Ayyubid period (13th cent.). *UTM coordinates:* 37S 248739 3713842.

Damascus, Saladin Mausoleum: The mausoleum of the Ayyubid Sultan Saladin (Salah al-Din) was built in the late 12th cent. It was restored in 1898 with the support of the German emperor Wilhelm II. *UTM coordinates:* 37S 249764 3711313.

Damascus, Sinan Pasha Mosque: Mosque built in the Ottoman period (16th cent.). *UTM coordinates:* 37S 249351 3710869.

Damascus, Takiya al-Sulaymaniya: Large complex including a mosque, a hospital, a madrasa, a takiya with a suq, built in the Ottoman period (16th cent.). *UTM coordinates:* 37S 248410 3711365.

Damascus, Umayyad Mosque: The mosque rose on Roman and Byzantine remains. Its main building periods were Umayyad, Hamdanid, Seljuk, Zangid, and Mamluk (8th-13th cent.). *UTM coordinates:* 37S 249817 3711247.

Hama, al-Nuri Mosque: Mosque built in the Zanjid period (12th cent). *UTM coordinates:* 37S 295239 3890348.

Hama, Azm Palace: Palace built in the Ottoman period (18th cent.). *UTM coordinates:* 37S 295337 3890213.

Hama, Great Mosque: Previously a Roman temple and a Byzantine church, it was converted into a mosque by the Umayyads (7th cent.) and remodelled in the Ayyubid and Mamluk periods (12th-14th cent.). *UTM coordinates:* 37S 294573 3890273.

Homs, Bab al-Masdud: Probably built in the Abbasid periods. Only part of the structure is preserved. *UTM coordinates:* 37S 290484 3844989 (approximate).

Homs, Citadel: The Citadel's chronology is uncertain, due to the massive demolitions carried ount in the 19th and 20th cent. Its main building periods were probably in the Ayyubid and Mamluk periods (12th-13th cent.). *UTM coordinates:* 37S 290710 3844747.

Homs, Great Mosque of al-Nuri: Mosque built in the Zanjid period (12th cent.), on the site where a Roman temple, a Byzantine church and an earlier Islamic mosque had already been erected. *UTM coordinates:* 37S 290752 3845575.

Masyaf, Masyaf Fortress: Its main building period was under the Ismailis (12th cent.), but the Castle was remodeled also later, especially in the Mamluk period (13th cent.). *UTM coordinates:* 37S 257740 3883604.

Qalat Siman, Church of Saint Simeon Stylites: Byzantine church, dedicated to St. Simeon Stylites, built in the 5th cent. *UTM coordinates:* 37S 306510 4023148.

Qalb Lawzah, Basilica: Byzantine church built in the 5th cent. *UTM coordinates:* 37S 282415 4005411.

Ruweiha, Bizzos Mausoleum: Tomb of the founder of the adjacent church, built in the 6th cent. *UTM coordinates:* 37S 291802 3957738.

Transjordan

Amman, Nymphaeum: Monumental fountain (Nymphaeum) built in the Roman period (2nd cent.). *UTM coordinates:* 36R 777544 3538702.

Amman, Qusayr al-Nuwaijis: Mausoleum built in the Roman period (2nd cent.). *UTM coordinates:* 36R 778056 3542952.

Amman, Roman Theatre: One of the largest Roman theatres in the Near East, built in the 2nd cent. *UTM coordinates:* 36R 777827 3538860.

Amman, Umayyad Palace (Audience Hall): Sort of vestibule at the entrance of the Umayyad palace, built in the 8th cent. It was restored and in part reconstructed in the 1990s. *UTM coordinates:* 36R 777332 3539254.

Iraq al-Amir, Qasr al-Abd: Monumental building (a palace or a temple) built in the Hellenistic period (2nd cent. BCE). *UTM coordinates:* 36R 760226 3534080.

Qusayr Amra: One of the 'desert castles' of Jordan, built during the Umayyad period (8th cent.). *UTM coordinates:* 37R 271586 3521000.

Not spotted Sites

Mesopotamia:

Baghdad: Mihrab of al-Khassaki Mosque; Shaykh Aquli Tomb; Harran, City Walls.

Syria:

Aleppo: City Walls; Khan al-Zait; Masjid Yusuf; Qastal Bab al-Maqam; Qastal Shabariq; Zawiya al-Haidary; Zawiya al-Junashiya.

Damascus: al-Rihaniya Madrasa; al-Shamiya al-Kubra Madrasa; Shaykh Muhammad ibn Ali ibn Nadif Mausoleum.

Bibliographic references

All quoted URLs were last visited on December 20th, 2022.

Sitography

ARCHNET: *Archnet Next. Open Access Library on the Built Environment of Muslim Societies*: https://www.archnet.org/

Luminous-lint: http://www.luminous-lint.com

Monummamluk-Alep: webpage dedicated to Alep: http://monummamluk-syrie.org/

Pharos: Pharos. International Consortium of Photo Archives, http://pharosartresearch.org/

Syrie-medievale.com: http://syrie-medievale.com/

Syrian Heritage Archive: https://syrian-heritage.org/map/

Bibliography

Abbu, A. 1973. *The Ayyubid domed buildings of Syria.* Ph.D. thesis, Edinburgh University (https://era.ed.ac.uk/handle/1842/17084).

Abd al-Razik, M. 2019. Mosque of Othman Ibn Ogelbek in Aleppo. An architectural archaeological study. *Egyptian Journal of Archaeological and Restoration Studies* 9/1: 79-95.

Abdu, A.N. 1973. Qubbat al-Sulaybiyya. *Sumer* 29: 111-118.

Abdulrazzaq, A.T. 2020. *Archaeological study of al-Ukhaidir site using satellite SAR image and ground penetrating radar.* Thesis, University of Baghdad, M.Sc. Geology.

About, I. 2015. Les photographes ambulants. *Techniques & Culture* 64 (http://tc.revues.org/7611).

Abu Assaf, A. 1997. Homs. In E.M. Meyers (ed.) *The Oxford Encyclopedia of Archaeology in the Near East*: 89-90. Oxford: Oxford University Press.

Abujaber, R.S., Cobbing, F. 2005. *Beyond the River. Ottoman Transjordan in original photographs.* London: Stacey.

Adamo, N. 2020. *History of irrigation and agriculture in the land between the two rivers.* London: Science Press Ltd.

Adashinskaya, A. 2020. An 'ancient argonaut' in the service of the empire. The research expeditions of Nikodim Pavlovich Kondakov. *Art Historiographies in Central and Eastern Europe November 7, 2020.*

AKTC (Aga Khan Trust for Culture) 2006. *The Citadel of Masyaf. A brief account of project activities in Syria* (https://web.archive.org/web/20061206031107/http://www.akdn.org/hcsp/Syria/Syriapages16_23a.pdf).

Al-Amid, T.M. 1968. *The Abbasid architecture of Samarra in the reign of both al-Mu al-Mu'tasim and al-Mutawakkil.* Thesis, University of Edinburgh.

Al-Attar, I. 2019. *Baghdad. An urban history through the lens of literature.* London: Routledge.

Al-Husayni, M.B. 1966. al-Uhaydir. *Sumer* 22: 79-89.

Al-Janabi, T. 1975. *Studies in Medieval Iraqi architecture.* Thesis, Edinburgh University.

Al-Janabi, T. 1983. Islamic archaeology in Iraq. Recent excavations at Samarra. *World Archaeology* 14/3: 305-327.

Al-Saffar, M. 2018. Urban heritage and conservation in the historic centre of Baghdad. *International Journal of Architectural Heritage* 2/1: 23-36.

Albright, W.F. 1925. Bronze age mounds of Northern Palestine and the Hauran. The spring trip of the School in Jerusalem. *Bulletin of the American Schools of Oriental Research* 19: 5-19.

Allan, J. 2003. *The Creswell photographic archive at the Ashmolean Museum* (http://creswell.ashmolean.org/MoreInfo.html).

Allen, T. 1999. *Ayyubid Architecture.* California: Solipsist Press, (http://www.sonic.net/~tallen/palmtree/ayyarch/index.htm).

Alyehia, A.R., al-Issa, B. 2016. *The day after. Heritage protection initiative site monitors project damage report St. Simeon Russian airstrike May 12, 2016* (https://tda-hpi.org/en/content/615/648/damage-reports/damage-report-st.-simeon-russian-airstrike-may-12,-2016).

Anastasio, S. 2012. Qasr Shamamuk: storia dello scavo e della collezione fiorentina. In S. Anastasio, G. Conti, L. Ulivieri, *La collezione orientale del Museo Archeologico Nazionale di Firenze. I. I materiali di Qasr Shamamuk*: 5-70. Roma: Aracne.

Anastasio, S. 2013. The first Italian archaeological expedition to Mesopotamia. Recently retrieved documents concerning the 1930 survey trip to Iraq. *Mesopotamia* 48: 221-229.

Anastasio, S. 2017. Review to G. Vörös, *Machaerus II. The Hungarian Archaeological Mission in the Light of the American-Baptist and Italian-Franciscan Excavations and Surveys. Final Report 1968- 2015. Edizioni Terra Santa, Milano 2015,* in *Bibliotheca Orientalis* 74/5-6: 652-656.

Anastasio, S. 2020. Creswell, Keppel Archibald Cameron (1879-1974). *Luminous-Lint Photographers* (http://www.luminous-lint.com/app/photographer/Keppel_Archibald_Cameron__Creswell/A/).

Anastasio, S. 2022. The contribtion of historical archives to Jordan archeology. In P. Gilento (ed.) *Building between Eastern and Western Mediterranean Lands. Construction processes and transmission of knowledge from Late Antiquity to Early Islam*: 21-36. Leiden-Boston: Brill.

Anastasio, S., Arbeid, B. 2019. *Egitto, Iraq ed Etruria nelle fotografie di John Alfred Spranger. Viaggi e ricerche archeologiche (1929-1936)*. Oxford: Archaeopress.

Anastasio, S., Botarelli, L. 2015. *The 1927-1938 archaeological expedition to Transjordan in Renato Bartoccini's archives*. Oxford: Archaeopress.

Anonymous (H.H.), 1857. Esquisses du Golfe Persique. Recueil de huit photographies prises sur le lieux, par le major H. Ban. *La Lumière, 1857-04-11*: 57 (https://gallica.bnf.fr/ark:/12148/bpt6k58554163.item#).

Anonymous, 1869. Steel measuring tapes. *Scientific American* 21/14: 216.

Anonymous (R.D.) 1931. Fouilles de M. Ploix de Rotrou dans la citadella d'Alep. *Syria. Archéologie, art et histoire* 12/1: 95-96.

Anonymous 1945. Memorial: Frederick Gardner Clapp. *Bulletin of the American Association of Petroleum Geologists* 29: 402-405.

Anonymous (C.J.E) 1973. Obituary. Arthur Lionel Forster Smith, C.B.E., M.V.O., LL.D. *Iraq* 35/1: i-ii.

Apostolou, I. 2013. Photographes français et locaux en Orient méditerranéen au XIXe siècle. *Bulletin du Centre de recherche français à Jérusalem* 24 (http://bcrfj.revues.org/7008).

Armando, S. 2011. Monneret de Villard, Ugo. *Dizionario Biografico degli Italiani* 75 (https://www.treccani.it/enciclopedia/monneret-de-villard-ugo_%28Dizionario-Biografico%29/).

ASOR (American Schools of Oriental Research) 1876. *Catalogue of photographs: taken expressly for the American Palestine Exploration Society, during a reconnaissance East of the Jordan in the Autumn of 1875*. New York-Beirut: ASOR.

Aubenas, S., Lacarrière, J. (eds) 1999. *Voyage en Orient*. Paris: Hazan.

AUC (American University in Cairo) 2003. *The Papers of Sir Keppel Archibald Cameron Creswell* (https://web.archive.org/web/20040816032845/http://develop.aucegypt.edu/gcaw/creswell/index.html).

Badger, G.P. 1852. *The Nestorians and their rituals*, vol. 1. London: Masters.

Baedeker, K. 1898. *Palestine and Syria. Handbook for travellers (third edition, revised and augmented)*. Leipzig: Baedeker.

Baedeker, K. 1912. *Palestine et Syrie, routes principales a travers la Mésopotamie et la babylonie L'ile de Chypre, manuel du voyageur*. Lepizig: Baedeker (https://gallica.bnf.fr/ark:/12148/bpt6k203297k?rk=42918).

Bair, B. 2011. The American Colony Photography Department: Western consumption and 'Insider' Commercial Photography. *Jerusalem Quarterly, Winter 2011* (https://www.palestine-studies.org/en/node/78392).

Banks, E.J. 1912. *Bismya or the lost city of Adab*. New York: Putnam's Sons.

Banse, E. 1919. *Die Türkei*. Berlin-Braunschweig-Hamburg: Westermann.

Barry, M.-É.É., 1881. *Mission scientifique de Mr. Ernest Chantre sous-directeur du Muséum de Lyon dans la haute Mésopotamie, le Kurdistan et le Caucase. Photographies de Mr le Capitaine Barry*. n.p.

Bartoccini, R. 1930. Gli scavi ad Amman. *La rivista illustrata del Popolo d'Italia* 8/4: 51-55.

Bartoccini, R. 1933-1934. Scavi ad Amman della missione archeologica italiana. *Bollettino dell'Associazione Internazionale per gli Studi Mediterranei* 4: 10-15.

Bartoccini, R. 1941. Un decennio di ricerche e di scavi italiani in Transgiordania. *Bollettino del R. Istituto di archeologia e storia dell'arte* IX/1-6: 75-81.

Bassem, W. 2015. Stepping back 1,300 years into Iraq's Ukhaidir palace. *Al-Monitor, Dec. 3, 2015* (https://www.al-monitor.com/originals/2015/12/iraq-karbala-ukhaidir-palace-neglect-history.html#ixzz77MAYgErS).

Basset, M.R. 1921. Nécrologie: Henri Pognon. *Journal Asiatique* 17: 337.

Beattle, A. 1996. Hama. In K.A. Berney, T. Ring (eds) *International dictionary of historic places*, vol. 4: 315-318. Chicago-Londin: Fitzroy Dearborn.

Bedford, F., Thompson, W.M. 1867. *The Holy Land, Egypt, Etc., Photographs taken for H.R.H. The Prince of Wales*. London [albumen silver prints].

Beke, E. 1865. *Jacob's flight, or, A pilgrimage to Harran and thence in the patriarch's footsteps into the Promised Land*. London: Longmans Green.

Bell, G. 1911. *Amurath to Amurath*. London: Heinemann.

Bell, G. 1914. *Palace and mosque at Ukhaidir. A study in early Mohanmadan architecture*. Oxford: Clarendon Press.

Bell, G. 1919. *Syria. The desert and the sown*. London: Heinemann [2nd impr.].

Biscop, J.-L., Sodini, J.-P. 1989. Travaux à Qal'at Sem'an. *Publications de l'École française de Rome* 123: 1675-1695.

Blair, S.S. 1991. Surveyor versus Epigrapher. *Muqarnas* 8: 66-73.

Blakely, J. 1997. Frederick Jones Bliss. In E.M. Meyers (ed.) *Oxford Encyclopedia of Archaeology in the Near East*: 332-333. Oxford: Oxford university Press.

Bliss, F.J. 1895. Narrative of an expedition to Moab and Gilead in March 1895. *Palestine Exploration Fund Quarterly Statement* 27/3: 203-235.

Boardman, J. 1991. *The Cambridge Ancient History 3/2. The Assyrian and Babylonian empires and other states of the Near East, from the eighth to the sixth centuries BC*. Cambridge: University Press.

Bobzin, H. 1997. Moritz, Bernhard. *Neue Deutsche Biographie* 18: 148.

Bohrer, Fr.N. 2011. *Photography and archaeology*. London: Reaktion Books.

Bonfils, A. 1876. *Catalogue des vues photographiques de l'Orient. Égypte, Palestine (Terre sainte), Syrie, Grèce & Constantinople...* Alais: Brugueirolle.

Bonfils, A. 1877-1878. *Souvenirs d'Orient: Égypte. Palestine. Syrie. Grèce.* Alais: n.p.

Borel, L. 2006. Recherches récentes sur le domaine d'Iraq al-Amir: nouveaux éléments sur le paysage construit. *Topoi* 14: 265-286.

Bostan, I. 1992. Birecik. *TDV İslâm Ansiklopedisi* 6: 187-189 (https://islamansiklopedisi.org.tr/birecik).

Bosworth, C.E. 2003. Harran. *Encyclopaedia Iranica* 12/1: 13-14.

Bowen Thompson, E. 1872. *The daughters of Syria. A Narrative of efforts by the late Mrs. Bowen Thompson, for the evangelization of the Syrian Females.* London: Seeley, Jackson, & Halliday.

Breniquet, C. 2008. Samarra-Kultur. Keramik. *Reallexikon der Assyriologie und Vorderasiatischen Archäologie* 11/7-8: 612-615.

Brey, W. 1984. William H. Rau's photographic experience in the East. *Stereo World* 2/2: 4-11.

Brisch, Kl. 1974. Sir Archibald Creswell, 13. September 1879 bis 8. April 1974. *Kunst des Orients* 9/1-2: 176-182.

Brossard-Gabastou, L. 2013. *Auguste Salzmann (1824-1872): pionnier de la photographie et de l'archéologie au Proche-Orient.* Paris: Harmattan.

Brown, E. 1999. The world's first daguerreotype images: Canadian travel photographer Pierre Gustave Gaspard Joly de Lotbinière. *The Archivist* 118: 22–29.

Brünnow, R.-E., Domaszewski, A. von 1904-1909. *Die Provincia Arabia auf Grund zweier in den Jahren 1897 und 1898 unterommenen Reisen und der Berichte früherer Reisender beschrieben von Rudolf Ernst Brünnow und Alfred v. Domaszewski.* Strassburg: Trübner.

Bruno A., 1966. The Preservation and Restoration of Taq-i Kisra. *Mesopotamia* 1, 1966: 89-108.

Buckingham, J.S. 1827. *Travels in Mesopotamia.* London: Colburn.

Burckhardt, J.L. 1882. *Travels in Syria and the Holy Land.* London: Darf.

Burns, K. 1991. Cairo's Creswell Collection. A legacy of love. *American Libraries* 22/10: 940-941, 943-944.

Burns, R. 1992. *Monuments of Syria: an historical guide.* London-New York: Tauris.

Burton, R.F., Tyrwhitt-Drake, Ch.F. 1872. *Unexplored Syria.* London: Tinsley Brothers.

Butler, H.C. 1903. *Publications of an American archaeological expedition to Syria in 1899-1900, II. Architecture and other arts.* New York: DeVinne Press.

Butler, H.C. 1929. *Early Churches in Syria, fourth to seventh centuries.* Princeton: Princeton University.

Butler, H.C. et al. 1907-1930. *Syria: publications of the Princeton University Archaeological Expeditions to Syria in 1904-5 and 1909.* Leiden: Brill [26 volumes: Div. 2/A:1-7, 2/B: 1-6, Div. 3/A: 1-7, Div. 3/B: 1-6] (https://digi.ub.uni-heidelberg.de/diglit/syria).

Cahun, L. 1884. *Excursions sur les bords de l'Euphrate.* Paris: Chateroux.

Casari, M. 2014. Bernard Berenson and Islamic culture. 'Thought and Temperament'. In J. Connors, L.A. WaLdman (eds) *Bernard Berenson: formation and heritage*: 173-205. Cambridge, MS: Villa I Tatti.

Çelik, B. 2019. Harran ve çevresinde Paleolitik Çağ. In M. Önal, S.I. Mutlu, S. Mutlu (eds) *Harran ve Çevresi. Arkeoloji*: 13-20. Şanlıurfa: Şurkav Yayınları.

Célimon-Paul, A.-C. 2009. Enlart, Camille. *Dictionnaire critique des historiens de l'art actifs en France de la Révolution à la Première Guerre mondiale* (https://www.inha.fr/fr/ressources/publications/publications-numeriques/dictionnaire-critique-des-historiens-de-l-art/enlart-camille.html?search-keywords=enlart+).

Chandra Makoond, N. 2015. *Advanced computational modelling of Taq-Kisra, Iraq.* MSc Dissertation, Czech Technical University in Prague (https://issuu.com/nirvanchandramakoond/docs/advanced_computational_modelling_of).

Chesney, F.R. 1850. *An expedition for the survey of the rivers Tigris and Euphrates.* London: Longman.

Chevedden, P.E. 1981. Bonfils & Son, Egypt, Greece and the Levant. *History of Photography, January 1981*: 82.

Chevedden, P.E. 1984. Making light of everything. Early photography of the Middle East and current photomania. *Middle East Studies Association Bulletin* 18/2: 151-174.

Chmyreva, I. 2010. *The History of European Photography. 1900-2000 / Volume I: 1900-1939.* Bratislava: Vaclav Macek.

Coke, R. 1927. *Baghdad, the city of peace.* London: Butterworth.

Combe, E. 1965. L'œuvre de K.A.C. Creswell. In C.L. Geddes (ed.) *Studies in Islamic art and architecture in honour of Professor K.A.C. Creswell*: 1-7. Cairo: American University in Cairo.

Conder, C.R. Major 1889. *The Survey of the Eastern Palestine*, London: P.E.F.

Courtellemont, G. 1994. *Le pionnier photographe de Mahomet.* Nimes: Lacour.

Creswell, K.A.C. 1912. A comparison of the Hebrew Sephirot with the Paut Neteru of Egypt. *The Occult Review, Dec. 1912*: 349-357.

Creswell, K.A.C. 1913a. The mihrab from Kashan. *The Burlington Magazine* 23/125: 302.

Creswell, K.A.C. 1913b. The origin of the Persian double dome. *The Burlington Magazine* 24/128: 94-99.

Creswell, K.A.C. 1922. *The origin of the cruciform plan of Cairene madrasas (Extrait du Bulletin de l'Institut français d'archéologie orientale, t. 21).* Cairo: Institut Français d'Archéologie Orientale.

Creswell, K.A.C. 1926. The evolution of the minaret, with special reference to Egypt. *The Burlington Magazine for Connoisseurs* 48/276; 134-135+137-140.

Creswell, K.A.C. 1932. *Early Muslim Architecture, Umayyads, Early 'Abbasids and Tulunids, Part I: Umayyads, A.D. 622-750.* Oxford: Clarendon Press.

Creswell, K.A.C. 1940. *Early Muslim Architecture, Umayyads, Early 'Abbasids and Tulunids. Part 2: Early 'Abbasids, Umayyads of Cordova, Aghlabids, Tulunids, and Samanids, A.D. 751-905.* Oxford: Clarendon Press.

Creswell, K.A.C. 1952. *The Muslim Architecture of Egypt I, Ikhshids and Fatimids, A.D. 939-1171.* Oxford: Clarendon Press.

Creswell, K.A.C. 1958. *A short account of Early Muslim architecture.* Middlesex: Penguin Books [edition revised by James Allan: Aldershot: Scolar, 1989].

Creswell, K.A.C. 1959a. *The Muslim Architecture of Egypt, II, Ayyubids and Early Bahrite Mamluks, A.D. 1171-1326.* Oxford: Clarendon Press.

Creswell, K.A.C. 1959b. The Great Mosque of Ḥama. In R. Ettinghausen (ed.) *Aus der Welt der Islamischen Kunst:* 48-53. Berlin: Mann Verlag.

Crowley, M. 2014. How the fate of one holy site could plunge Iraq back into civil war. *Time, June 26* (https://time.com/2920692/iraq-isis-samarra-al-askari-mosque/).

Daiber, V. 2022a. Madrasa al-Zahiriyya. *Discover Islamic Art, Museum with no frontiers* (https://islamicart.museumwnf.org/database_item.php?id=monument;ISL;sy;Mon01;18;en).

Daiber, V. 2022b. Qasr al-Azm. *Discover Islamic Art, Museum with no frontiers* (https://islamicart.museumwnf.org/database_item.php?id=monument;ISL;sy;Mon01;21;en).

Daiber, V. 2022c. Takiyya al-Sulaymaniyya. *Discover Islamic Art, Museum with no frontiers* (https://islamicart.museumwnf.org/database_item.php?id=monument;ISL;sy;Mon01;19;en).

Daiber, V. 2022d. Umayyad Mosque. *Discover Islamic Art, Museum with no frontiers* (https://islamicart.museumwnf.org/database_item.php?id=monument;ISL;sy;Mon01;11;en).

Daiber, V. 2022e. Utrush Mosque. *Discover Islamic Art, Museum with no frontiers* (https://islamicart.museumwnf.org/database_item.php?id=monument;ISL;sy;Mon01;34;en).

de Beylié, L. 1907. *Prome et Samara: voyage archéologique en Birmanie et en Mésopotamie.* Paris: Leroux.

de Clerq, L. 1859. *Voyage en Orient et en Espagne Vol. 1: Villes, Monuments et Vues pittoresques de Syrie.* Paris: J. Blondeau et Antonin [album of albumen silver prints].

de Clerq, L. 1860. *Voyage en Orient et en Espagne Vol. 2: Chateaux du Temps des Croisades en Syrie.* Paris: J. Blondeau et Antonin [album of albumen silver prints].

de Saulcy, F., 1865. *Voyage en Terre Sainte I*, Paris: Didier.

de Tarragon, J.-M. 2019. Holy Land pilgrimage through historical photography. *Jerusalem Quarterly* 78: 93-111.

de Vogüé, M.-E.-M. 1864. Ruines d'Araq-el-Émir. *Revue Archéologique* 10: 52-62.

de Vogüé, M.-E.-M. 1865. *Syrie centrale: architecture civile et religieuse du Ier au VIIe siècle, tomes I-II.* Paris: Noblet et Baudry.

della Valle, P. 1843. *Viaggi di Pietro della Valle, il pellegrino: descritti da lui medesimo in lettere familiari all'erudito suo amico Mario Schipano, divisi in tre parti cioè: La Turchia, La Persia, e l'India, colla vita dell'autore* [consulted edition: Brighton: Gancia, 1843].

Desautels, J., Aubin, G., Blanchet, R. 2011. *Voyage en Orient (1839-1840). Journal d'un voyageur curieux du monde et d'un pionnier de la daguerréotypie.* Laval: Université Laval.

Devonshire, H. 1917. *Rambles in Cairo.* Cairo: The Sphinx Printing Press.

Díaz-Andreu, M. 2007. *A world history of nineteenth-century archaeology. Nationalism, colonialism, and the past.* Oxford: Oxford University Press.

Dieulafoy, M. 1885. *L'Art antique de la Perse. Achéménides, Parthes, Sassanides. Cinquième partie: Monuments parthes et sassanides.* Paris: Librairie des imprimeries réunies.

Draper, P. 2005. The early use of the pointed arch revisited. *Architectural History* 48: 1-20.

du Camp, M. 1852. *Égypte, Nubie, Palestine et Syrie. Dessins photographiques recueillis pendant les années 1849, 1850, et 1851.* Paris, Gide & J. Baudry.

Durukan, A. 2011. Some considerations on the Mamluk remains of Birecik (Sanluirfa). *Proceedings of the first international congress on Islamic archaeology, Istanbul 8-10 April 2005*: 37-73.

Dussaud, R. 1927. *Topographie historique de la Syrie antique et médiévale.* Paris: I.F.P.O..

El-Hage, B. 2000. *Des photographes à Damas, 1840-1918*, Paris, Marval.

Engin, A. 2003. Birecik and its surroundings from the Palaeolithic age to the end of the Roman period. In A. Durukan (ed.) *The cultural heritage in the towns Birecik, Halfeti, Suruç, Bozova and Rumkale:* 9-23. Ankara: T.C. Başbakanlık Güneydoğu Anadolu Projesi Bölge Kalkınma İdaresi Başkanlığı.

Eschner, K., 2017. How hoop skirts led to tape measures. *Smithsonian Magazine Juli 14.2017* (https://www.smithsonianmag.com/smart-news/how-hoop-skirts-led-tape-measures-180963995/).

Ettinghausen, R. 1957. Bibliography of the writings of K.A.C. Creswell. In honor of his seventy-fifth birthday-September 13, 1954. *Ars Orientalis* 2: 509-512.

Falls, Capt. C., Becke, Major A.F., 1930 *Military operations. Egypt and Palestine. From June 1917 to the end of the war, Part II.* London: Majesty's Stationery Office.

Fitzherbert, T. 1991. The Creswell photographic archive at the Ashmolean Museum, Oxford. *Muqarnas* 8: 125-127.

Foliard, D. 2016. Orientalismes? Pionniers français et britanniques de la photographie au Levant. *Études photographiques* 34 (http://journals.openedition.org/etudesphotographiques/3605).

Foss, C. 1996. Dead cities of the Syrian hill country. *Archaeology* 49/5: 48-53.

Fowden, G. 2004. *Qusayr 'Amra. Art and the Umayyad elite in late antique Syria*. Oakland: University of California Press.

Frankfort, H. 1936. *Progress of the work of the Oriental Institute in Iraq, 1934-1935 (OIC 29)*. Chicago: The University of Chicago Press.

Frecker, P. n.d. Tancrède Dumas. *Luminous-Lint*, (http://www.luminous-lint.com/app/photographer/Tancrede_Dumas/).

Frith, Fr. 1858. *Egypt and Palestine. Photographed and described by Francis Frith. Volumes I-II*. London: J.S. Virtue [albumen silver prints].

Gaube, H. 2007. A history of the city of Aleppo. In S. Bianca (ed.) *Medieval citadels between East and West*: 73-102. Turin: Aga Khan Trust for Culture.

Gaube, H., Wirth, E. 1984. *Aleppo. Historische und geographische Beiträge zur baulichen Gestaltung, zur sozialen Organisation und zur wirtschaftlichen Dynamik einer vorderasiatischen Fernhandelsmetropole*. Wiesbaden: Reichert.

Gautier, L. 1896. *Au delà du Jourdain: souvenirs d'une excursion faite en mars 1894*. Gèneve: Rey et Malavallon, Imprimeurs.

Gavin, C. 1982. *The Image of the East. Nineteenth-century Near Eastern photographs by Bonfils from the collection of the Harvard Semitic Museum*. Chicago: Univ. of Chicago Press.

Gentelle, P. 2003. *Traces d'eau. Un géographe chez les archéologues*, Paris: Belin.

Gibson, S., Chapman, R.L. 1996. A note on T.E. Lawrence as photographer in the wilderness of Zin. *Palestine Explorattion Quarterly Statement* 218: 99-102.

Gilento, P. 2022. The study of Near Eastern building techniques and the legacy of Howard Crosby Butler. In P. Gilento (ed.) *Building between Eastern and Western Mediterranean Lands. Construction processes and transmission of knowledge from Late Antiquity to Early Islam*: 37-60. Leiden-Boston: Brill.

Gioffredi Superbi, F., 2010. The photograph and Bernard Berenson: The story of a collection. *Visual Resources* 26/3: 289-303.

Girault de Prangey, G. 1846. *Monuments arabes d'Égypte, de Syrie et d'Asie mineure, dessinés et mesurés de 1842 à 1845*. Paris: de Prangey.

Gonnella, J. 2007. Introduction to the Citadel of Aleppo. In S. Bianca (ed.) *Medieval citadels between East and West*: 103-138. Turin: Aga Khan Trust for Culture.

Gonnella, J. 2012. Inside out: The Mamluk Throne Hall in Aleppo. In D. Behrens-Abouseif (ed.) *The arts of the Mamluks in Egypt and Syria. Evolution and impact*: 223-246. Göttingen: V&R Unipress Gmb.

Gonnella, J., Khayyata, W., Kohlmeyer, J.K. 2005. *Die Zitadelle von Aleppo*. Münster: Rhema.

Gordon, B., el-Hage, B. 2014. *Cities, citadels, and sights of the Near East: Francis Bedford's nineteenth-century photographs of Egypt, the Levant, and Constantinople*. Cairo: The American University in Cairo Press.

Goupil-Fesquet, Fr.A.A. 1843. *Voyage d'Horace Vernet en Orient, rédigé par M. Goupil Fesquet*. Paris: Challamel.

Grabar, O. 1991. K.A.C. Creswell and his work. *Muqarnas* 8: 1-3.

Gran-Aymerich, E. 2006. Jane Dieulafoy (1851-1916). In G.M. Cohen, M.S. Joukowsky (eds) *Breaking ground: pioneering women archaeologists*. Ann Arbor: University of Michigan Press.

Green, J., Teeter, E., Larson J.A. (eds) 2012, *Picturing the Past. Imaging and imagining the ancient Middle East (Oriental Institute Museum Publications 34)*. Chicago: The University of Chicago Press.

Gunter, A.C., Hauser, S.R. (eds) 2005. *Ernst Herzfeld and the development of Near Eastern Studies, 1900-1950*. Leiden: Brill.

Hallote, R. 2007. Photography and the American contribution to early 'Biblical' Archaeology, 1870-1920. *Near Eastern Archaeology* 70/1: 26-41.

Hamid, A. 1974. New lights on the 'Ashiq palace of Samarra. *Sumer* 30: 183-194.

Hamilton, R.W. 1991. Keppel Archibald Cameron Creswell, 1879-1974. *Muqarnas* 8: 128-136.

Hammad, M. 2004. *Architectures Ayyoubides, le style austère à Alep. Photographies d'architecture. Exposition 10-22 Mars 2004*. Paris: Centre Culturel Arabe Syrien.

Hannavy, (ed.) 2008. *Encyclopedia of nineteenth-century photography*. New York-Oxford: Routledge.

Hannoosh, M. 2016. Practices of photography. Circulation and mobility in the nineteenth-century Mediterranean. *History of Photography* 40/1: 3-27 (http://dx.doi.org/10.1080/03087298.2015.1123830).

Hansen, P.H. 2004. Stark, Dame Freya Madeline (1893–1993). *Oxford Dictionary of National Biography*. Oxford: Oxford University Press (https://doi.org/10.1093/ref:odnb/38280).

Harding G.L., 1959. *The Antiquities of Jordan*, New York: Lutterworth Press.

Harlan, D. 2022. Fragmented archives: an example of the photographs of J.A. Spranger in the SPHS Collection (https://www.bsa.ac.uk/2022/05/04/fragmented-archives-an-example-of-the-photographs-of-j-a-spranger-in-the-sphs-collection/).

Hasan K.I. 1977, Taharriyat atariyya qurb al-Uhaydir [in Arabic]. *Sumer* 33: 119-125.

Hasan, H. 2007. Introduction to the Citadel of Masyaf. In S. Bianca (ed.) *Medieval citadels between East and West*: 181-214. Turin: Aga Khan Trust for Culture.

Hasan, H. 2008. *The Citadel of Masyaf. Description, history, site plan and visitor tour*. Syria: Aga Khan Trust for Culture and the Syrian Directorate, General of Antiquities and Museums (https://archive.archnet.org/collections/104/publications/5214).

Hauser, S.R. 2003. Herzfeld, Ernst i. Life and work. *Encyclopædia Iranica* 12/3: 290-293 (https://iranicaonline.org/articles/herzfeld-ernst-i-1).

Healey, J.F., Liddel, P., Önal, M. 2020. New Greek inscriptions from Harran Castle. *Zeitschrift für Papyrologie und Epigraphik* 216: 133-146.

Helbig, K. 2016. La Trace de Rome? Aerial photography and archaeology in Mandate Syria and Lebanon. *History of Photography* 40/3:283-300 (DOI:10.1080/09639489.2016.1171464).

Herzfeld, E. 1922, Max van Berchem. *Der Islam* 12: 206-213.

Herzfeld, E. 1923. *Die Ausgrabungen von Samarra I, Der Wandschmuck der Bauten von Samarra und seine Ornamentik*. Berlin: Reimer.

Herzfeld, E. 1927. *Die Ausgrabungen von Samarra III, Die Malereien von Samarra*. Berlin: Reimer.

Herzfeld, E. 1930. *Die Ausgrabungen von Samarra V, Die vorgeschichtliche Töpfereien*. Berlin: Reimer.

Herzfeld, E. 1942. Damascus: Studies in Architecture: I. *Ars Islamica* 9: 1-53.

Herzfeld, E. 1943. Damascus: Studies in Architecture: II. *Ars Islamica* 10: 13-70.

Herzfeld, E. 1946. Damascus: Studies in Architecture: III. *Ars Islamica* 11-12: 1-71.

Herzfeld, E. 1948a. Damascus: Studies in Architecture: IV. *Ars Islamica* 13: 118-138.

Herzfeld, E. 1948b, *Die Ausgrabungen von Samarra VI, Geschichte der Stadt Samarra*. Hamburg: Eckardt & Meestorff.

Herzfeld, E. 1954. *Matériaux pour un corpus Inscriptionum Arabicarum. Part 2: Syrie du Nord. Inscriptions et monuments d'Alep, T.2. Planches*. Cairo: Institut Française d'Archéologie Orientale.

Herzfeld, E. 1955. *Matériaux pour un corpus Inscriptionum Arabicarum. Part 2: Syrie du Nord. Inscriptions et monuments d'Alep, T.1-1*. Cairo: Institut Française d'Archéologie Orientale.

Herzfeld, E. 1956. *Matériaux pour un corpus Inscriptionum Arabicarum. Part 2: Syrie du Nord. Inscriptions et monuments d'Alep, T.1-2*. Cairo: Institut Française d'Archéologie Orientale.

Hitrowo, B. von 1896. Gutachten, betreffend die Nothwendigkeit neuer photographischer Aufnahmen der Ruinen Palästina's und Syriens. *Zeitschrift des Deutschen Palästina-Vereins* 19: 137-143.

Hornstein, Ch.A. 1898. A visit to Kerak and Petra. *Palestine Exploration Fund Quarterly Statement* 30/2: 94-103.

Howe, K.St. 1997. *Revealing the Holy Land: the photographic exploration of Palestine*. Santa.Barbara, CA: Santa Barbara Museum of Art.

Hull, E., Kitchener E.H.H. 1885. *Mount Seir, Sinai and Western Palestine: Being a narrative of a scientific expedition*. London: P.E.F.

IAN (Islamic Art Network) 2004. *Creswell's Cairo: then and now. A joint exhibition of photographs from the Creswell Collection in the Rare Books and Special Collections Library of the American University* (http://www.islamic-art.org/CreswellExhibition/index.asp).

Imbert, Fr. 2015. Le prince al-Walid et son bain: itinéraires épigraphiques à Qusayr 'Amra. *Bulletin des Etudes Orientales* 64: 321-363.

Ingholt, H. 1942. The Danish excavations at Hama on the Orontes. *American Journal of Archaeology* 4/4: 469–476.

Isaacson, W. 2007. *Einstein. His life and universe*. New York: Simon & Schuster.

Jacobsen, Th., Lloyd, S. 1935. *Sennacherib's aqueduct at Jerwan (OIP 24)*. Chicago: The University of Chicago Press.

Jacobson, D.M. 2016. The PEF and its photographic collection. *City of David Studies of Ancient Jerusalem* 11: 53-73 (https://www.academia.edu/40154254/The_PEF_and_Its_Photographic_Collection).

Janulardo, E. 2015. Per un'archeologia del moderno. Gio Ponti, Le Corbusier, Gropius a Baghdad. *Forma Urbis* 20/8: 33-37.

Jarrar, S., Riedlmayer, A., Spurr, J.B. 1994. *Resources for the study of islamic architecture. Historical section*. Cambridge, MA: Aga Khan Program for Islamic Architecture (https://archnet.org/publications/2704).

Jaussen, A., Savignac, R. 1922. *Mission archéologique en Arabie. III. Les châtaux arabes de Qeseir 'Amra, Harane et Tuba*. Paris: Geuthner.

Jones, Lieut J.F. 1857. *Memoirs. Journal of a steam-trip to the north of Baghdad (April 1846), and others along the tract of the Nahrwan canal (submitted in April 1950), through Kurdistan to the frontier of Turkey and Persia (1844), research in the median wall of Xenophon, along the Tigris and on the site of the ancient Opis, Baghdad (1855), Nineveh, Assyria (1852)*. Bombay: Govt. at Bombay Education Society's Press.

Kadoi, Y. (ed.) 2016. *Arthur Upham Pope and a new survey of Persian art*. Leiden-Boston: Brill.

Kadoi, Y. 2021. *The power of duplication. Medieval Persian painting through photographs ca 1890-1920* (https://bilderfahrzeuge.hypotheses.org/5320).

Kafescioğlu, Ç. 1999. 'In The Image of Rum'. Ottoman architectural patronage in sixteenth-century Aleppo and Damascus. *Muqarnas* 16: 70–96.

Karnouk, G. 1991. The Creswell's Library: A legacy. *Muqarnas* 8: 117-124.

Kawtharani, W. 2013. *The Ottoman Tanzimat and the Constitution*. Doha: Arab Center for Research & Policy Studies.

Keall, E.J. 2011. Asvan e-Kesra. *Encyclopaedia Iranica* 3/2: 155-159.

Keenan, B., Beddow, T. 2000. *Damascus. Hidden treasures of the old city*. London: Thames & Hudson.

Kenfield, Sh.T. 2010. Archaeological archives, Department of Art and Archaeology, Princeton University. *Anabases* 11: 219-226 (https://journals.openedition.org/anabases/893).

Kennedy, H. 2005. *When Baghdad ruled the Muslim world*. Cambridge, MA: Da Capo Press.

Kenney, E. 2009. *Power and patronage in Medieval Syria. The architecture and urban works of Tankiz Al-Nasiri*. Chicago: Middle East Documentation Center.

Kenney, E. 2012. A Mamluk monument reconstructed. An achitectural history of the mosque and mausoleum of Tankiz al-Nasiri in Damascus. In D. Behrens-Abouseif (ed.) *The arts of the Mamluks in Egypt and Syria. Evolution and impact*: 141-161. Goettingen: Bonn University Press.

Khalil, J., Strika, V. 1987. *The Islamic architecture of Baghdad. The results of a joint Italian-Iraqi survey*. Napoli: Istituto Universitario Orientale.

Khoury, N.N.N., 1998. The Mihrab: From Text to Form. *International Journal of Middle East Studies* 30/1: 1-27.

Killick, R., Roaf, M. 1983. Excavations in Iraq 1981-82. *Iraq* 45/2: 199-224.

King, G. 2002. Archaeological fieldwork at the Citadel of Homs, Syria: 1995-1999. *Levant* 34/1: 39-58.

Klic, L. 2021. Linked open images: visual similarity for the Semantic Web. *Semantic Web* 1: 1-12, (https://content.iospress.com/articles/semantic-web/sw212893).

Knox, J. 2003. *Robert Byron. A Biography*. London: J.Murray.

Kondakov, N.P. 1904, *Archeologitscheskojo Puteschestwije pa Sirij i Palestine* [in Russian]. St. Petersburg: Imperial Akademia (https://archive.org/details/arkheologichesko00kond).

Koppes, Cl.R. 1976. Captain Mahan, General Gordon, and the origins of the term 'Middle East.' *Middle Eastern Studies* 12/1: 95-98.

Koulouris, S. 2018. The Creswell Online Network: documenting Islamic architecture through early photography. In I. Chrysakis, L. Harami, D. Angelakis, G. Bruseker (eds) *CIDOC 2018 Conference: Generating and tracing the 'Provenance of Knowledge', Book of Abstracts*: 85. Heraklion: Institute of Computer Science, Foundation for Research and Technology Hellas.

Koulouris, S. 2022. Making connoisseurship 'something like an exact science'. *Art Documentation: Journal of the Art Libraries Society of North America* 41/1: 70-83.

Koulouris, S. 2023. Capturing the Byzantine world. In G. Bernardi (ed.) *Medieval Hellenism and the Mediterranean ecumene as seen by Bernard Berenson and his circle*. Turnhout: Brepols.

Koutsoumpos, N. 2019. *A special individual: J.A. Spranger photographs Greece of the interwar period*. Paper given at the Photographic Encounters 2019 (Chania, Crete, 3-4 May) (https://www.academia.edu/42287452).

Lafi, N. 2017. Building and destroying authenticity in Aleppo. Heritage between conservation, transformation, destruction, and re-invention. In Ch. Bernhardt, M. Sabrow, A. Saupe (eds) *Gebaute Geschichte. Historische Authentizität im Stadtraum*: 206-228. Wallstein (https://halshs.archives-ouvertes.fr/halshs-01560321).

Lallemand, Ch. 1866. *La Syrie. Costumes, voyages, paysages*. Paris: Librairie Du Petit Journal.

Lamm, C.J. 1928. *Die Ausgrabungen von Samarra IV. Das Glas*. Berlin: Reimer.

Lammers, U. 2015. *Sieben Leben: Wissenschaftlerbiografien an der kulturwissenschaftlichen Abteilung der Technischen Hochschule Braunschweig im Nationalsozialismus*. Braunschweig: Digitale Bibliothek der TU Braunschweig.

Lapp, N.L., 1980: *The Excavations at Araq El-Emir. Volume I. (The Annual of the American Schools of Oriental Research 47)*. Winona Lake: Eisenbraun.

Larché, F. 2005. *Iraq al-Amir: le château du Tobiade Hyrcan. Volume II, Restitution et reconstruction (BAH 172)*. Beyrouth: I.F.P.O. [with contributions by F. Braemer et de B. Geyer].

Lassner, J. 1970. *The topography of Baghdad in the Early Middle Ages*. Detroit: Wayne State University Press.

Lawrence, T.E. 1939. *Oriental Assembly (edited by A. W. Lawrence. With photographs by the author)*. London: Williams and Norgate Ltd.

Le Bon, G. 1889. *Les premières civilisations*. Paris: Marpon & Flammarion.

Le Strange, G. 1901. *Baghdad during the Abbasid Caliphate*. Oxford: Clarendon Press.

Lederman, E. 2015. *K.A.C. Creswell's Middle East views at the V&A* (https://www.vam.ac.uk/blog/caring-for-our-collections/k-a-c-creswell-and-the-victoria-and-albert-museum).

Lee, J., Bain R.E.M., Vincent, J. 1894. *Earthly footsteps of the Man of Galilee*. New York-St. Louis: Thompson.

Lees, G.R. 1895. Across Southern Bashan. *The Geographical Journal* 5/1: 1-27.

Lees, G.R. 1909. *Life and adventure beyond Jordan*. New Yorkppleton.

Leisten, Th. 2003. *Excavation of Samarra. I. Architecture. Final report on the first campaign*. Mainz a.R.: von Zabern.

Lenzen, Ch.J. 2003. The desert and the sown. An introduction to the archeological and historiographic challenge. *Mediterranean Archaeology* 16: 5-12.

Libbey, W., Hoskins Fr.E. 1905. *The Jordan valley and Petra*. New York: Putnam's sons.

Liverani, M. 1988. *Antico Oriente. Storia società economia.* Roma-Bari: Laterza.

Lloyd, S. 1954. 159. Henri Frankfort: 1897-1954. *Man* 54: 106.

Lloyd, S., Brice, W. 1951. Harran. *Anatolian Studies* 1:77-111.

Lock, P. 1990. D.G. Hogarth (1862–1927): '...A Specialist in the Science of Archaeology.' *The Annual of the British School at Athens* 85: 175-200.

Loosley, E. 2012. *The architecture and liturgy of the Bema in Fourth-to-Sixth-century Syrian churches.* Leiden: Brill.

Lorent, J.A. 1845. *Wanderungen im Morgenlande während den Jahren 1842-1843.* Mannheim: Löffler.

Loud, G. 1936. *Khorsabad, Part 1 (OIP 38).* Chicago: The University of Chicago Press.

Lukitz, L 2004. Gertrude Bell. *Oxford Dictionary of National Biography.* Oxford: Oxford University Press.

Luynes, H., duc de 1871-1874. *Voyage d'exploration à la mer Morte a Petra et sur la rive gauche du Jourdain.* Paris: Bertrand.

Mackenzie, D. 1911a. *Megalithic monuments of Rabbath Ammon at Ammān.* London: Palestine Exploration Fund.

Mackenzie, D.1911b. Reports from Dr. Duncan Mackenzie. *Palestine Exploration Fund Quarterly Statement* 43: 8-11.

Mahan, A.T. 1902. The Persian Gulf and international relations. *National Review, Sept. 1902:* 27-45.

Mallowan, M.E.L. 1960. Sir Leonard Woolley. *Expedition Magazine* 3/1: n.p. (http://www.penn.museum/sites/expedition/?p=571).

Massignon, L. 1909. Note sur le château d'Al Okhaïder. *Comptes rendus des séances de l'Académie des Inscriptions et Belles-Lettres* 53/3: 202-212.

Massignon, L. 1910. *Mission en Mésopotamie (1907-1908), Tome 1.* Cairo: Impr. de l'Institut français d'archéologie orientale.

Massignon, L. 1912. *Mission en Mésopotamie (1907-1908), Tome 2.* Cairo: Impr. de l'Institut français d'archéologie.

Meinecke, M. 1992. *Die Mamlukische Architektur in Ägypten und Syrien (648/1250 bis 923/1517).* Glückstadt: Augustin.

Merrill, S. 1877. Modern researches in Palestine. *Journal of the American Geographical Society of New York* 9: 109-125.

Merrill, S. 1881. *East of the Jordan.* New York: Charles Scribner's sons.

Michell, G. (ed.) 1978. *Architecture of the Islamic World.* London: Thames and Hudson.

Moaz, A., 1998. Processes of urban development in an Islamic city. The north-weestern suburb in Damascus from the twelfth to the nineteenth centuries. *Iichiko* 47: 55-80.

Moaz, A., Takieddine, Z. 2022a. Hospital (Bimaristan) al-Qaymari. *Discover Islamic Art, Museum with no frontiers* (https://islamicart.museumwnf.org/database_item.php?id=monument;ISL;sy;Mon01;9;en).

Moaz, A., Takieddine, Z. 2022b. Madrasa al-'Adiliyya. *Discover Islamic Art, Museum with no frontiers* (https://islamicart.museumwnf.org/database_item.php?id=monument;ISL;sy;Mon01;39;en).

Moaz, A., Takieddine, Z. 2022c. Madrasa al-Sahiba. *Discover Islamic Art, Museum with no frontiers* (https://islamicart.museumwnf.org/database_item.php?id=monument;ISL;sy;Mon01;8;en).

Moaz, A., Takieddine, Z. 2022d. Mausoleum of Saladin (Salah al-Din). *Discover Islamic Art, Museum with no frontiers* (https://islamicart.museumwnf.org/database_item.php?id=monument;ISL;sy;Mon01;14;en).

Momigliano, N. 2013. Duncan Mackenzie and the Palestine Exploration Fund. *Palestine Exploration Quarterly* 128/2: 139-170.

Moritz, B. 1916. *Bilder aus Palastina, Nord-Arabien un dem Sinai. 100 Bilder nach Photographien mit erläuterndem Text.* Berlin: Reimer.

Mortensen E. 2018. The early research history of Jerash: a short outline. In Lichtenberger, A., Raja, R. (eds) *The archeology and hostory of Jerash. 110 Years of excavations:* 167-186. Turnhout: Brepols.

Moscrop, J.J. 1996. *The Palestine Exploration Fund: 1865-1914.* Thesis submitted for the degree of Doctor of Philosophy at the University of Leicester.

Moulton, J. 1926-1927. The American Exploration Society. *The Annual of the American Schools of Oriental Research* 8: 55-78.

Moulton, J. 1928. East of the Jordan Fifty years ago. *Bulletin of the American Schools of Oriental Research* 30: 8-10.

Mouton, J.M., Guilhot, J.-O., Piaton, Cl. 2018. *Portes et murailles de Damas de l'antiquité aux premiers Mamlouks.* Beyrouth: I.F.P.O.

Musil, A. 1907. *Kusejr 'Amra.* Wien: Kaiserliche Akademie der Wissenschaften.

Musil, A. 1907-1908. *Arabia Petra. I. Moab. II. Edom.* Wien: Hölder.

Nicholson, J. 2005. *The Hejaz railway.* London: Stacey International Publishers.

Niebuhr, C. 1776-1780. *Voyages en Arabie et en d'autres pays circonvoisins.* Amsterdam: Baalde.

Nippa, A. c. 1994. *Lesen in alten Photographien aus Baalbek.* Zürich: Völkerkundenmuseum der Universität Zürich [published between 1994 and 1996].

Nir, Y. 1985. *The History of photography in the Holy Land 1839-1899.* Philadelphia: University of Pennsylvania Press.

Northedge, A. 1991. Creswell, Herzfeld, and Samarra. *Muqarnas* 8: 74-93.

Northedge, A. (ed.) 1992. *Studies on Roman and Islamic Amman. Volume I: History, site and architecture.* Oxford: Oxford University Press.

Northedge, A. 1993. An Interpretation of the palace of the caliph at Samarra (Dar al-Khilafa or Jawsaq al Khaqani). *Ars Orientalis* 23: 143-170.

Northedge, A. 2006. The Qubbat al-Sulaybiyya and its interpretation. In P.L. Baker, B. Brend (eds) *Sifting sands, reading signs. Studies in honour of Prof. Géza Fehérvári*: 71-82. London: Furnace Publishing (https://www.academia.edu/39681561/Qubbat_al_Sulaibiyya_and_its_interpretation).

Northedge, A. 2008. *Archaeological Atlas of Samarra, 1. Historical topography of Samarra*. London: British School of Archaeology in Iraq (https://www.bisi.ac.uk/content/samarra-studies-publication-series).

Northedge, A. 2014. Samarra Today: the present situation of the site and studies. *Beiträge zur Islamischen Kunst und Archäologie* 4: 78-94.

Northedge, A., Kennet, D. 2015. *Archaeological Atlas of Samarra, 2/1-3*. London: British School of Archaeology in Iraq, (https://www.bisi.ac.uk/content/samarra-studies-publication-series).

Nour, H.M. 2017. The Great Mosque of Harran. Historical architectural study. *Annals of Arab Archaeologists* 20/20: 834-857.

O'Kane, B. 2009. *Creswell photographs re-examined. New perspectives on Islamic architecture*. Cairo: American University in Cairo Press.

O'Reilly, I.E. 1983. Near Eastern archaeology in historic photographs. *The Biblical Archaeologist* 46/4: 244-250.

Önal, M., Mutlu, S.I., Mutlu, S. (eds) 2019. *Harran ve Çevresi. Arkeoloji*. Şanlıurfa: Şurkav Yayınları.

Onne, E. 1980. *Photographic heritage of the Holy Land, 1839-1914*. Manchester UK: Institute of Advanced Studies, Manchester Polytechnic.

Ousterhout, R.G. 2016. *John Henry Haynes. A photographer and archaeologist in the Ottoman empire 1881-1900*. Oxford: Archaeopress.

Owen, W. 2017a. *Emergency archeology 1: a dig in the V&A's photography archive* (https://medium.com/the-many/emergency-archeology-a-dig-in-the-photographic-archive-9292b7189028).

Owen, W. 2017b. *Emergency archeology 2: prototyping a digital archive of Islamic architecture* (https://medium.com/the-many/emergency-archeology-2-prototyping-a-digital-archive-of-islamic-architecture-aee5b4b0b07).

Owen, W. 2017c. *Emergency archeology 3: a century of change at Aleppo's Madrasa al-Halawiyya* (https://medium.com/@wdowen/emergency-archeology-3-a-century-of-change-at-aleppos-madrasa-al-halawiyya-722900eb29aa).

Öztunçay, B. 1992. *James Robertson: Pioneer of photography in the Ottoman empire*. Istanbul: Eren.

Pagliarulo, G. 2011. Photographs to read: Berensonian annotations. In C. Caraffa (ed.) *Photo archives and the photographic memory of art history*: 181-191. Berlin and Munich: Deutscher Kunstverlag.

Palumbo, G., Atzori, A. (eds) 2014. *Qusayr 'Amra site management plan*. Amman: UNESCO.

Parapetti, R. 2017. The lost Mirjaniya Madrasa of Baghdad, Reconstructions and additional notes. *Mesopotamia* 52: 1-9.

Parrot, H. 1941. Henri de Genouillac. *Syria. Archéologie, art et histoire* 22/3-4: 299-300.

Parry Janis, E. 1987. *The photography of Gustave Le Gray*. Chicago: Art Institute of Chicago and the University of Chicago Press.

Parsons, A. 1808. *Travels in Asia and Africa*. London: Longman, Hurst, Rees and Orme [edited by Rev. J. Berjew].

Perez, N.H. 1988. *Focus East. Early photography in the Near East (1839-1885)*. New York: Abrams.

Peters, J.P. 1893. Notes of eastern travel. *The American Journal of Archaeology and of the History of the Fine Arts* 8/3: 325-334.

Pieri, D. 2015. *Les fouilles de la Via Sacra à Qalat Seman (2007-2010). Architecture, stratigraphie et mobilier. Archéologie et Préhistoire*. Paris: Université Paris 1 Panthéon-Sorbonne (https://hal.archives-ouvertes.fr/tel-01941211/).

Place, V. 1867. *Ninive et l'Assyrie*. Paris: Imprimerie Impériale.

Poidebard, A. 1934. *La trace de Rome dans le désert de Syrie. Le limes de Trajan à la conquête arabe. Recherches aériennes (1925-1932) (Bibliothèque archéologique et historique du Service des Antiquités de Syrie 18)*. Paris: Geuthner.

Pope-Hennessy, J. 1988. Berenson, Bernard. *Dizionario biografico degli Italiani* 34. Roma: Treccani, (https://www.treccani.it/enciclopedia/bernard-berenson_(Dizionario-Biografico)).

Preusser, C. 1911. *Nordmesopotamische Baudenkmäler Altchristlicher und Islamischer Zeit*. Leipzig: Hinrichs

Puchstein, O., Krencker, D., Schulz, B., Kohl, H. 1902. Zweiter Jahresbericht über die Ausgrabungen in Baalbeck. *Jahrbuch des Kaiserlich Deutschen Archaeologischen Instituts* 17: 87-123.

Raboisson, A. 1886. *En Orient*. Paris: Librairie Catholique de l'Oeuvre de Saint-Paul.

Raby, J. 1991. Reviewing the reviewers. *Muqarnas* 8: 5-11.

Raby, J. 2004. Nur al-Din, the Qastal al-Shuaybiyya, and the classical revival. *Muqarnas* 21: 289-310.

Randy, A. 2009. July 14, 1868: Tape measure clicks in. *Wired*, 07.14.2009 (https://www.wired.com/2009/07/dayintech-0714/).

Raphael (Père) 1904. *Album de la Mission de Mésopotamie et d'Arménie confiée aux Frères Mineurs Capucins de la Province de Lyon, 40 phot. prises en 1904 par le frère Raphaël* (https://gallica.bnf.fr/ark:/12148/btv1b531680094/f40.item).

Raymond, A. 1998. *La ville arabe, Alep, à l'époque ottomane: (XVIe-XVIIIe siècles)*. Damas: I.F.P.O. [new online edition] (http://books.openedition.org/ifpo/505).

Resig, R. 2014. Using computer vision to increase the research potential of photo archives. *Journal of Digital Humanities* 3: 2.

Reuther, O. 1910. *Das Wohnhaus in Baghdad und andere Staedten des Irak*. Berlin: Wasmuth 1910.

Reuther, O. 1912. *Ocheïdir, nach Aufnahmen von Mitgliedern der Babylon-Expedition der Deutschen Orient-Gesellschaft*. Leipzig: Hinrichs.

Reuther, O. 1930. *Die Ausgrabungen der deutschen Ktesiphon-Expedition im Winter 1918-29*. Berlin: Staatliche Museen in Berlin.

Rice, D.S. 1952. Medieval Harran. Studies on its topography and monuments, I. *Anatolian Studies* 2: 36-84.

Rice, D.S. 1955. A Muslim shrine at Harran. *Bulletin of the School of Oriental and African Studies* 17/3: 436-448.

Roberts, J. 1853. *Photographic views of Constantinople*. London: Joseph Cundall.

Robinson, Ch. (ed.) 2001. *A Medieval Islamic city reconsidered. An interdisciplinary approach to Samarra*. Oxford: Oxford University Press.

Robinson, Ch. 2003. *Islamic historiography*. Cambridge: Cambridge University Press.

Rocke, M. 2001. Una sorta di sogno d'estasi. In A. Boscaro, M. Bossi (eds) *Firenze, il Giappone e l'Asia Orientale*: 367-384 Florence: Olschki.

Rogers, J.M. 1991. Architectural history as literature: Creswell's reading and methods. *Muqarnas* 8: 45-54.

Rose, V. 2017. Les fouilles d'Henry Viollet à Samarra. *Annales islamologiques* 51: 167-190 (https://journals.openedition.org/anisl/3449?lang=en).

Rosovsky, N. 1997. Palestine and the nineteenth century. In K.St. Howe, *Revealing the Holy Land. The photographic exploration of Palestine*: 11-15. Santa Barbara, CA: Santa Barbara Museum of Art.

Rousseau, G.B., 1899. *Voyage de Baghdad à Alep*. Paris: André.

Saba, M. 2017. *Samarra* (https://www.archnet.org/authorities/3929).

Sachau, E. 1883. *Reise in Syrien und Mesopotamien*. Leipzig: Brockhaus.

Sack, D. 1985. Damasco: lo sviluppo storico di una capitale. In *Da Ebla a Damasco. Diecimila anni di archeologia in Siria*: 148-152. Milano: Electa.

Sack, D. 1989. *Damaskus. Entwicklung und Struktur einer orientalisch-islamischen Stadt*. Mainz a.R.: Verlag Philipp von Zabern.

Sader, S., Scheffler, Th., Neuwirth, A. 1998. *Baalbek. Image and monument 1898-1998*. Stuttgart: Steiner.

Salmon, G. 1904, *Introduction topographique à l'histoire de Baghdad*. Paris: Bouillon.

Sarre, F., 1925, *Ausgrabungen von Samarra II. Die Keramik von Samarra*. Berlin: Reimer.

Sarre, Fr., Herzfeld, E. 1911a. *Archäologische Reise im Euphrat- und Tigris-Gebiet, I*. Berlin: Reimer.

Sarre, Fr., Herzfeld, E. 1911b. *Archäologische Reise im Euphrat- und Tigris-Gebiet, III*. Berlin: Reimer.

Sarre, Fr., Herzfeld, E. 1920a. *Archäologische Reise im Euphrat- und Tigris-Gebiet, II*. Berlin: Reimer.

Sarre, Fr., Herzfeld, E. 1920b. *Archäologische Reise im Euphrat- und Tigris-Gebiet, IV*. Berlin: Reimer.

Sarre, F., Martin, F.R. 1912. *Die Ausstellung von Meisterwerken muhammedanischer Kunst in München*. Munich: Bruckmann.

Sarre, F., Martin, F.R., Dreger, M. 1912. *Meisterwerke muhammedanischer Kunst auf der Ausstellung München 1910: Teppiche, Waffen, Miniaturen, Buchkunst, Keramik, Glas und kristall, Stein-, Holz-und Elfenbeinarbeiten, Stoffe, Metall, Verschiedenes*. Munich: Bruckmann.

Saunders, B. 2019. Seguaci americani della Scuola Romana di fotografia: Nathan Flint Baker, Leavitt Hunt e Richard Morris Hunt/ American Pupils of the Roman School of Photography: Nathan Flint Baker, Leavitt Hunt and Richard Morris Hunt. *Rivista di studi di fotografia* 5/9: 8-29 (https://doi.org/10.14601/RSF-25767).

Sauvaget, J. 1931. *Inventaire des monuments musulmans de la ville d'Alep*. Paris: Geuthner.

Sauvaget, J. 1932. *Les monuments historiques de Damas*. Beyrouth: I.F.P.O. (https://books.openedition.org/ifpo/3611).

Sauvaget, J. 1938. *Les monuments ayyoubides de Damas, I*. Paris: Boccard (https://books.openedition.org/ifpo/3787).

Sauvaget, J. 1940. *Les monuments ayyoubides de Damas, II*. Paris: Boccard (https://books.openedition.org/ifpo/3787).

Sauvaget, J. 1948. *Les monuments ayyoubides de Damas, III*. Paris: Boccard (https://books.openedition.org/ifpo/3787).

Sauvaget, J. 1949. La plan antique de Damas. *Syria. Archéologie, art et histoire* 26: 314-358.

Sauvaire, H. 1894-1896. Description de Damas. *Journal asiatique, mars-avril, mai-juin, novembre-décembre 1894 and mars-avril, mai-juin 1896* (https://archive.org/details/in.ernet.dli.2015.69523).

Scanlon, G.T. 1975. Sir Archibald Creswell (1879-1974). *Bulletin of the British Society for Middle Eastern Studies* 1/2: 110-111.

Scheffler, Th. 1998. *The Kaiser in Baalbek: Tourism, archaeology, and the politics of imagination* (https://www.academia.edu/28271704).

Schmid, H. 1980. *Die Madrasa des Kalifen al-Mustansir in Baghdad (Baghdader Forschungen 3)*. Mainz a.R.: von Zabern.

Schmid, S.G. 2008. The Hellenistic period and the Nabataeans. In R.B. Adams (ed.) *Jordan. An archaeological reader*: 353-411. London: Equinox.

Schultz, R.W., Barnsley, S.H. 1901. *The monastery of Saint Luke of Stiris, in Phocis and the dependent monastery of Saint Nicolas in the Fields, near Skripou, in Bœotia*. London: Macmillan.

Schulz, B., Strzygowski, J., 1904. Kulturbesitz Mschatta. Bericht über die Aufnahme der Ruine von Bruno Schulz und kunstwissenschaftliche Untersuchung von Josef Strzygowski. *Jahrbuch der Königlich Preussischen Kunstsammlungen* 25/4: 205-373.

Seyrig, H. 1963. Le R. P. René Mouterde. *Syria. Archéologie, art et histoire* 40: 226-227.

Sheehi, S., Ennis, H., Heeren, A. *et al.* 2017. Photography. *The Routledge Encyclopedia of Modernism*. London: Taylor and Francis.

Sinclair, T.A. 1990. *Eastern Turkey. An architectural and archeological survey. Volume IV*. London: The Pindar Press.

Singer, I., Kahn, Z. 1901-1906. Cahun, David Léon: 492-493. *The Jewish Encyclopedia*. New York: Funk & Wagnalls.

Sobczak, K. 2015. Transition from the Temple of Jupiter to the Great Mosque of Damascus in architecture and design. *Studia Ceranea* 5: 311–320.

Sobieszek, R.A., Gavin, C.E.S. 1980. *Remembrances of the Near East. The photographs of Bonfils, 1867-1907*. Chicago: OIP.

Solomon-Godeau, A. 1981. A Photographer in Jerusalem, 1855. Auguste Salzmann and His Time. *October* Vol. 18, Autumn: 90-107.

Speiser, E.A. 1935. *Excavations at Tepe Gawra*. Philadelphia: University of Pennsylvania Press.

Stapp, W. 2008. Hunt, Leavitt (1831-1907), Baker, Nathan Flint (c. 1822-1891). In J. Hannavy (ed.) *The Encyclopedia of Nineteenth-Century Photography*: 729-731. London: Taylor & Francis.

Streck, M. 1900. *Die alte Landschaft Babylonien*. Leiden: Brill.

Tabbaa, Y. 1997. *Constructions of power and piety in Medieval Aleppo*. University Park, PA: The Pennsylvania State University Press.

Takieddine, Z., Abd al-Ghafour, S. 2022a. Madrasat al-Firdaws. *Discover Islamic Art, Museum with no frontiers* (https://islamicart.museumwnf.org/database_item.php?id=monument;ISL;sy;Mon01;4;en).

Takieddine, Z., Abd al-Ghafour, S. 2022b. Mihrab of the Madrasa al-Halawiyya. *Discover Islamic Art, Museum with no frontiers* (https://islamicart.museumwnf.org/database_item.php?id=monument;ISL;sy;Mon01;5;en).

Takieddine, Z., Abd al-Ghafour, S. 2022c. The Minaret of the Umayyad Mosque of Aleppo. *Discover Islamic Art, Museum with no frontiers* (https://islamicart.museumwnf.org/database_item.php?id=monument;ISL;sy;Mon01;2;en&pageD=N).

Tate, G. 1992 *Les campagnes de la Syrie Nord*. Beyrouth: I.F.P.O. (https://books.openedition.org/ifpo/4334).

Tchalenko, G. 1953. *Villages antiques de la Syrie du nord. Le massif du Bélus à l'époque romaine, voll. 1-2*. Paris: Institut français d'archéologie de Beyrouth.

Tchalenko, G. 1974. La Basilique de Qalbloze. *Les annales archéologiques arabes syriennes* 24: 9-15.

Tchalenko, J. 2019. Georges Tchalenko 1905–1987: Biographical Material. In J. Tchalenko, E. Loosley Leeming, *Notes on the sanctuary of St. Symeon Stylites at Qal'at Sim'an*: 1-27. Leiden: Brill.

Tchalenko, J., Loosley Leeming, E. 2019. *Notes on the sanctuary of St. Symeon Stylites at Qal'at Sim'an*. Leiden: Brill.

Terunean, V. 2010. *Mémoire arménienne: photographies du camp de réfugiés d'Alep, 1922-1936*. Beirut: Presses de l'Université Saint-Joseph.

Thiersch, H., Hölscher, G. 1904. Reise durch Phönizien und Palästina. *Mitteilungen der Deutschen Orient-Gesellschaft* 23: 1-25.

Thomson, W.M., 1886, *The Land and the Book. Lebanon Damascus and beyond Jordan*. London: Nelson and Sons.

Toubia, S. 2008. *Sarrafian Liban 1900-1930*. Mansourieh: Editions Aleph.

Tovell, J. 1992. The Creswell Library of Islamic art and architecture at the American University in Cairo Part One: In the Presence of the original owner, 1956-73. *Art Libraries Journal* 17/4: 13-22.

Tovell, J. 1993. The Creswell Library of Islamic art and architecture at the American University in Cairo Part Two: The evolution of a teaching library 1973-1992. *Art Libraries Journal* 18/1: 39-48.

Tristram, H.B. 1865. *The Land of Israel. A journal of travels in Palestine*. London: Clay, Son & Taylor.

Tristram, H.B. 1873. *The Land of Moab*. London: Murray.

UNESCO 2016. *WHC/16/40.COM/7A.Add. Item 7A of the Provisional Agenda: State of conservation of the properties inscribed on the List of World Heritage in Danger* (https://whc.unesco.org/en/sessions/40COM/documents/).

UNESCO 2019. *WHC/19/43.COM/7A.Add. Item 7A of the Provisional Agenda: State of conservation of the properties inscribed on the List of World Heritage in Danger* (https://whc.unesco.org/en/sessions/43com/documents).

UNESCO/UNITAR, 2018. *Five years of conflict. The state of cultural heritage in the ancient city of Aleppo*. Paris: UNESCO (https://whc.unesco.org/en/activities/946/).

Upton, J.M. 1932. The Expedition to Ctesiphon, 1931-1932. *The Metropolitan Museum of Art Bulletin* 27/8:185+188-197.

Vaczek, L., Buckland, G. 1981. *Travelers in ancient lands. A portrait of the Middle East, 1839-1919*. Boston: New York Graphic Society.

van Berchem, M. Fatio, E. 1914. *Voyage en Syrie*. Cairo: Imprimerie de l'Insititut Française d'Archéologie.

van Berchem, M., Strzygowski, J. 1910. *Amida. Materiaux pour l'épigraphie et l'histoire Musulmanes du Diyar-Bekr*. Heidelberg: Winter's Universitätbuchandlung.

Vârtejanu-Joubert, M. 2019. Débuts de la photographie, débuts de l'archive photographique: Bonfils au Harvard Semitic Museum. *Martor* 24: 13-26.

Vernoit, S. 1997. The Rise of Islamic archaeology. *Muqarnas* 14: 1-10.

Veselá, M. 2012. *Alois Musil (1868-1944): Archaeology of Late Antiquity and the beginning of Islamic archeology in the Middle East* (Doctoral thesis, Université de Paris I Panthéon-Sorbonne). Pilsen: n.p.

Vibert-Gigue, Cl., Bisheh, Gh. 2007. *Les pientures de Qusayr 'Amra: Un bain omeyyade dans la bâdiya jordanienne* (Bibliothèque archéologique et historique, T. 179). Beyrouth: I.F.P.O.

Viollet, H. 1909. Le palais de Al-Mutasim, fils d'Haroun-al-Raschid, à Samara et de quelques monuments arabes peu connus de la Mésopotamie. *Comptes rendus des séances de l'Académie des Inscriptions et Belles-Lettres* 53/5: 370-375.

Viollet, H. 1913. Fouilles à Samara en Mésopotamie. Un palais musulman du IXe siècle. *Mémoires présentés par divers savants à l'Académie des Inscriptions et Belles-Lettres* 12: 685-718.

Waller, F. 1982. Jakob August Lorent, A forgotten German travelling photographer. *The Photographic Collector* 3: 21-39.

Ward, W.H. 1885. The Wolfe Expedition. *Journal of the Society of Biblical Literature and Exegesis* 5/1-2: 56-60.

Warren, Lt.-Col. Ch. 1870. Expedition East of the Jordan, July and August, 1867. *Palestine Exploration Fund Quarterly Statement* 4: 284-306.

Warren, Lt.-Col. Ch. 1880. Eastern Palestine. *Palestine Exploration Fund Quarterly Statement* 12: 171-172.

Warren, N. 2009. Detecting the past: K.A.C. Creswell, photography and the landscape of Cairo. In B. O'Kane (ed.) *Creswell photographs re-examined. New perspectives on Islamic architecture*: 293-327. Cairo: American University in Cairo Press.

Watenpaugh, H.Z. 2005. Deviant Dervishes. Space, gender, and the construction of antinomian piety in Ottoman Aleppo. *International Journal of Middle East Studies* 37/4: 535–565.

Weber, S. 2009. *Damascus. Ottoman Modernity and Urban Transformation (1808-1918)*. Århus: Aarhus University Press.

Wellsted, J.R. 1840. *Travels in the cilty of the Caliphs*. London: Colburn Publisher.

Wheelhouse, C.G. 2006. *Narrative of a Yacht Voyage in the Mediterranean 1849-1850. Photographic Sketches from the Shores of the Mediterranean*. Edition by Folios Limited in collaboration with the National Museum of Photography, Film and Television.

Wiet, G. 1971. *Baghdad. Metropolis of the Abbasid caliphate*. Oklahoma: University of Oklahoma Press.

Will, E., Larché F. 1991. *Iraq al-Amir, le château du Tobiade Hyrca (BAH 132)*. Beyrouth: I.F.P.O..

Willey, P. 2005. *The Eagle's Nest. Ismaili Castles in Iran and Syria*. London-New York: Tauris.

Wilson, K., Lauinger, J., Phillips, M.L. et al. 2012. *Bismaya. Recovering the lost city of Adab (OIP 138)*. Chicago: The University of Chicago Press.

Wulzinger, K., Watzinger, C. 1921. *Damaskus, die antike Stadt* (Wiss. Veröff. d. deutsch-türkischen Denkmalschutz kommandos, Heft 4). Berlin & Leipzig: de Gruyter.

Wulzinger, K., Watzinger, C. 1924. *Damaskus, die islamische Stadt* (Wiss. Veröff. d. deutsch-türkischen Denkmalschutz kommandos, Heft 5). Berlin 6 Leipzig: de Gruyter.

Yardımcı, N. 2004a. Harran. In S. Anastasio, M. Lebeau, M. Sauvage (eds.) *Atlas of Preclassical Upper Mesopotamia (Subartu 13)*: 154. Turnhout: Brepols.

Yardımcı, N. 2004b. *Harran Ovası Yüzey Araştırması I-II/ Archaeological Survey in the Harran Plain I-II*. Istanbul: Arkeoloji ve Sanat Yayınlar

Yoshitake, R. 2013. Early Applications of domical vault in Jordan. *Journal of Architectural and Planning Research* 78/693: 2387-2397.

Zannier, I. 1986. *Verso Oriente. Fotografie di Antonio e Felice Beato*. Firenze: Alinari.

Zevi, F. 1984. Photographers and Egypt in XIXth century. In Zevi, F., Bosticco, S., *Photographers and Egypt in XIXth century*: 11-19. Firenze: Alinari.

Zuckerman, B.M. 2000. Peter Bergheim's Holy Land stereoviews. *Stereo World* 26/6: 10-17.

موجز

بلاد الرافدين وسوريا وشرق الأردن ضمن مجموعة صور أرشيبالد كريسويل في مكتبة بيرينسون

ولد أرشيبالد كريسويل (Archibald Creswell) في لندن في 13 أيلول/سبتمبر عام 1879. درس الهندسة في فينسبري.

في عام 1916، خلال الحرب العالمية الأولى، تم تعيينه في مصر ليلتحق بسلاح الطيران الملكي. ومنذ ذلك الحين، قضى معظم حياته في القاهرة وأصبحت العمارة الإسلامية موضوع دراسته الرئيسي.

في عامي 1919-1920، عمل مفتشاً للآثار في "إدارة اللنبي العسكرية لأراضي العدو المحتلة": في تلك الفترة، قام كريسويل بالعديد من الرحلات في شتى بلاد الشرق الأدنى، ملتقطاً للعديد من الصور.

بعد الحرب العالمية الأولى، رعى الملك فؤاد ملك مصر أعماله لإنجاز دراسة مكثفة للعمارة الإسلامية، وفي عام 1931، بدأ كريسويل بتدريس الفن والعمارة الإسلامية في جامعة فؤاد الأول بالقاهرة وبقي فيها حتى عام 1951. استمر في العيش بمفرده في القاهرة دون زواج طالما كانت صحته تسمح بذلك. في عام 1973، انتقل إلى إنجلترا، وتوفي في لندن في 8 أبريل 1974.

يعتبر كريسويل مؤسس اختصاص العمارة الإسلامية في التاريخ الحديث. ما تزال منشوراته أدوات بحث أساسية للباحثين في هذا الموضوع. لكي نذكر أعماله الرئيسية وحسب، يمكن الإشارة إلى العناوين التالية: (Early Muslim Architecture) العمارة الإسلامية المبكرة (مجلدان، 1932-1940)؛ (The Muslim Architecture of Egypt) العمارة الإسلامية في مصر (مجلدان، 1952-1959).

اعتبر كريسويل التصوير الفوتوغرافي أداة لا يمكن الاستغناء عنها لتسجيل وتوثيق المشغولات المعمارية (artefacts)، وهذا هو سبب التقاطه لآلاف الصور التي تحتفظ بها اليوم عدة مراكز أرشفة: متحف أشموليان في مدينة أكسفورد، ومتحف فيكتوريا وألبرت في مدينة لندن، والجامعة الأمريكية في القاهرة، ومكتبة الفنون الجميلة في هارفارد، ومكتبة بيرينسون في فيلا إي تاتي في فلورنسا. هذه الأخيرة هي المجموعة المعروضة في هذا المجلد.

فيلا إي تاتي (Villa I Tatti) هو مركز أبحاث تابع لجامعة هارفارد، أسسه برنارد بيرينسون (Bernard Berenson) (1865-1959)، وهو ناقد فني ذائع الصيت. اكتسب ثروة مذهلة بفضل نشاطه كمستشار فني. أصبح منزله (Villa I Tatti) مركزاً ثقافياً في فلورنسا، ومجهزاً بمكتبة غنية، وأرشيف للصور الفوتوغرافية التي تركز على فن الرسم الإيطالي في عصر النهضة. تحتفظ المكتبة بإجمالي 2930 صورة تبرع بها كريسويل، توجد على ظهر معظمها ملاحظات مكتوبة بخط اليد، والتي توضح بالتفصيل المواضيع المصورة. تتعلق الصور بمعالم أثرية في مصر وسوريا وفلسطين والعراق والأردن ولبنان وتونس وتركيا. قام بيرينسون بتقديم التمويل لكريسويل في العديد من المرات.

الصور التي أرسلها كريسويل لبيرينسون ليست نتيجة مبيعات فعلية، غير أنها مرتبطة بأنشطة الرعاية التي يوفرها بيرينسون.

في المجلد تم تحليل الصور المرتبطة بشرق تركيا (البيرة أو بيره جك، حران) وبالعراق (سامراء، قنطرة حربا، بغداد، طاق كسرى، الأخيضر) وبسوريا (قلعة سمعان، قلب لوزة، رويحة، حلب، مسكنة، مصياف، حماه، حمص، دمشق) وبالأردن (عمان، عراق الأمير، قصير عمرة). إجمالاً، يمكن تأريخها بين عامي 1919 و1930.

يوجد في المجلد، بعد كتالوج الصور، ملحق يقدم قائمة بالمصورين المعروف بأنهم عملوا في بلاد الرافدين وسوريا والأردن، من بداية تاريخ التصوير إلى سنوات صور كريسويل.

يحتوي الكتاب على عنوان ويب يتيح للمستخدم تحديد الموقع الجغرافي على خرائط جوجل المخصصة (Google My Maps) للمواقع وللمعالم الأثرية التي صورها كريسويل.

ما تزال العديد من المواقع والمعالم الأثرية التي صورها كريسويل قائمة، لكن هناك العديد من المواقع والمعالم الأخرى (خاصة في حلب ودمشق) التي لم تعد موجودة، أو التي أجريت عليها تعديلات كبيرة. لهذا السبب، تعد مجموعة صور كريسويل مصدراً استثنائياً لدراسة المعالم الأثرية القديمة، وخاصة لجميع مشاريع الحفاظ عليها وترميمها.

Stefano Anastasio

Translated by Chadi Hatoum

ستيفانو أناستاسيو

ترجمة: شادي حسن حاطوم